ARCANA

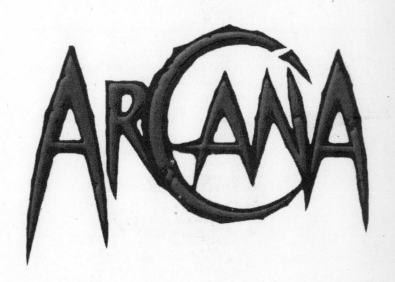

Arcana Vol. 2
Created by So-Young Lee

Translation - Youngju Ryu
English Adaptation - Barbara Randall Kesel
Copy Editor - Emily Wing
Retouch and Lettering - Lucas Rivera
Production Artist - Eric O. Pineda
Cover Design - Thea Willis

Editor - Bryce P. Coleman
Digital Imaging Manager - Chris Buford
Production Managers - Jennifer Miller and Mutsumi Miyazaki
Managing Editor - Jill Freshney
VP of Production - Ron Klamert
Publisher and E.I.C. - Mike Kiley
President and C.O.O. - John Parker
C.E.O. - Stuart Levy

A  Manga

TOKYOPOP Inc.
5900 Wilshire Blvd. Suite 2000
Los Angeles, CA 90036

E-mail: info@TOKYOPOP.com
Come visit us online at www.TOKYOPOP.com

ISBN: 1-59532-482-8
First TOKYOPOP printing: September 2005
10 9 8 7 6 5 4 3 2 1
Printed in Canada

VOLUME 2
SO-YOUNG LEE

HAMBURG // LONDON // LOS ANGELES // TOKYO

THE JOURNEY THUS FAR...

INEZ, A YOUNG ORPHAN GIRL WITH THE UNIQUE
ABILITY TO COMMUNICATE WITH ALL ANIMALS,
HAS BEEN CHARGED WITH AN INCREDIBLE
MISSION. SHE MUST JOURNEY OUTSIDE THE
CONFINES OF HER COUNTRY AND ENLIST THE
AID OF A GUARDIAN DRAGON TO PROTECT
HER KINGDOM FROM THE ONSLAUGHT OF THE
RETURNING DEMON HORDES! ARMED WITH
ONLY A MYSTICAL AMULET, AND ACCOMPANIED
BY YULAN, A MYSTERIOUS MEMBER OF THE
KING'S COURT, INEZ MUST SUMMON ALL HER
COURAGE IF SHE IS TO SUCCEED.

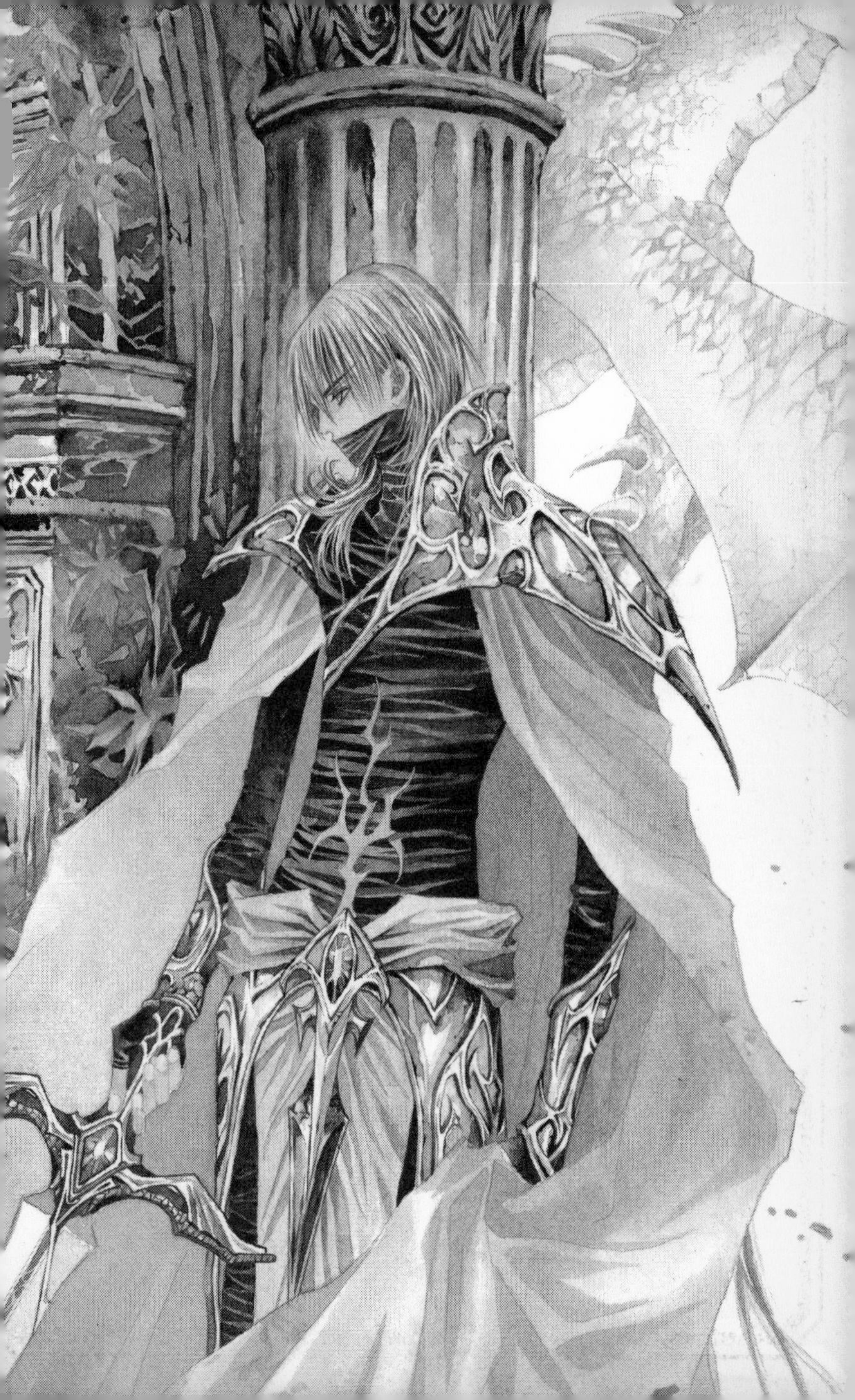

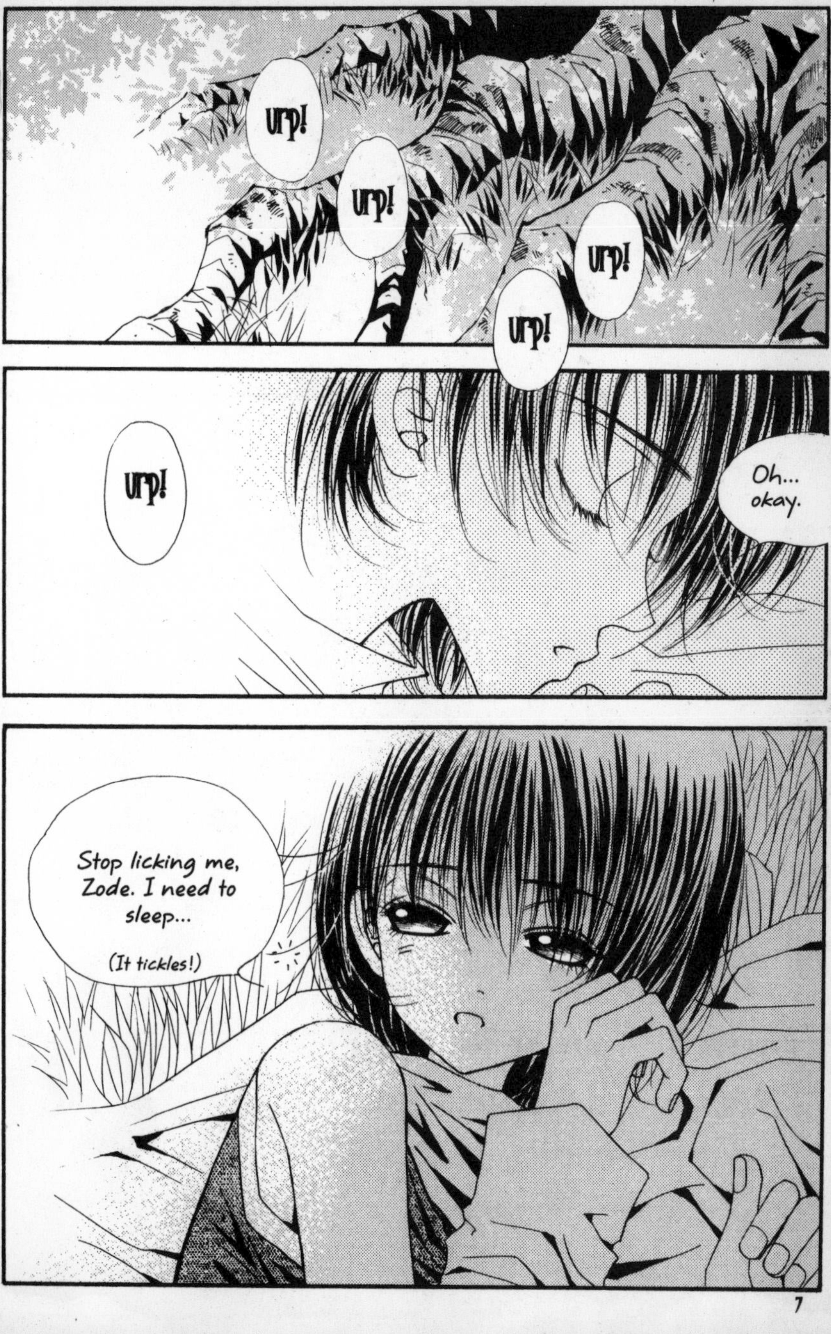
Urp!
Urp!
Urp!
Urp!
Urp!
Oh... okay.
Stop licking me, Zode. I need to sleep...
(It tickles!)

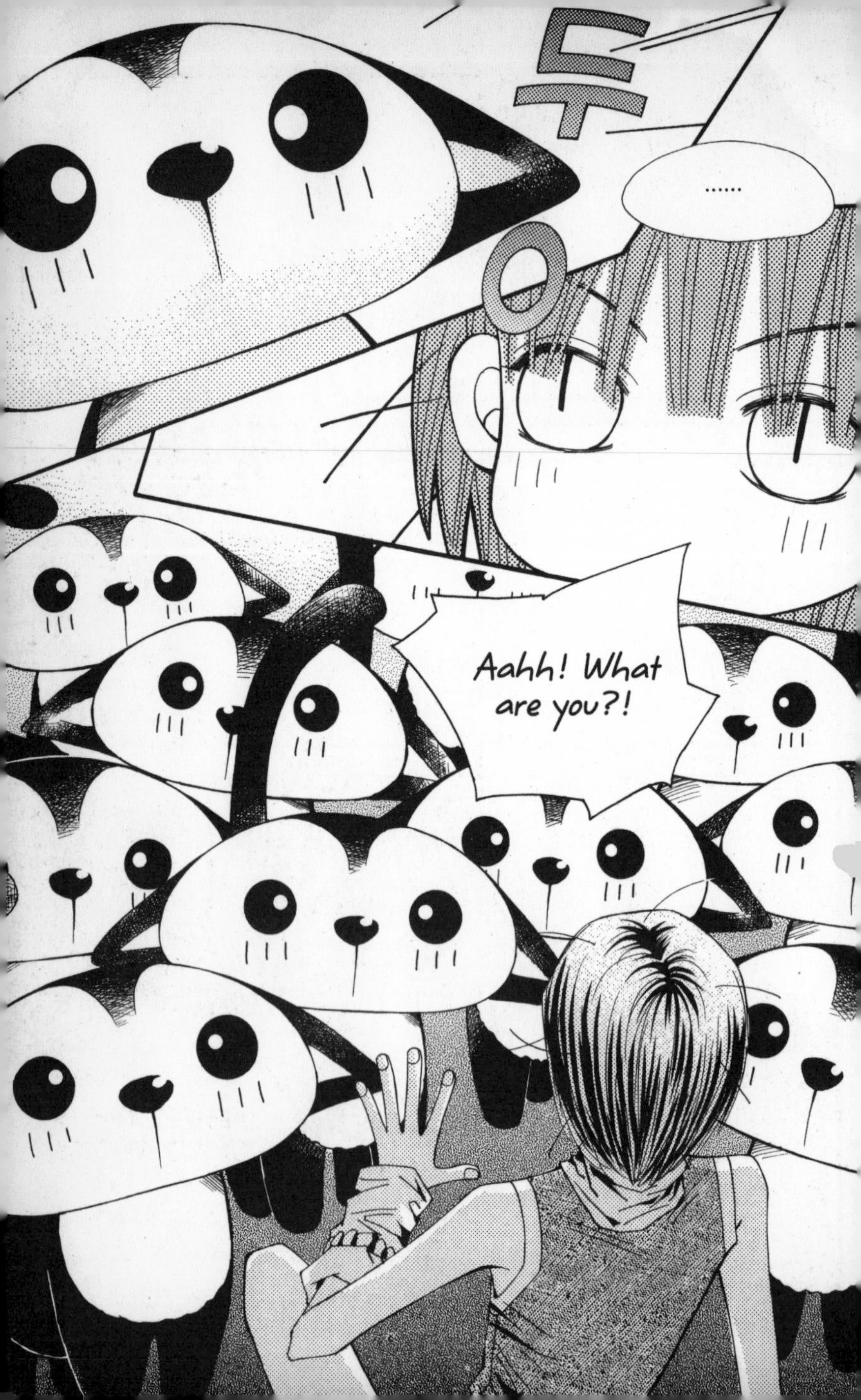
……
Aahh! What are you?!

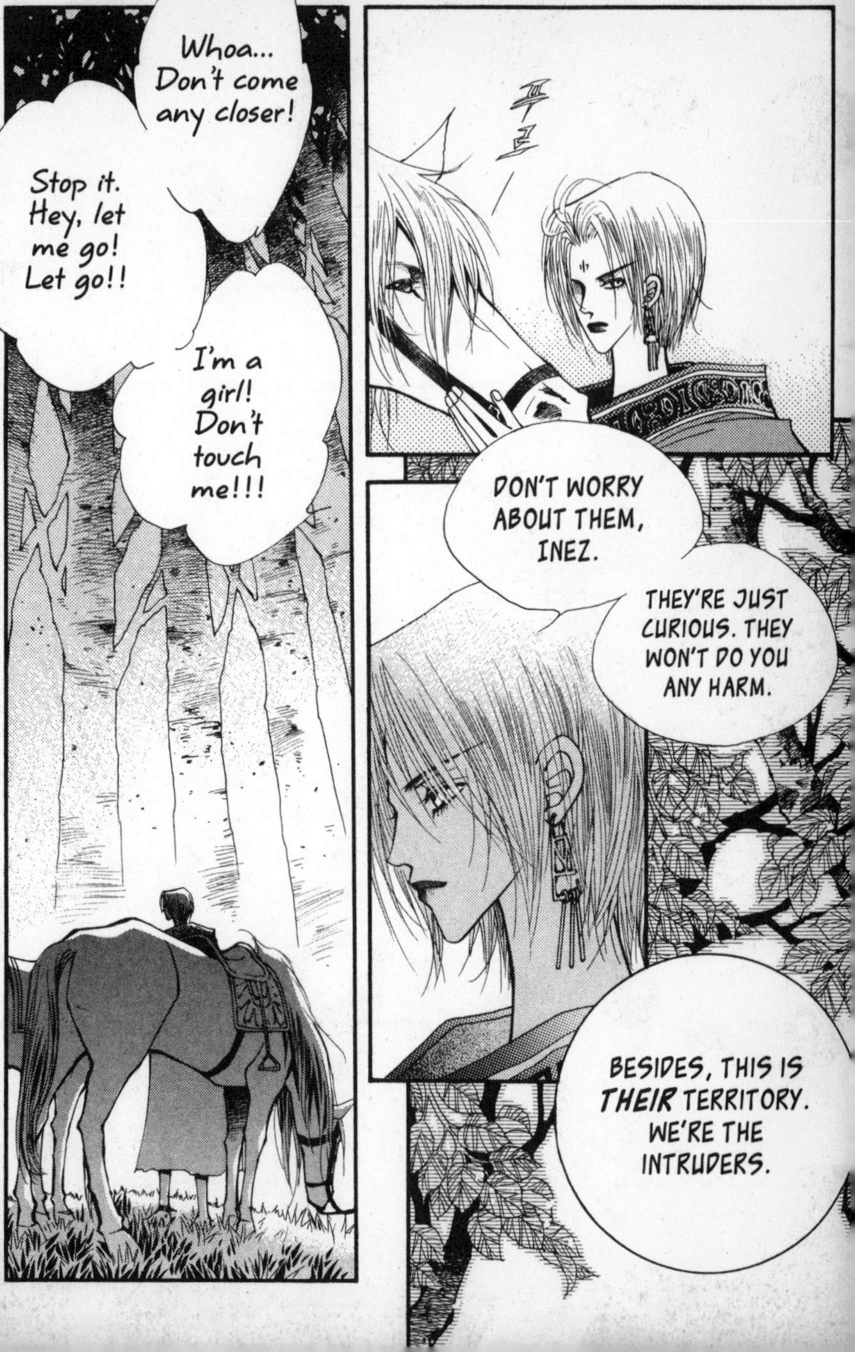
Whoa... Don't come any closer!
Stop it. Hey, let me go! Let go!!
I'm a girl! Don't touch me!!!
DON'T WORRY ABOUT THEM, INEZ.
THEY'RE JUST CURIOUS. THEY WON'T DO YOU ANY HARM.
BESIDES, THIS IS *THEIR* TERRITORY. WE'RE THE INTRUDERS.

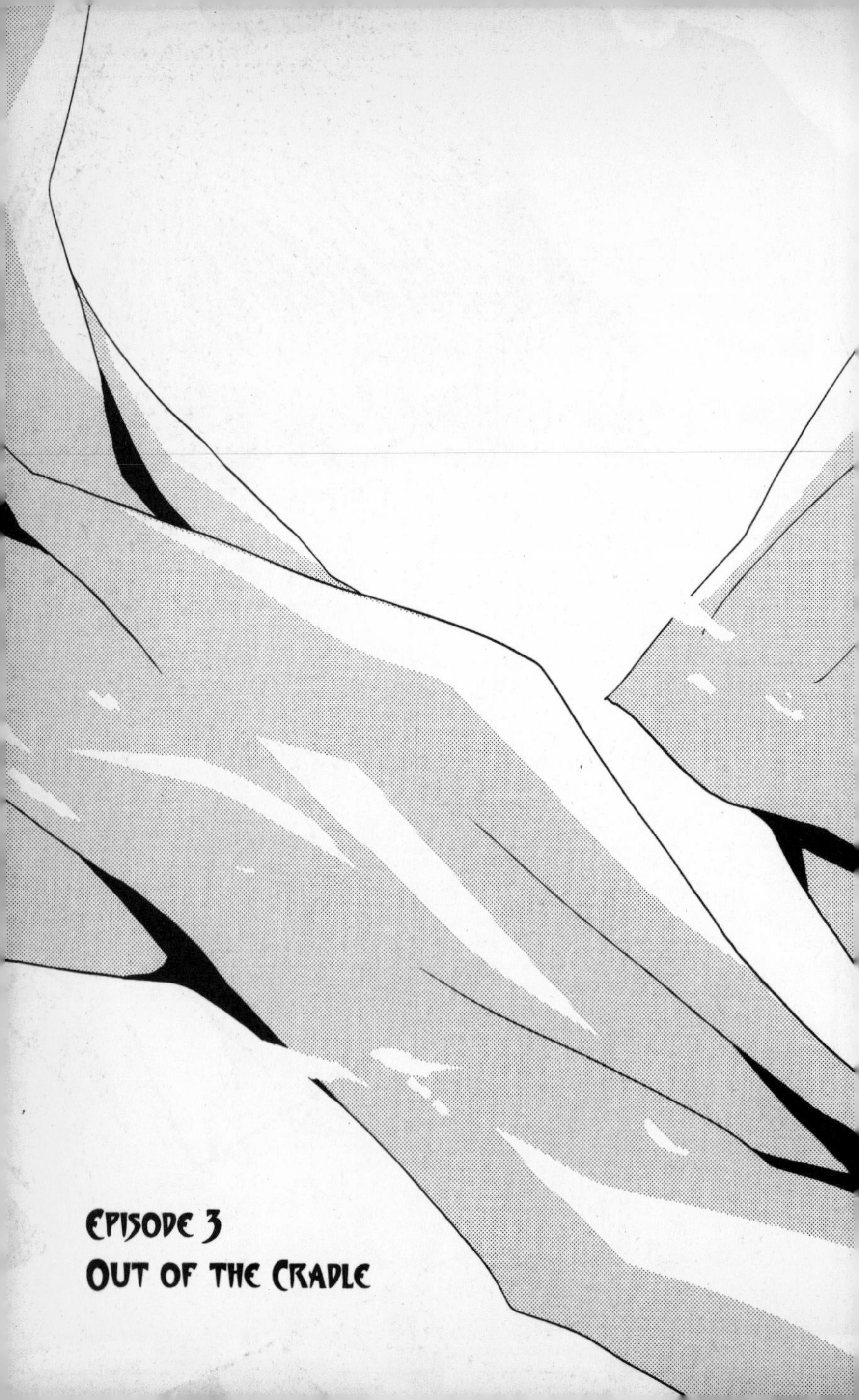

Episode 3
Out of the Cradle

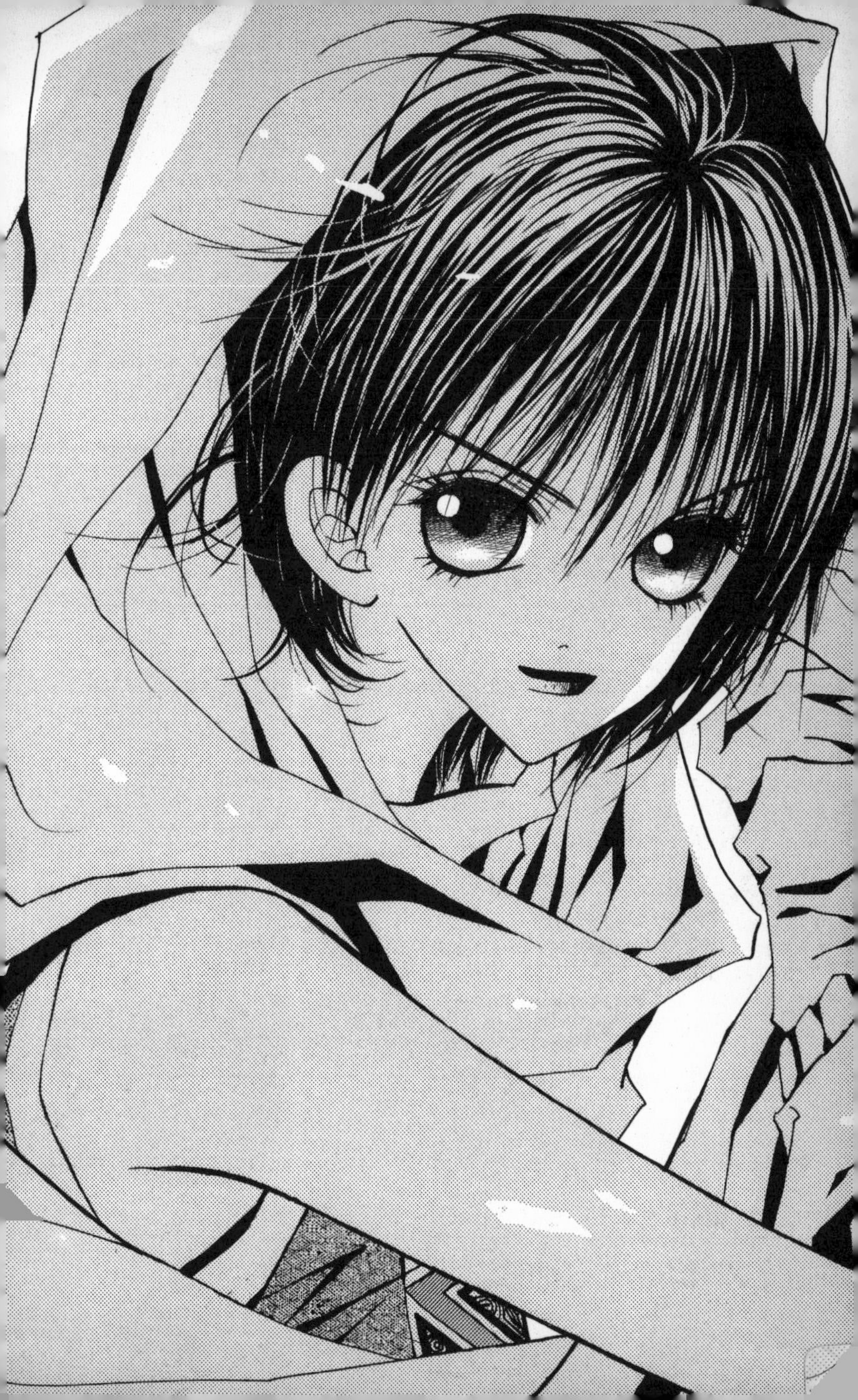

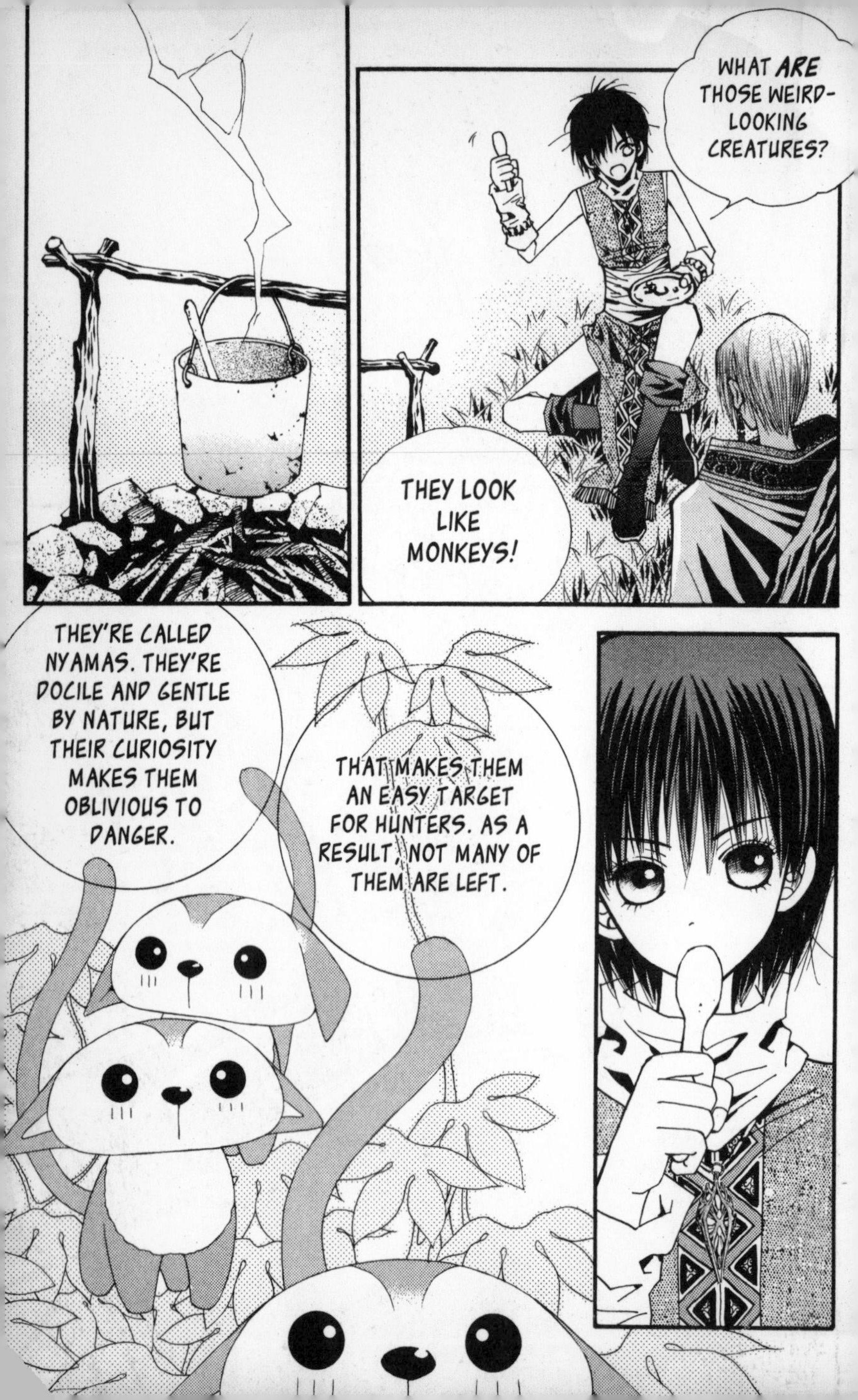
WHAT ARE THOSE WEIRD-LOOKING CREATURES?
THEY LOOK LIKE MONKEYS!
THEY'RE CALLED NYAMAS. THEY'RE DOCILE AND GENTLE BY NATURE, BUT THEIR CURIOSITY MAKES THEM OBLIVIOUS TO DANGER.
THAT MAKES THEM AN EASY TARGET FOR HUNTERS. AS A RESULT, NOT MANY OF THEM ARE LEFT.

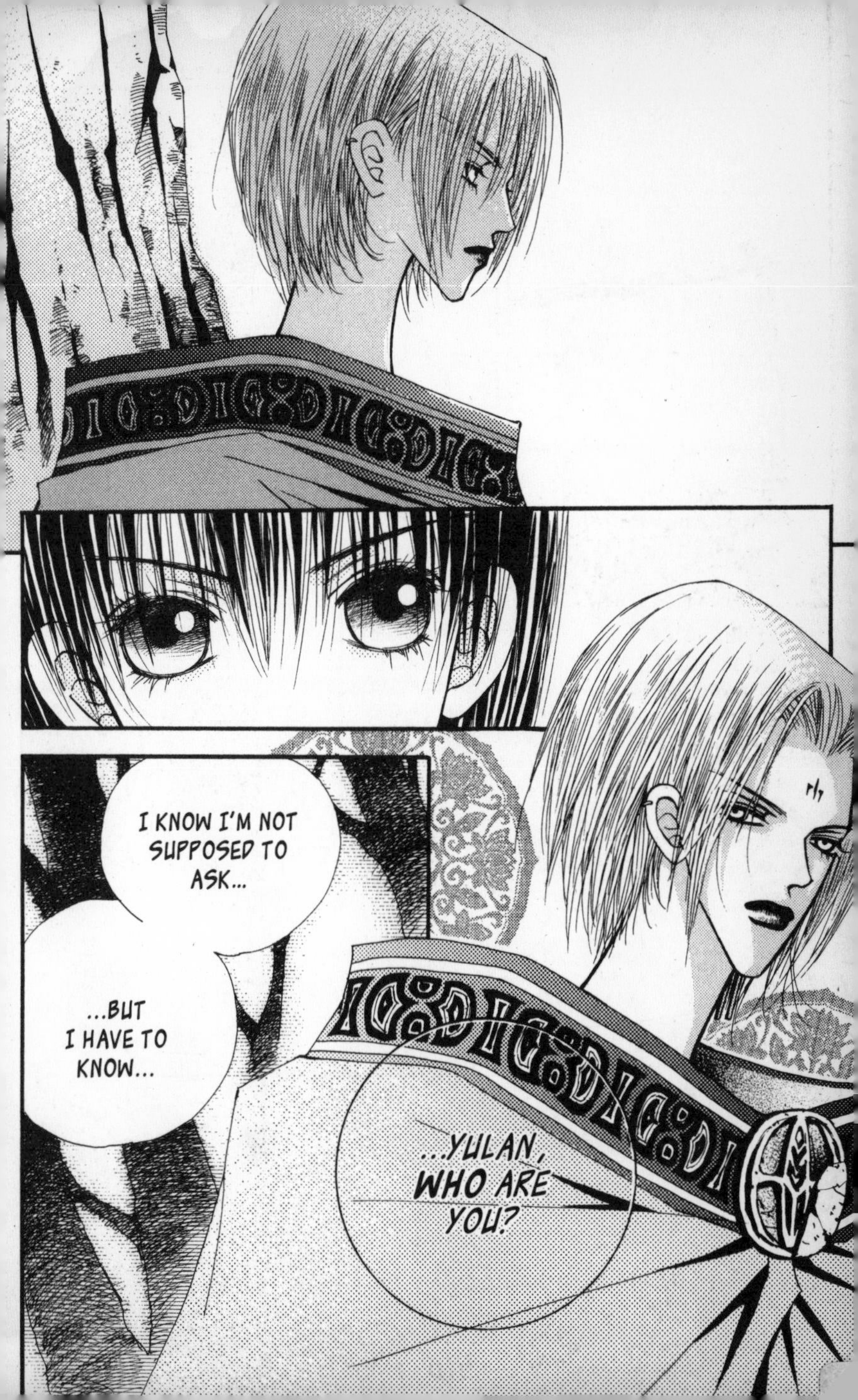
I KNOW I'M NOT SUPPOSED TO ASK...
...BUT I HAVE TO KNOW...
...YULAN, WHO ARE YOU?

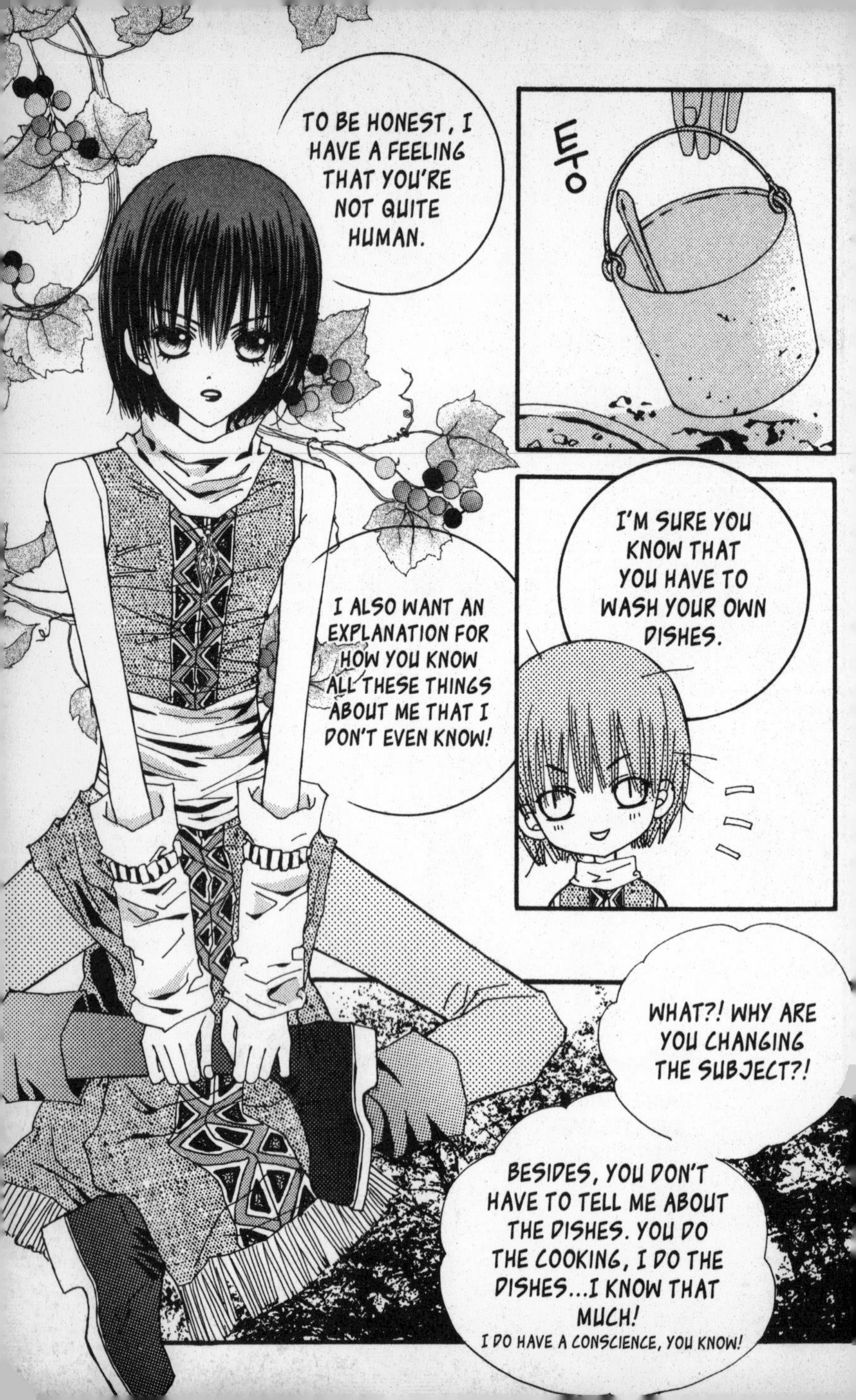
TO BE HONEST, I HAVE A FEELING THAT YOU'RE NOT QUITE HUMAN.
I ALSO WANT AN EXPLANATION FOR HOW YOU KNOW ALL THESE THINGS ABOUT ME THAT I DON'T EVEN KNOW!
퉁
I'M SURE YOU KNOW THAT YOU HAVE TO WASH YOUR OWN DISHES.
WHAT?! WHY ARE YOU CHANGING THE SUBJECT?!
BESIDES, YOU DON'T HAVE TO TELL ME ABOUT THE DISHES. YOU DO THE COOKING, I DO THE DISHES...I KNOW THAT MUCH!
I DO HAVE A CONSCIENCE, YOU KNOW!

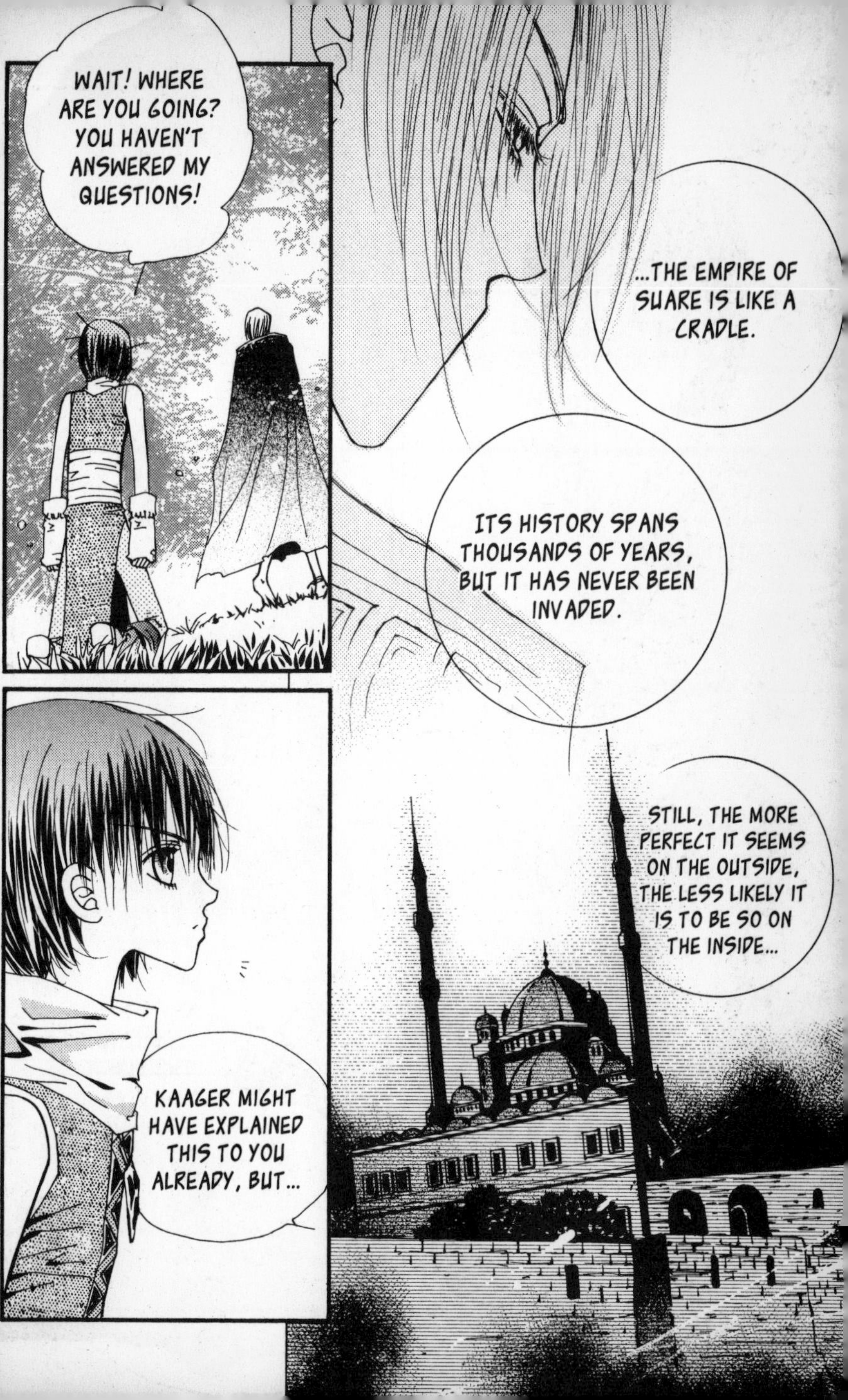
WAIT! WHERE ARE YOU GOING? YOU HAVEN'T ANSWERED MY QUESTIONS!
KAAGER MIGHT HAVE EXPLAINED THIS TO YOU ALREADY, BUT...
...THE EMPIRE OF SUARE IS LIKE A CRADLE.
ITS HISTORY SPANS THOUSANDS OF YEARS, BUT IT HAS NEVER BEEN INVADED.
STILL, THE MORE PERFECT IT SEEMS ON THE OUTSIDE, THE LESS LIKELY IT IS TO BE SO ON THE INSIDE...

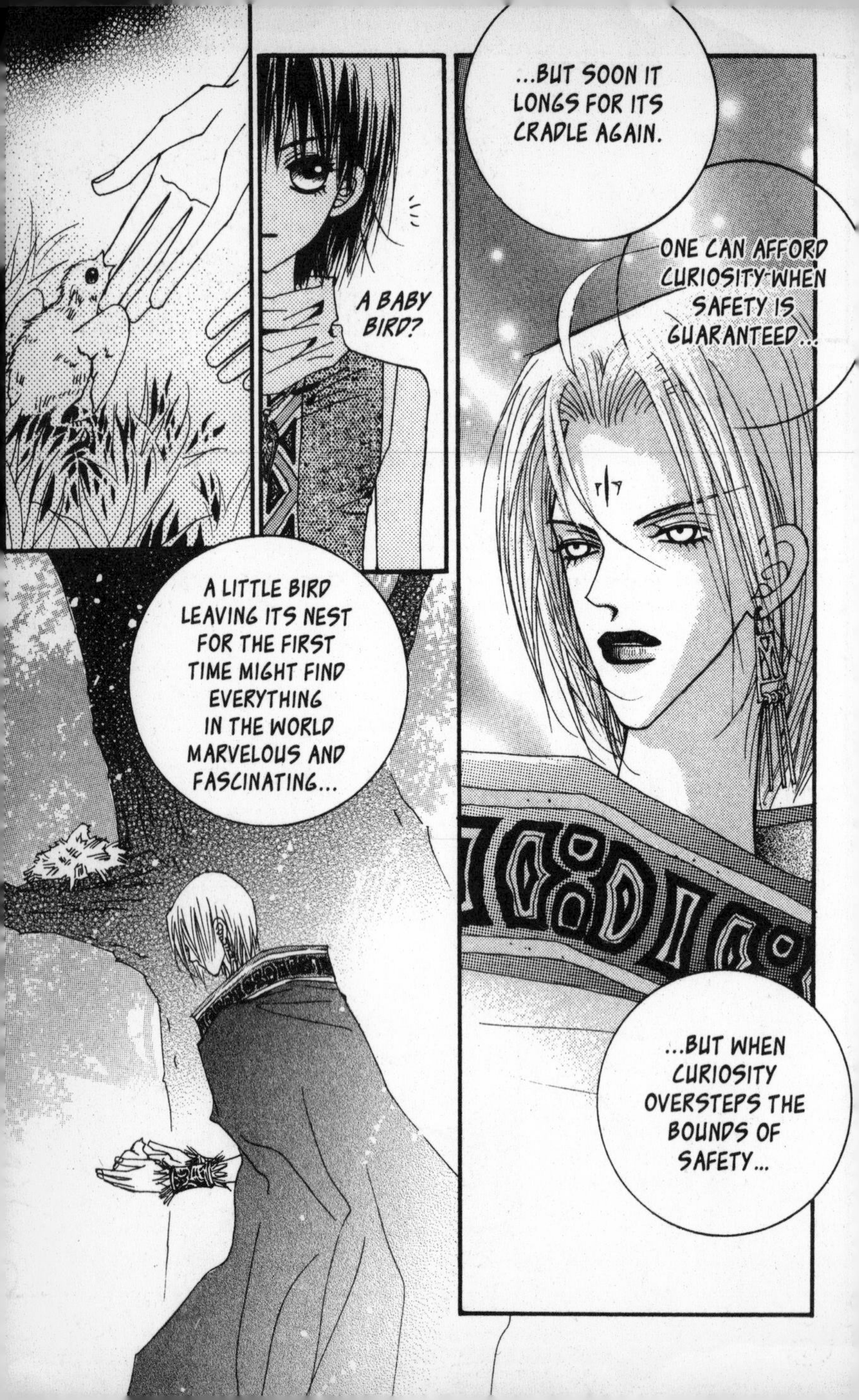
A BABY BIRD?
A LITTLE BIRD LEAVING ITS NEST FOR THE FIRST TIME MIGHT FIND EVERYTHING IN THE WORLD MARVELOUS AND FASCINATING...
...BUT SOON IT LONGS FOR ITS CRADLE AGAIN.
ONE CAN AFFORD CURIOSITY WHEN SAFETY IS GUARANTEED...
...BUT WHEN CURIOSITY OVERSTEPS THE BOUNDS OF SAFETY...

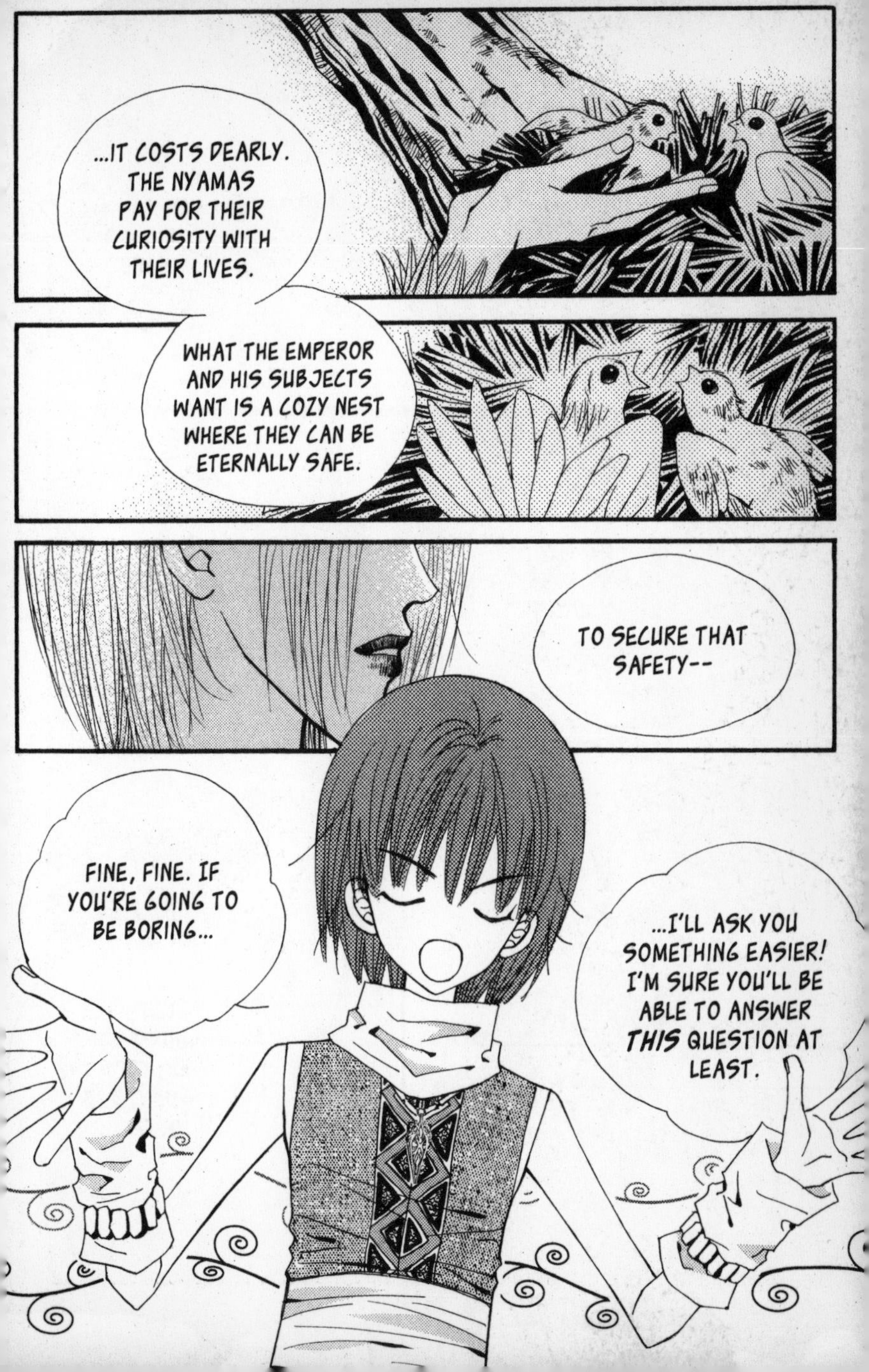
...IT COSTS DEARLY. THE NYAMAS PAY FOR THEIR CURIOSITY WITH THEIR LIVES.
WHAT THE EMPEROR AND HIS SUBJECTS WANT IS A COZY NEST WHERE THEY CAN BE ETERNALLY SAFE.
TO SECURE THAT SAFETY--
FINE, FINE. IF YOU'RE GOING TO BE BORING...
...I'LL ASK YOU SOMETHING EASIER! I'M SURE YOU'LL BE ABLE TO ANSWER *THIS* QUESTION AT LEAST.

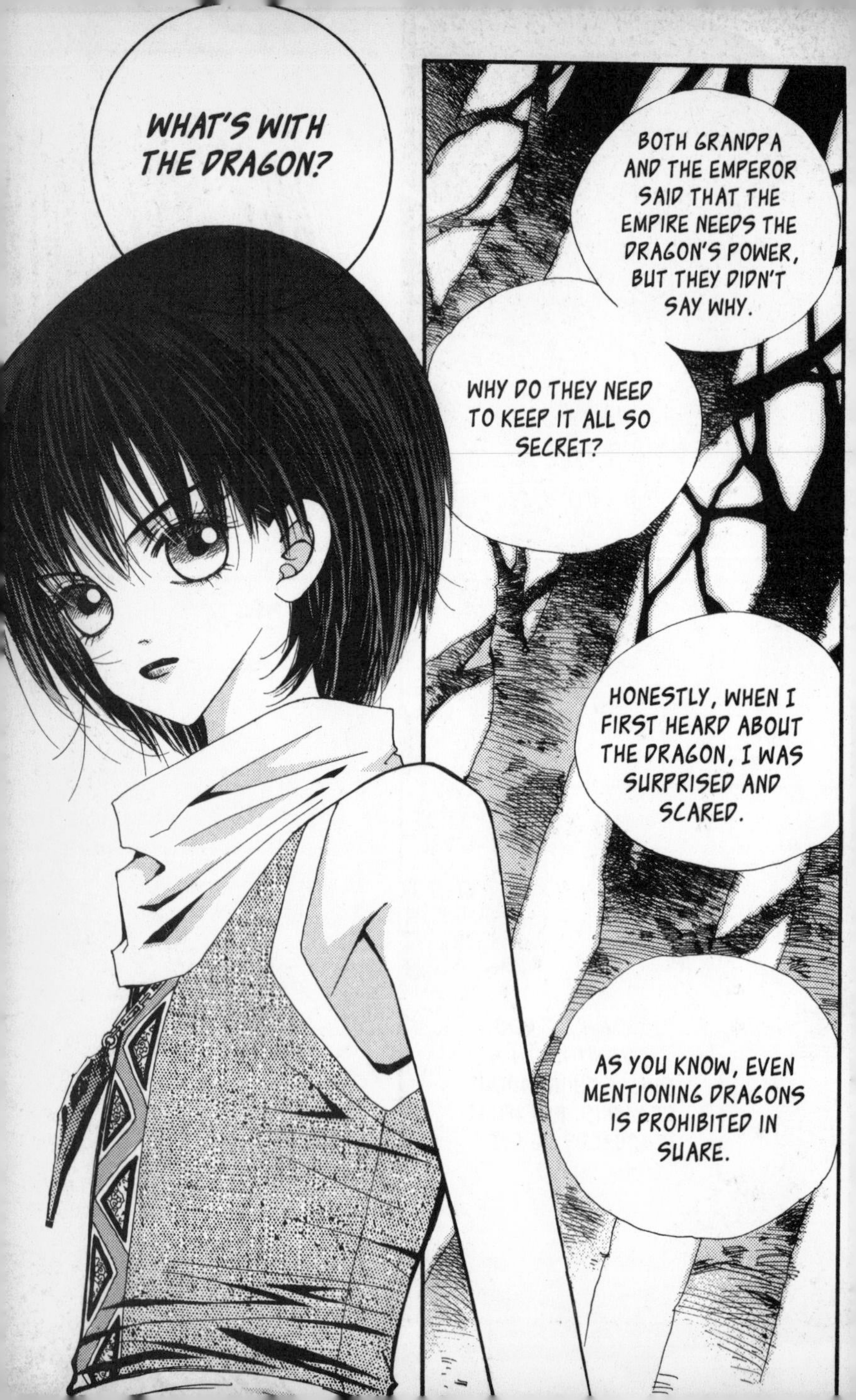
WHAT'S WITH THE DRAGON?
BOTH GRANDPA AND THE EMPEROR SAID THAT THE EMPIRE NEEDS THE DRAGON'S POWER, BUT THEY DIDN'T SAY WHY.
WHY DO THEY NEED TO KEEP IT ALL SO SECRET?
HONESTLY, WHEN I FIRST HEARD ABOUT THE DRAGON, I WAS SURPRISED AND SCARED.
AS YOU KNOW, EVEN MENTIONING DRAGONS IS PROHIBITED IN SUARE.

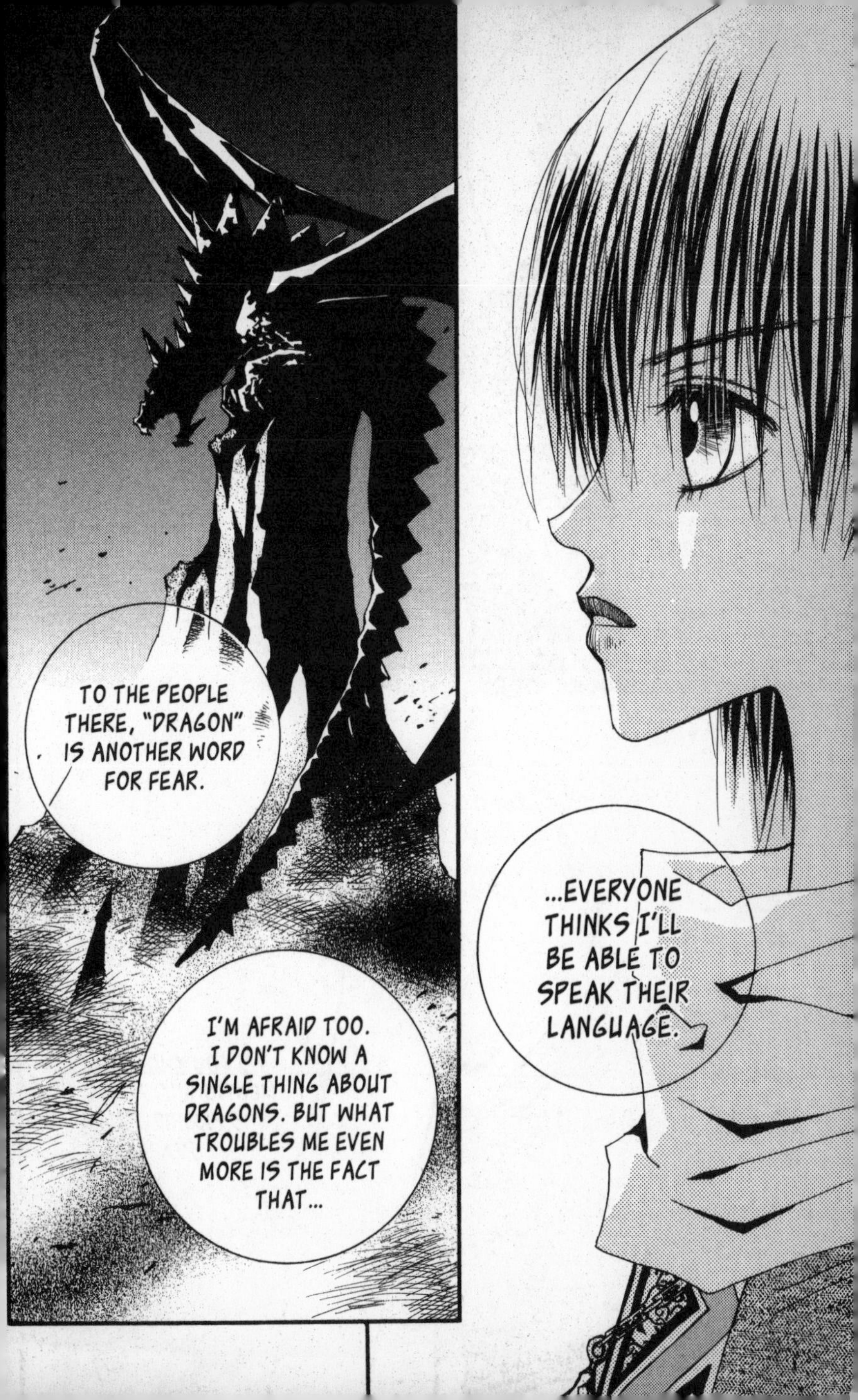
TO THE PEOPLE THERE, "DRAGON" IS ANOTHER WORD FOR FEAR.
I'M AFRAID TOO. I DON'T KNOW A SINGLE THING ABOUT DRAGONS. BUT WHAT TROUBLES ME EVEN MORE IS THE FACT THAT...
...EVERYONE THINKS I'LL BE ABLE TO SPEAK THEIR LANGUAGE.

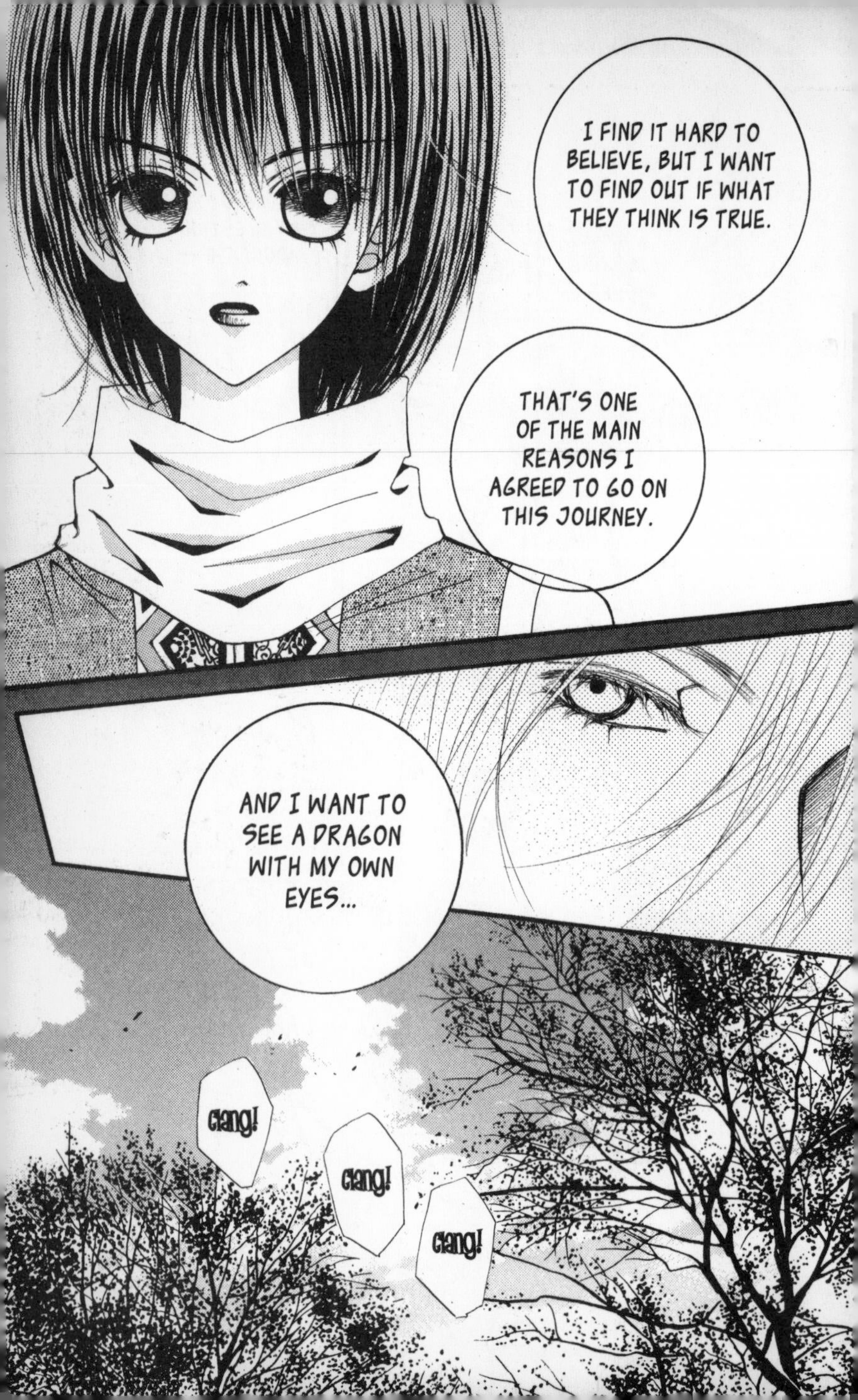

I FIND IT HARD TO BELIEVE, BUT I WANT TO FIND OUT IF WHAT THEY THINK IS TRUE.
THAT'S ONE OF THE MAIN REASONS I AGREED TO GO ON THIS JOURNEY.
AND I WANT TO SEE A DRAGON WITH MY OWN EYES...
Clang!
Clang!
Clang!

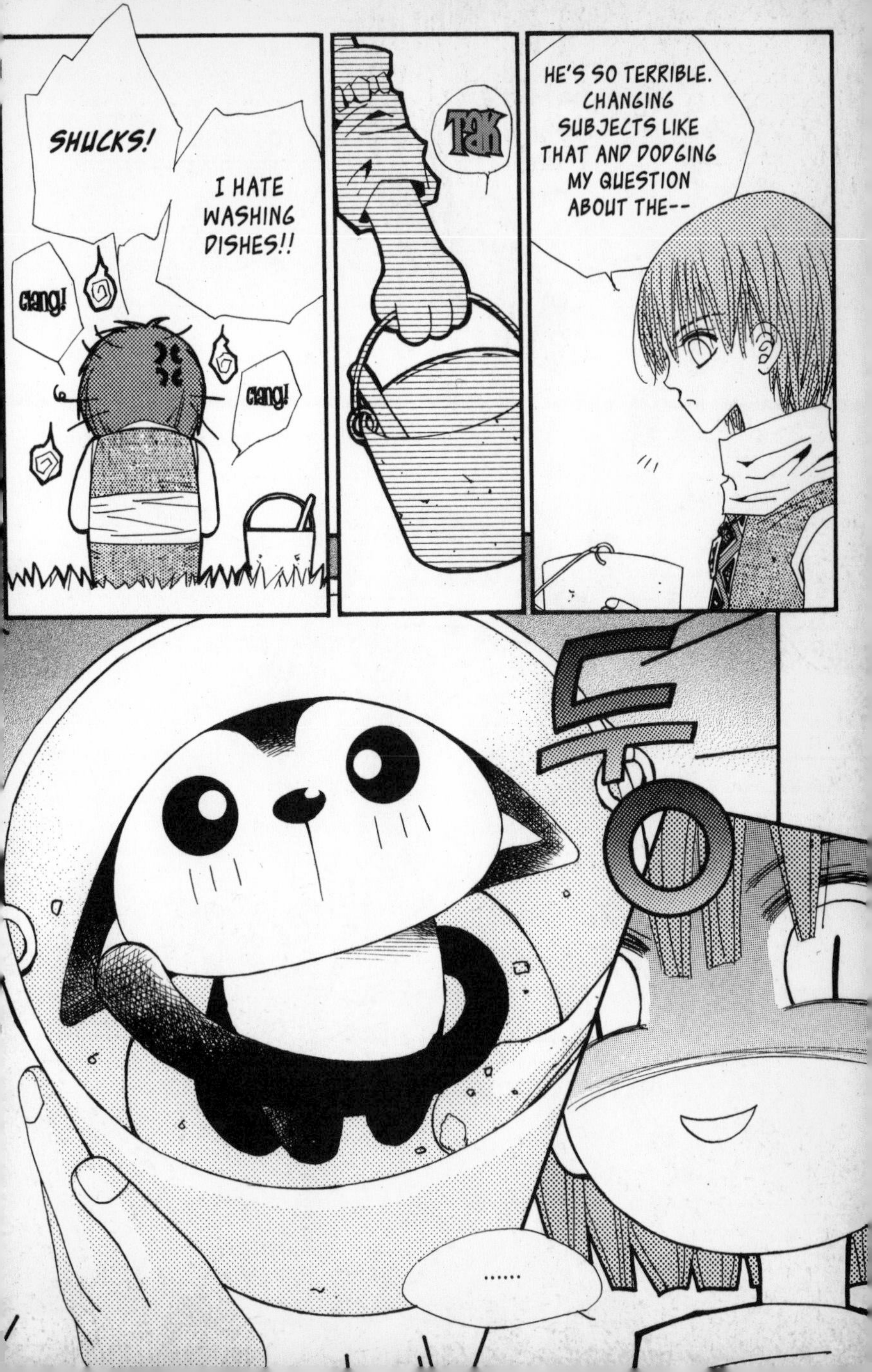
SHUCKS!
I HATE WASHING DISHES!!
CLANG!
CLANG!
TAK
HE'S SO TERRIBLE. CHANGING SUBJECTS LIKE THAT AND DODGING MY QUESTION ABOUT THE--
......

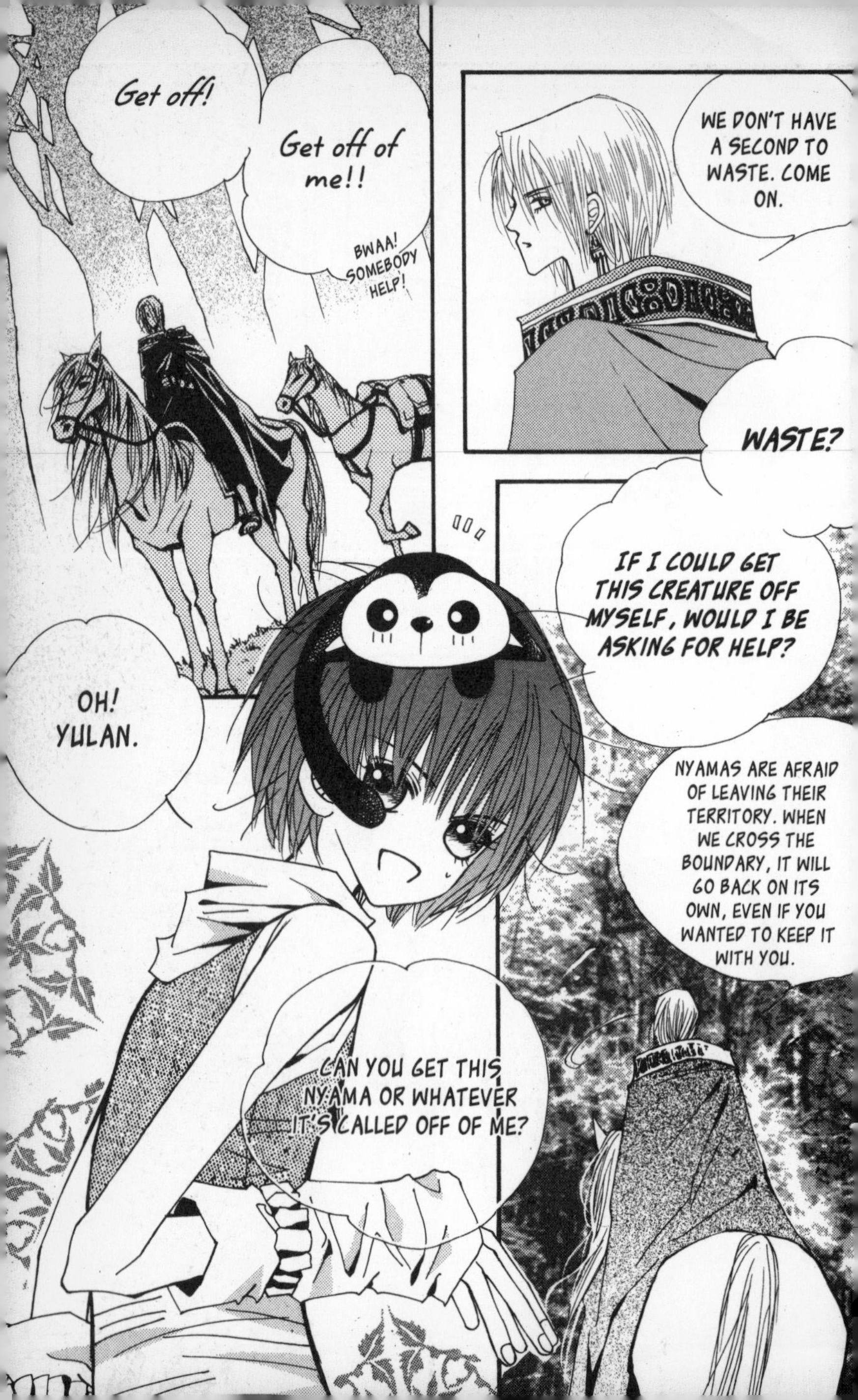
Get off!
Get off of me!!
BWAA! SOMEBODY HELP!
WE DON'T HAVE A SECOND TO WASTE. COME ON.
WASTE?
IF I COULD GET THIS CREATURE OFF MYSELF, WOULD I BE ASKING FOR HELP?
OH! YULAN.
NYAMAS ARE AFRAID OF LEAVING THEIR TERRITORY. WHEN WE CROSS THE BOUNDARY, IT WILL GO BACK ON ITS OWN, EVEN IF YOU WANTED TO KEEP IT WITH YOU.
CAN YOU GET THIS NYAMA OR WHATEVER IT'S CALLED OFF OF ME?

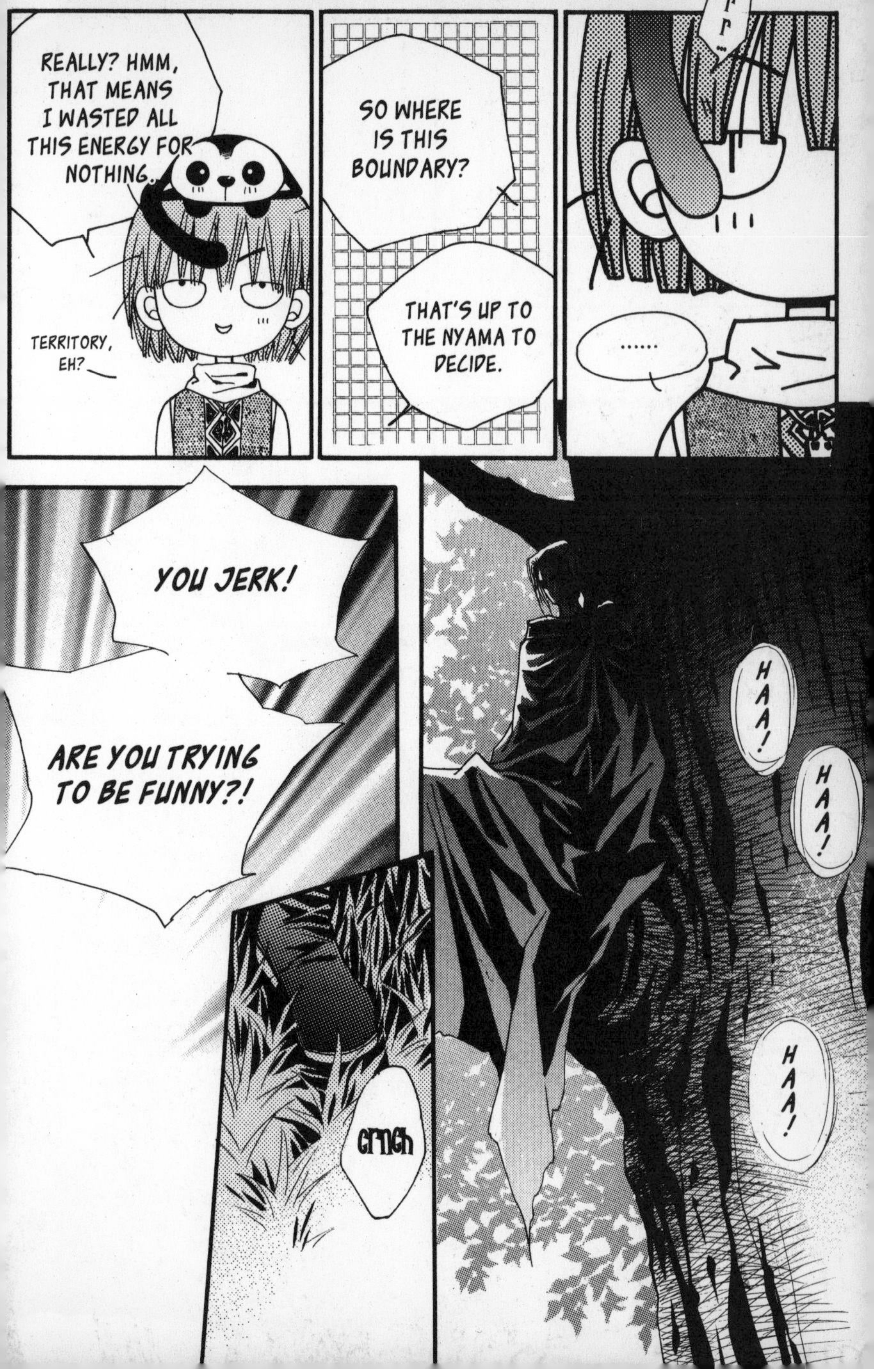
REALLY? HMM, THAT MEANS I WASTED ALL THIS ENERGY FOR NOTHING.
TERRITORY, EH?
SO WHERE IS THIS BOUNDARY?
THAT'S UP TO THE NYAMA TO DECIDE.
srr...
......
YOU JERK!
ARE YOU TRYING TO BE FUNNY?!
crnch
HAA!
HAA!
HAA!

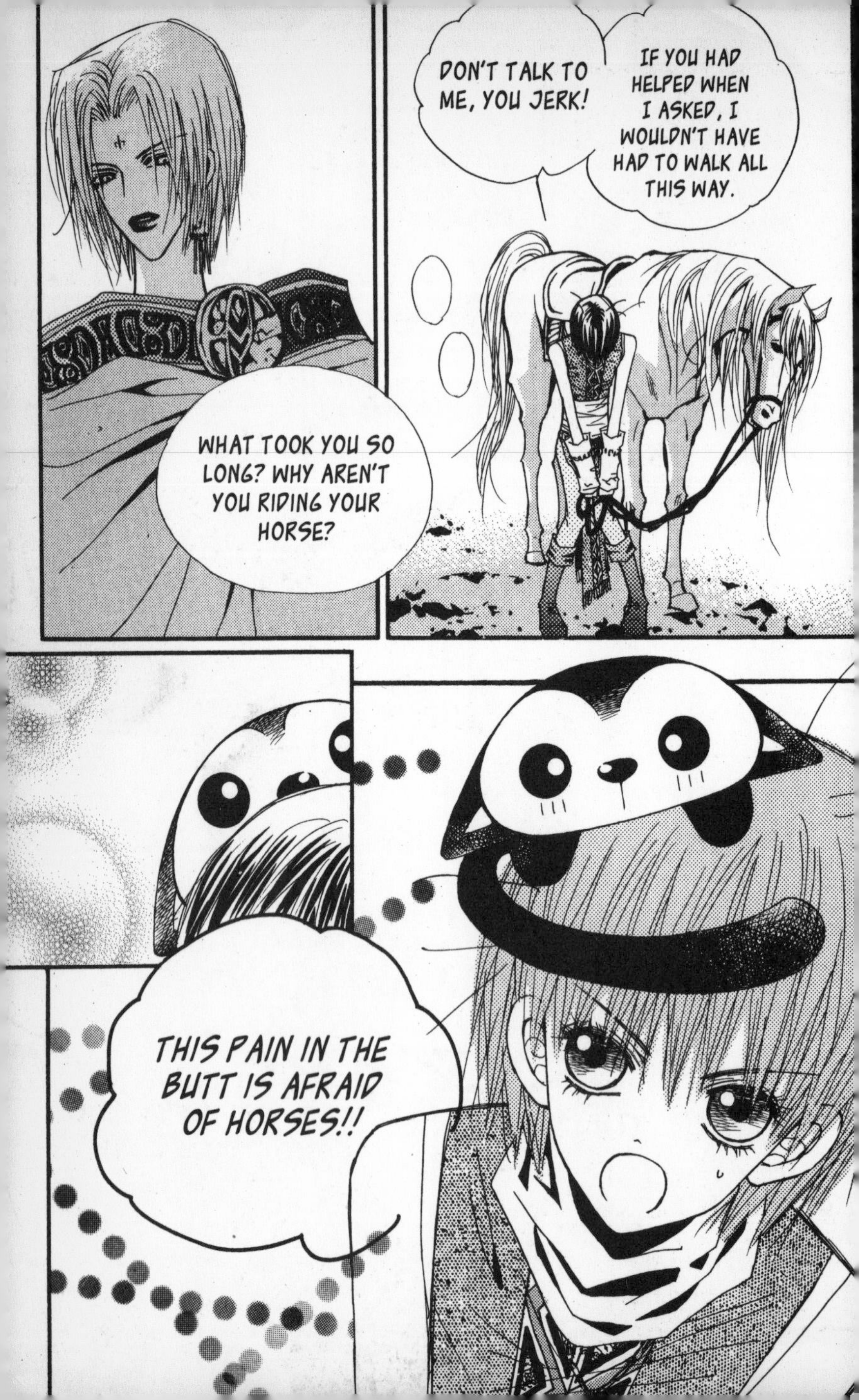
WHAT TOOK YOU SO LONG? WHY AREN'T YOU RIDING YOUR HORSE?
DON'T TALK TO ME, YOU JERK!
IF YOU HAD HELPED WHEN I ASKED, I WOULDN'T HAVE HAD TO WALK ALL THIS WAY.
THIS PAIN IN THE BUTT IS AFRAID OF HORSES!!

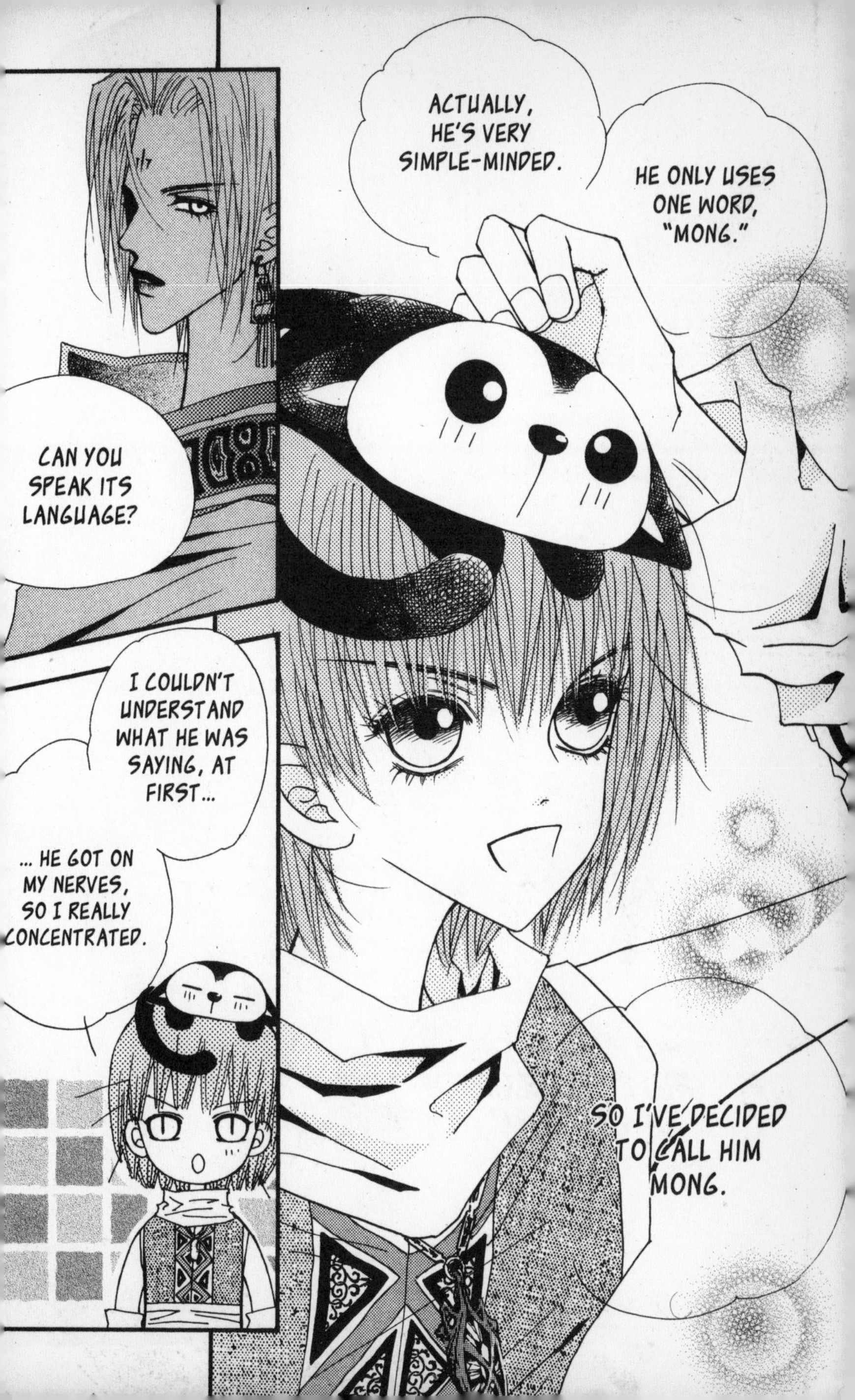
CAN YOU SPEAK ITS LANGUAGE?
I COULDN'T UNDERSTAND WHAT HE WAS SAYING, AT FIRST...
... HE GOT ON MY NERVES, SO I REALLY CONCENTRATED.
ACTUALLY, HE'S VERY SIMPLE-MINDED.
HE ONLY USES ONE WORD, "MONG."
SO I'VE DECIDED TO CALL HIM MONG.

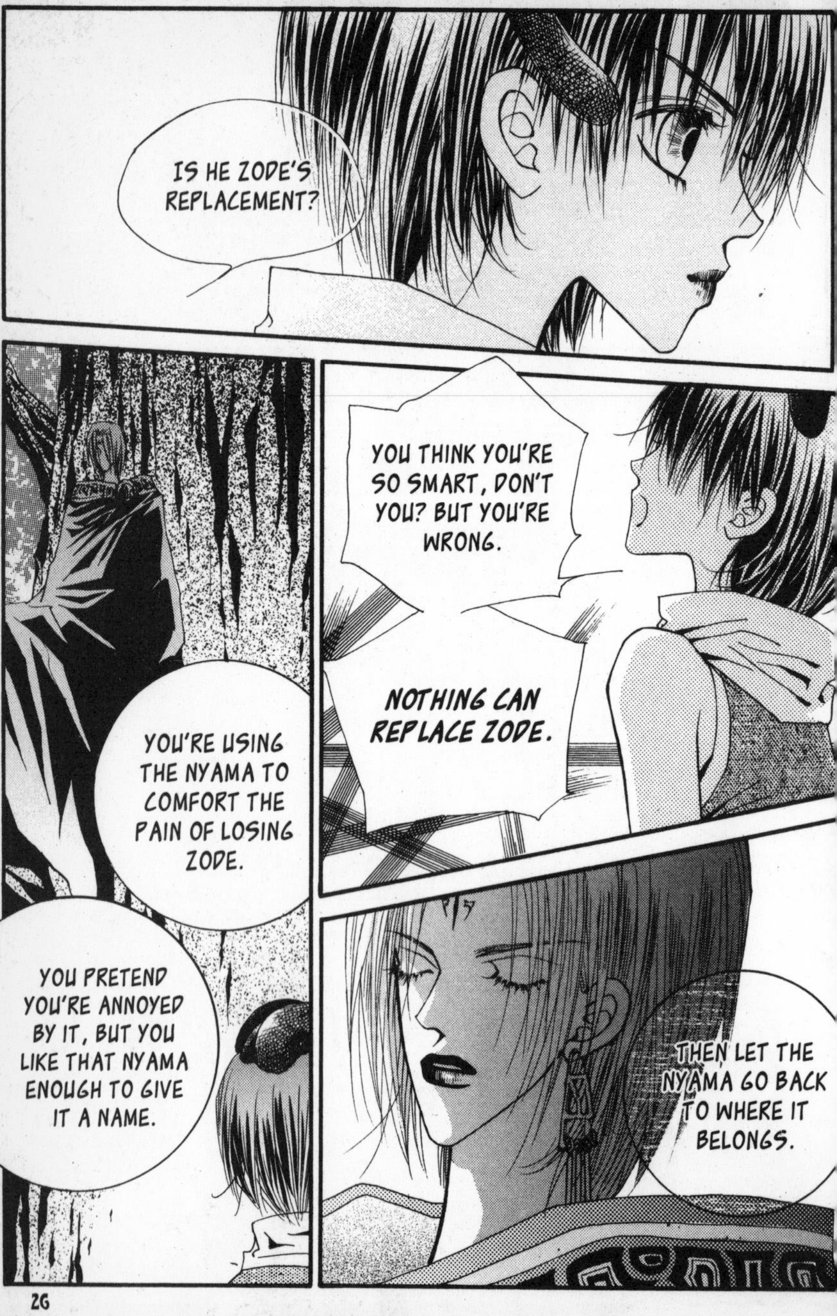
IS HE ZODE'S REPLACEMENT?
YOU'RE USING THE NYAMA TO COMFORT THE PAIN OF LOSING ZODE.
YOU PRETEND YOU'RE ANNOYED BY IT, BUT YOU LIKE THAT NYAMA ENOUGH TO GIVE IT A NAME.
YOU THINK YOU'RE SO SMART, DON'T YOU? BUT YOU'RE WRONG.
NOTHING CAN REPLACE ZODE.
THEN LET THE NYAMA GO BACK TO WHERE IT BELONGS.

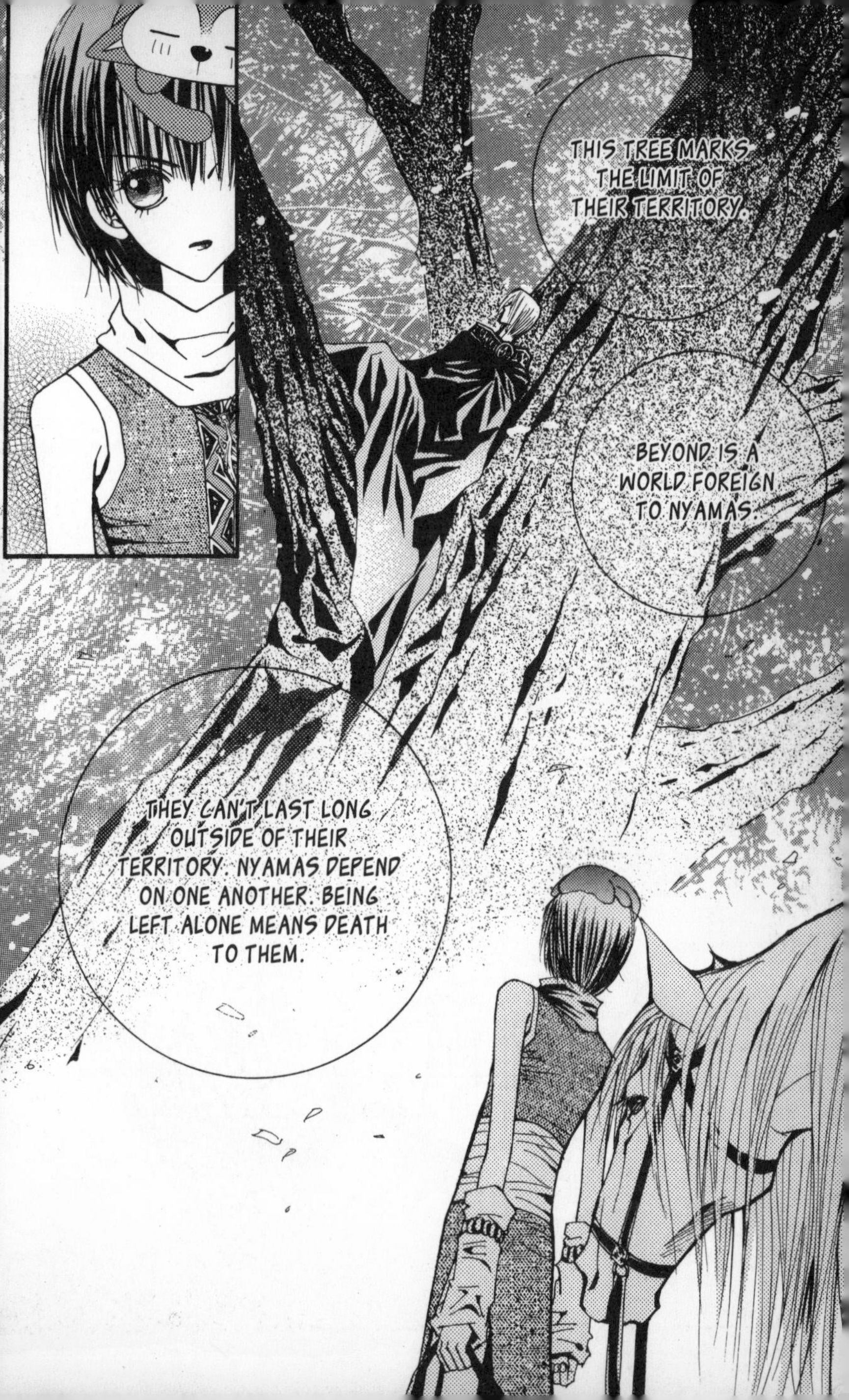
THIS TREE MARKS THE LIMIT OF THEIR TERRITORY.
BEYOND IS A WORLD FOREIGN TO NYAMAS.
THEY CAN'T LAST LONG OUTSIDE OF THEIR TERRITORY. NYAMAS DEPEND ON ONE ANOTHER. BEING LEFT ALONE MEANS DEATH TO THEM.

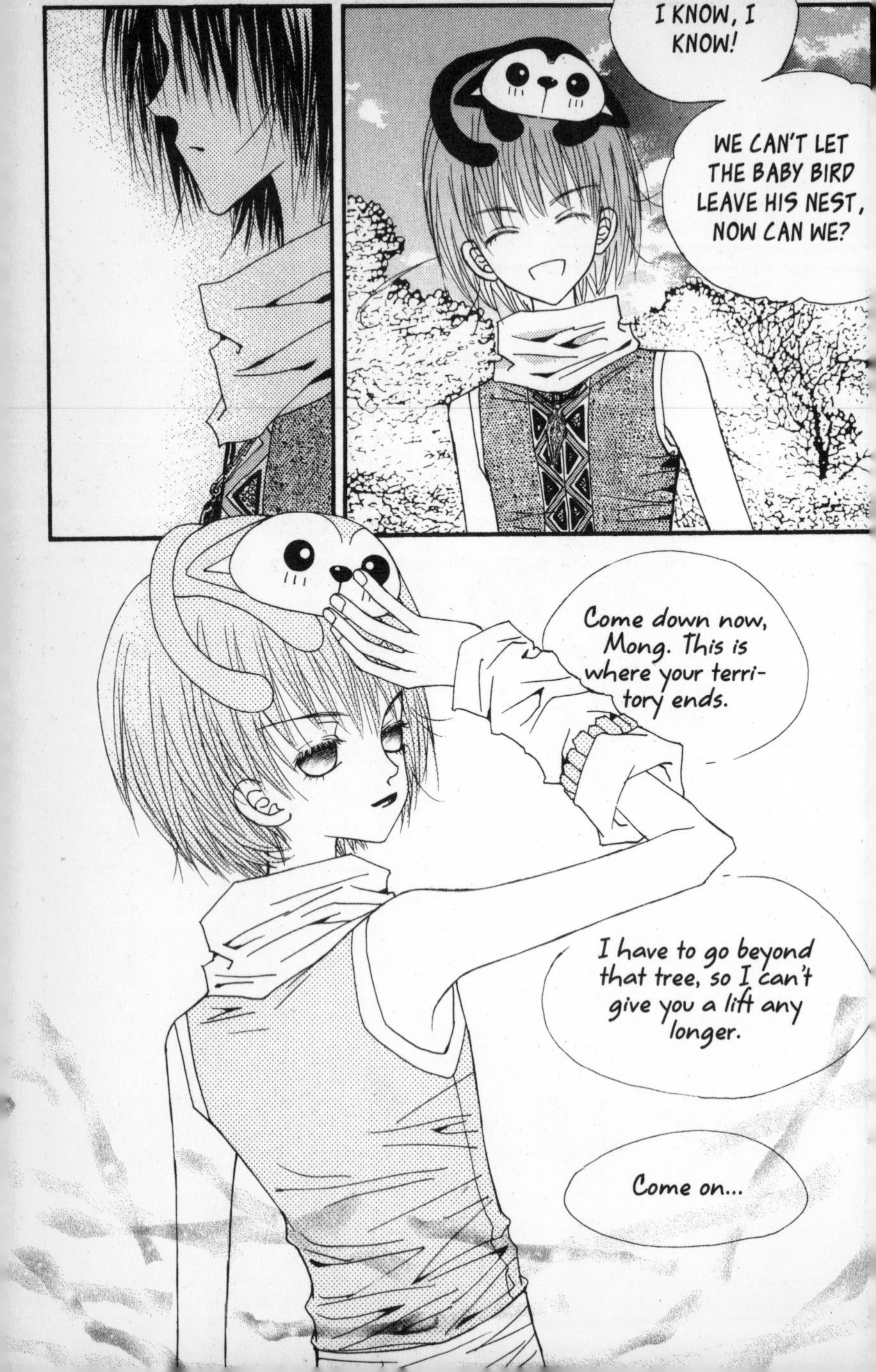
I KNOW, I KNOW!
WE CAN'T LET THE BABY BIRD LEAVE HIS NEST, NOW CAN WE?
Come down now, Mong. This is where your terri-tory ends.
I have to go beyond that tree, so I can't give you a lift any longer.
Come on...

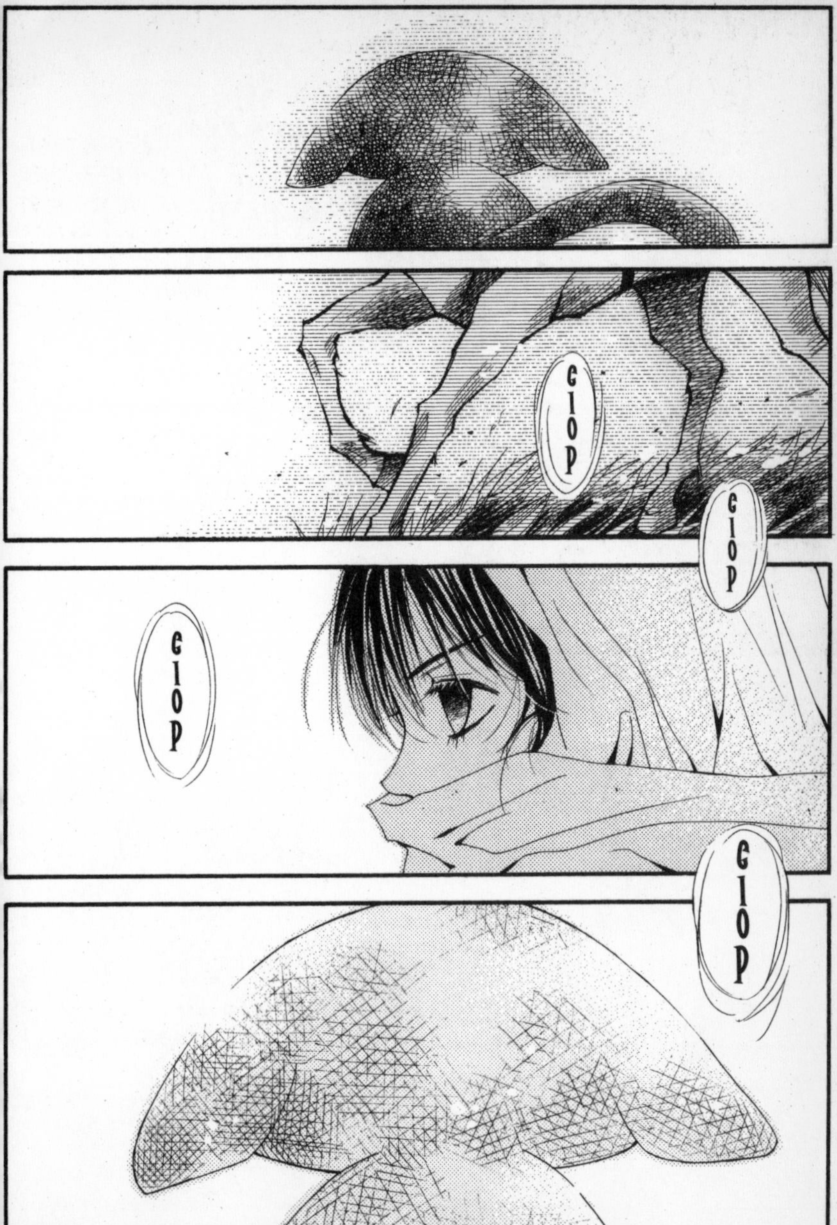
GLOP
GLOP
GLOP
GLOP

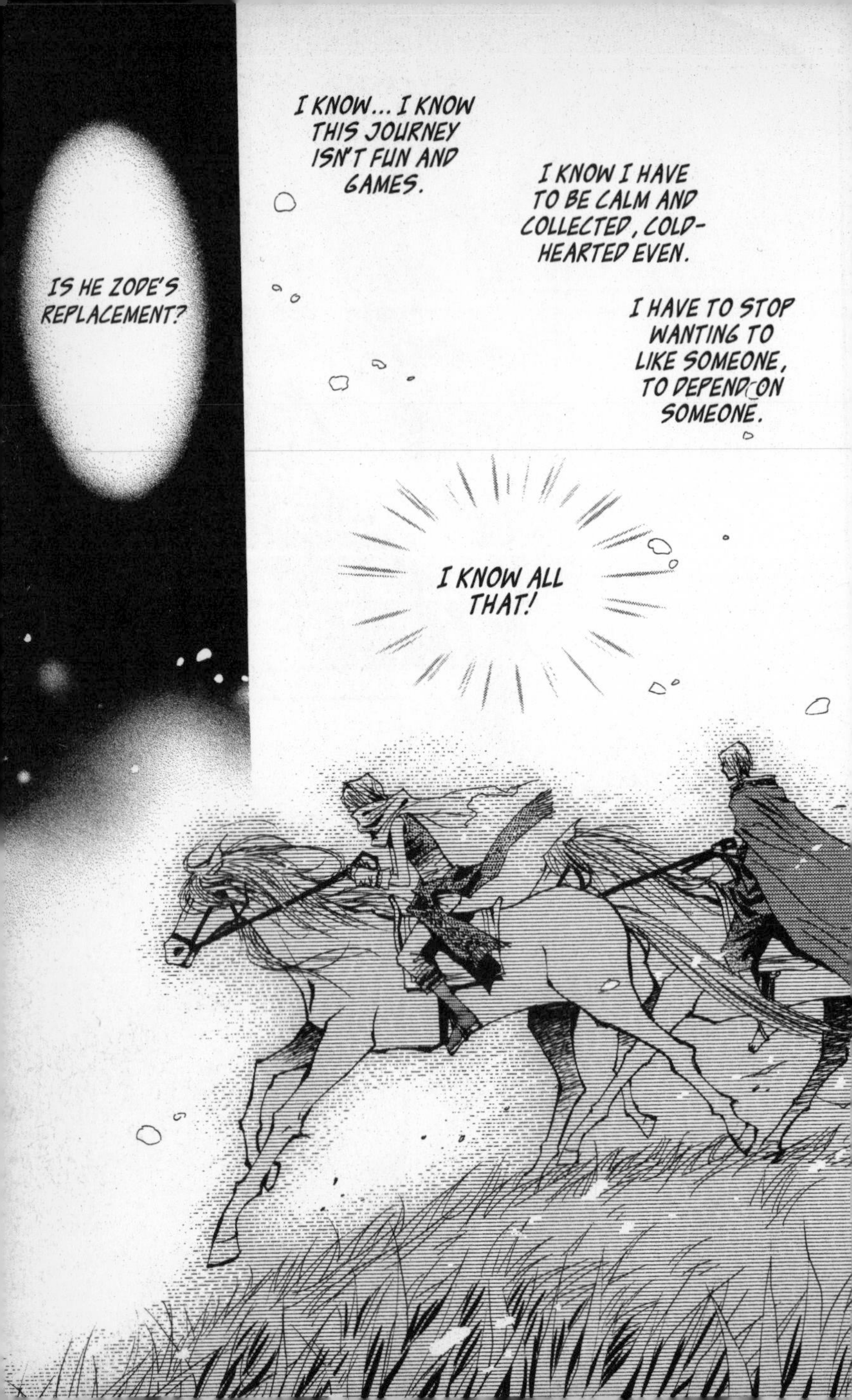
IS HE ZODE'S REPLACEMENT?
I KNOW... I KNOW THIS JOURNEY ISN'T FUN AND GAMES.
I KNOW I HAVE TO BE CALM AND COLLECTED, COLD-HEARTED EVEN.
I HAVE TO STOP WANTING TO LIKE SOMEONE, TO DEPEND ON SOMEONE.
I KNOW ALL THAT!

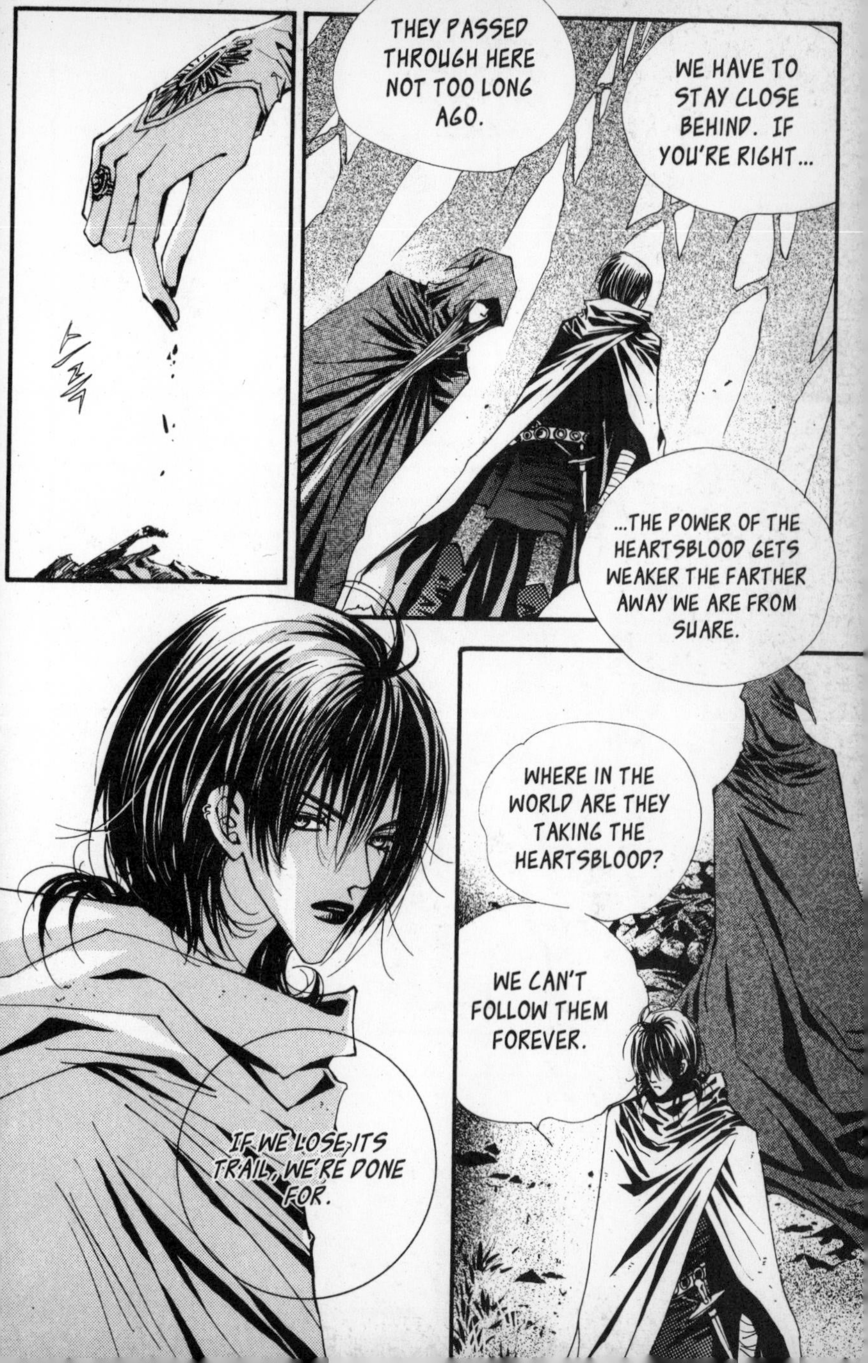
THEY PASSED THROUGH HERE NOT TOO LONG AGO.
WE HAVE TO STAY CLOSE BEHIND. IF YOU'RE RIGHT...
...THE POWER OF THE HEARTSBLOOD GETS WEAKER THE FARTHER AWAY WE ARE FROM SUARE.
IF WE LOSE ITS TRAIL, WE'RE DONE FOR.
WHERE IN THE WORLD ARE THEY TAKING THE HEARTSBLOOD?
WE CAN'T FOLLOW THEM FOREVER.

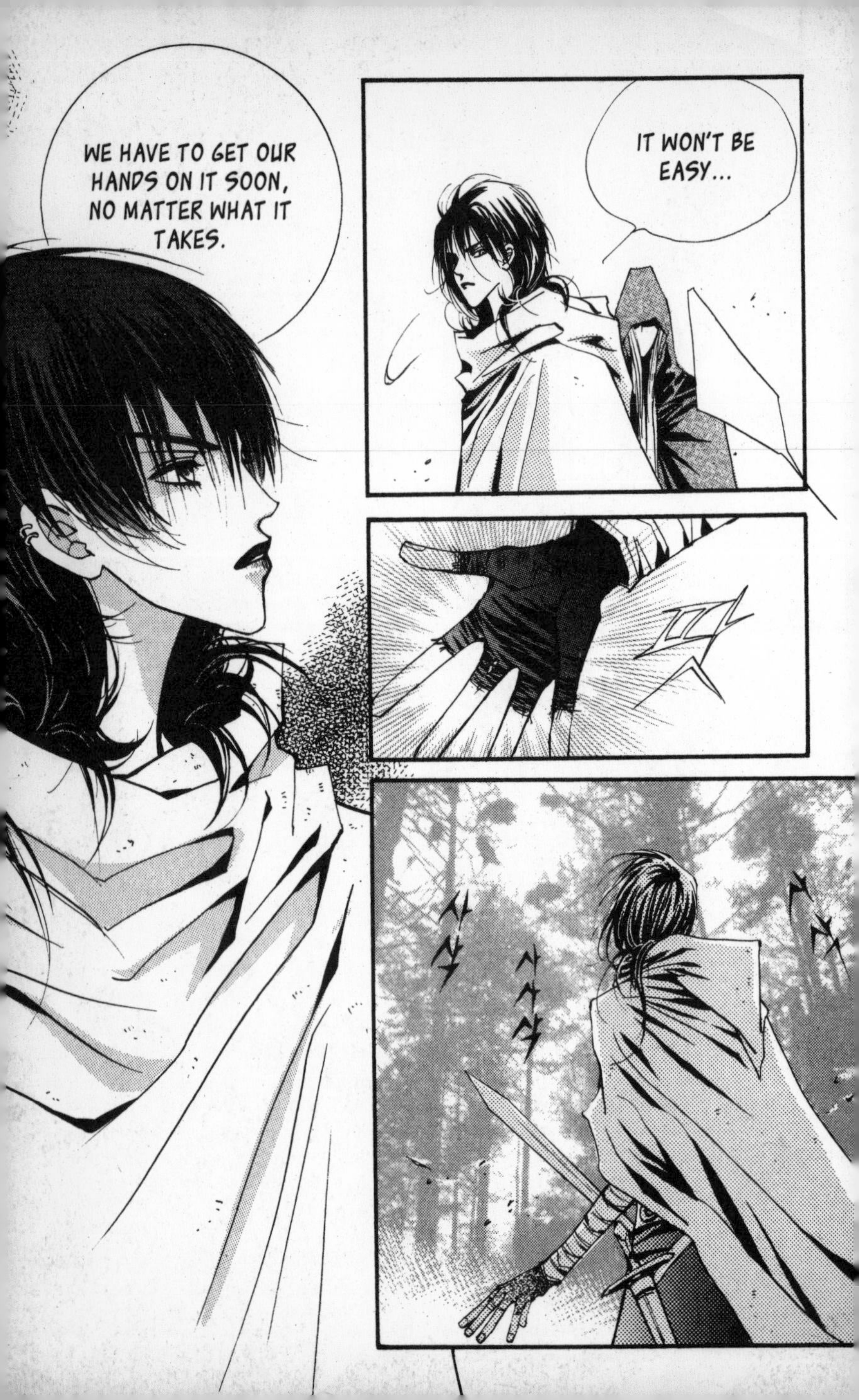
WE HAVE TO GET OUR HANDS ON IT SOON, NO MATTER WHAT IT TAKES.
IT WON'T BE EASY...

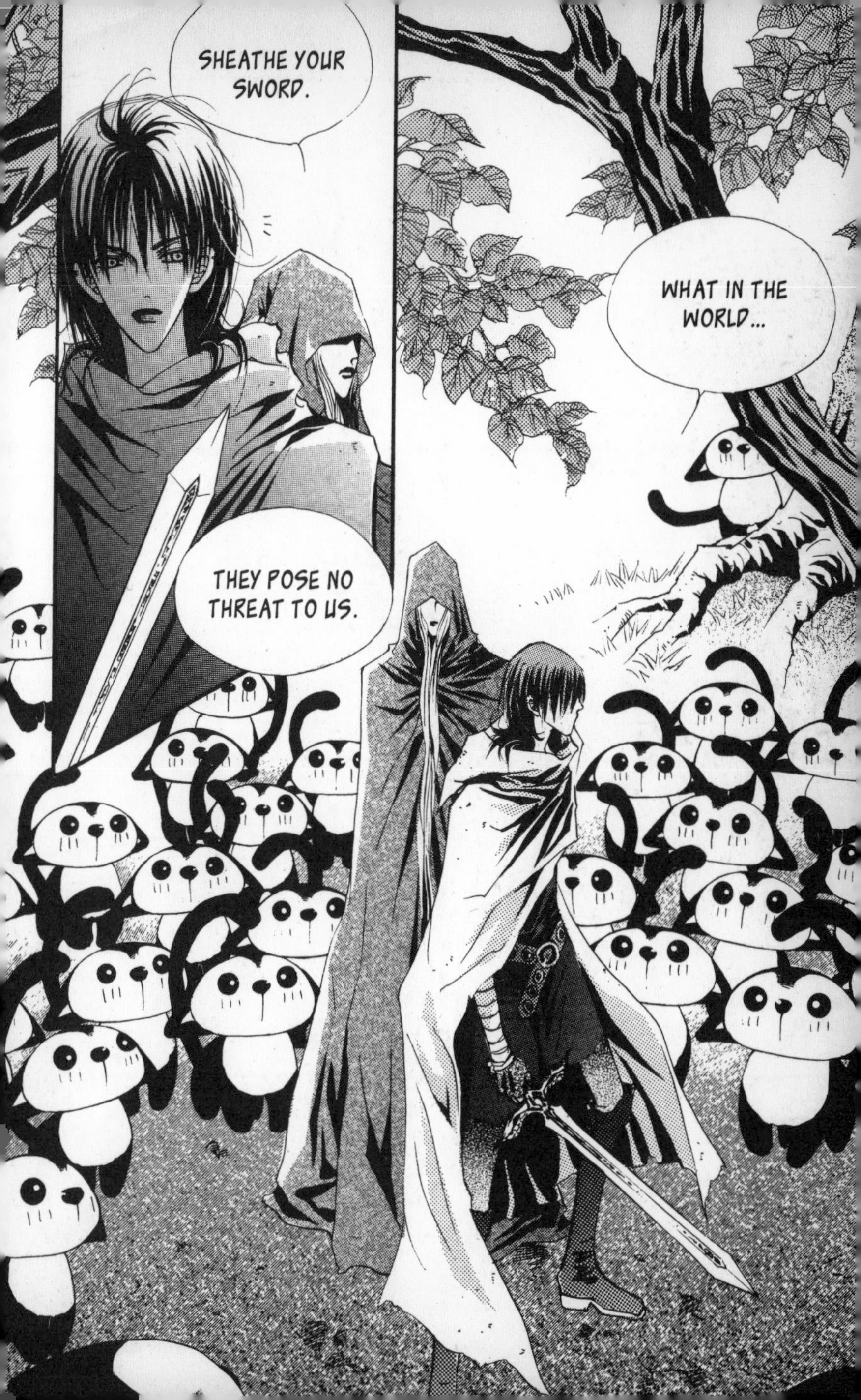
SHEATHE YOUR SWORD.
THEY POSE NO THREAT TO US.
WHAT IN THE WORLD...

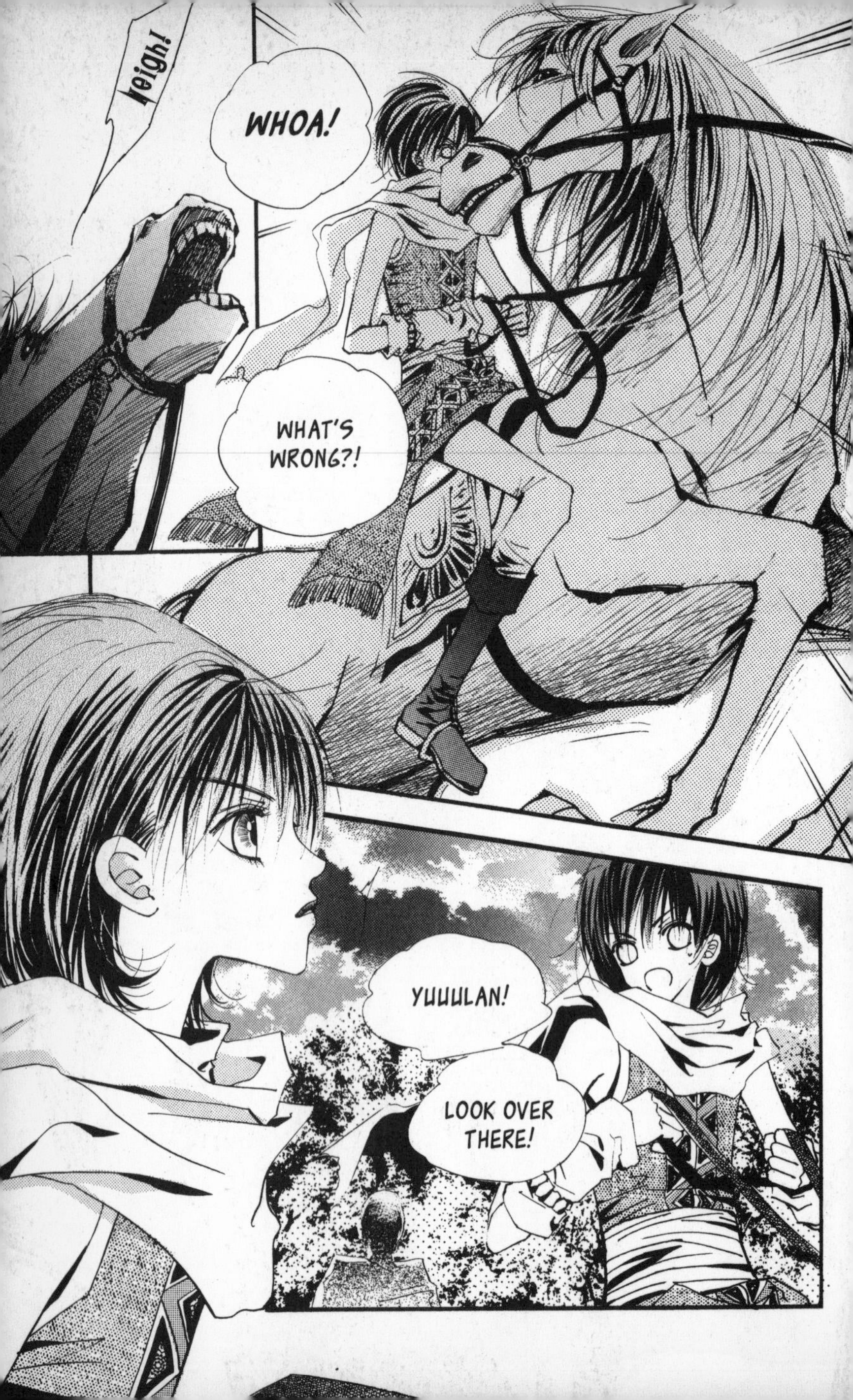
neigh!
WHOA!
WHAT'S WRONG?!
YUUULAN!
LOOK OVER THERE!

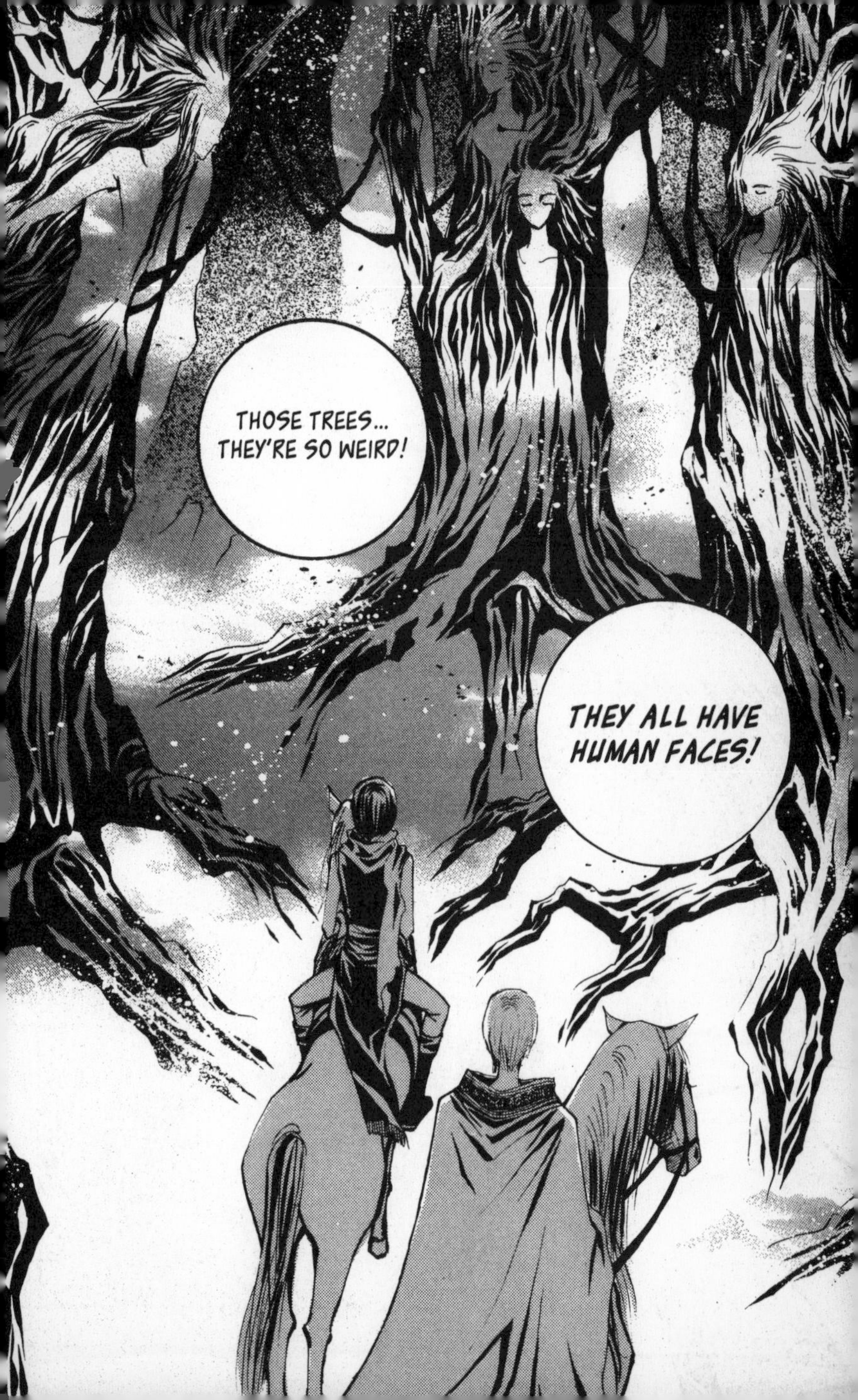
THOSE TREES... THEY'RE SO WEIRD!
THEY ALL HAVE HUMAN FACES!

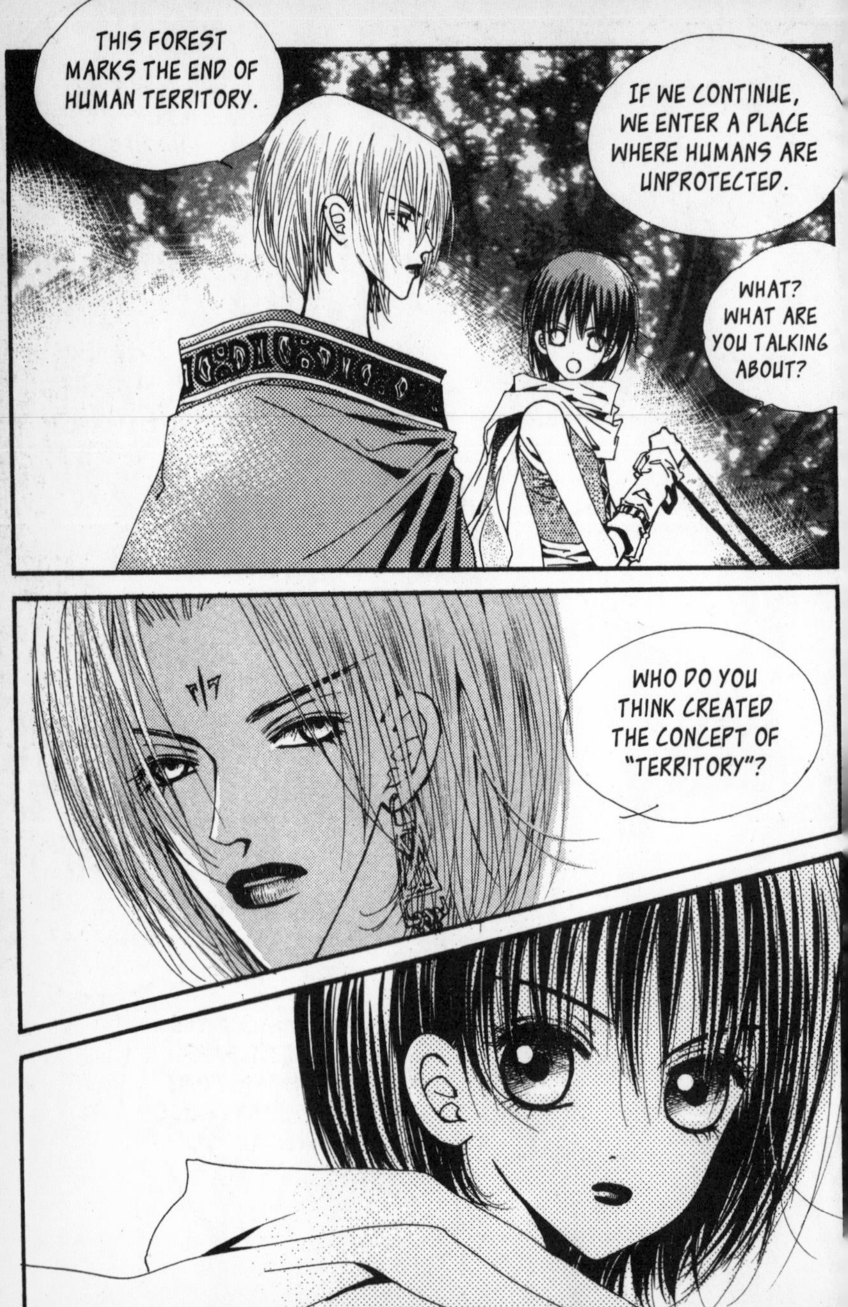
THIS FOREST MARKS THE END OF HUMAN TERRITORY.
IF WE CONTINUE, WE ENTER A PLACE WHERE HUMANS ARE UNPROTECTED.
WHAT? WHAT ARE YOU TALKING ABOUT?
WHO DO YOU THINK CREATED THE CONCEPT OF "TERRITORY"?

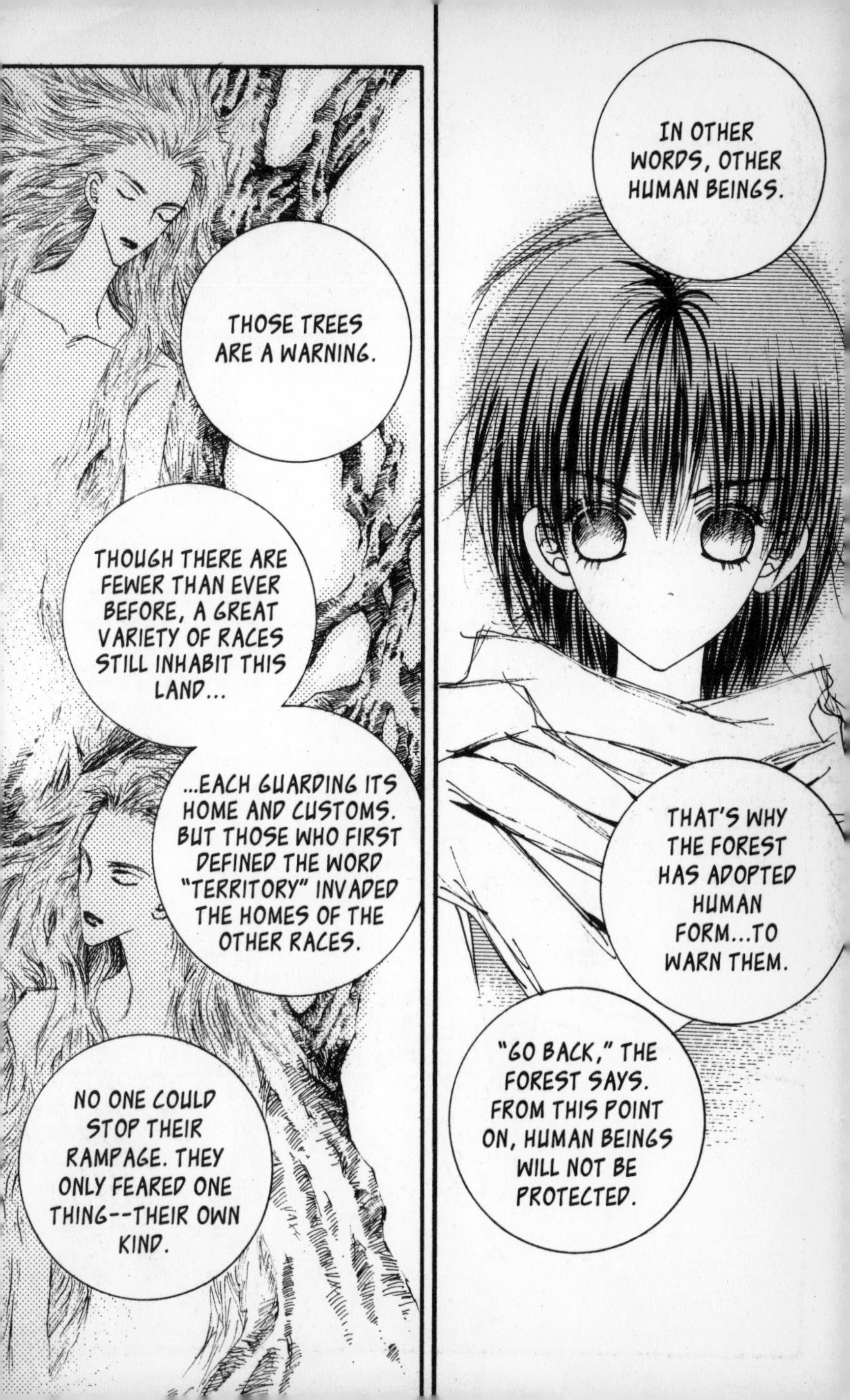
THOSE TREES ARE A WARNING.
THOUGH THERE ARE FEWER THAN EVER BEFORE, A GREAT VARIETY OF RACES STILL INHABIT THIS LAND...
...EACH GUARDING ITS HOME AND CUSTOMS. BUT THOSE WHO FIRST DEFINED THE WORD "TERRITORY" INVADED THE HOMES OF THE OTHER RACES.
NO ONE COULD STOP THEIR RAMPAGE. THEY ONLY FEARED ONE THING--THEIR OWN KIND.
IN OTHER WORDS, OTHER HUMAN BEINGS.
THAT'S WHY THE FOREST HAS ADOPTED HUMAN FORM...TO WARN THEM.
"GO BACK," THE FOREST SAYS. FROM THIS POINT ON, HUMAN BEINGS WILL NOT BE PROTECTED.

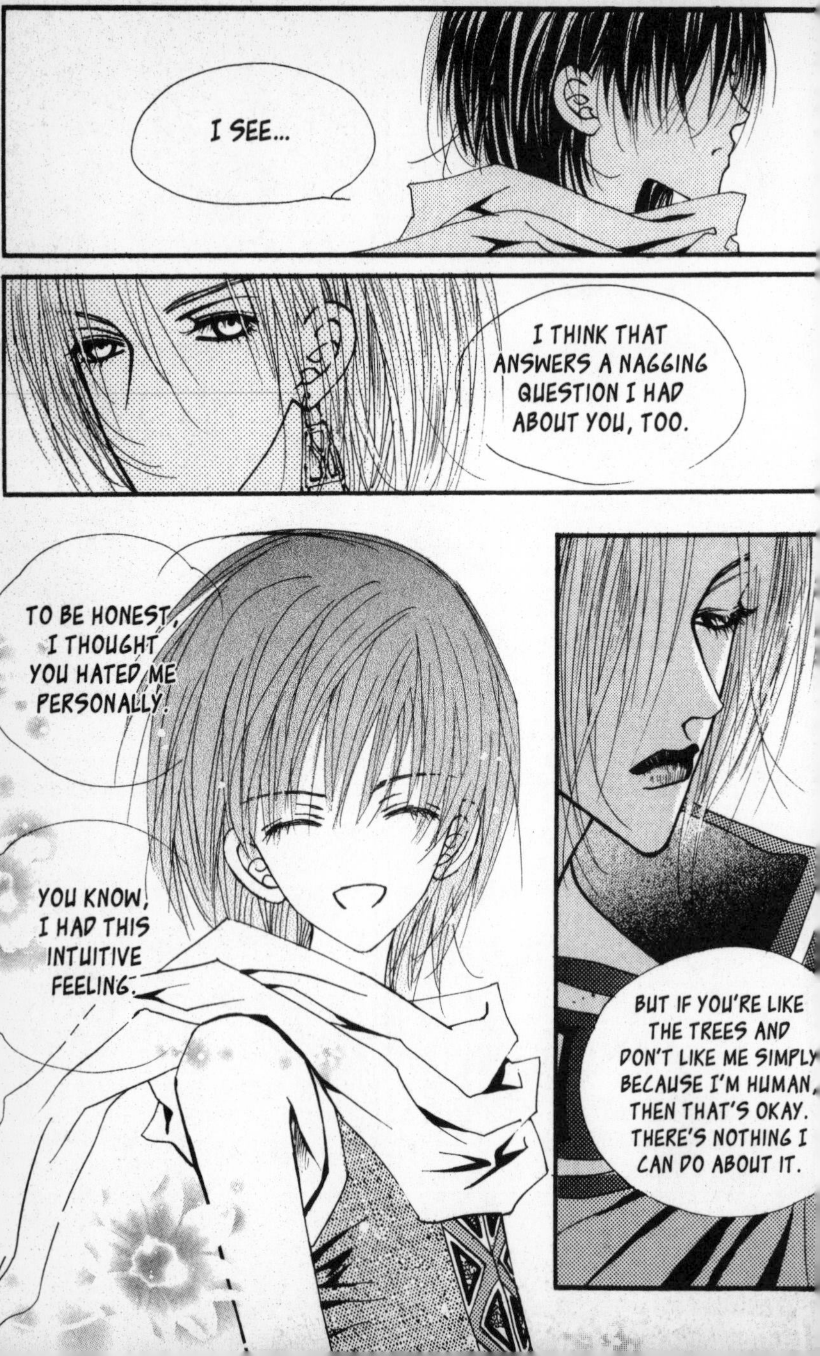
I SEE...
I THINK THAT ANSWERS A NAGGING QUESTION I HAD ABOUT YOU, TOO.
TO BE HONEST, I THOUGHT YOU HATED ME PERSONALLY.
YOU KNOW, I HAD THIS INTUITIVE FEELING.
BUT IF YOU'RE LIKE THE TREES AND DON'T LIKE ME SIMPLY BECAUSE I'M HUMAN, THEN THAT'S OKAY. THERE'S NOTHING I CAN DO ABOUT IT.

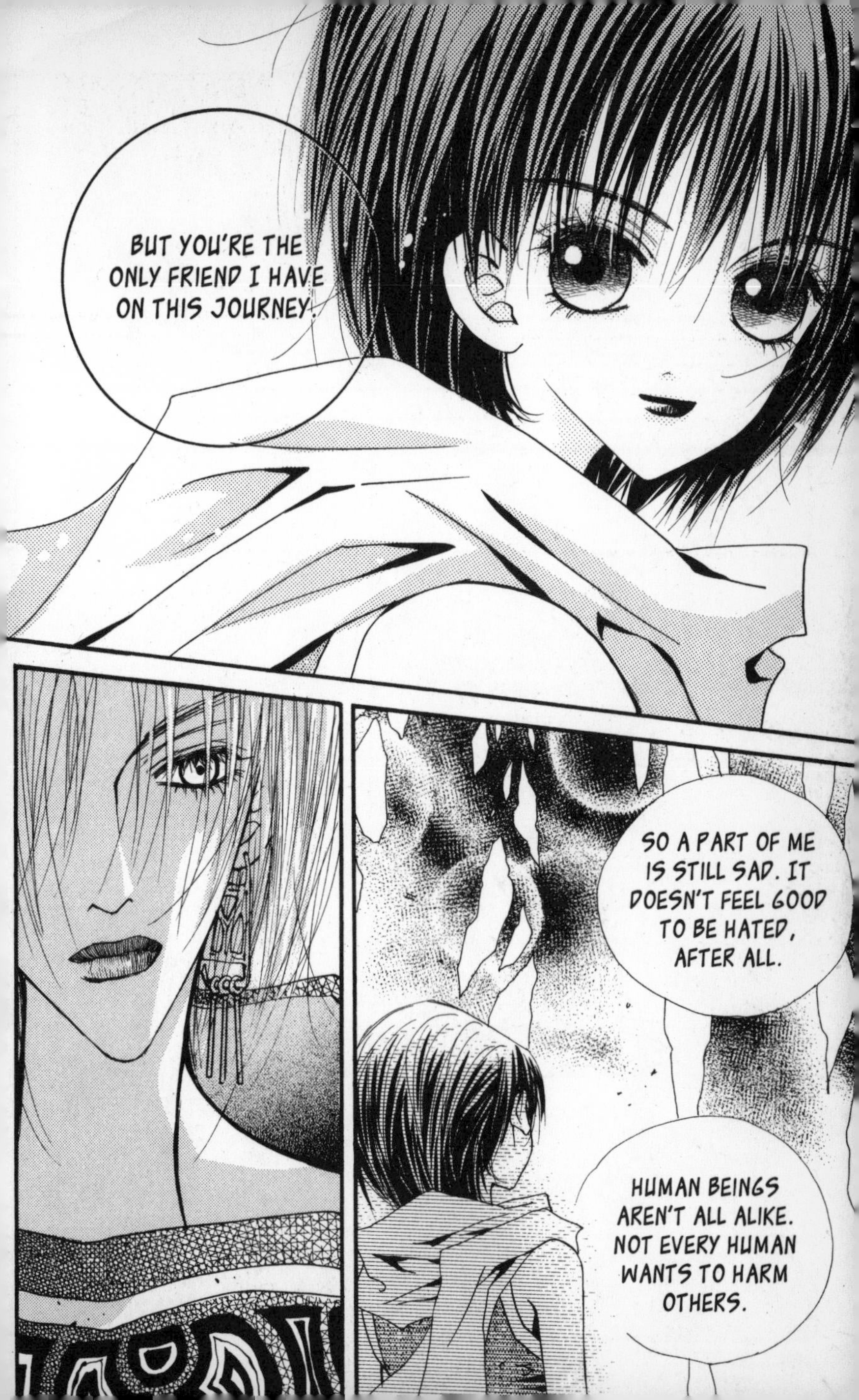
BUT YOU'RE THE ONLY FRIEND I HAVE ON THIS JOURNEY.
SO A PART OF ME IS STILL SAD. IT DOESN'T FEEL GOOD TO BE HATED, AFTER ALL.
HUMAN BEINGS AREN'T ALL ALIKE. NOT EVERY HUMAN WANTS TO HARM OTHERS.

NOT ALL OF THE OTHER RACES FEEL AN AVERSION TOWARD HUMANS EITHER.

SOME WOULD EVEN SACRIFICE THEMSELVES FOR THEIR HUMAN FRIENDS.

YOU HAD A FRIEND LIKE THAT TOO, DIDN'T YOU?

?!

THE FIRST ONE TO BUILD THE WALL HAS TO BE THE FIRST TO BREAK IT DOWN.

ONCE THE WALL IS GONE, THE HORIZON OPENS, AND MARVELOUS THINGS CAN FILL THE SPACE WHERE A BARRIER ONCE STOOD.

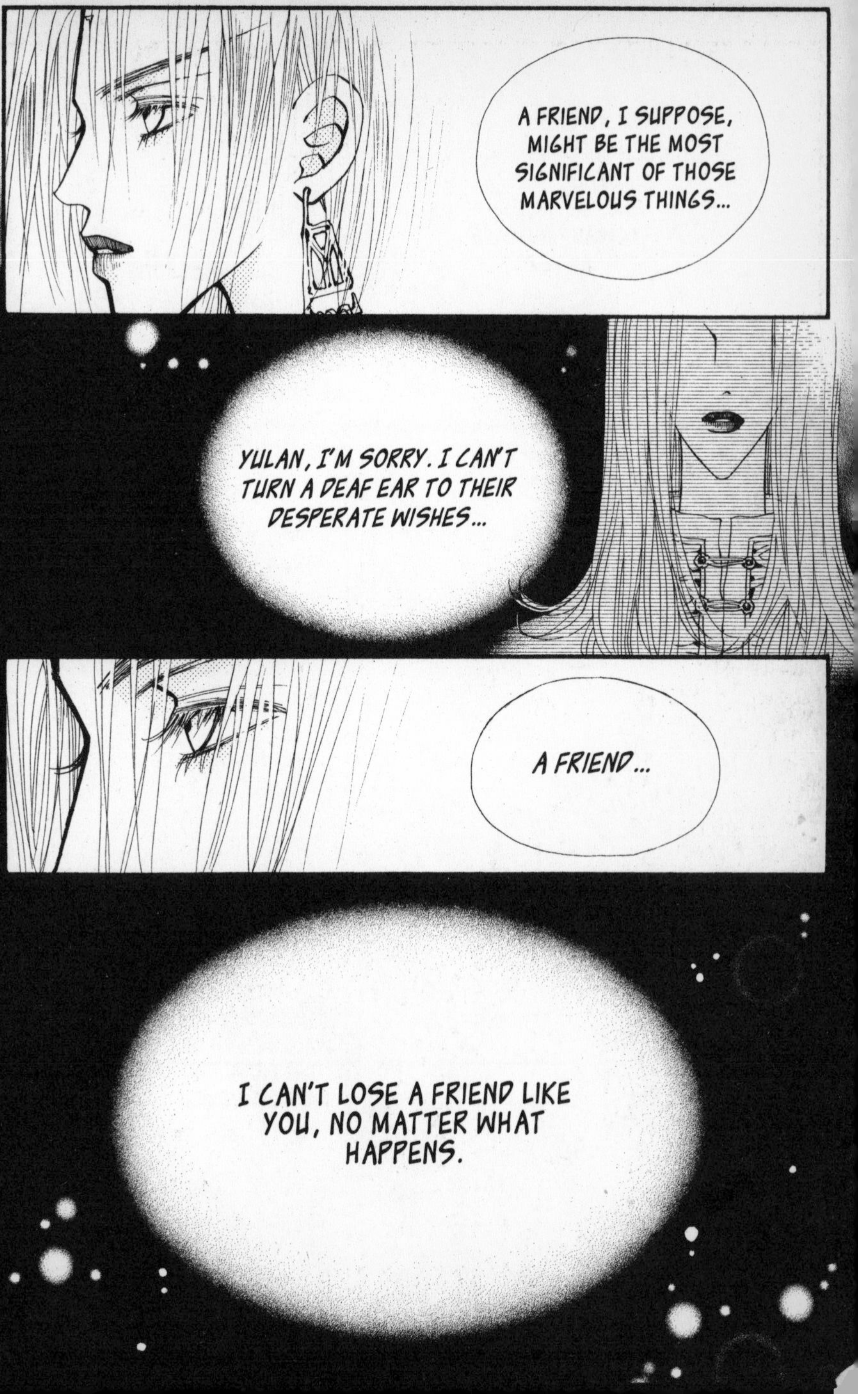
A FRIEND, I SUPPOSE, MIGHT BE THE MOST SIGNIFICANT OF THOSE MARVELOUS THINGS...
YULAN, I'M SORRY. I CAN'T TURN A DEAF EAR TO THEIR DESPERATE WISHES...
A FRIEND...
I CAN'T LOSE A FRIEND LIKE YOU, NO MATTER WHAT HAPPENS.

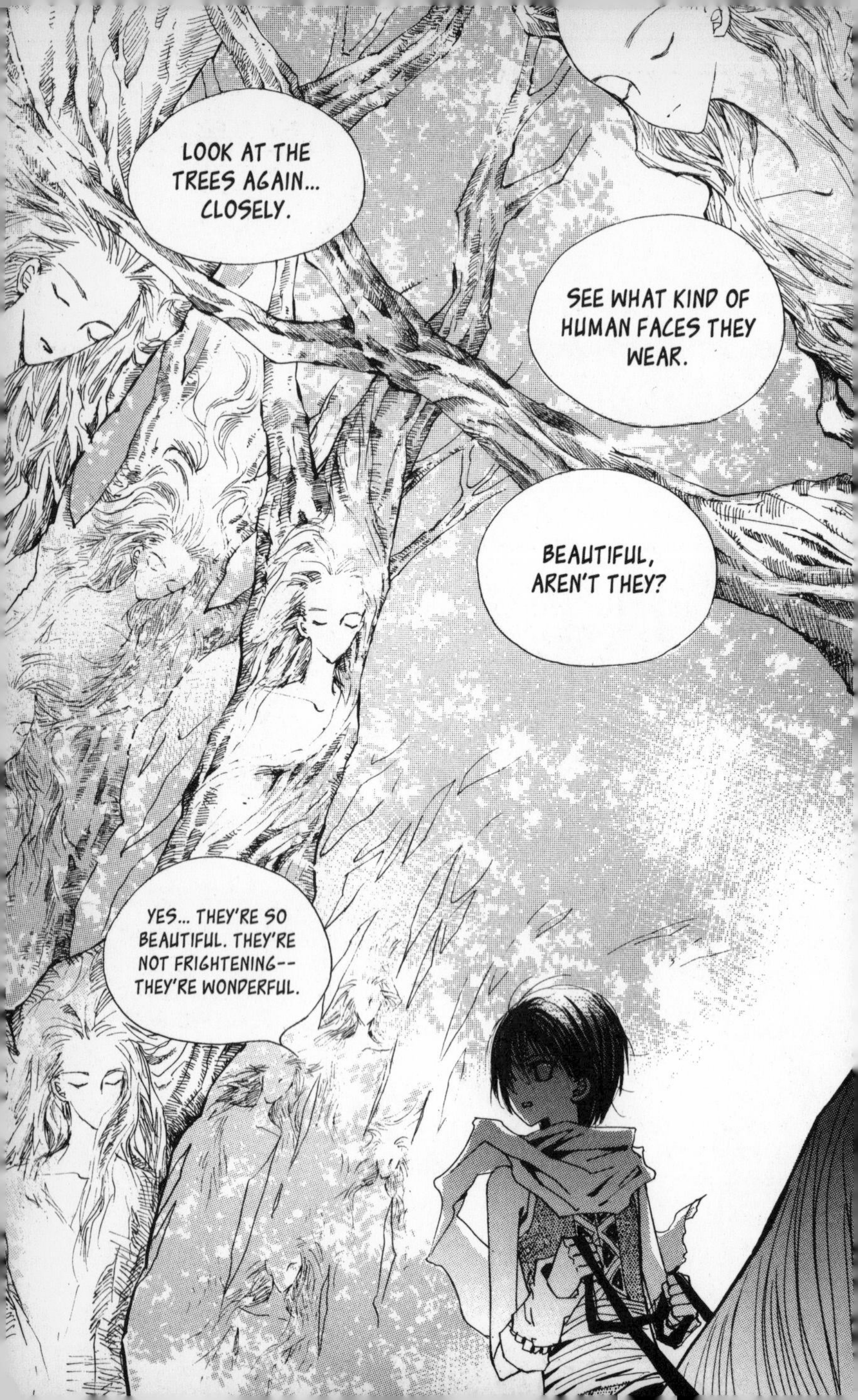
LOOK AT THE TREES AGAIN... CLOSELY.
SEE WHAT KIND OF HUMAN FACES THEY WEAR.
BEAUTIFUL, AREN'T THEY?
YES... THEY'RE SO BEAUTIFUL. THEY'RE NOT FRIGHTENING-- THEY'RE WONDERFUL.

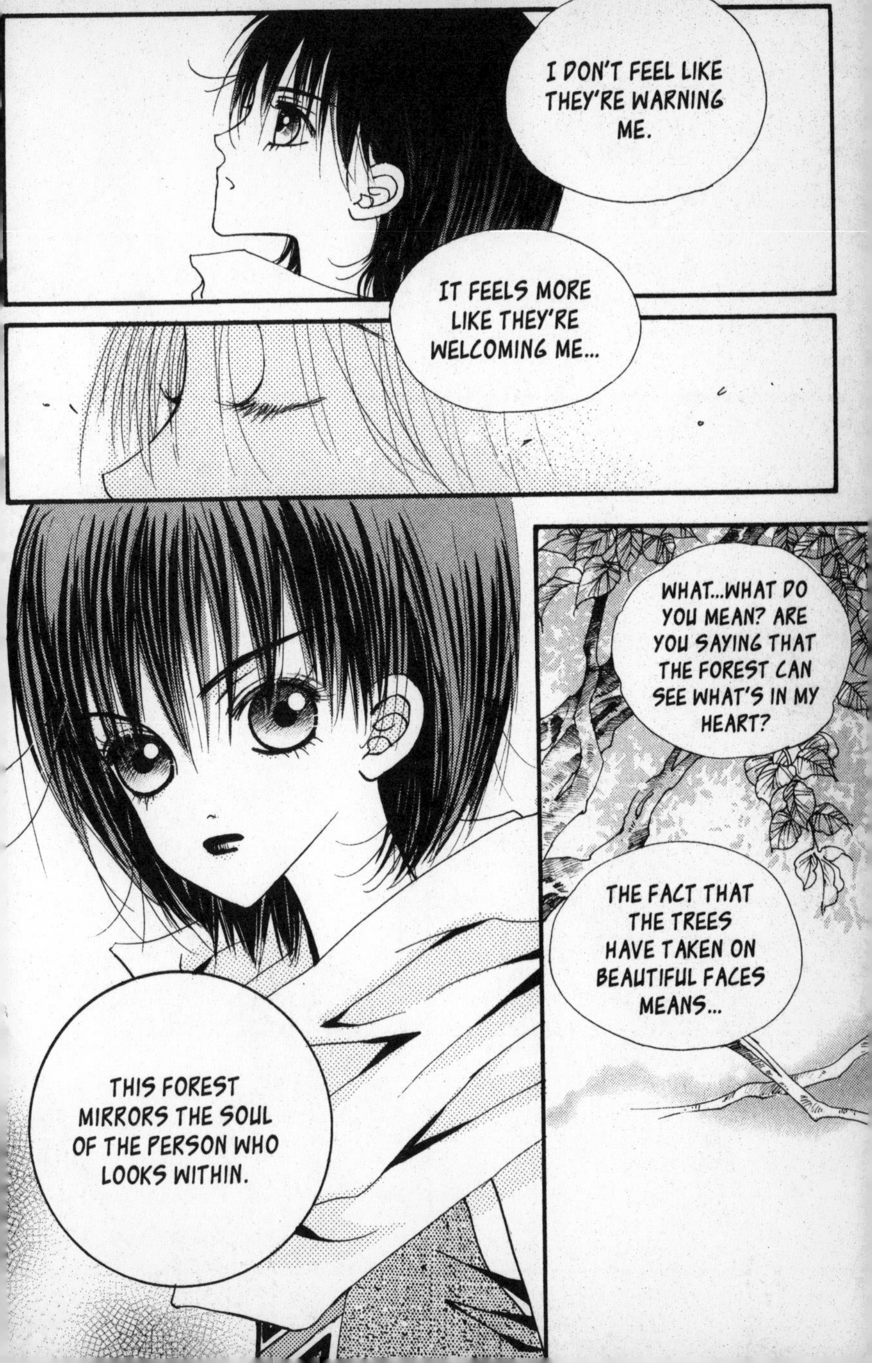
I DON'T FEEL LIKE THEY'RE WARNING ME.
IT FEELS MORE LIKE THEY'RE WELCOMING ME...
THIS FOREST MIRRORS THE SOUL OF THE PERSON WHO LOOKS WITHIN.
WHAT...WHAT DO YOU MEAN? ARE YOU SAYING THAT THE FOREST CAN SEE WHAT'S IN MY HEART?
THE FACT THAT THE TREES HAVE TAKEN ON BEAUTIFUL FACES MEANS...

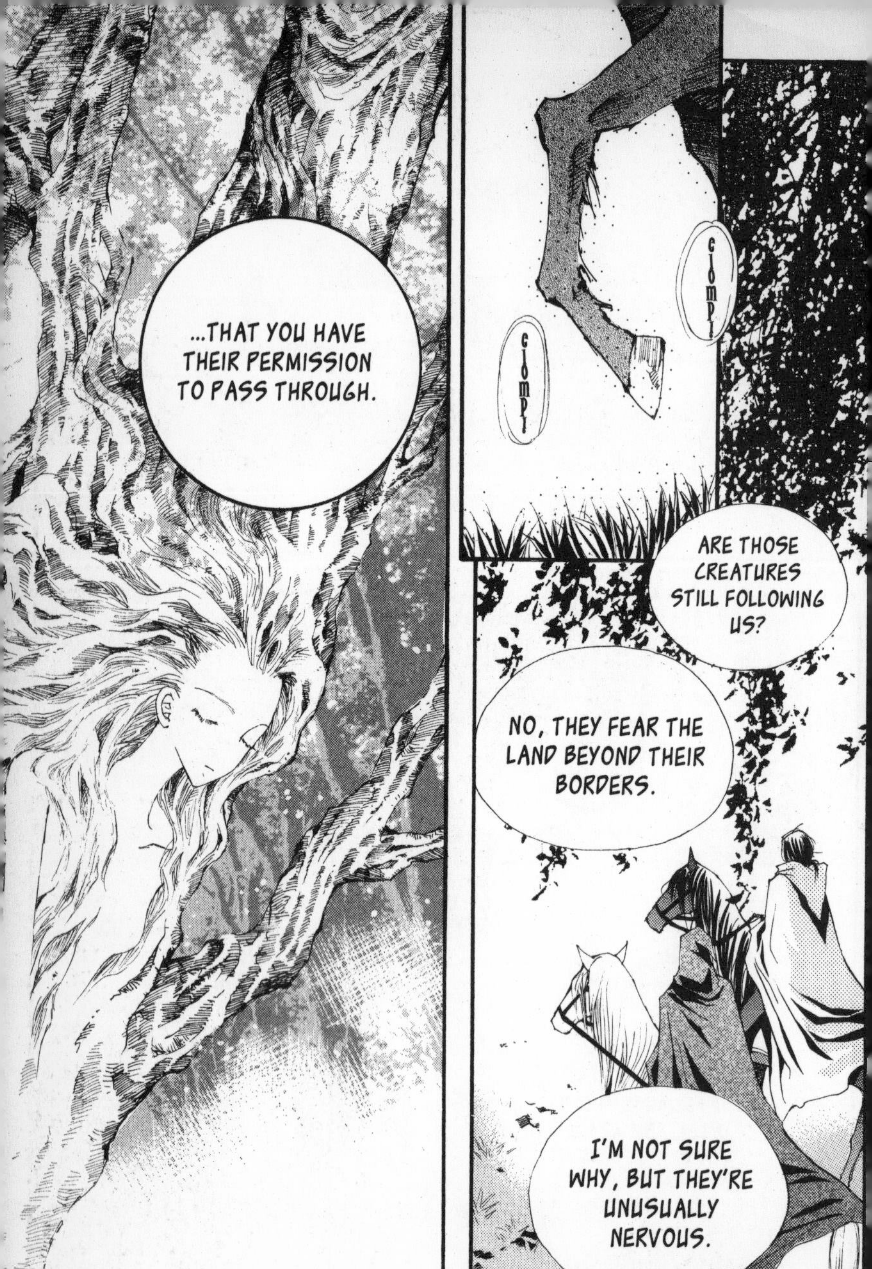
...THAT YOU HAVE THEIR PERMISSION TO PASS THROUGH.
GLOMP!
GLOMP!
ARE THOSE CREATURES STILL FOLLOWING US?
NO, THEY FEAR THE LAND BEYOND THEIR BORDERS.
I'M NOT SURE WHY, BUT THEY'RE UNUSUALLY NERVOUS.

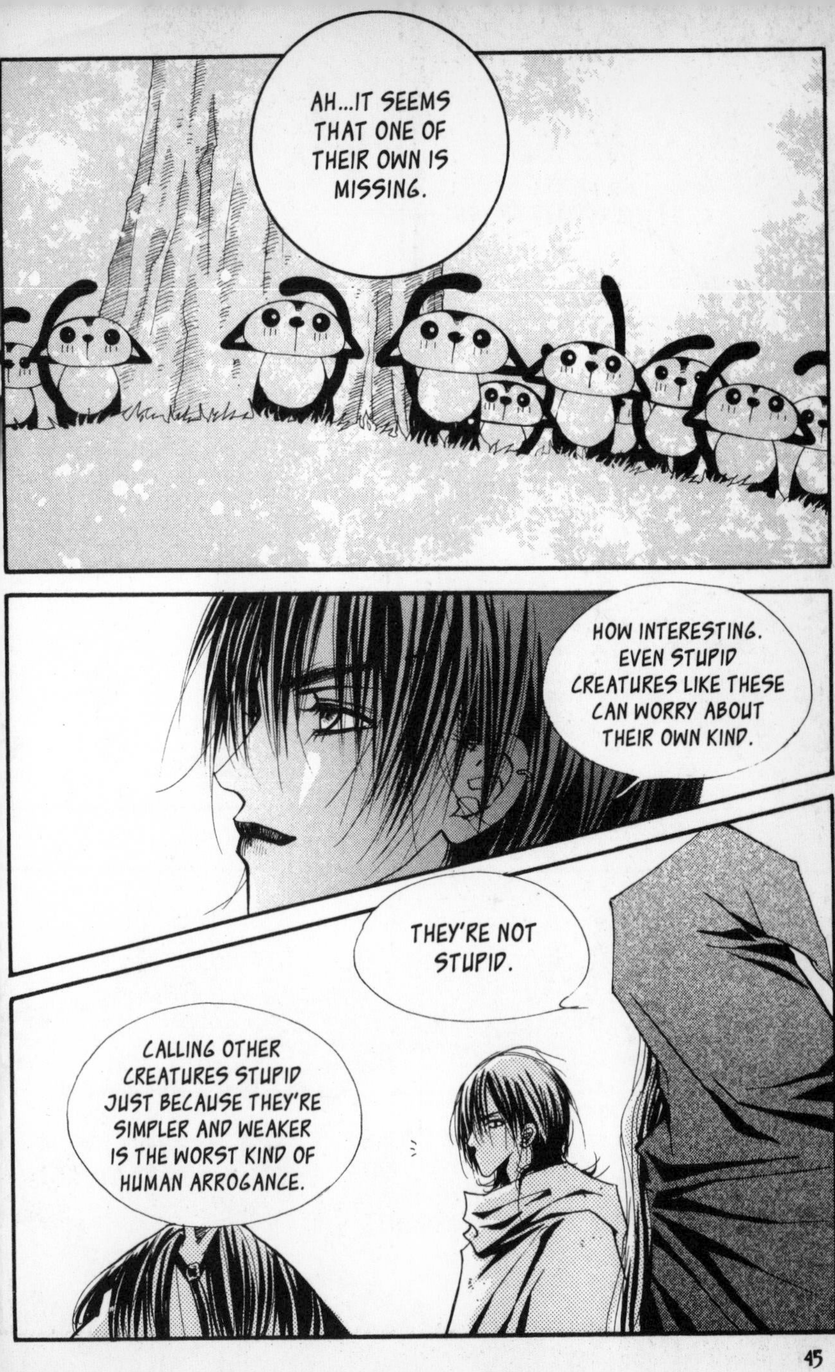
AH...IT SEEMS THAT ONE OF THEIR OWN IS MISSING.
HOW INTERESTING. EVEN STUPID CREATURES LIKE THESE CAN WORRY ABOUT THEIR OWN KIND.
THEY'RE NOT STUPID.
CALLING OTHER CREATURES STUPID JUST BECAUSE THEY'RE SIMPLER AND WEAKER IS THE WORST KIND OF HUMAN ARROGANCE.

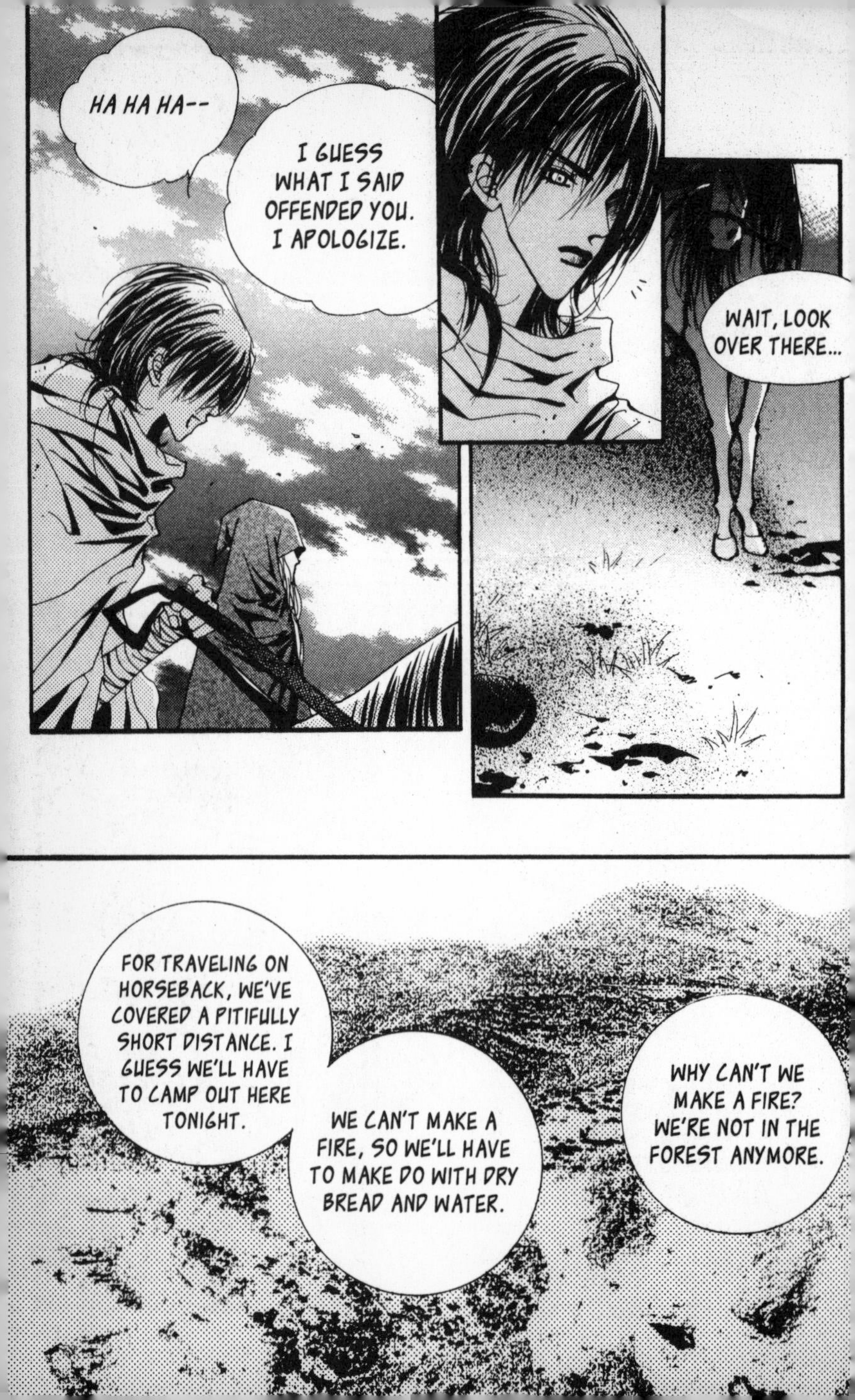
HA HA HA--
I GUESS WHAT I SAID OFFENDED YOU. I APOLOGIZE.
WAIT, LOOK OVER THERE...
FOR TRAVELING ON HORSEBACK, WE'VE COVERED A PITIFULLY SHORT DISTANCE. I GUESS WE'LL HAVE TO CAMP OUT HERE TONIGHT.
WE CAN'T MAKE A FIRE, SO WE'LL HAVE TO MAKE DO WITH DRY BREAD AND WATER.
WHY CAN'T WE MAKE A FIRE? WE'RE NOT IN THE FOREST ANYMORE.

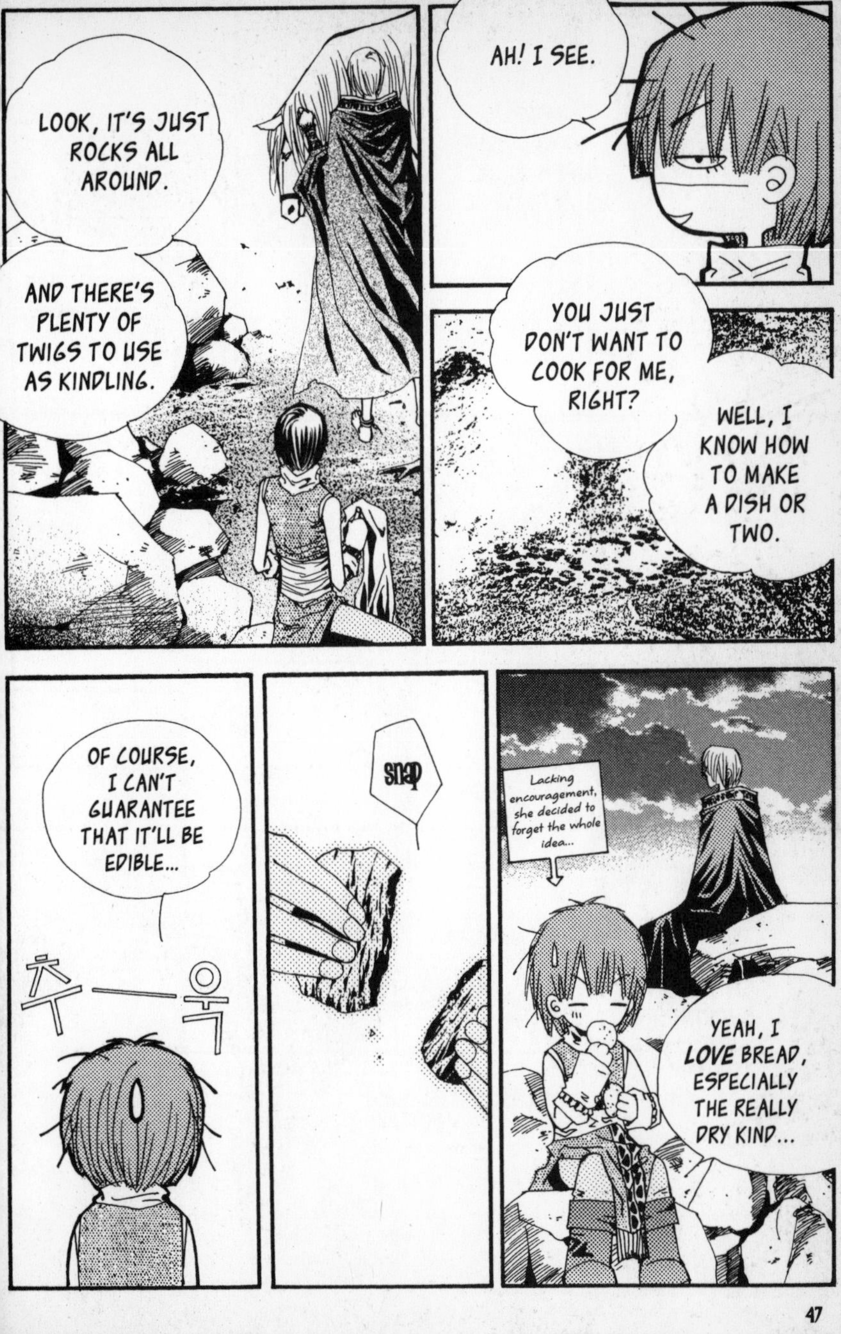
LOOK, IT'S JUST ROCKS ALL AROUND.
AND THERE'S PLENTY OF TWIGS TO USE AS KINDLING.
AH! I SEE.
YOU JUST DON'T WANT TO COOK FOR ME, RIGHT?
WELL, I KNOW HOW TO MAKE A DISH OR TWO.
OF COURSE, I CAN'T GUARANTEE THAT IT'LL BE EDIBLE...
추—욱
SNAP
Lacking encouragement, she decided to forget the whole idea...
YEAH, I *LOVE* BREAD, ESPECIALLY THE REALLY DRY KIND...

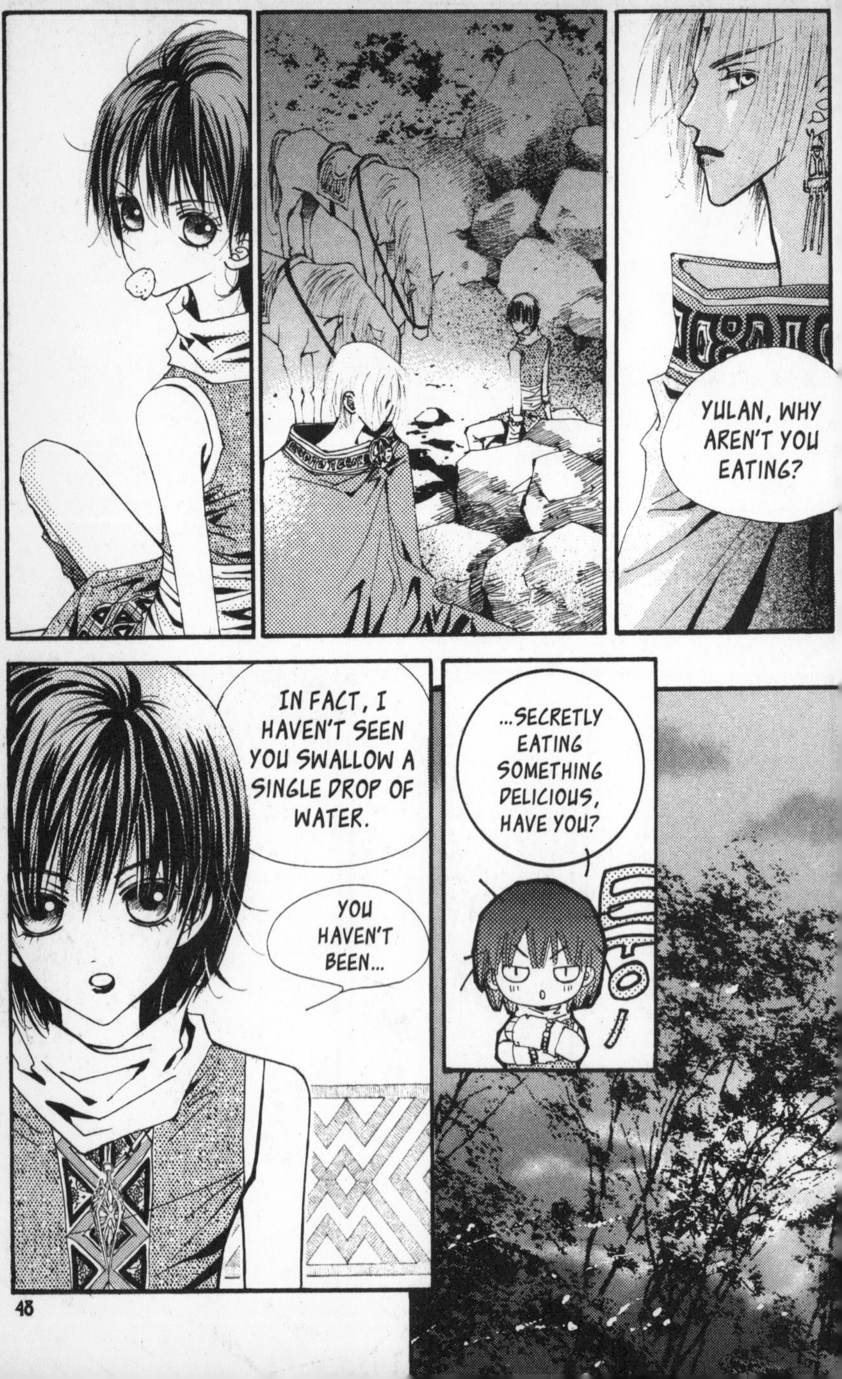
YULAN, WHY AREN'T YOU EATING?
IN FACT, I HAVEN'T SEEN YOU SWALLOW A SINGLE DROP OF WATER.
YOU HAVEN'T BEEN...
...SECRETLY EATING SOMETHING DELICIOUS, HAVE YOU?

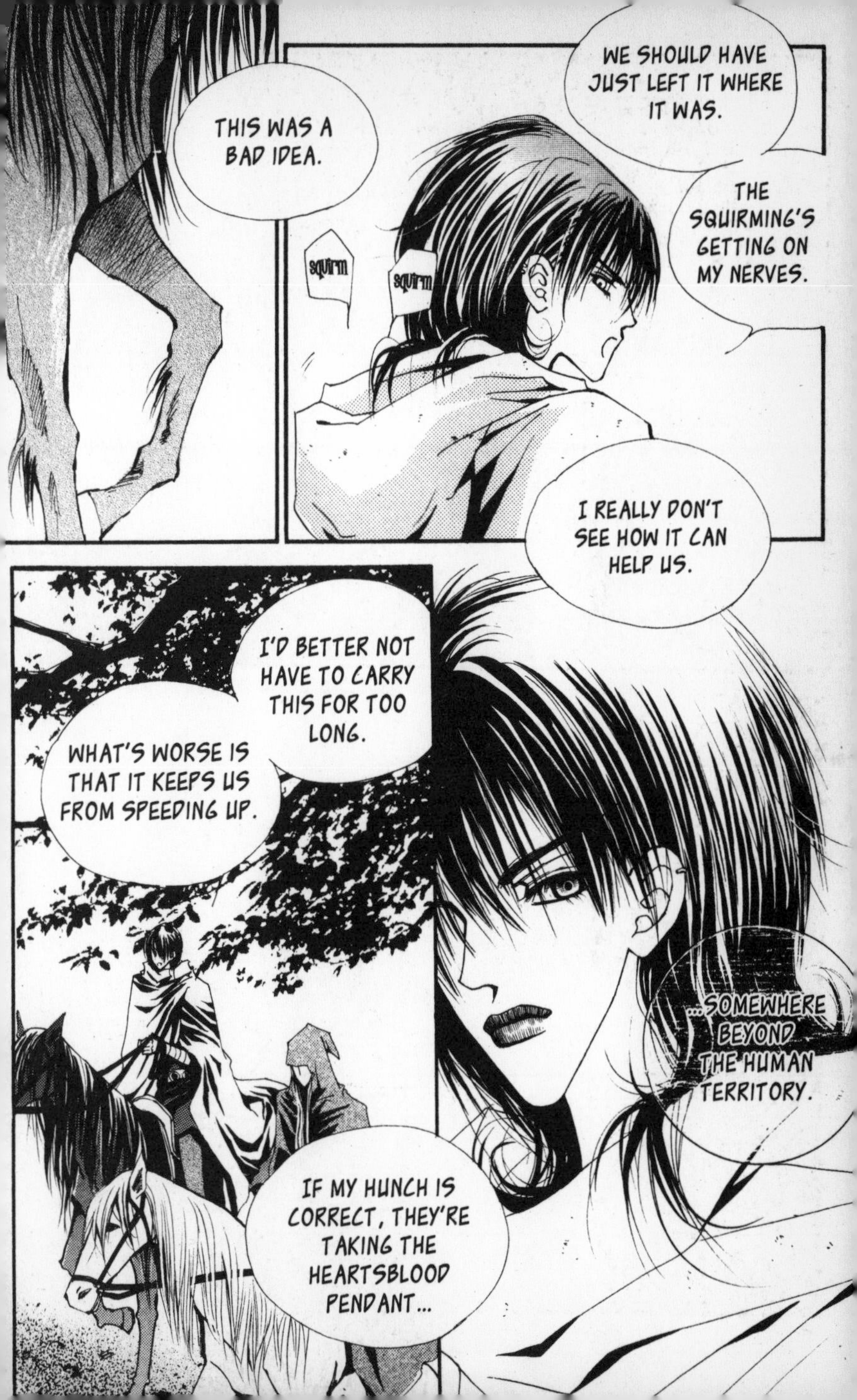
THIS WAS A BAD IDEA.
WE SHOULD HAVE JUST LEFT IT WHERE IT WAS.
squirm
squirm
THE SQUIRMING'S GETTING ON MY NERVES.
I REALLY DON'T SEE HOW IT CAN HELP US.
I'D BETTER NOT HAVE TO CARRY THIS FOR TOO LONG.
WHAT'S WORSE IS THAT IT KEEPS US FROM SPEEDING UP.
IF MY HUNCH IS CORRECT, THEY'RE TAKING THE HEARTSBLOOD PENDANT...
...SOMEWHERE BEYOND THE HUMAN TERRITORY.

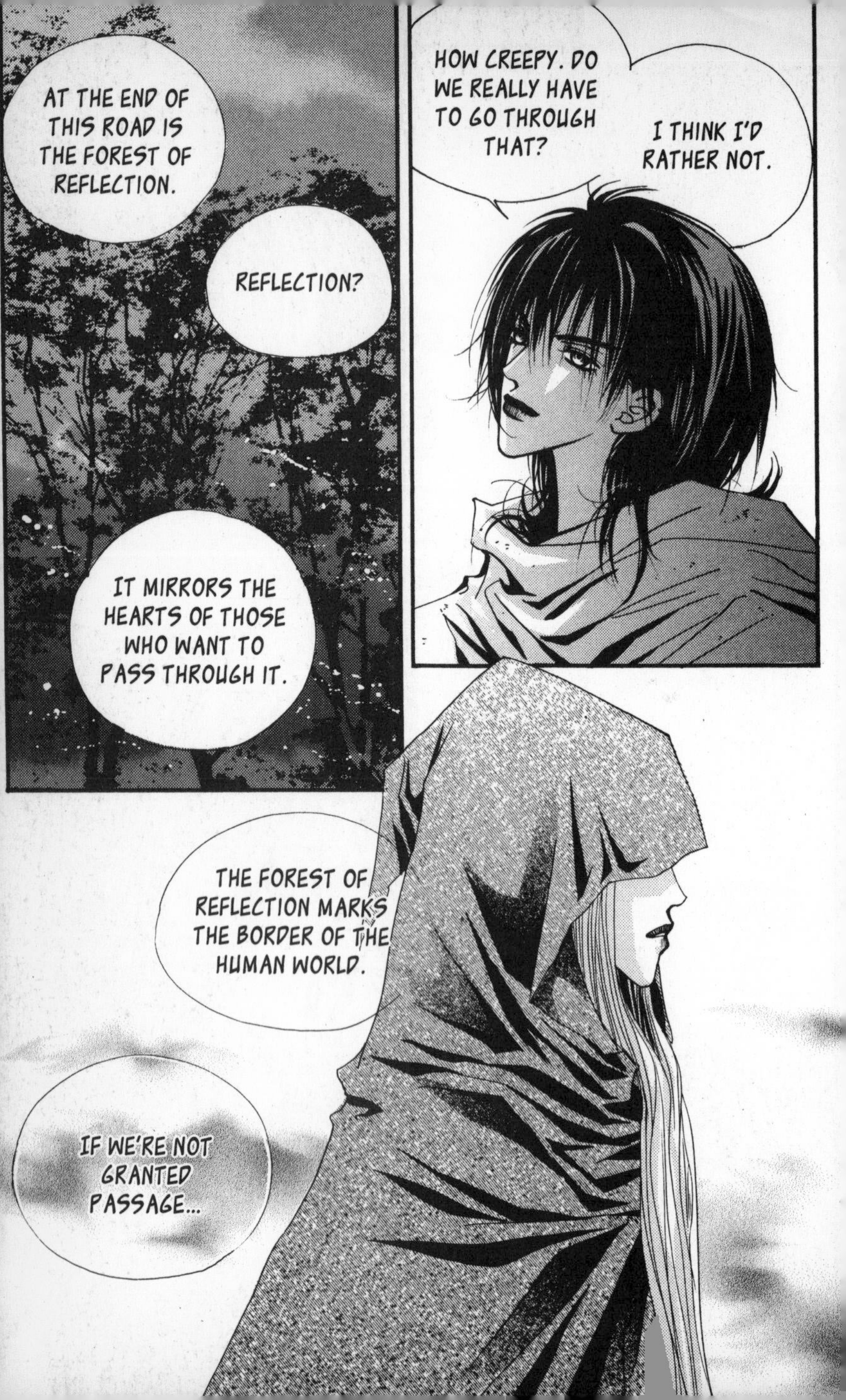
AT THE END OF THIS ROAD IS THE FOREST OF REFLECTION.
REFLECTION?
IT MIRRORS THE HEARTS OF THOSE WHO WANT TO PASS THROUGH IT.
HOW CREEPY. DO WE REALLY HAVE TO GO THROUGH THAT?
I THINK I'D RATHER NOT.
THE FOREST OF REFLECTION MARKS THE BORDER OF THE HUMAN WORLD.
IF WE'RE NOT GRANTED PASSAGE...

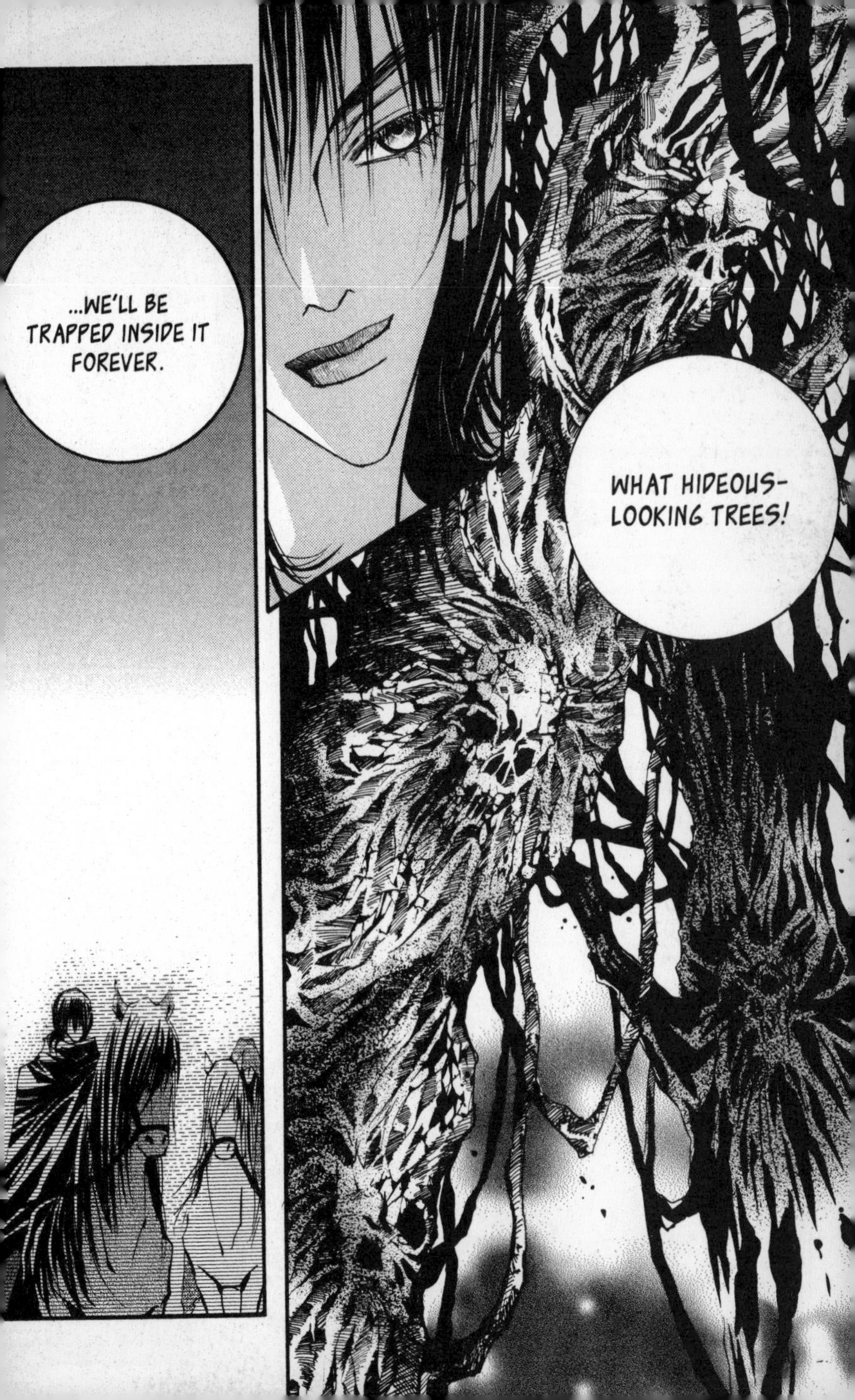
...WE'LL BE TRAPPED INSIDE IT FOREVER.
WHAT HIDEOUS-LOOKING TREES!

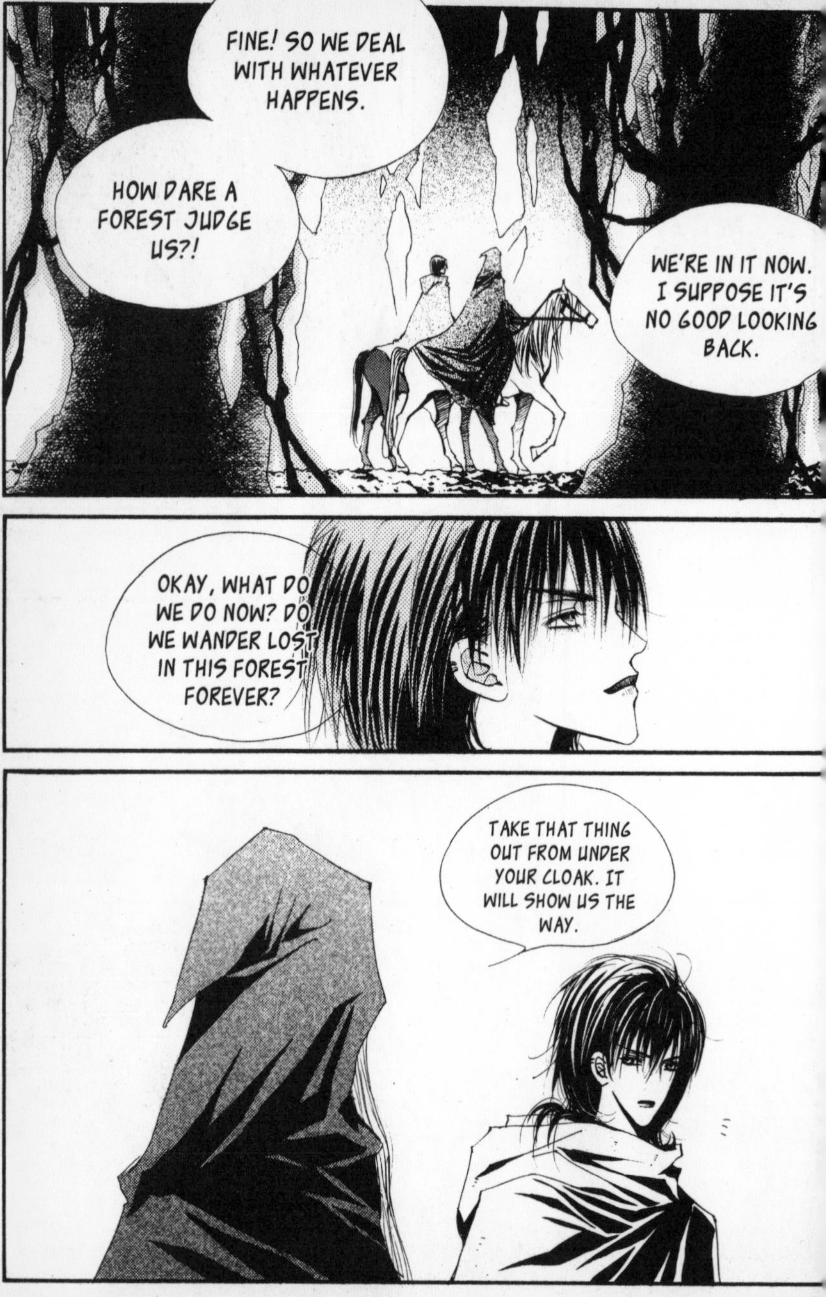
FINE! SO WE DEAL WITH WHATEVER HAPPENS.
HOW DARE A FOREST JUDGE US?!
WE'RE IN IT NOW. I SUPPOSE IT'S NO GOOD LOOKING BACK.
OKAY, WHAT DO WE DO NOW? DO WE WANDER LOST IN THIS FOREST FOREVER?
TAKE THAT THING OUT FROM UNDER YOUR CLOAK. IT WILL SHOW US THE WAY.

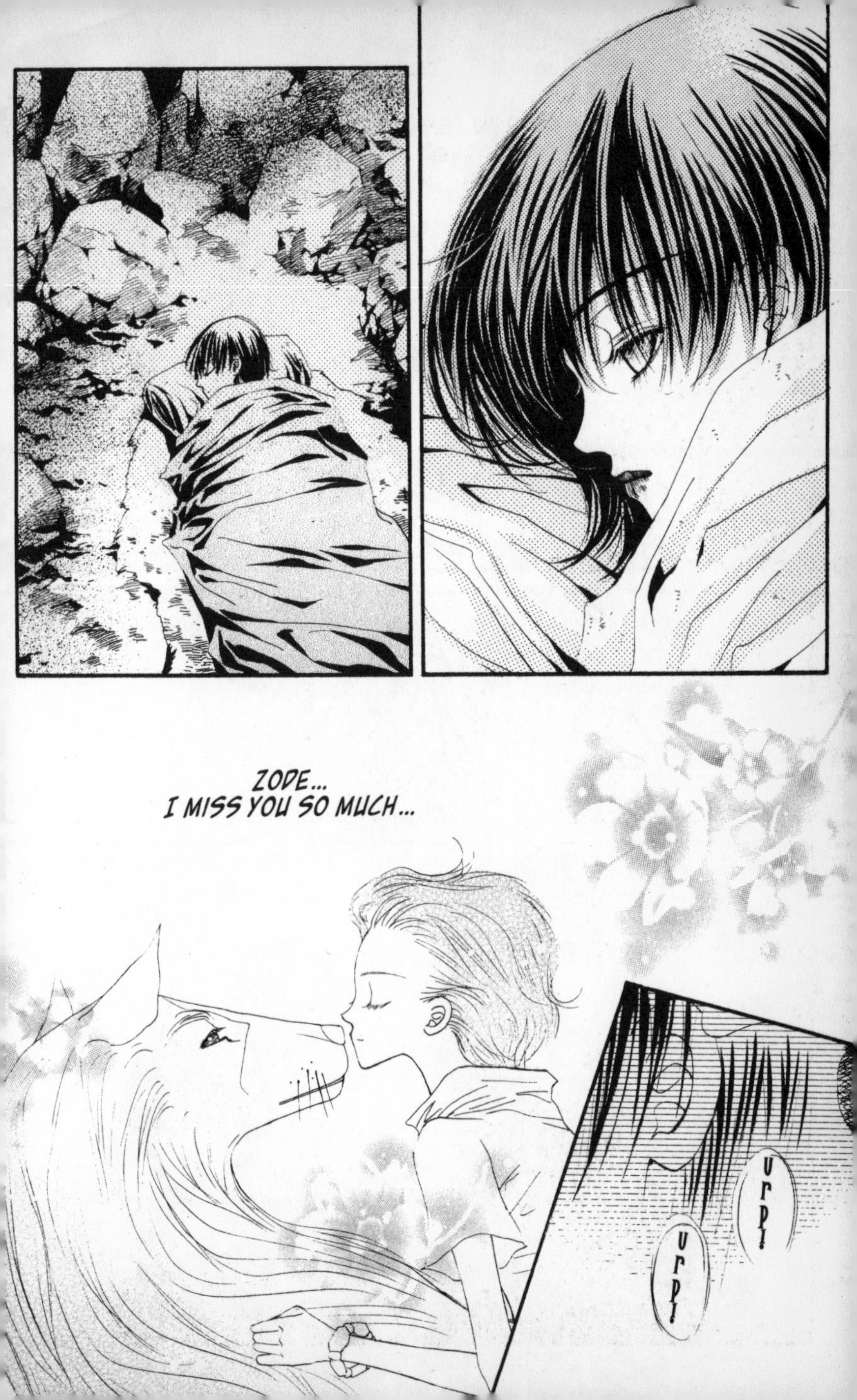
ZODE...
I MISS YOU SO MUCH...
URP!
URP!

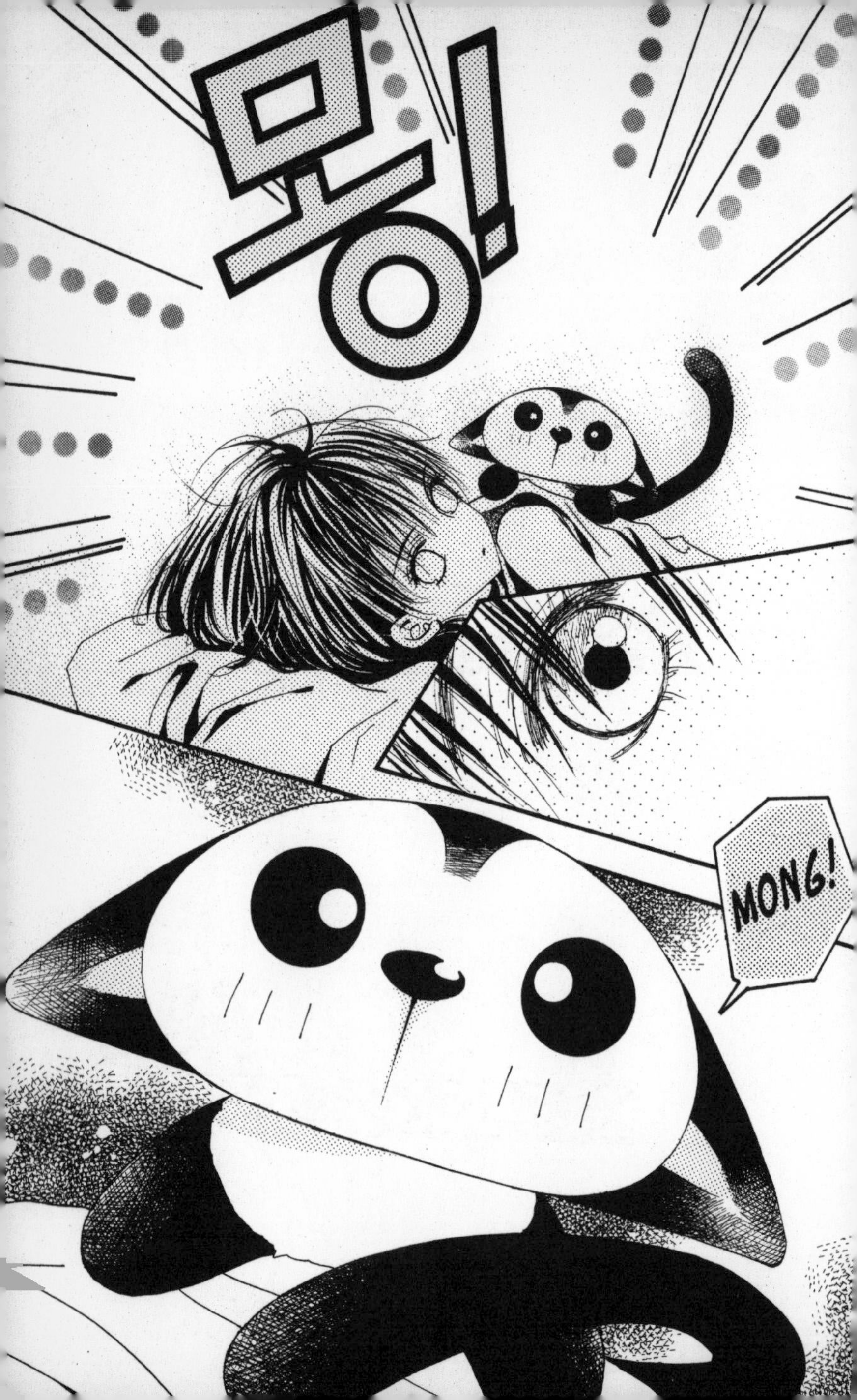
몽!
MONG!

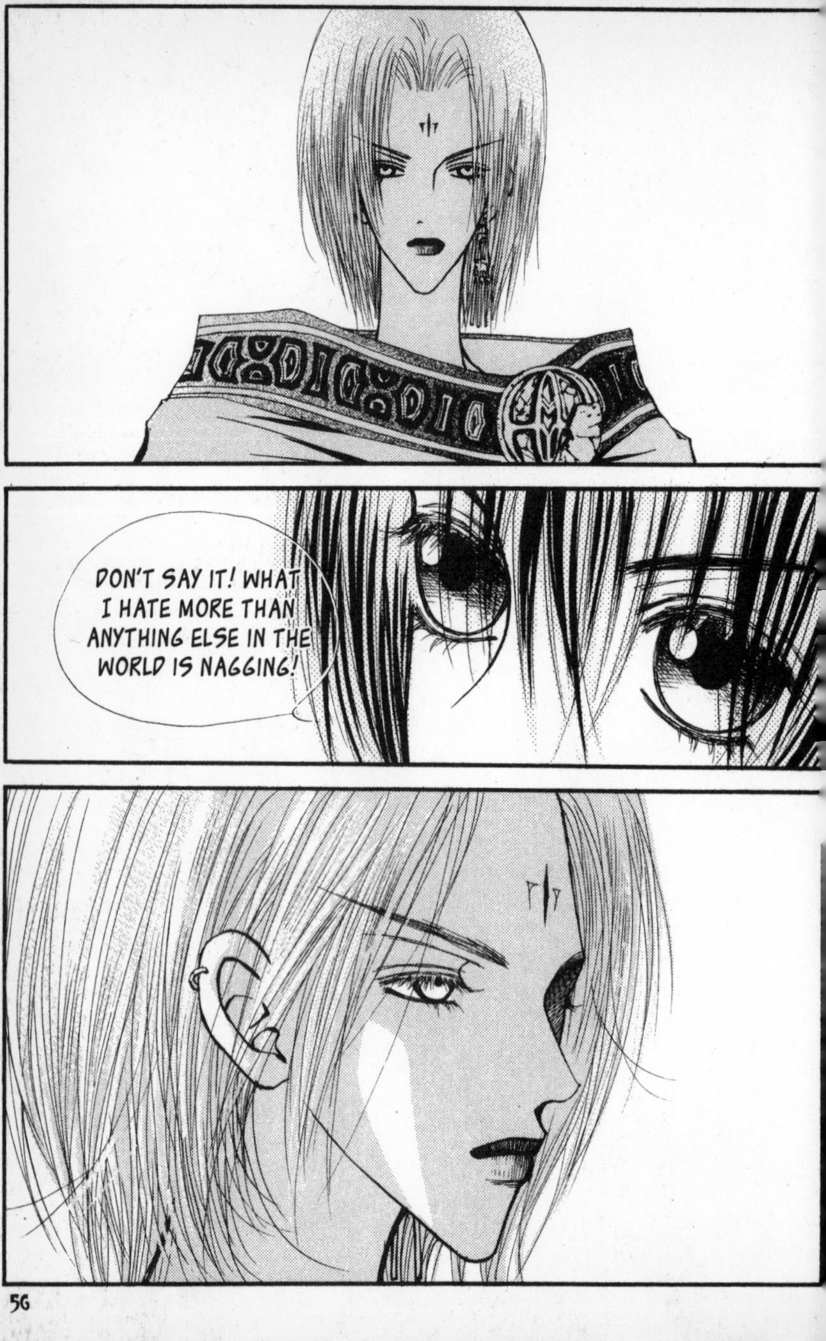
DON'T SAY IT! WHAT I HATE MORE THAN ANYTHING ELSE IN THE WORLD IS NAGGING!

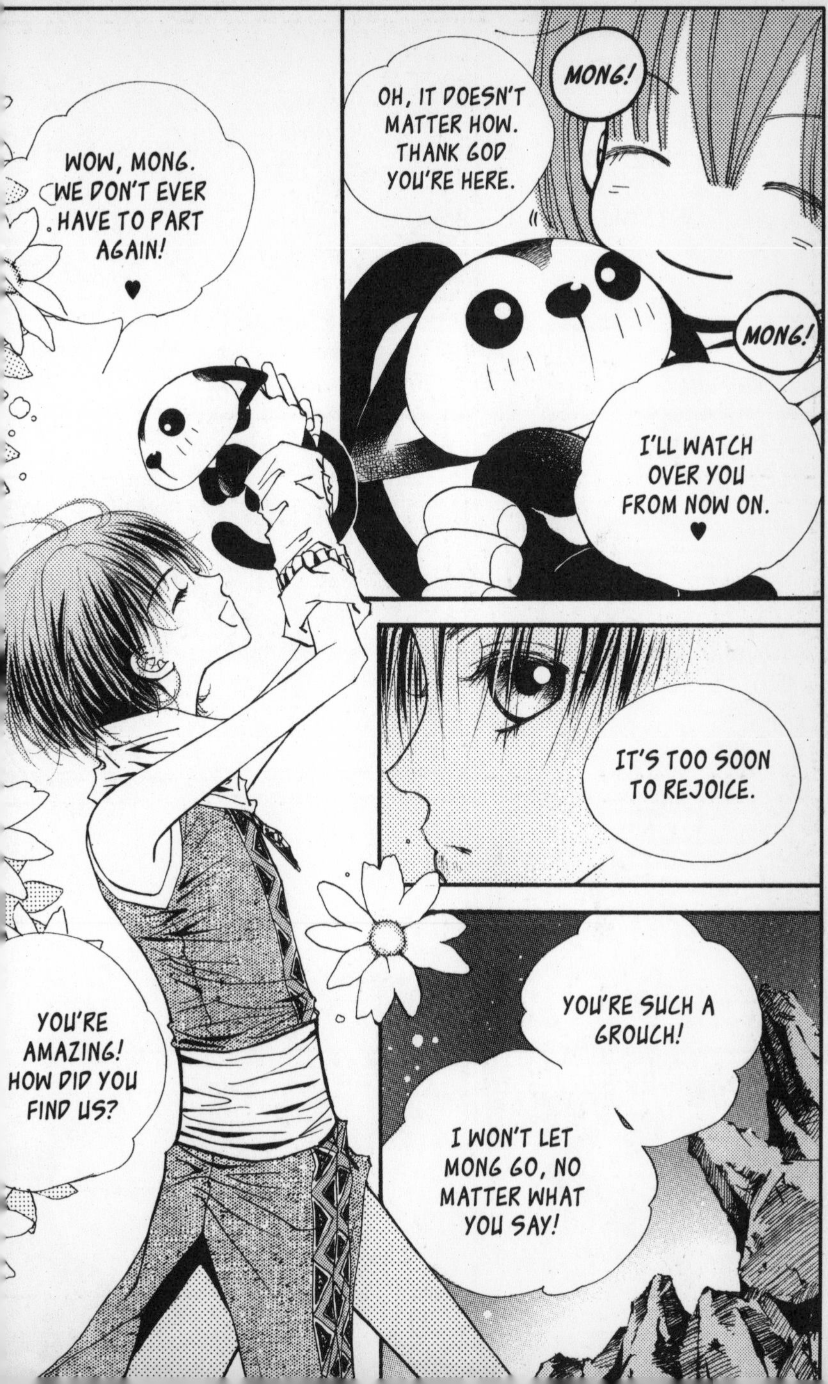
WOW, MONG. WE DON'T EVER HAVE TO PART AGAIN! ♥
YOU'RE AMAZING! HOW DID YOU FIND US?
OH, IT DOESN'T MATTER HOW. THANK GOD YOU'RE HERE.
MONG!
MONG!
I'LL WATCH OVER YOU FROM NOW ON. ♥
IT'S TOO SOON TO REJOICE.
YOU'RE SUCH A GROUCH!
I WON'T LET MONG GO, NO MATTER WHAT YOU SAY!

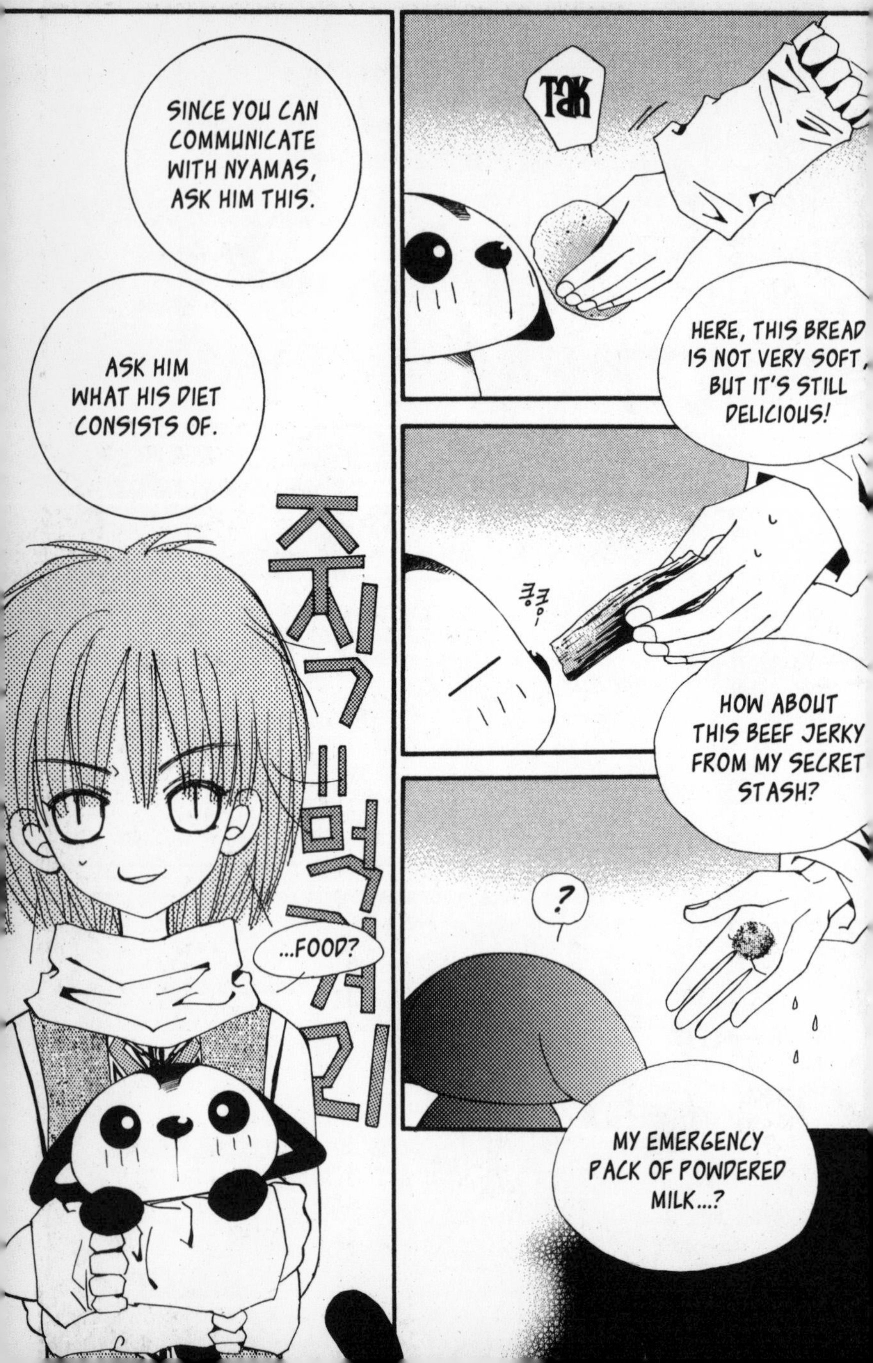
SINCE YOU CAN COMMUNICATE WITH NYAMAS, ASK HIM THIS.
ASK HIM WHAT HIS DIET CONSISTS OF.
...FOOD?
TAK
HERE, THIS BREAD IS NOT VERY SOFT, BUT IT'S STILL DELICIOUS!
HOW ABOUT THIS BEEF JERKY FROM MY SECRET STASH?
?
MY EMERGENCY PACK OF POWDERED MILK...?

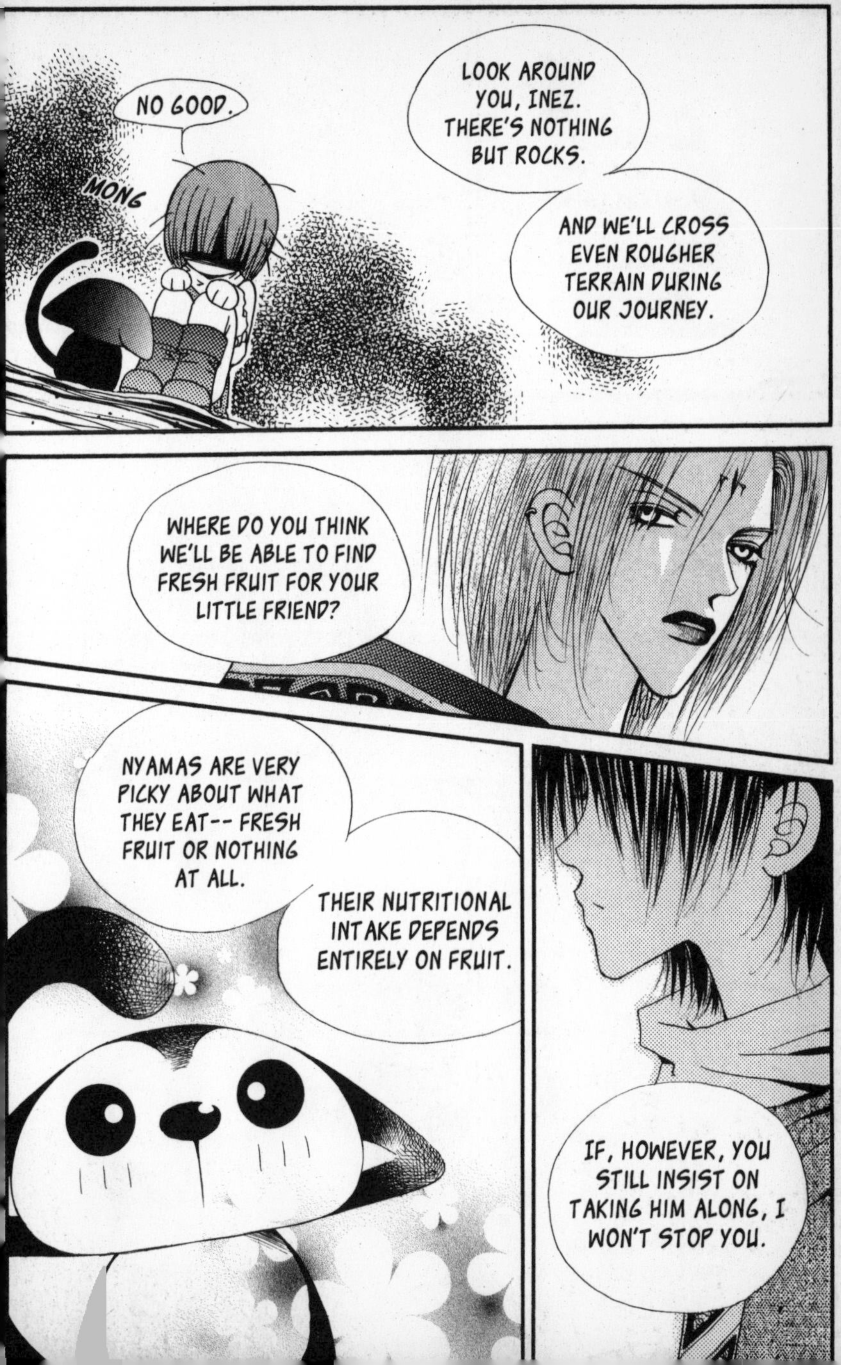
NO GOOD.
MONG
LOOK AROUND YOU, INEZ. THERE'S NOTHING BUT ROCKS.
AND WE'LL CROSS EVEN ROUGHER TERRAIN DURING OUR JOURNEY.
WHERE DO YOU THINK WE'LL BE ABLE TO FIND FRESH FRUIT FOR YOUR LITTLE FRIEND?
NYAMAS ARE VERY PICKY ABOUT WHAT THEY EAT-- FRESH FRUIT OR NOTHING AT ALL.
THEIR NUTRITIONAL INTAKE DEPENDS ENTIRELY ON FRUIT.
IF, HOWEVER, YOU STILL INSIST ON TAKING HIM ALONG, I WON'T STOP YOU.

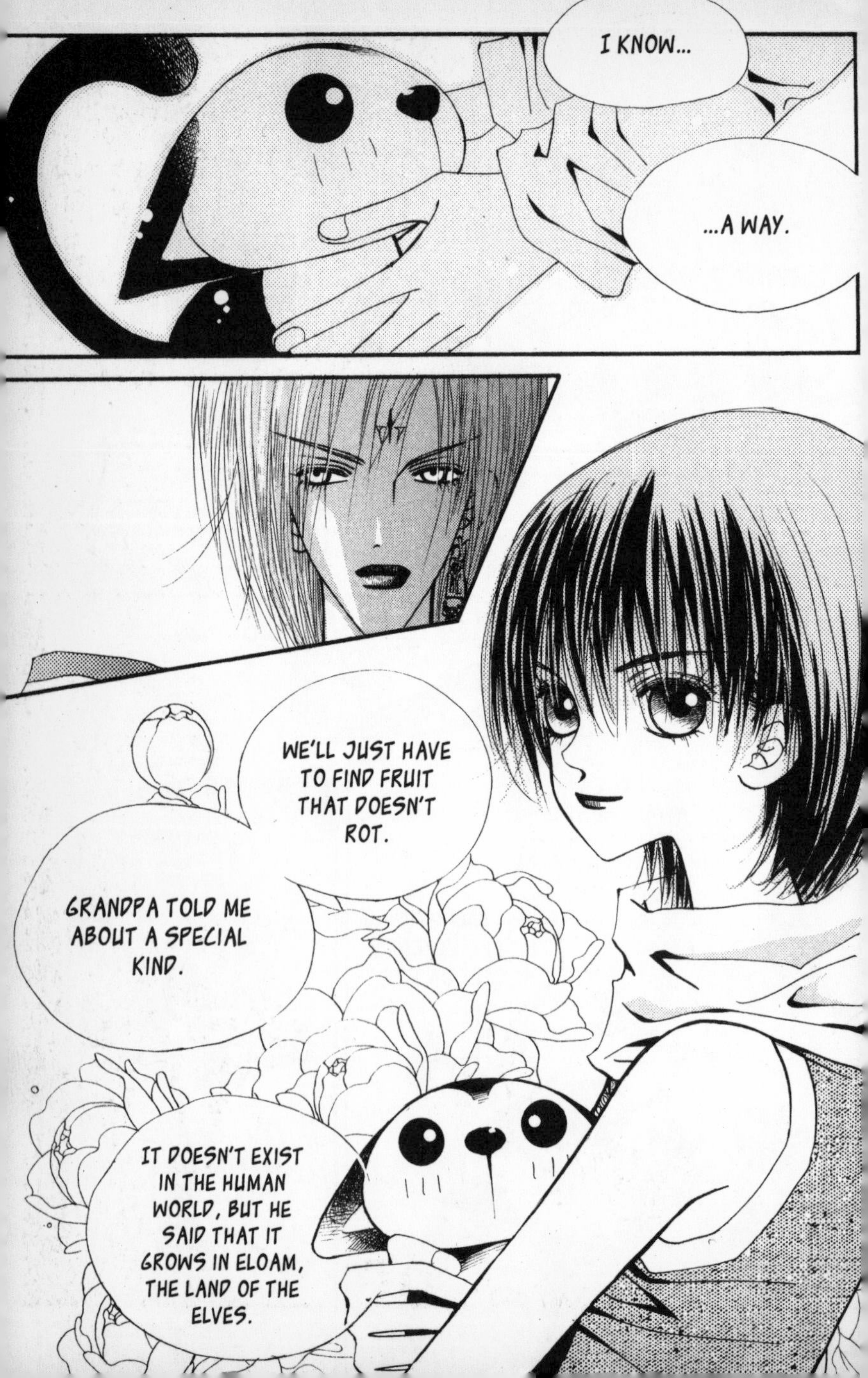
I KNOW...
...A WAY.
WE'LL JUST HAVE TO FIND FRUIT THAT DOESN'T ROT.
GRANDPA TOLD ME ABOUT A SPECIAL KIND.
IT DOESN'T EXIST IN THE HUMAN WORLD, BUT HE SAID THAT IT GROWS IN ELOAM, THE LAND OF THE ELVES.

JUST ONE BITE OF IT MAKES YOU FULL, HE SAID.

I DON'T WANT TO PART WITH YOU, MONG.

MONG.

THE LITTLE CRITTER IS OUR SAVIOR. HA HA HA.

IT GOT US OUT OF THE FOREST OF REFLECTION AND LED US STRAIGHT TO...

...THE HEARTSBLOOD.

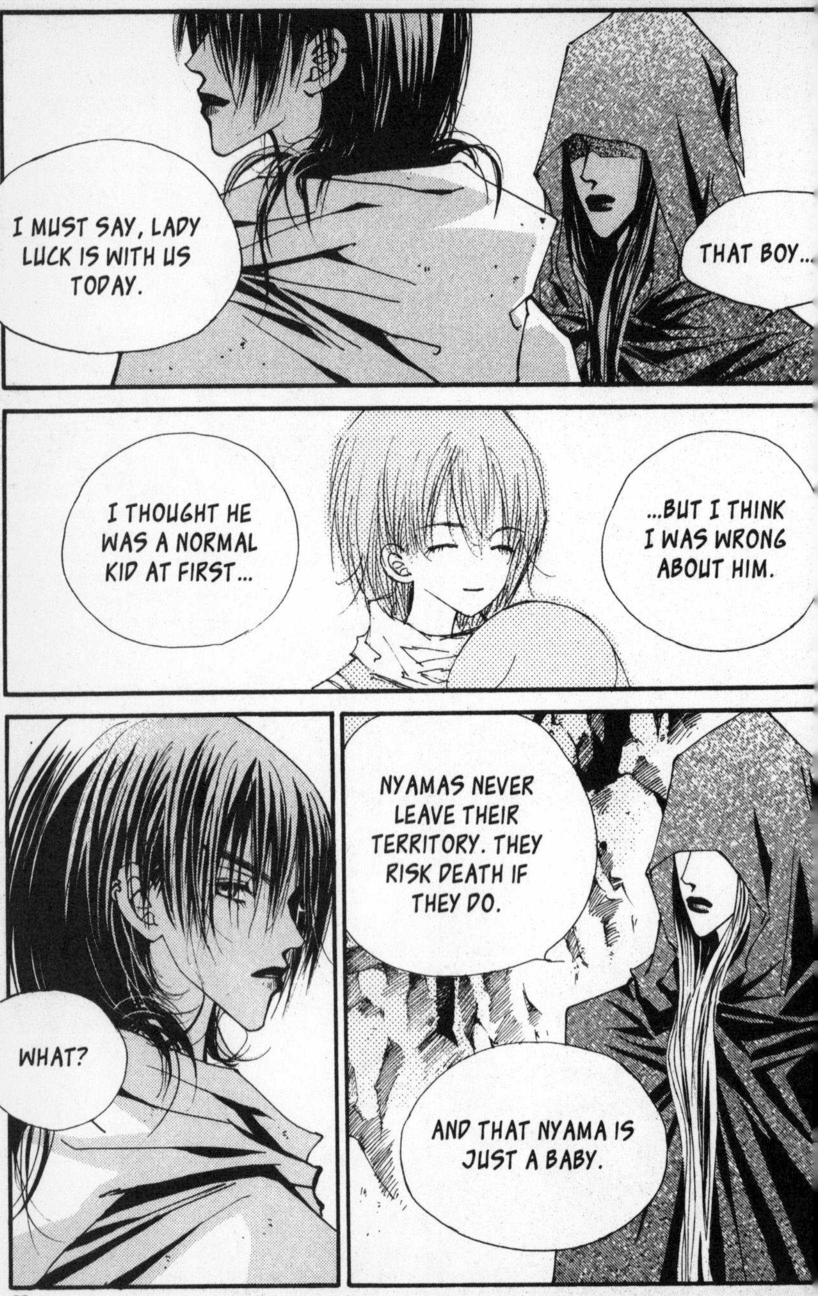
I MUST SAY, LADY LUCK IS WITH US TODAY.
THAT BOY...
I THOUGHT HE WAS A NORMAL KID AT FIRST...
...BUT I THINK I WAS WRONG ABOUT HIM.
WHAT?
NYAMAS NEVER LEAVE THEIR TERRITORY. THEY RISK DEATH IF THEY DO.
AND THAT NYAMA IS JUST A BABY.

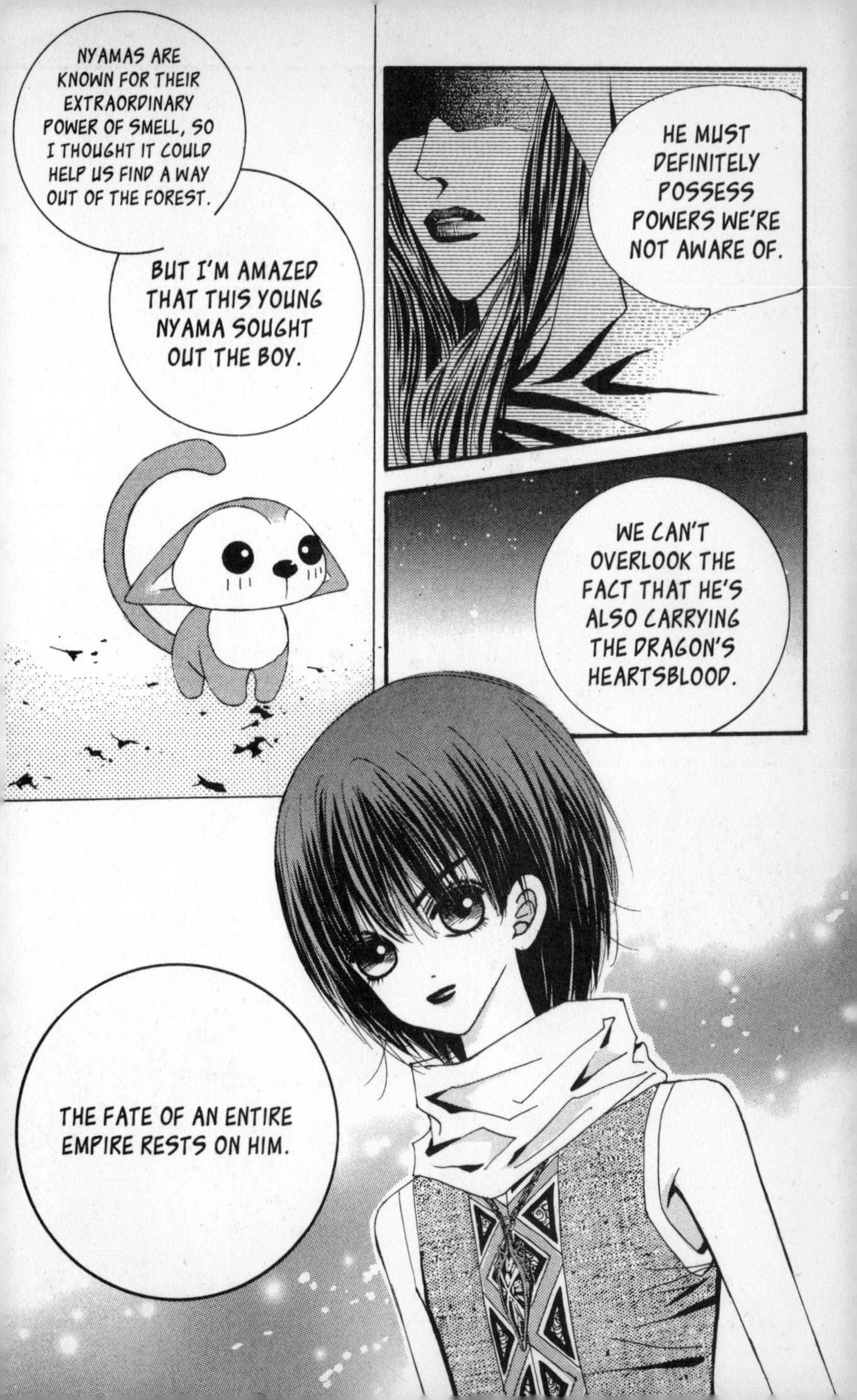
NYAMAS ARE KNOWN FOR THEIR EXTRAORDINARY POWER OF SMELL, SO I THOUGHT IT COULD HELP US FIND A WAY OUT OF THE FOREST.
BUT I'M AMAZED THAT THIS YOUNG NYAMA SOUGHT OUT THE BOY.
HE MUST DEFINITELY POSSESS POWERS WE'RE NOT AWARE OF.
WE CAN'T OVERLOOK THE FACT THAT HE'S ALSO CARRYING THE DRAGON'S HEARTSBLOOD.
THE FATE OF AN ENTIRE EMPIRE RESTS ON HIM.

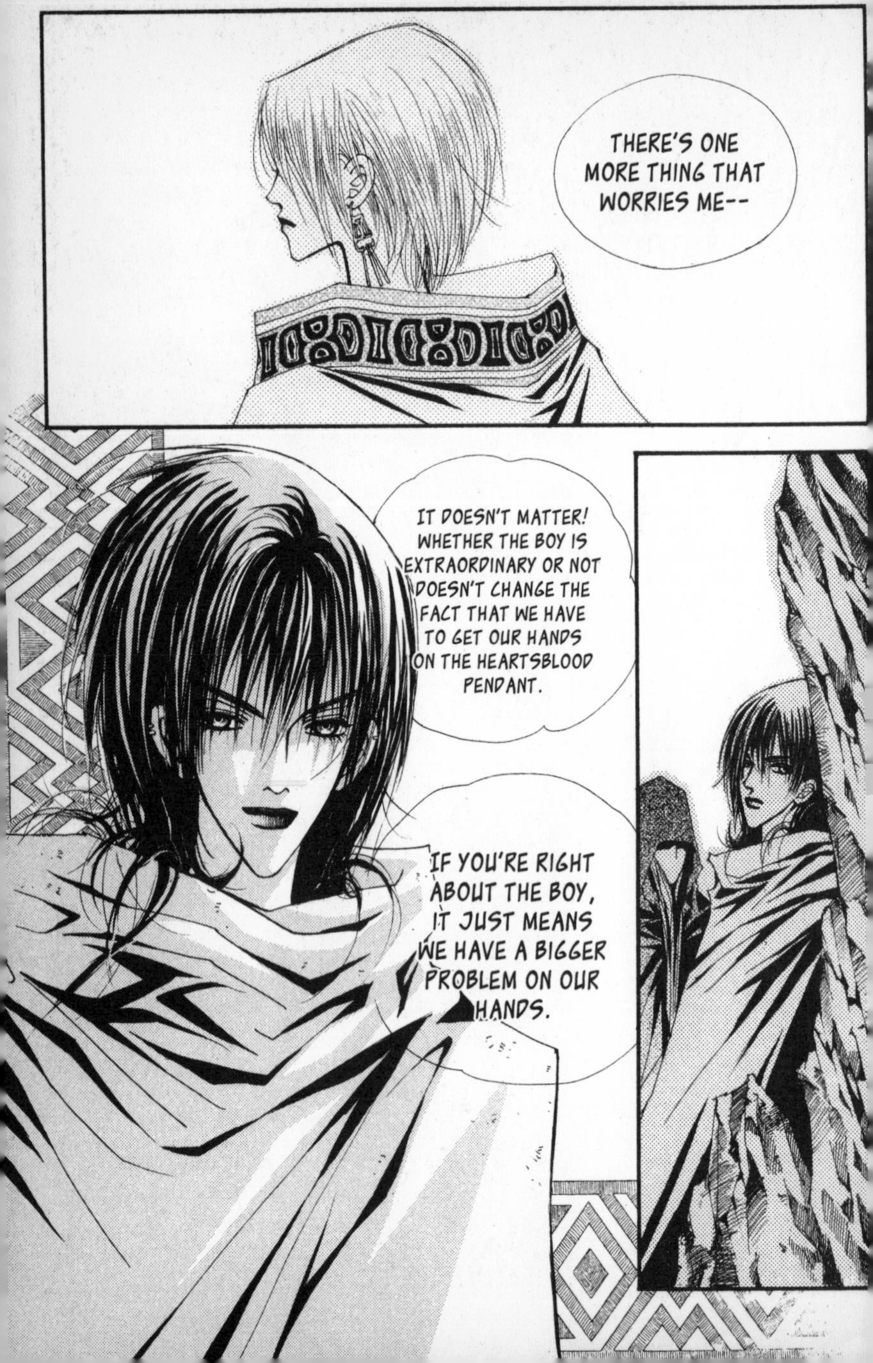
THERE'S ONE MORE THING THAT WORRIES ME--
IT DOESN'T MATTER! WHETHER THE BOY IS EXTRAORDINARY OR NOT DOESN'T CHANGE THE FACT THAT WE HAVE TO GET OUR HANDS ON THE HEARTSBLOOD PENDANT.
IF YOU'RE RIGHT ABOUT THE BOY, IT JUST MEANS WE HAVE A BIGGER PROBLEM ON OUR HANDS.

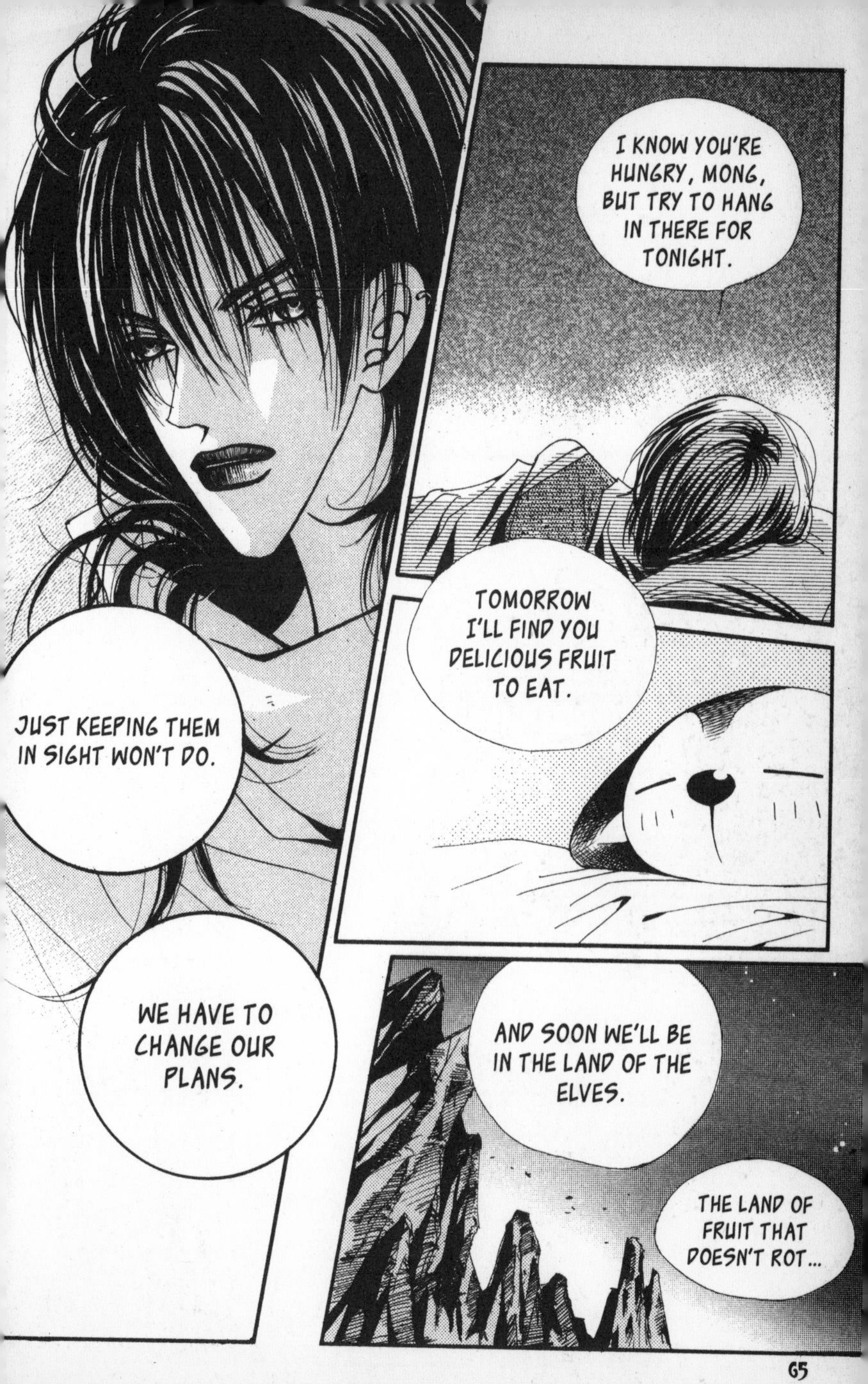
JUST KEEPING THEM IN SIGHT WON'T DO.
WE HAVE TO CHANGE OUR PLANS.
I KNOW YOU'RE HUNGRY, MONG, BUT TRY TO HANG IN THERE FOR TONIGHT.
TOMORROW I'LL FIND YOU DELICIOUS FRUIT TO EAT.
AND SOON WE'LL BE IN THE LAND OF THE ELVES.
THE LAND OF FRUIT THAT DOESN'T ROT...

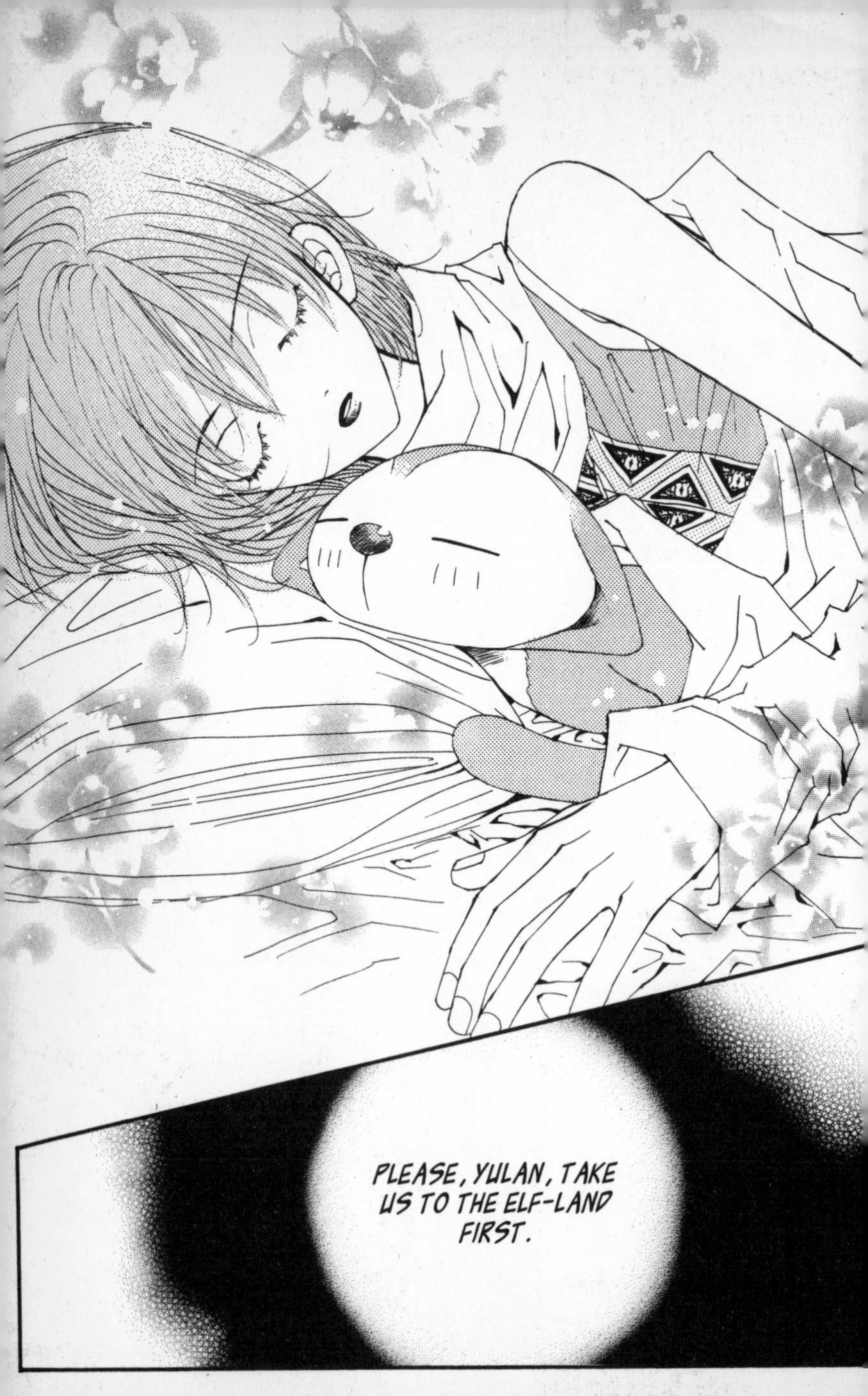
PLEASE, YULAN, TAKE US TO THE ELF-LAND FIRST.

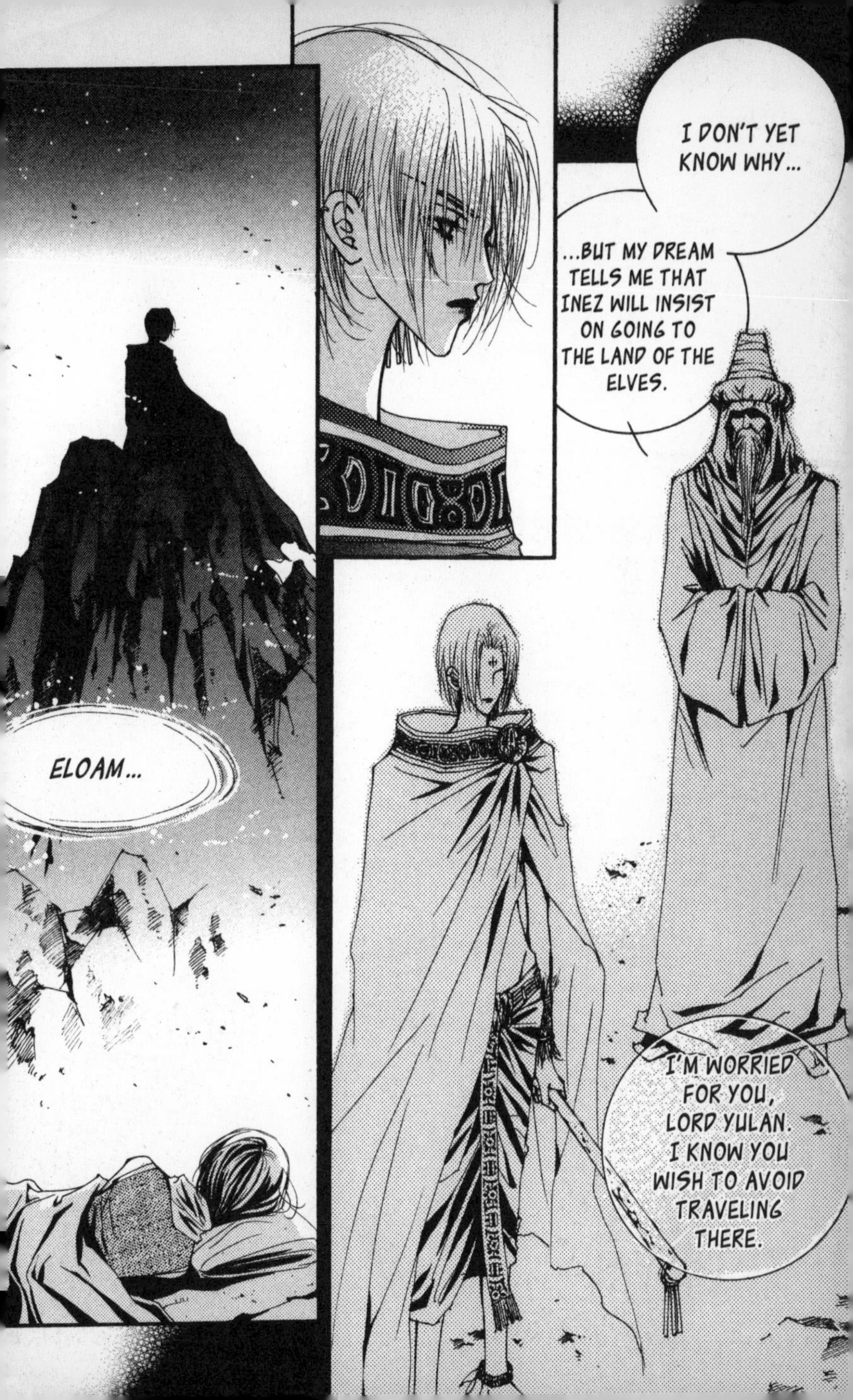
ELOAM...
I DON'T YET KNOW WHY...
...BUT MY DREAM TELLS ME THAT INEZ WILL INSIST ON GOING TO THE LAND OF THE ELVES.
I'M WORRIED FOR YOU, LORD YULAN. I KNOW YOU WISH TO AVOID TRAVELING THERE.

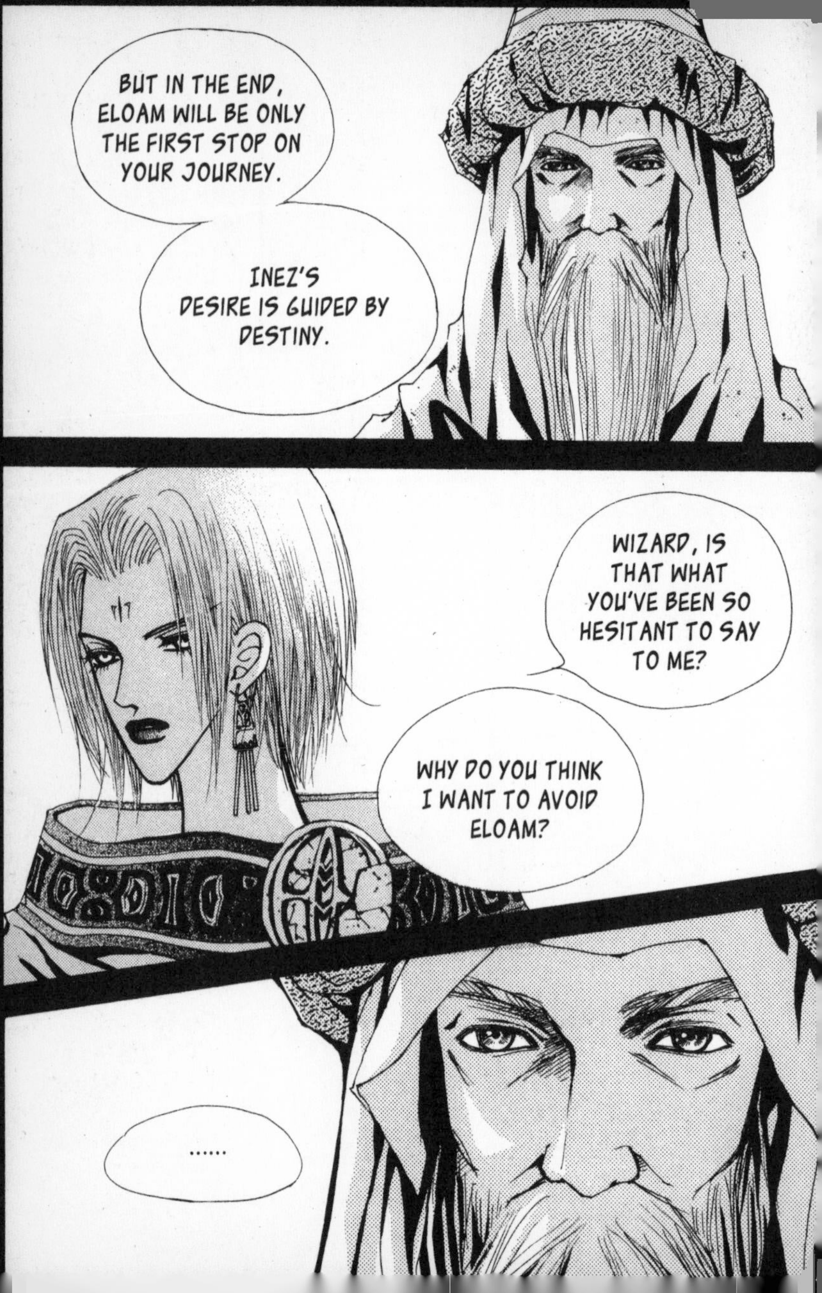
BUT IN THE END, ELOAM WILL BE ONLY THE FIRST STOP ON YOUR JOURNEY.
INEZ'S DESIRE IS GUIDED BY DESTINY.
WIZARD, IS THAT WHAT YOU'VE BEEN SO HESITANT TO SAY TO ME?
WHY DO YOU THINK I WANT TO AVOID ELOAM?
......

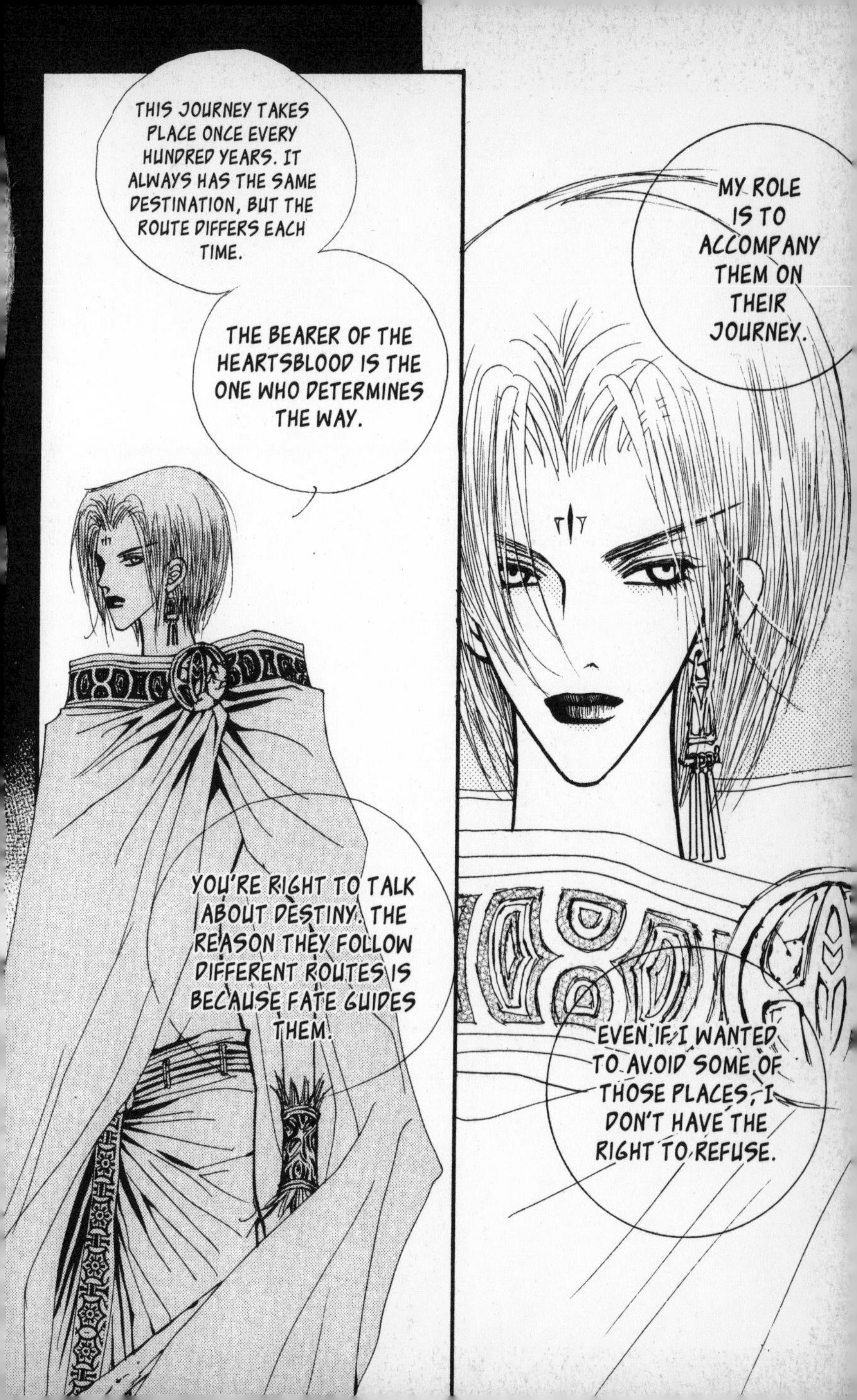

THIS JOURNEY TAKES PLACE ONCE EVERY HUNDRED YEARS. IT ALWAYS HAS THE SAME DESTINATION, BUT THE ROUTE DIFFERS EACH TIME.
THE BEARER OF THE HEARTSBLOOD IS THE ONE WHO DETERMINES THE WAY.
MY ROLE IS TO ACCOMPANY THEM ON THEIR JOURNEY.
YOU'RE RIGHT TO TALK ABOUT DESTINY. THE REASON THEY FOLLOW DIFFERENT ROUTES IS BECAUSE FATE GUIDES THEM.
EVEN IF I WANTED TO AVOID SOME OF THOSE PLACES, I DON'T HAVE THE RIGHT TO REFUSE.

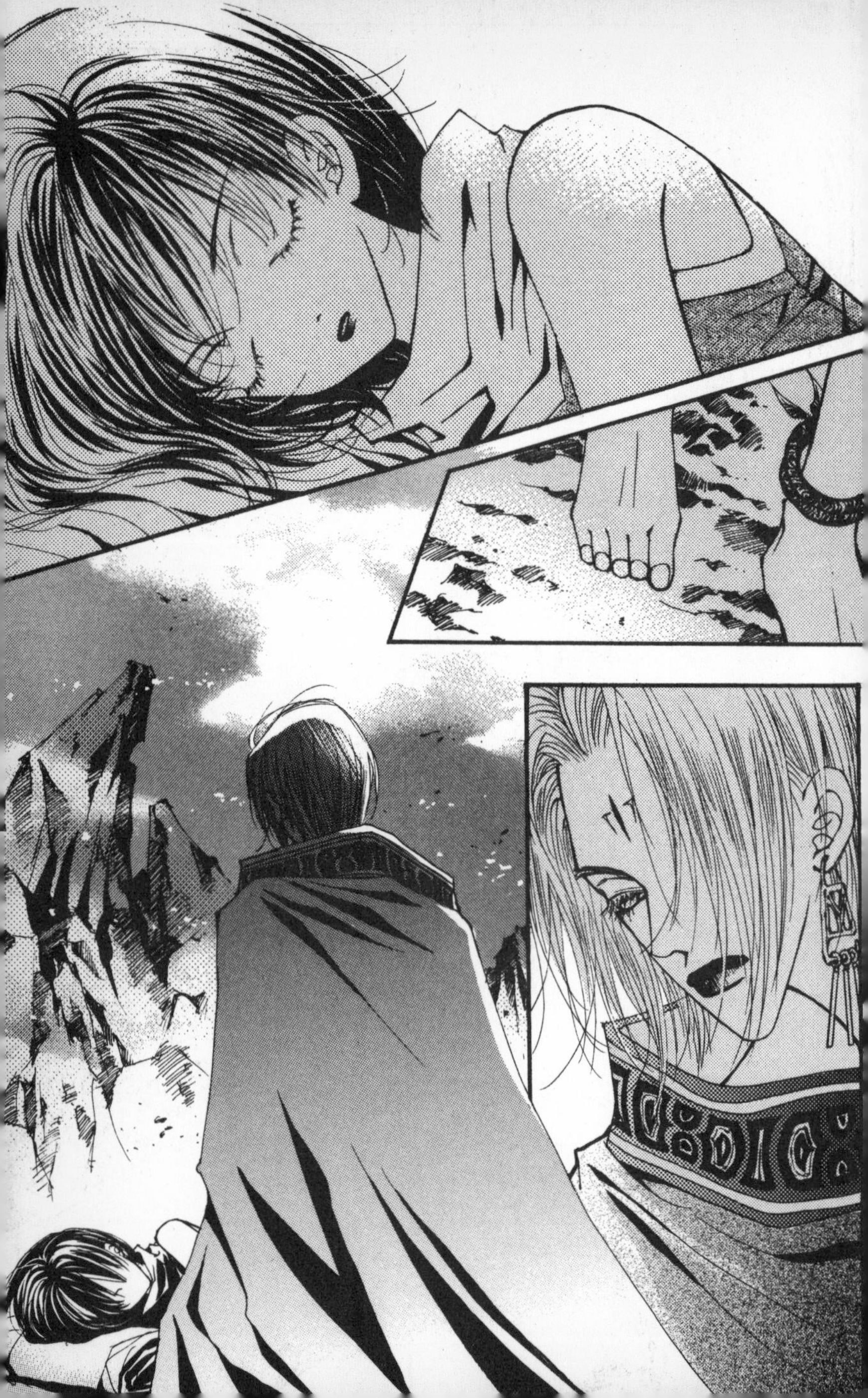

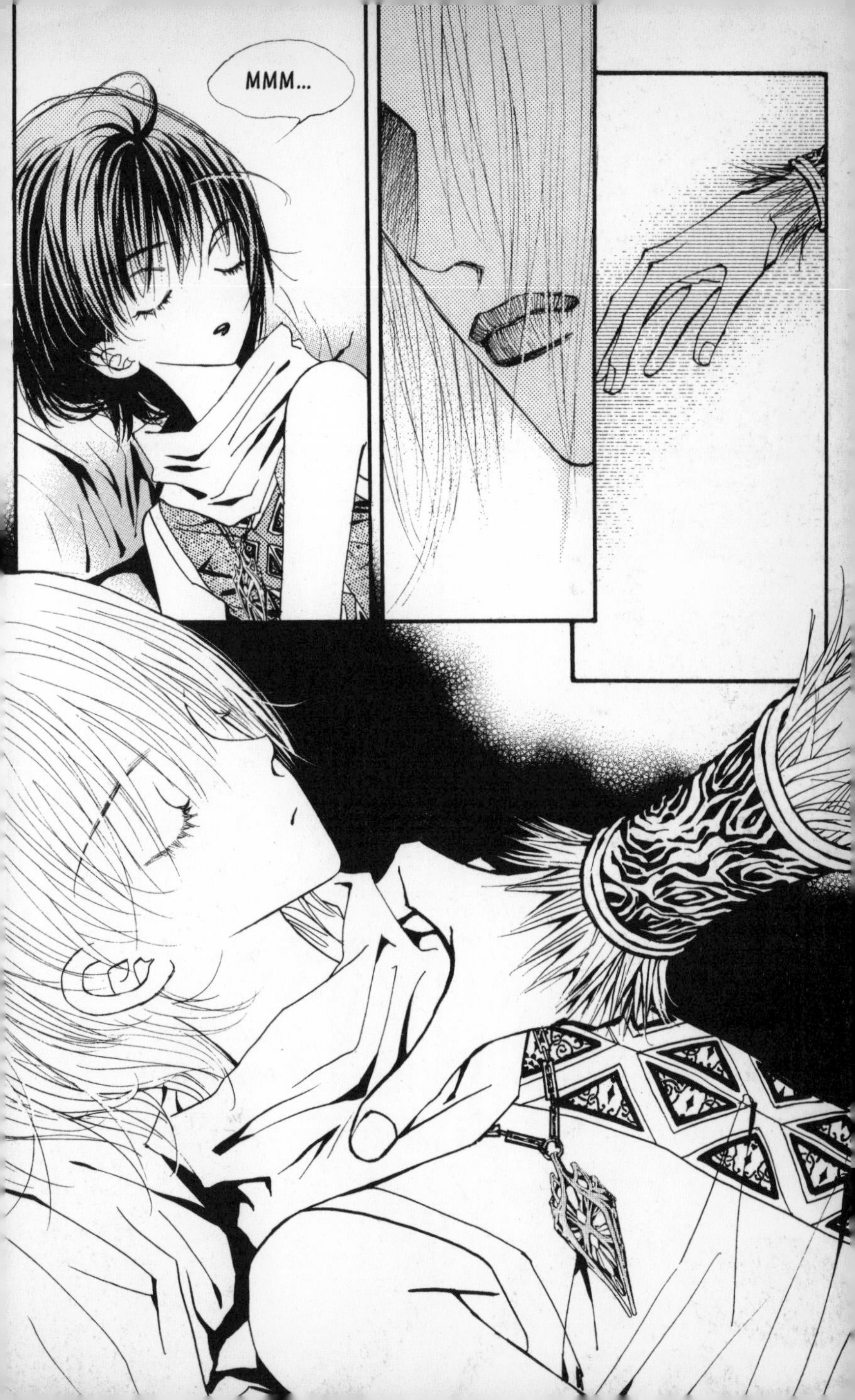
MMM...

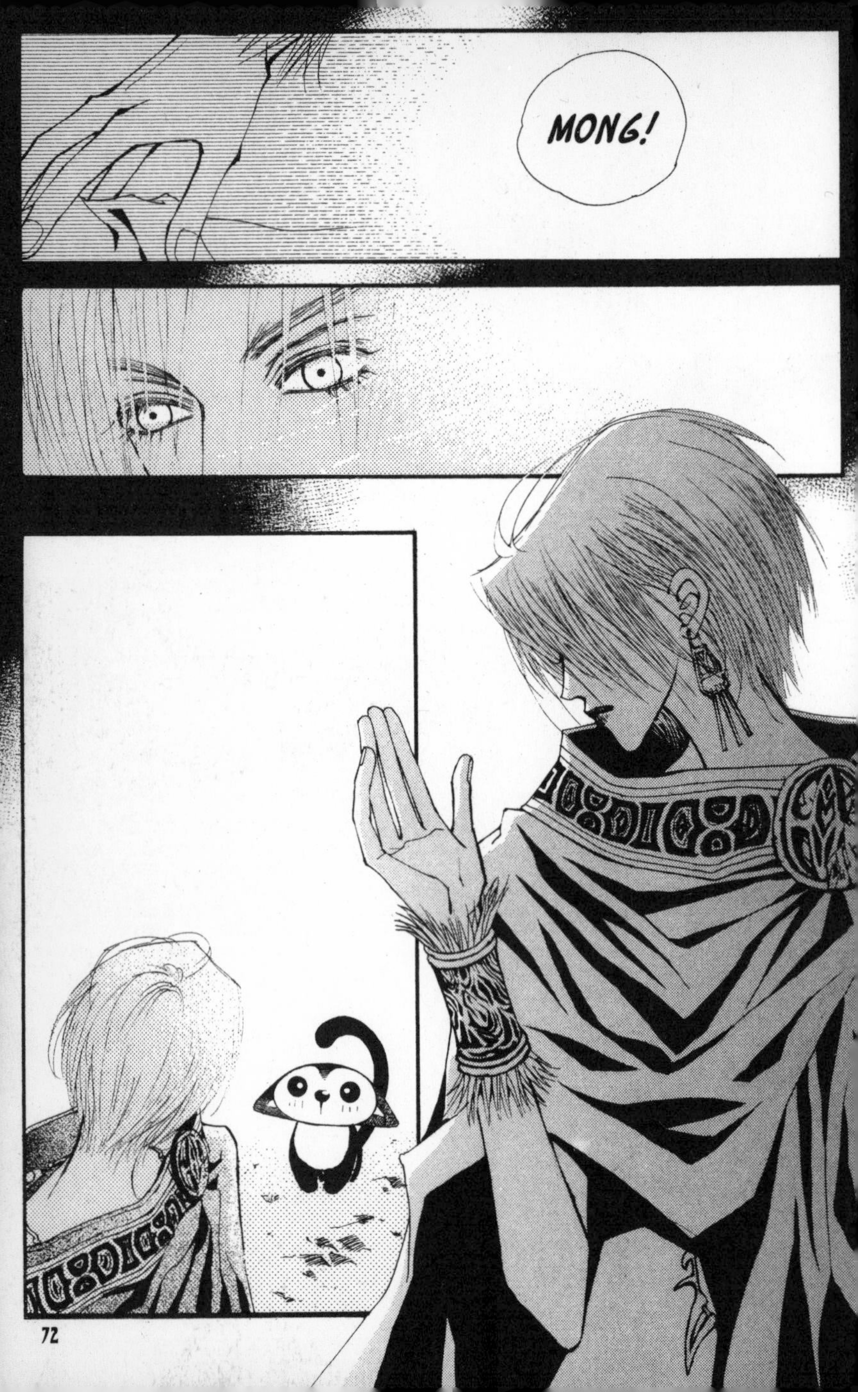
MONG!

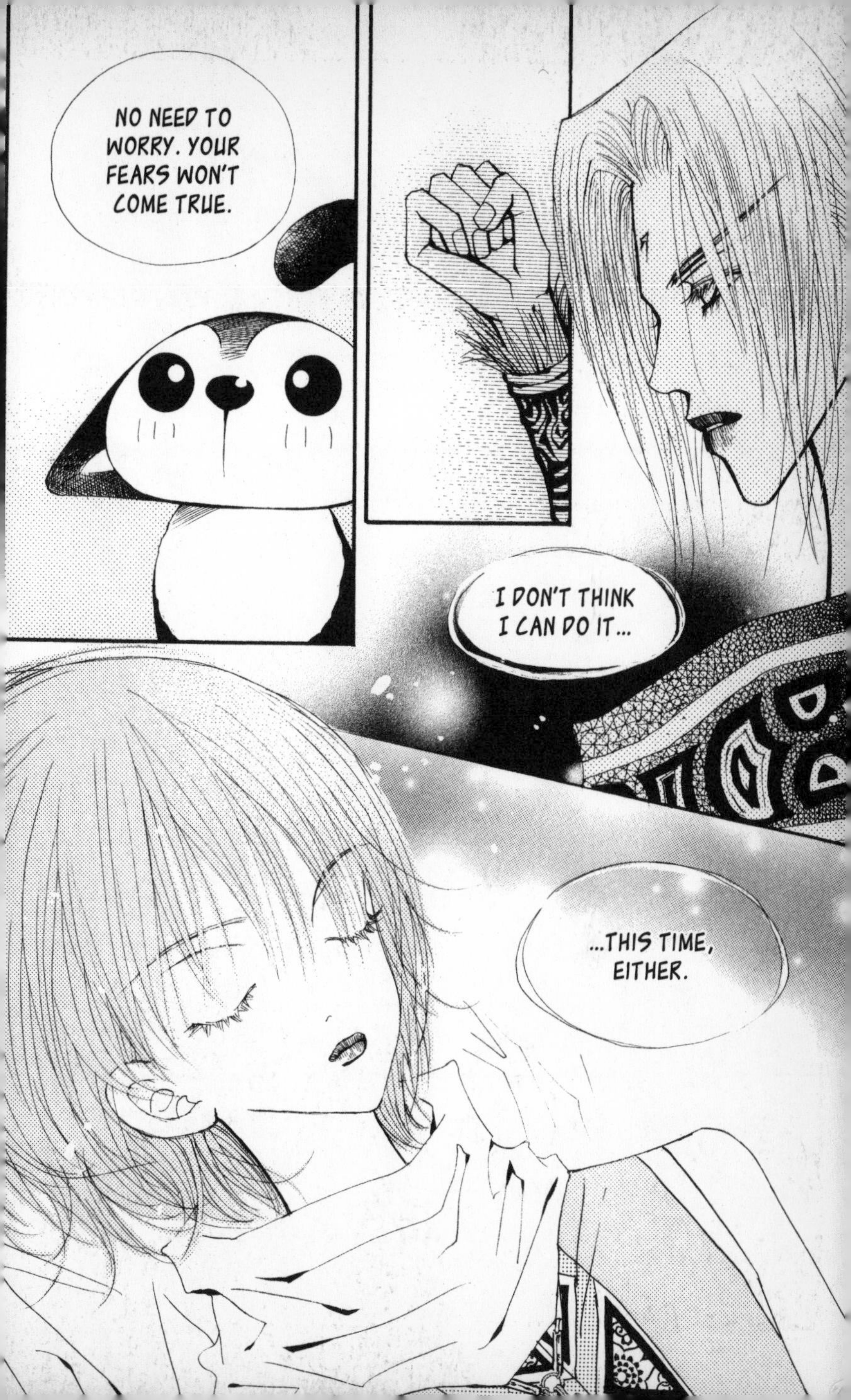
NO NEED TO WORRY. YOUR FEARS WON'T COME TRUE.
I DON'T THINK I CAN DO IT...
...THIS TIME, EITHER.

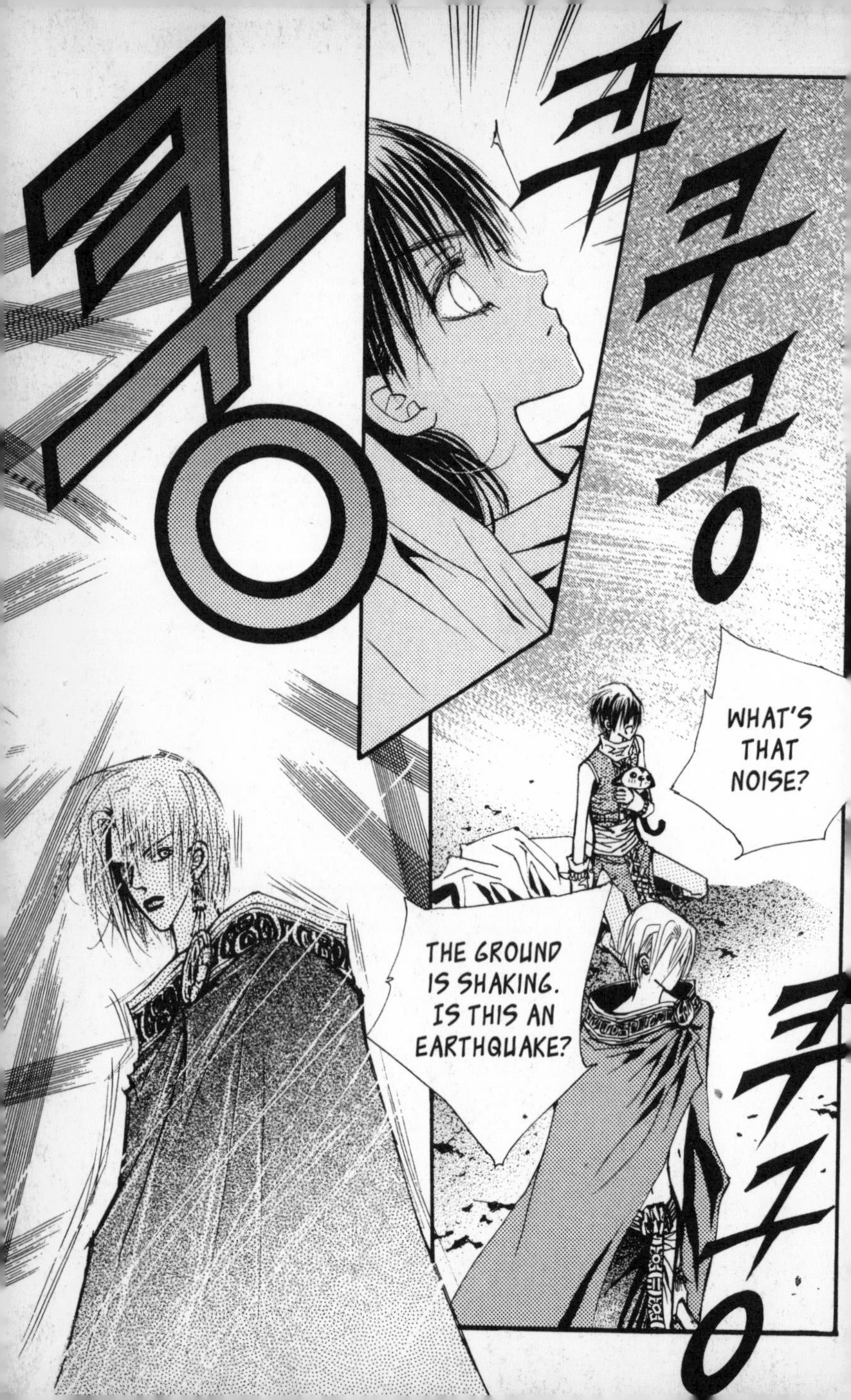
WHAT'S THAT NOISE?
THE GROUND IS SHAKING. IS THIS AN EARTHQUAKE?

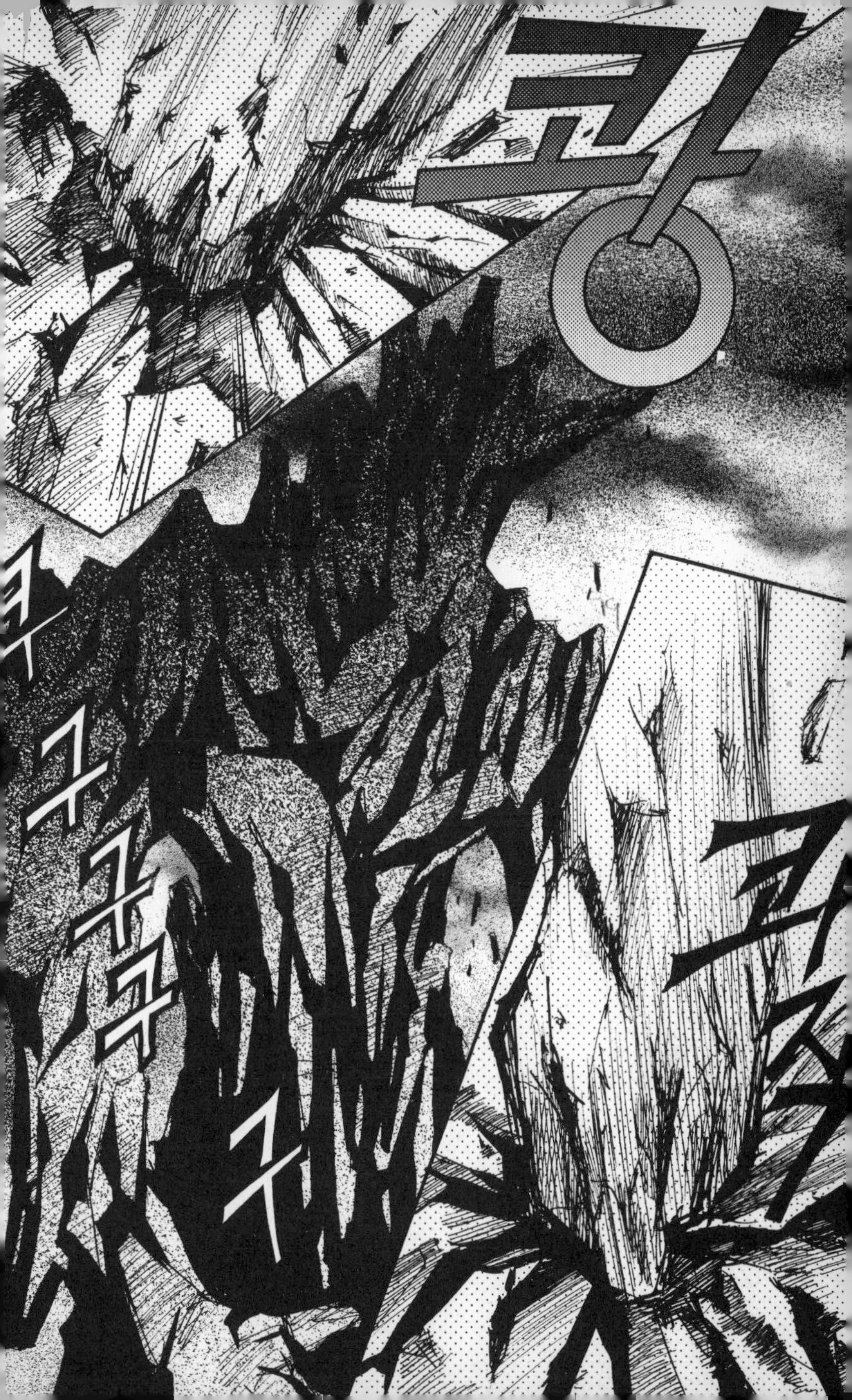

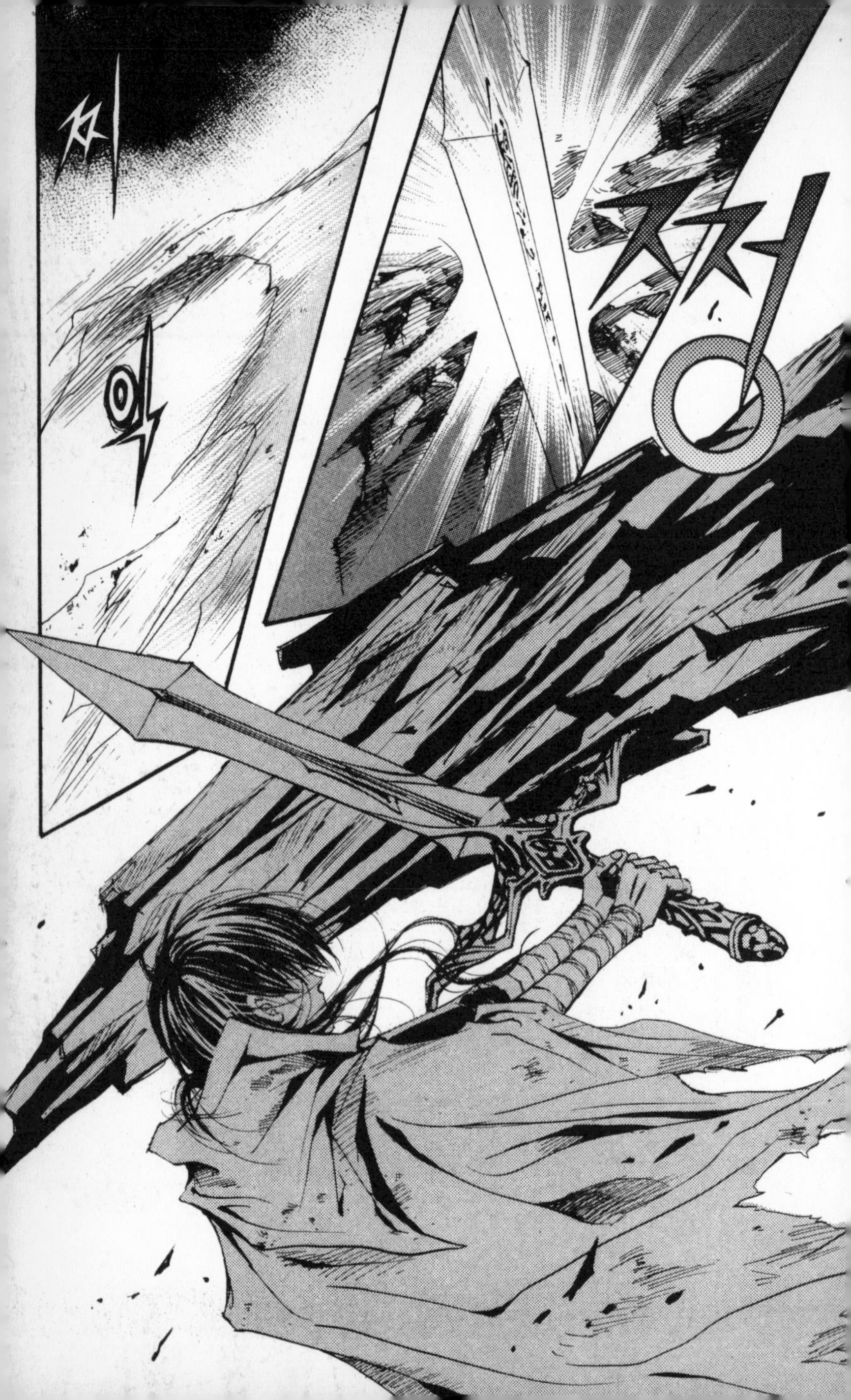
치
이
쩡

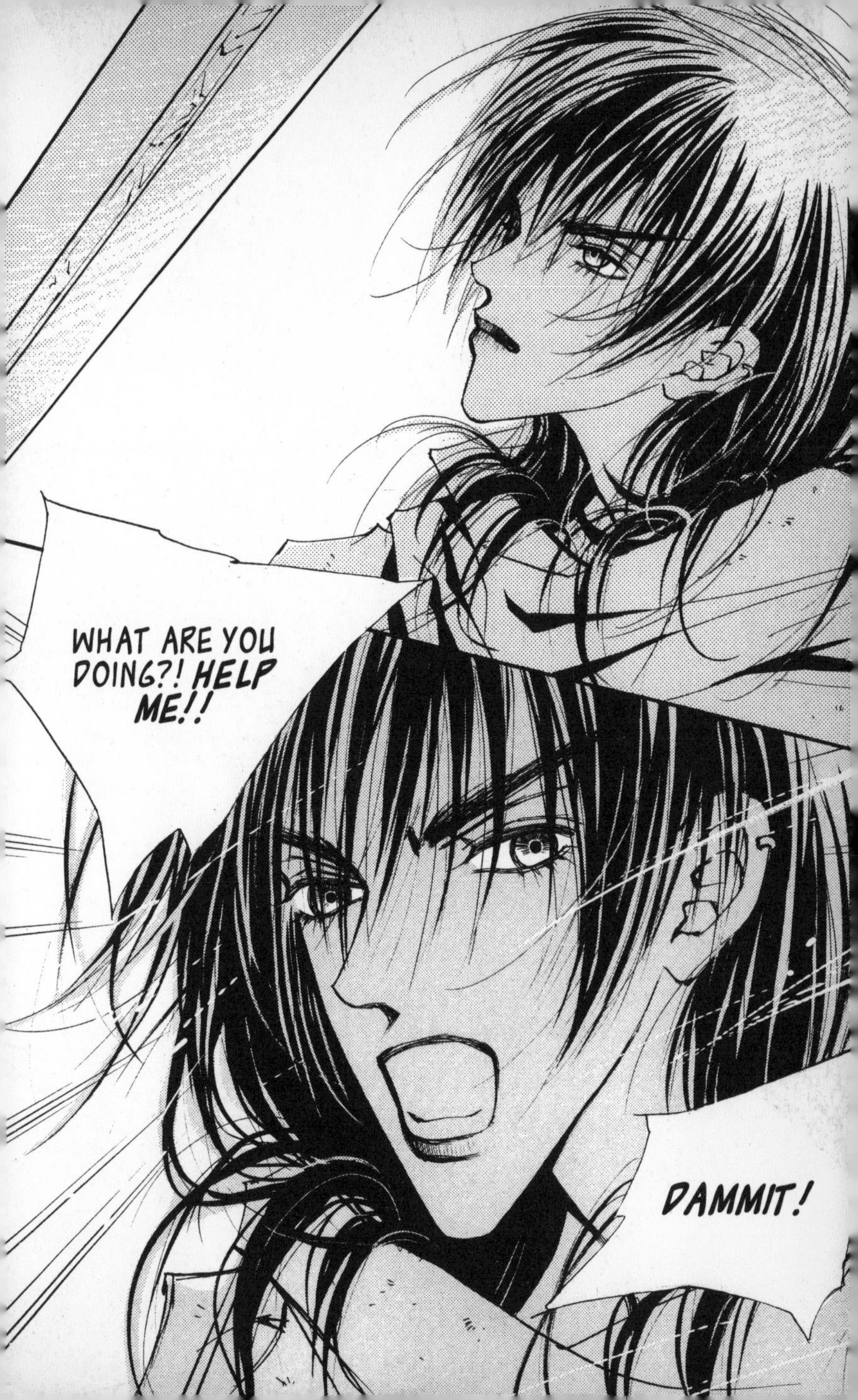
WHAT ARE YOU DOING?! HELP ME!!
DAMMIT!

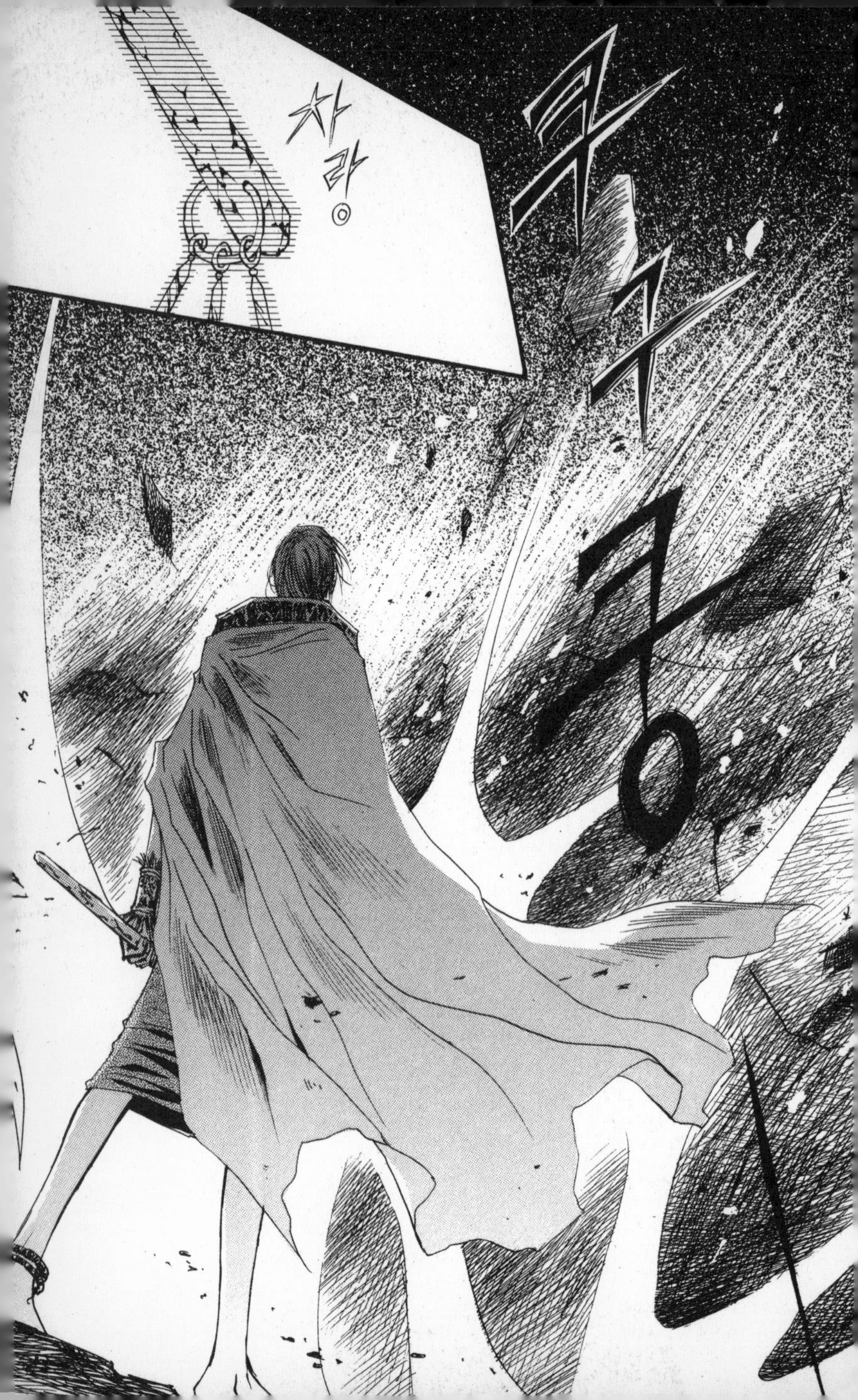
차랑
쿠구쿵

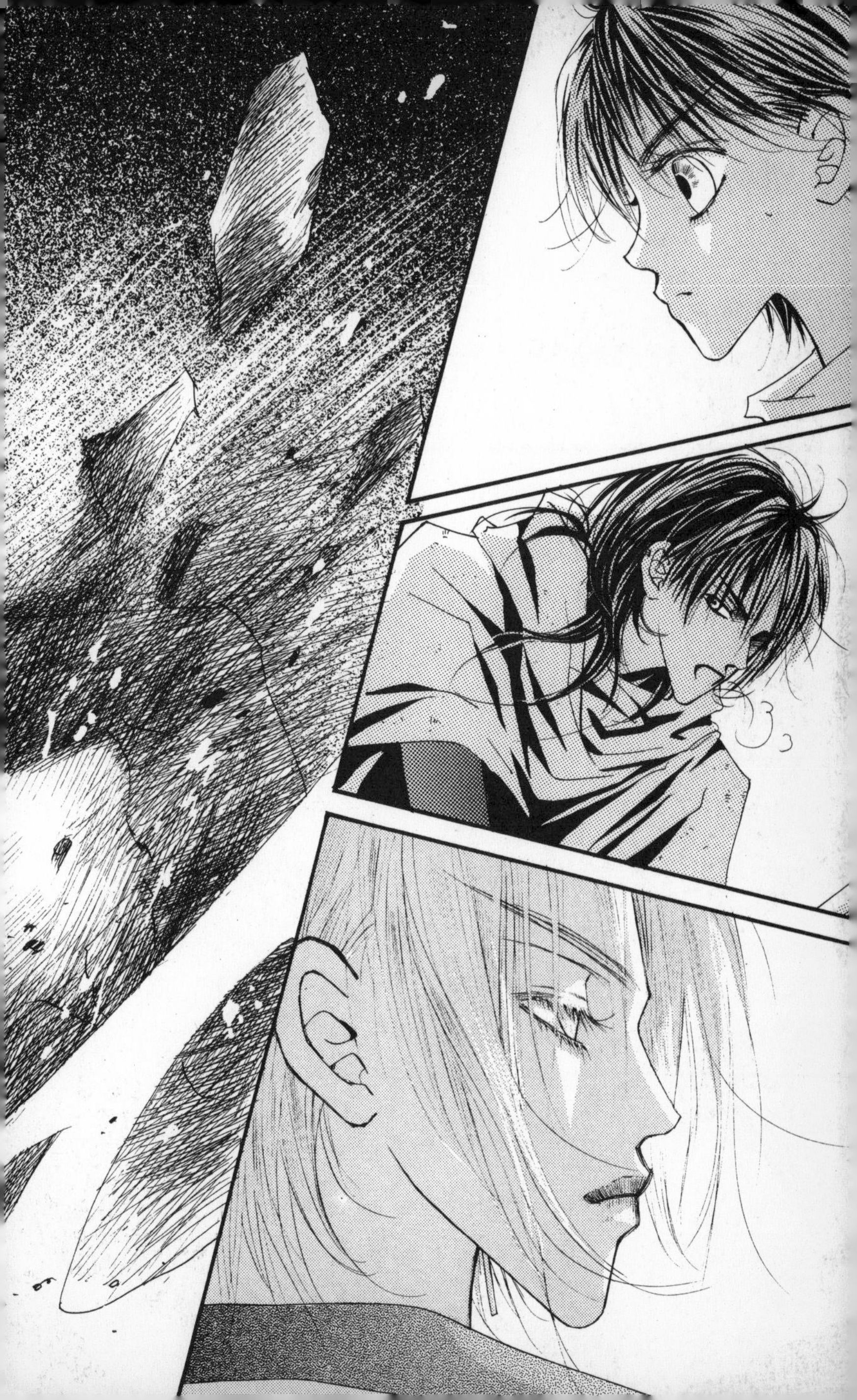

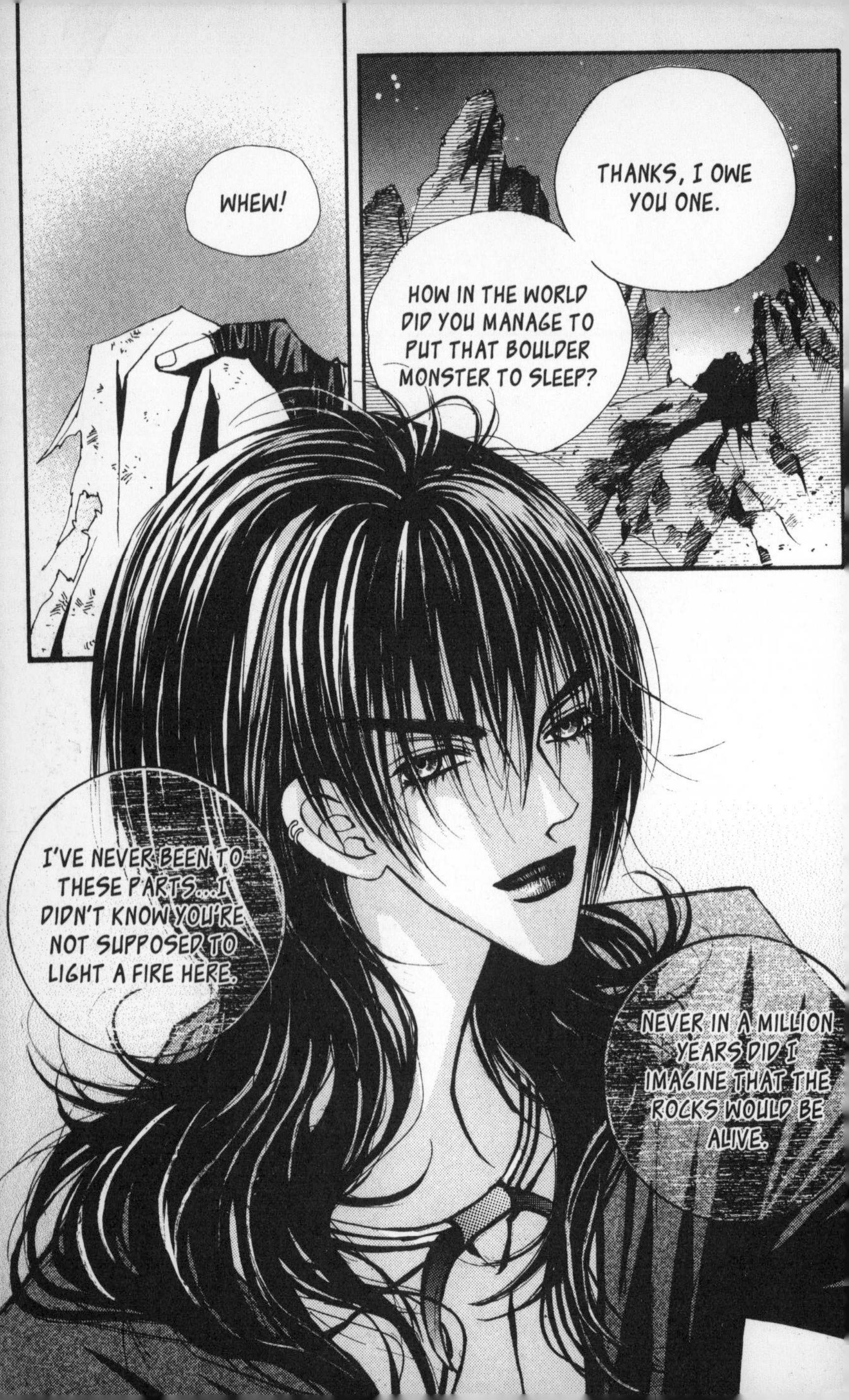
WHEW!
THANKS, I OWE YOU ONE.
HOW IN THE WORLD DID YOU MANAGE TO PUT THAT BOULDER MONSTER TO SLEEP?
I'VE NEVER BEEN TO THESE PARTS... I DIDN'T KNOW YOU'RE NOT SUPPOSED TO LIGHT A FIRE HERE.
NEVER IN A MILLION YEARS DID I IMAGINE THAT THE ROCKS WOULD BE ALIVE.

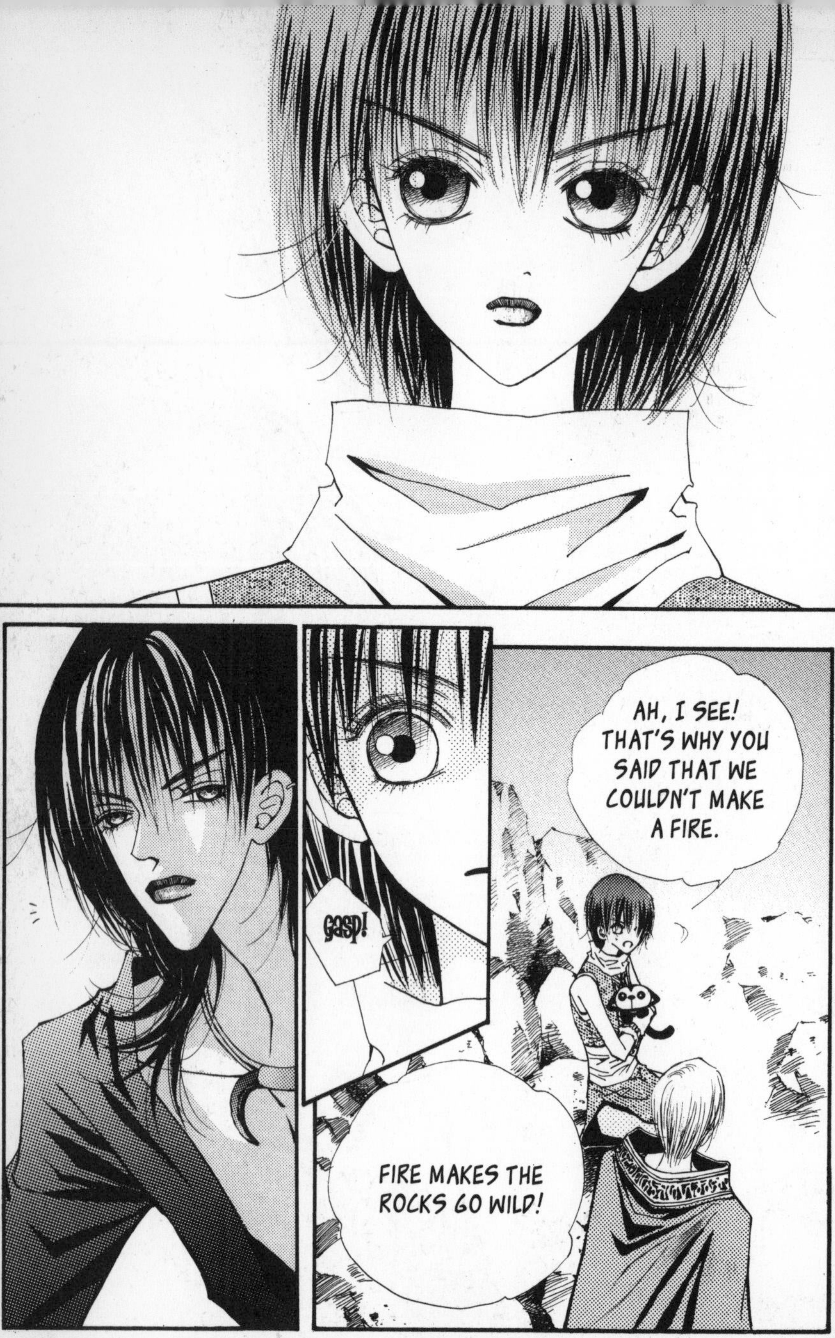
GASP!
AH, I SEE! THAT'S WHY YOU SAID THAT WE COULDN'T MAKE A FIRE.
FIRE MAKES THE ROCKS GO WILD!

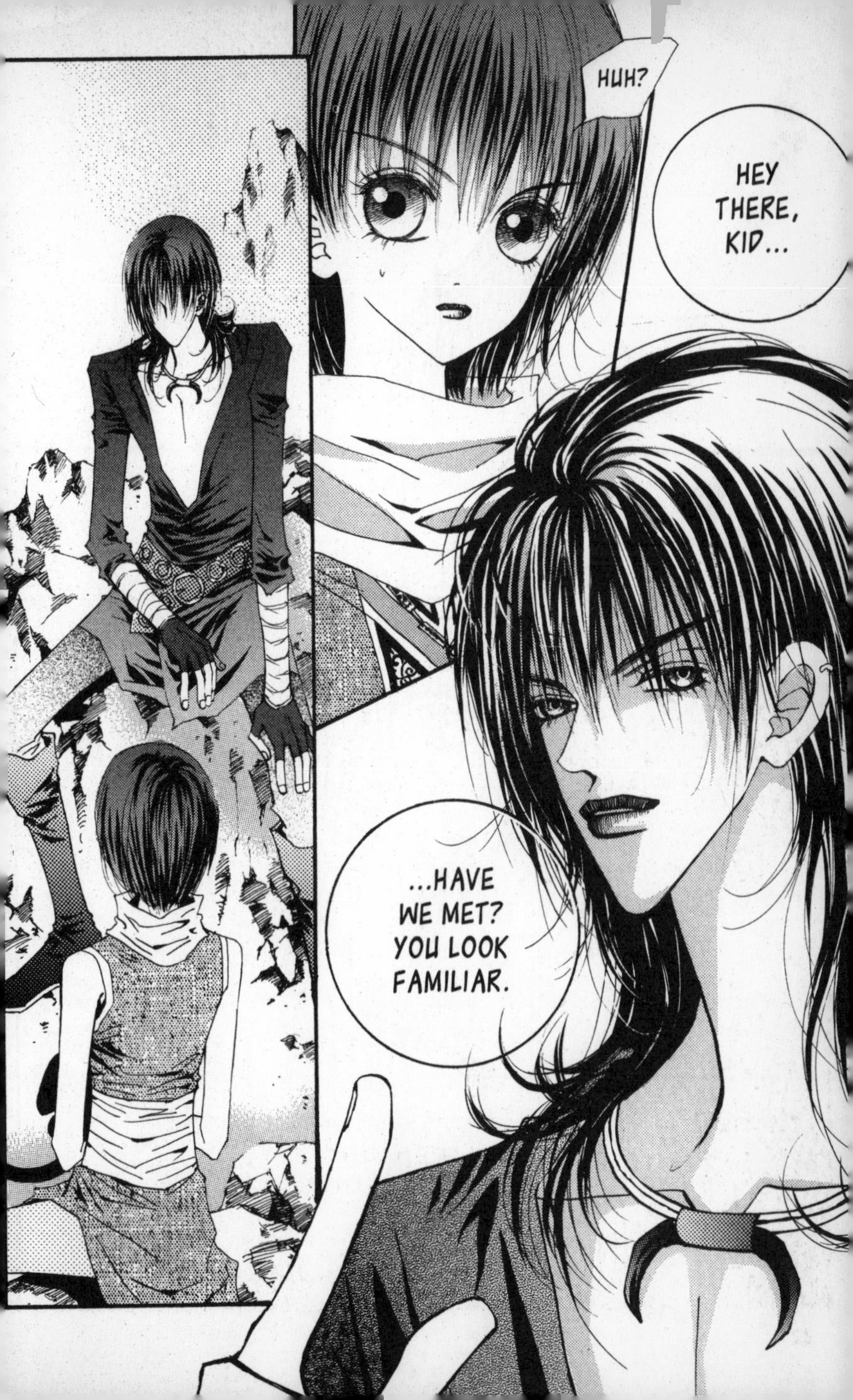
HUH?
HEY THERE, KID...
...HAVE WE MET? YOU LOOK FAMILIAR.

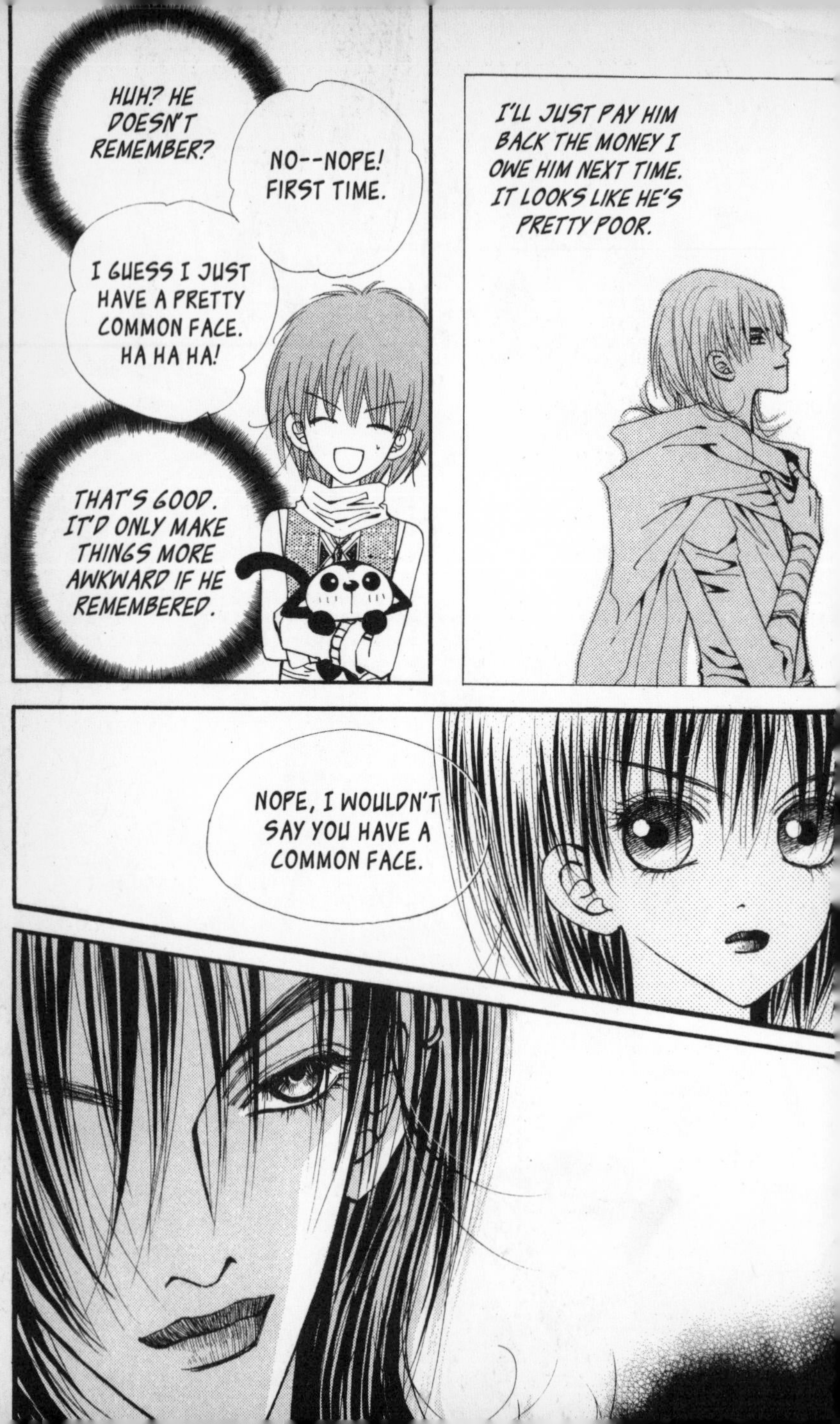
HUH? HE DOESN'T REMEMBER?
NO--NOPE! FIRST TIME.
I GUESS I JUST HAVE A PRETTY COMMON FACE. HA HA HA!
THAT'S GOOD. IT'D ONLY MAKE THINGS MORE AWKWARD IF HE REMEMBERED.
I'LL JUST PAY HIM BACK THE MONEY I OWE HIM NEXT TIME. IT LOOKS LIKE HE'S PRETTY POOR.
NOPE, I WOULDN'T SAY YOU HAVE A COMMON FACE.

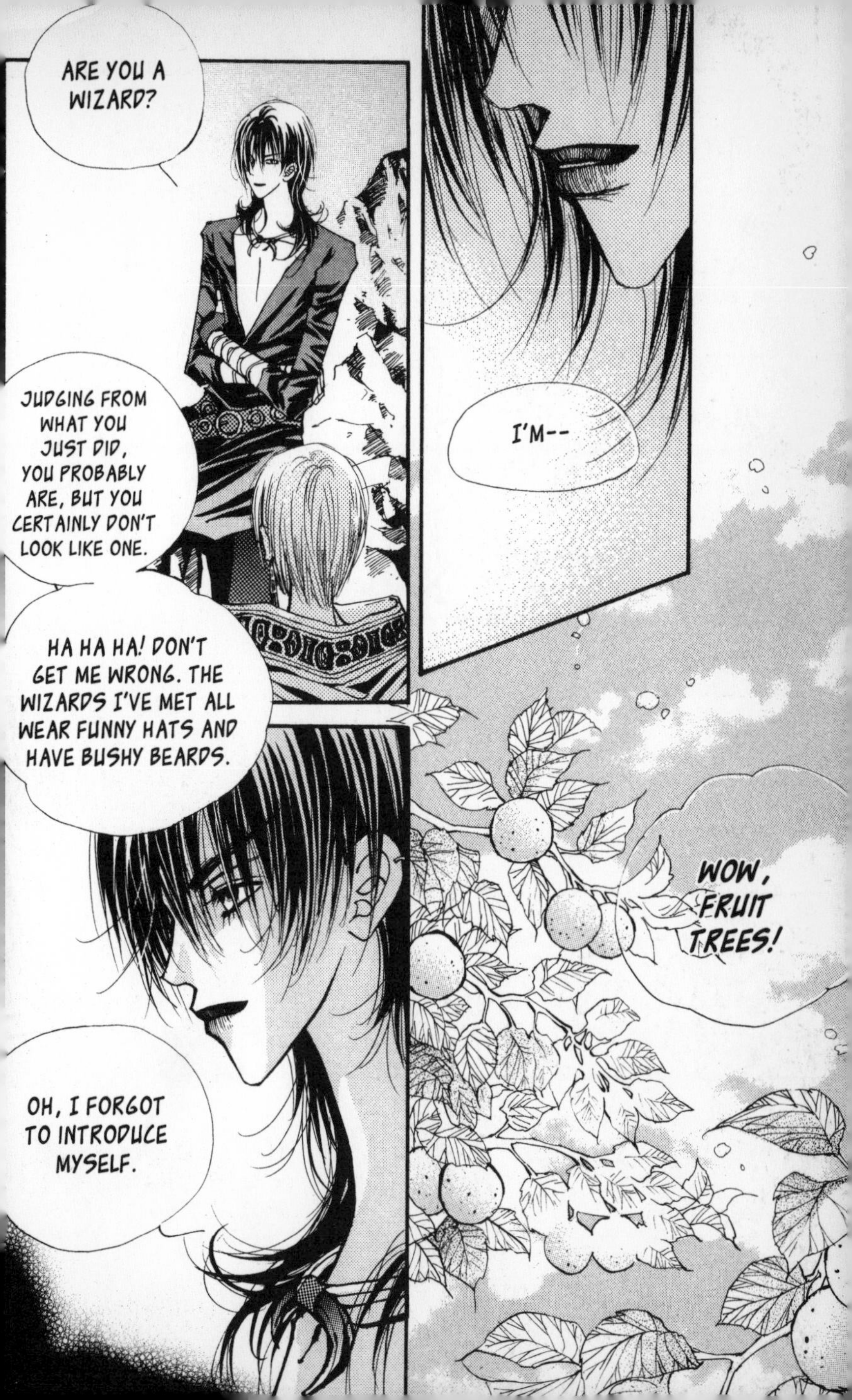
ARE YOU A WIZARD?
JUDGING FROM WHAT YOU JUST DID, YOU PROBABLY ARE, BUT YOU CERTAINLY DON'T LOOK LIKE ONE.
HA HA HA! DON'T GET ME WRONG. THE WIZARDS I'VE MET ALL WEAR FUNNY HATS AND HAVE BUSHY BEARDS.
I'M--
OH, I FORGOT TO INTRODUCE MYSELF.
WOW, FRUIT TREES!

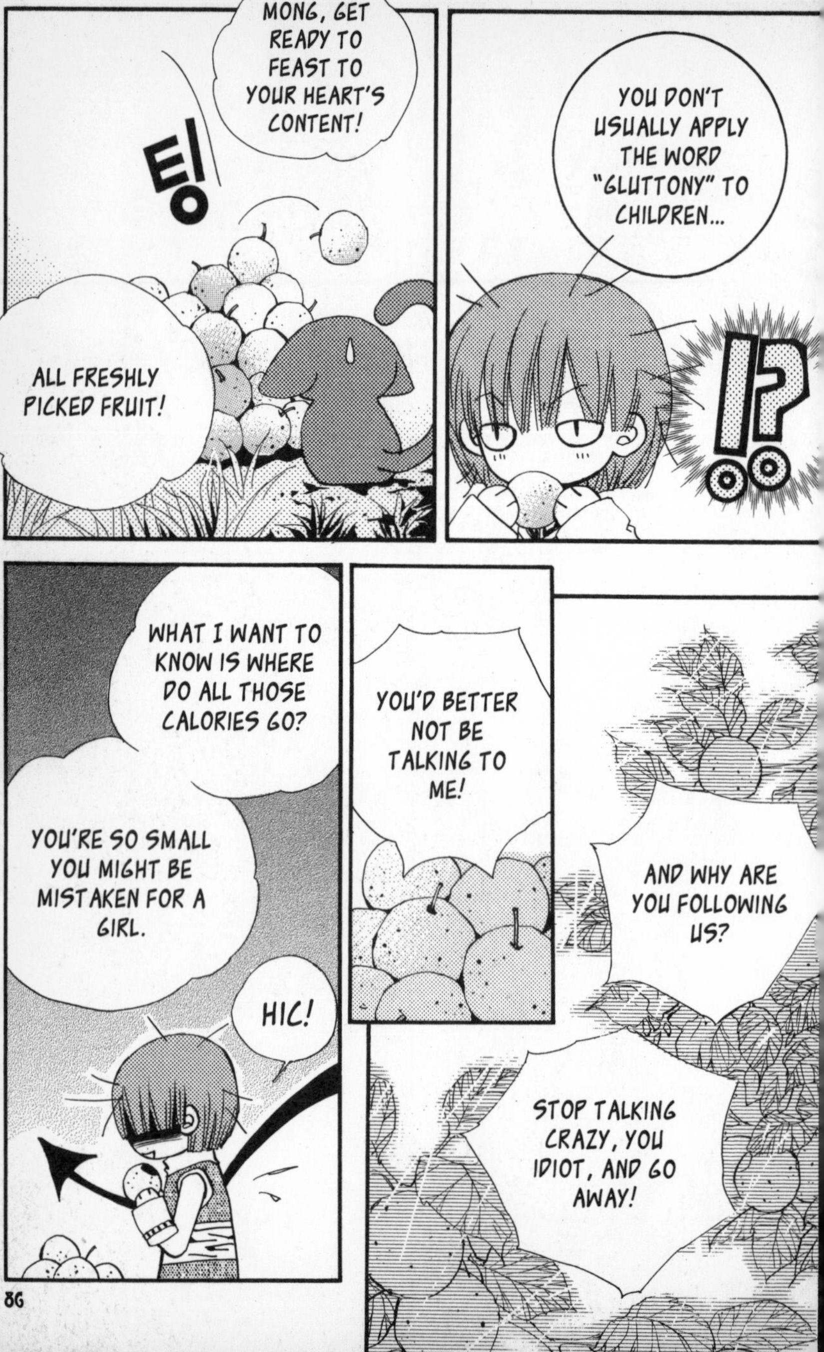
MONG, GET READY TO FEAST TO YOUR HEART'S CONTENT!
팅
ALL FRESHLY PICKED FRUIT!
YOU DON'T USUALLY APPLY THE WORD "GLUTTONY" TO CHILDREN...
!?
WHAT I WANT TO KNOW IS WHERE DO ALL THOSE CALORIES GO?
YOU'RE SO SMALL YOU MIGHT BE MISTAKEN FOR A GIRL.
HIC!
YOU'D BETTER NOT BE TALKING TO ME!
AND WHY ARE YOU FOLLOWING US?
STOP TALKING CRAZY, YOU IDIOT, AND GO AWAY!

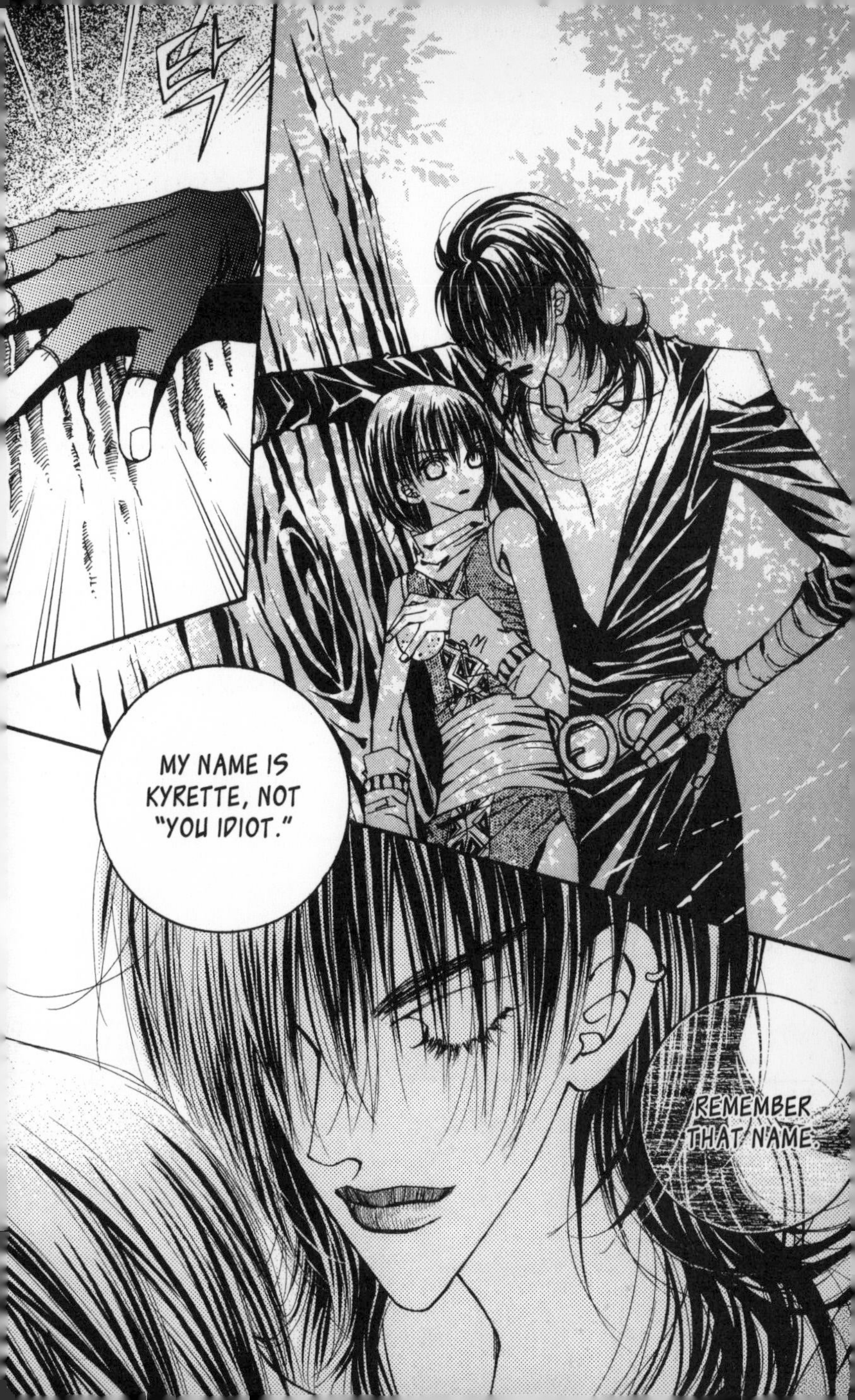
MY NAME IS KYRETTE, NOT "YOU IDIOT."
REMEMBER THAT NAME.

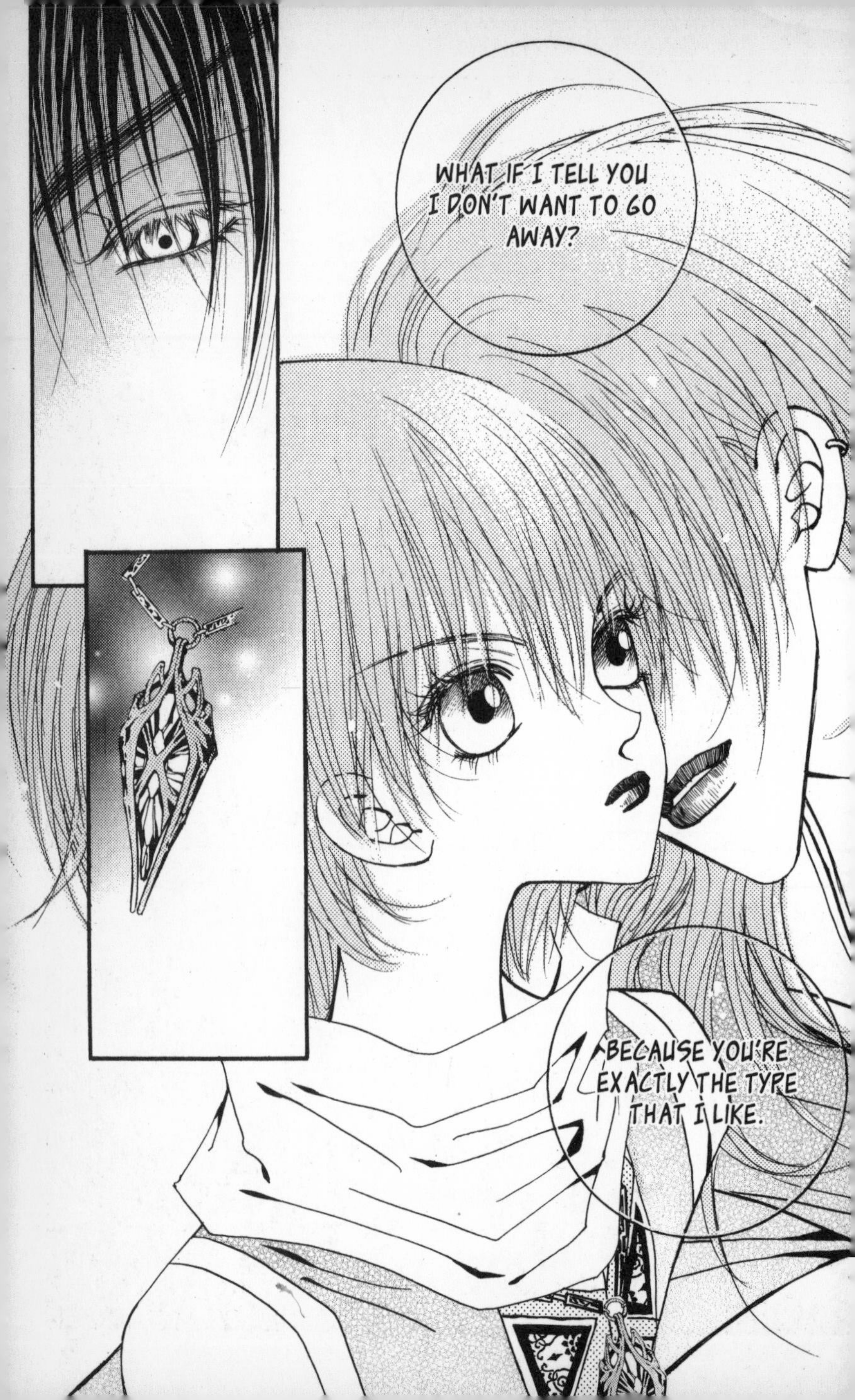
WHAT IF I TELL YOU I DON'T WANT TO GO AWAY?
BECAUSE YOU'RE EXACTLY THE TYPE THAT I LIKE.

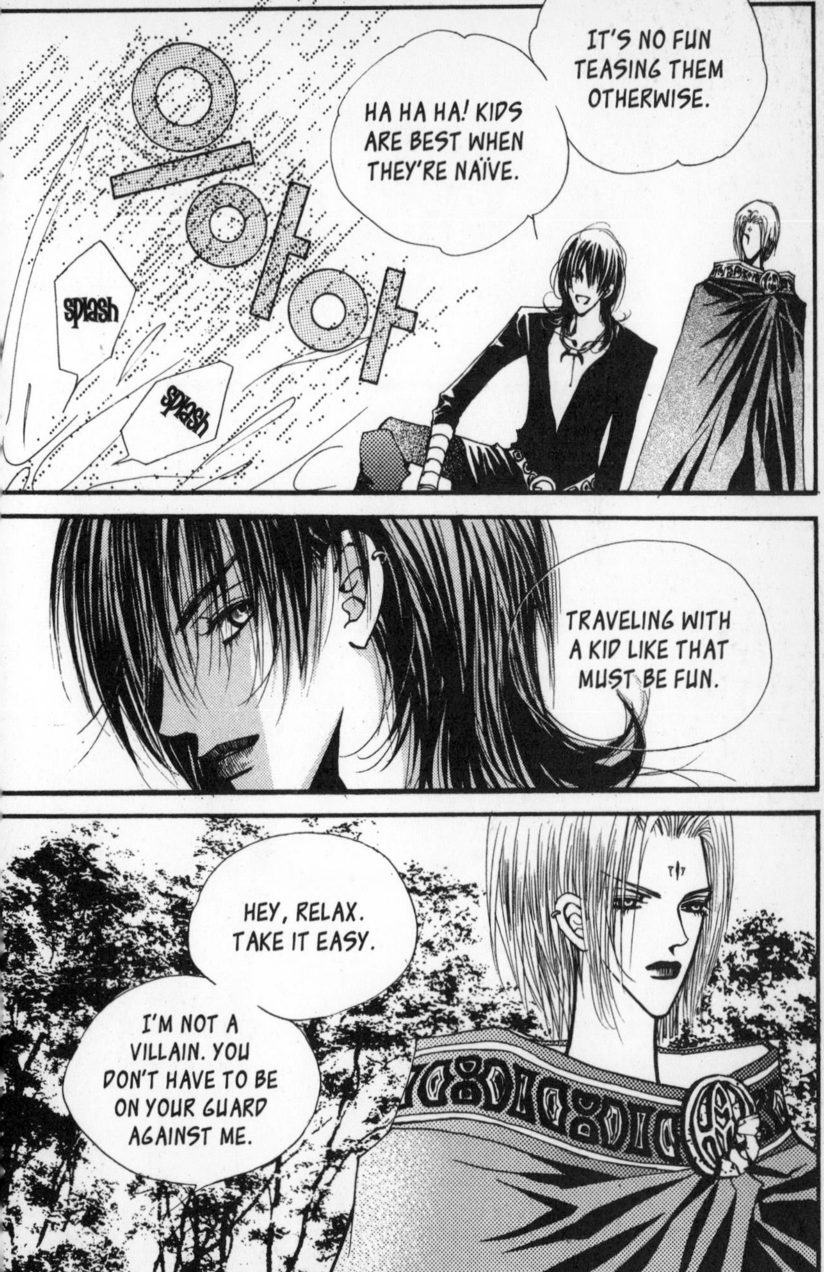

으아아
splash
splash
HA HA HA! KIDS ARE BEST WHEN THEY'RE NAÏVE.
IT'S NO FUN TEASING THEM OTHERWISE.
TRAVELING WITH A KID LIKE THAT MUST BE FUN.
HEY, RELAX. TAKE IT EASY.
I'M NOT A VILLAIN. YOU DON'T HAVE TO BE ON YOUR GUARD AGAINST ME.

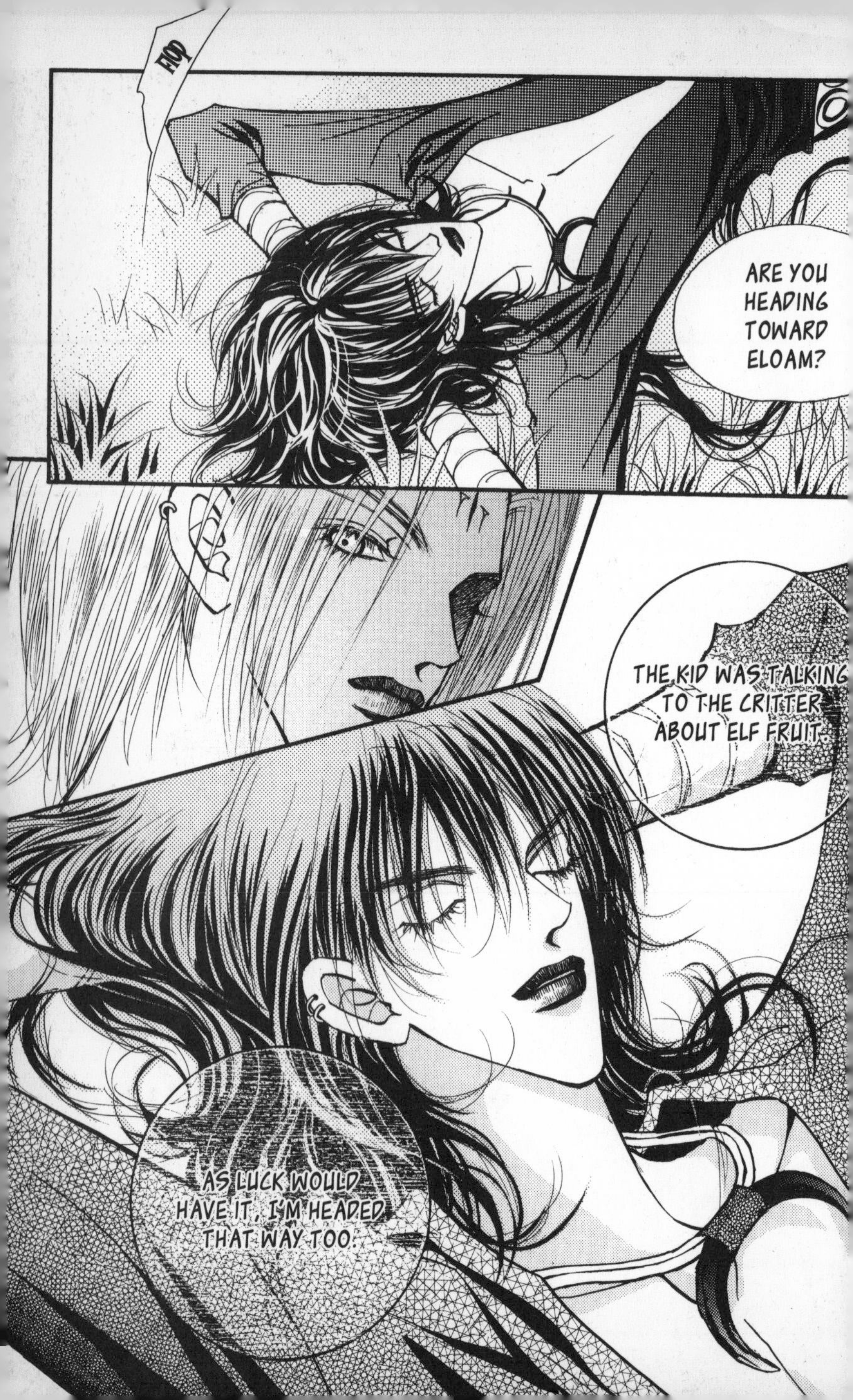
FLOP
ARE YOU HEADING TOWARD ELOAM?
THE KID WAS TALKING TO THE CRITTER ABOUT ELF FRUIT.
AS LUCK WOULD HAVE IT, I'M HEADED THAT WAY TOO.

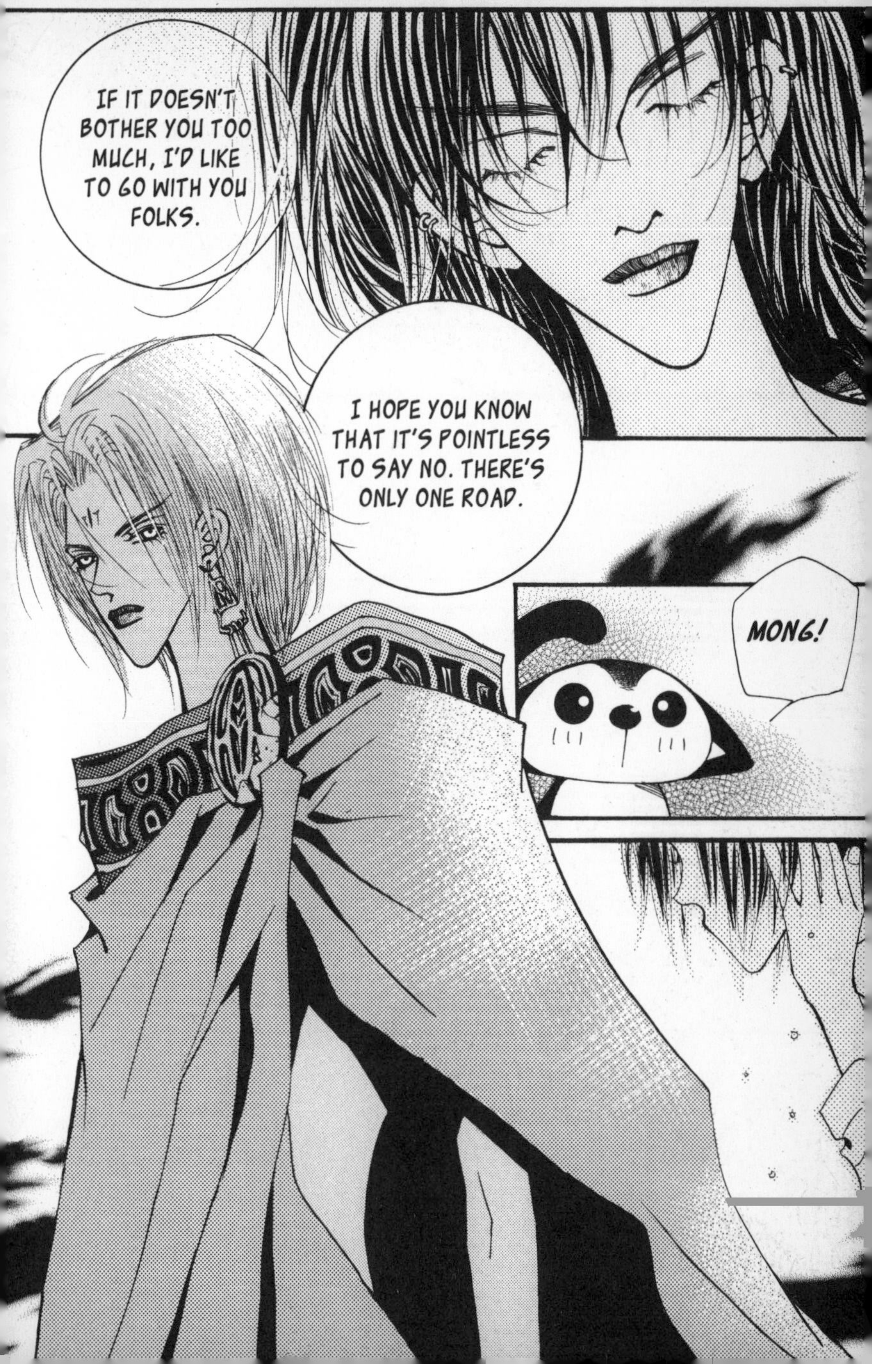
IF IT DOESN'T BOTHER YOU TOO MUCH, I'D LIKE TO GO WITH YOU FOLKS.
I HOPE YOU KNOW THAT IT'S POINTLESS TO SAY NO. THERE'S ONLY ONE ROAD.
MONG!

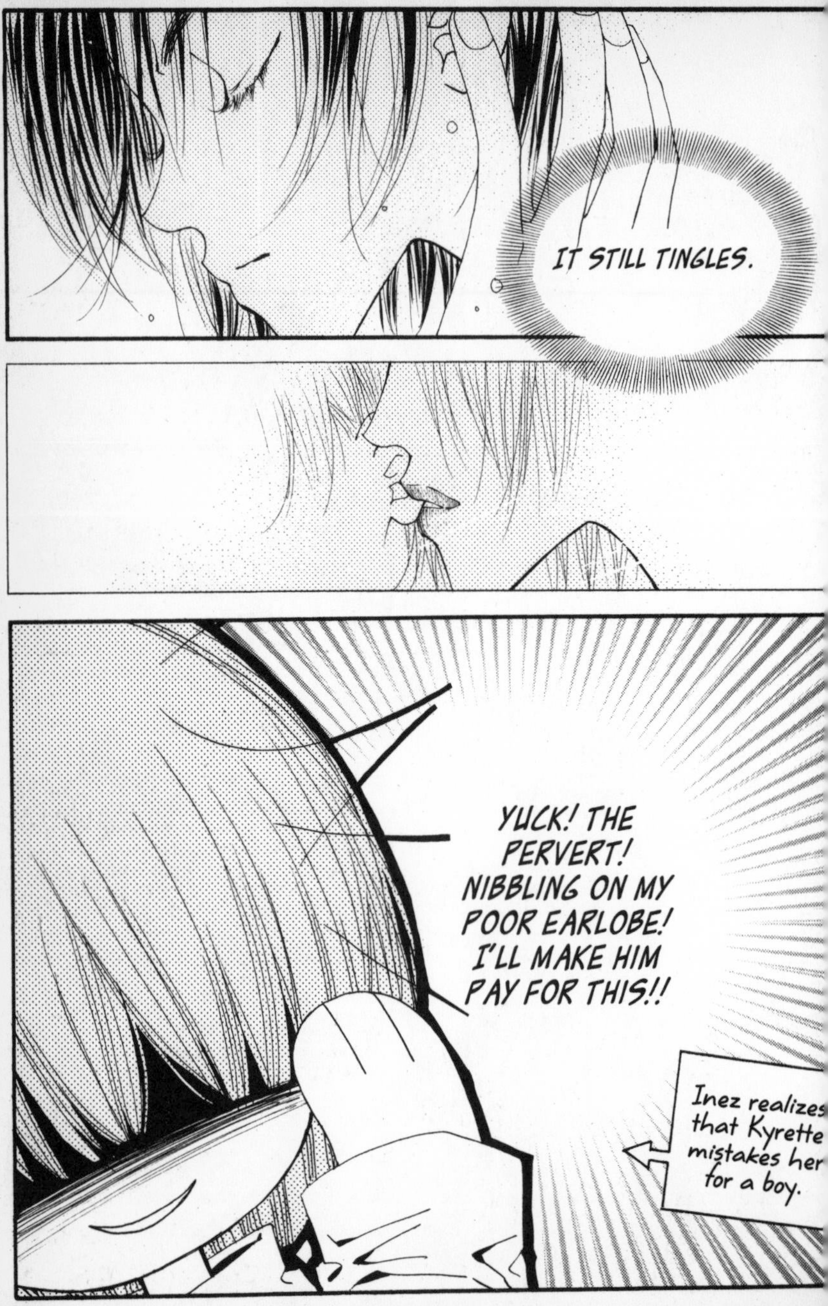
IT STILL TINGLES.
YUCK! THE PERVERT! NIBBLING ON MY POOR EARLOBE! I'LL MAKE HIM PAY FOR THIS!!
Inez realizes that Kyrette mistakes her for a boy.

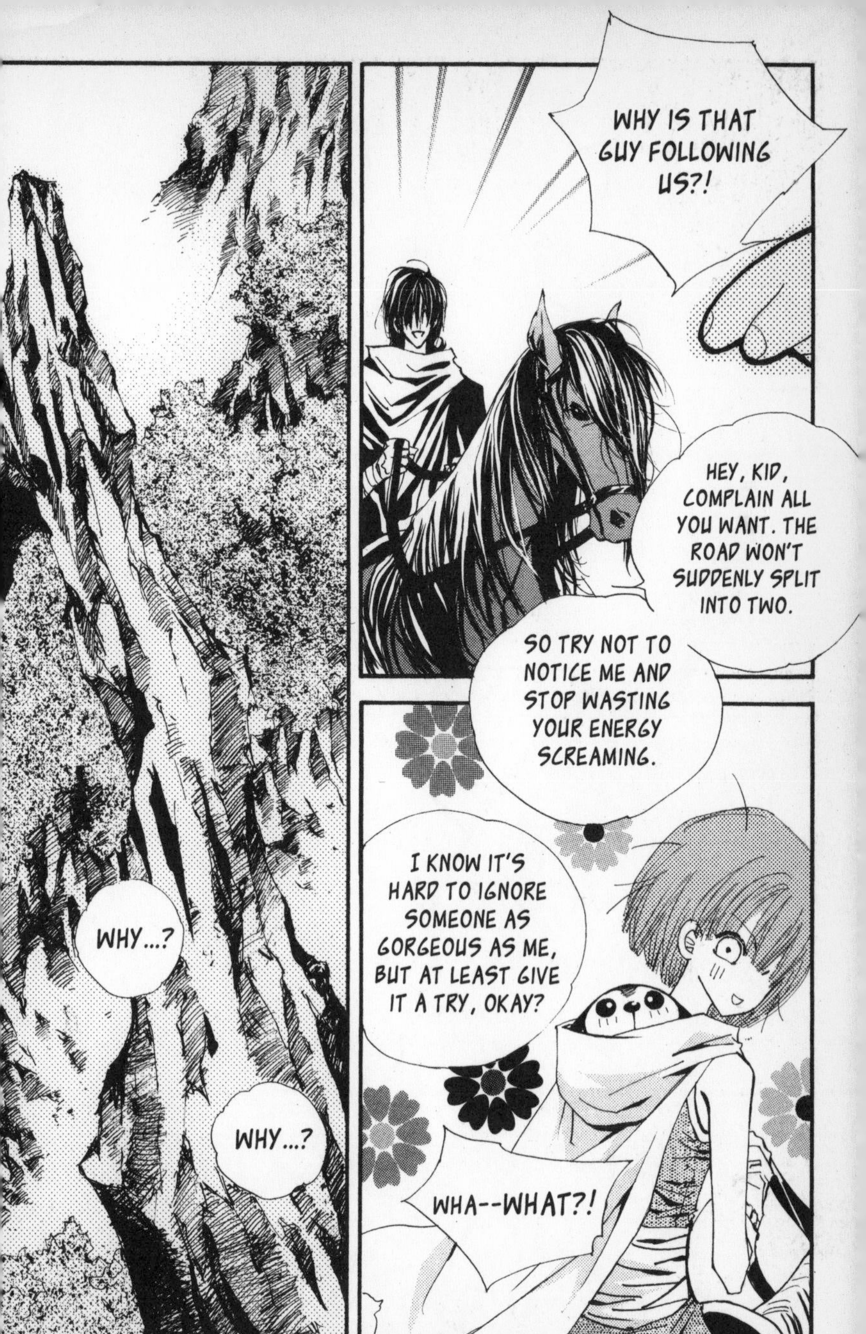
WHY...?
WHY...?
WHY IS THAT GUY FOLLOWING US?!
HEY, KID, COMPLAIN ALL YOU WANT. THE ROAD WON'T SUDDENLY SPLIT INTO TWO.
SO TRY NOT TO NOTICE ME AND STOP WASTING YOUR ENERGY SCREAMING.
I KNOW IT'S HARD TO IGNORE SOMEONE AS GORGEOUS AS ME, BUT AT LEAST GIVE IT A TRY, OKAY?
WHA--WHAT?!

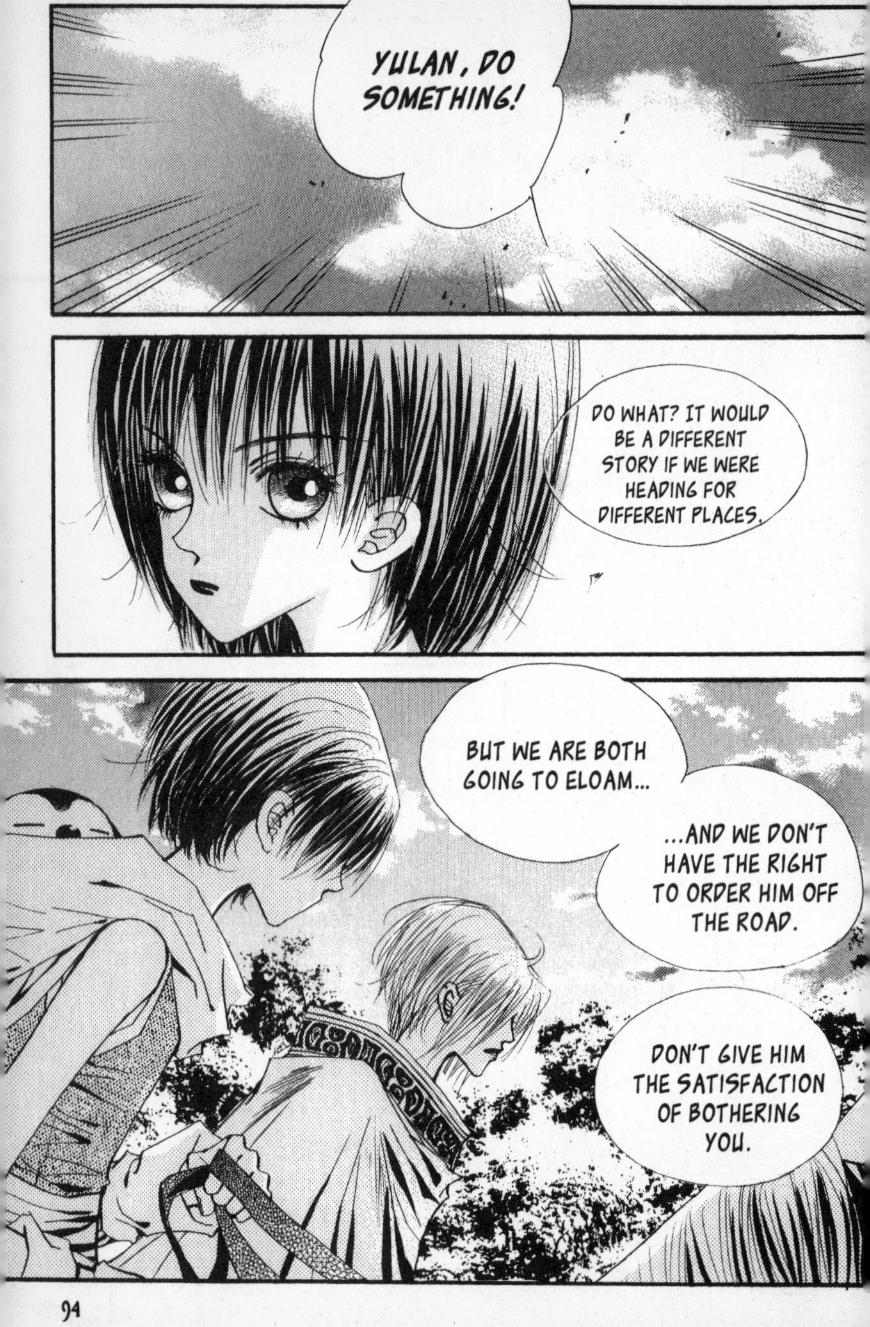
YULAN, DO SOMETHING!
DO WHAT? IT WOULD BE A DIFFERENT STORY IF WE WERE HEADING FOR DIFFERENT PLACES.
BUT WE ARE BOTH GOING TO ELOAM...
...AND WE DON'T HAVE THE RIGHT TO ORDER HIM OFF THE ROAD.
DON'T GIVE HIM THE SATISFACTION OF BOTHERING YOU.

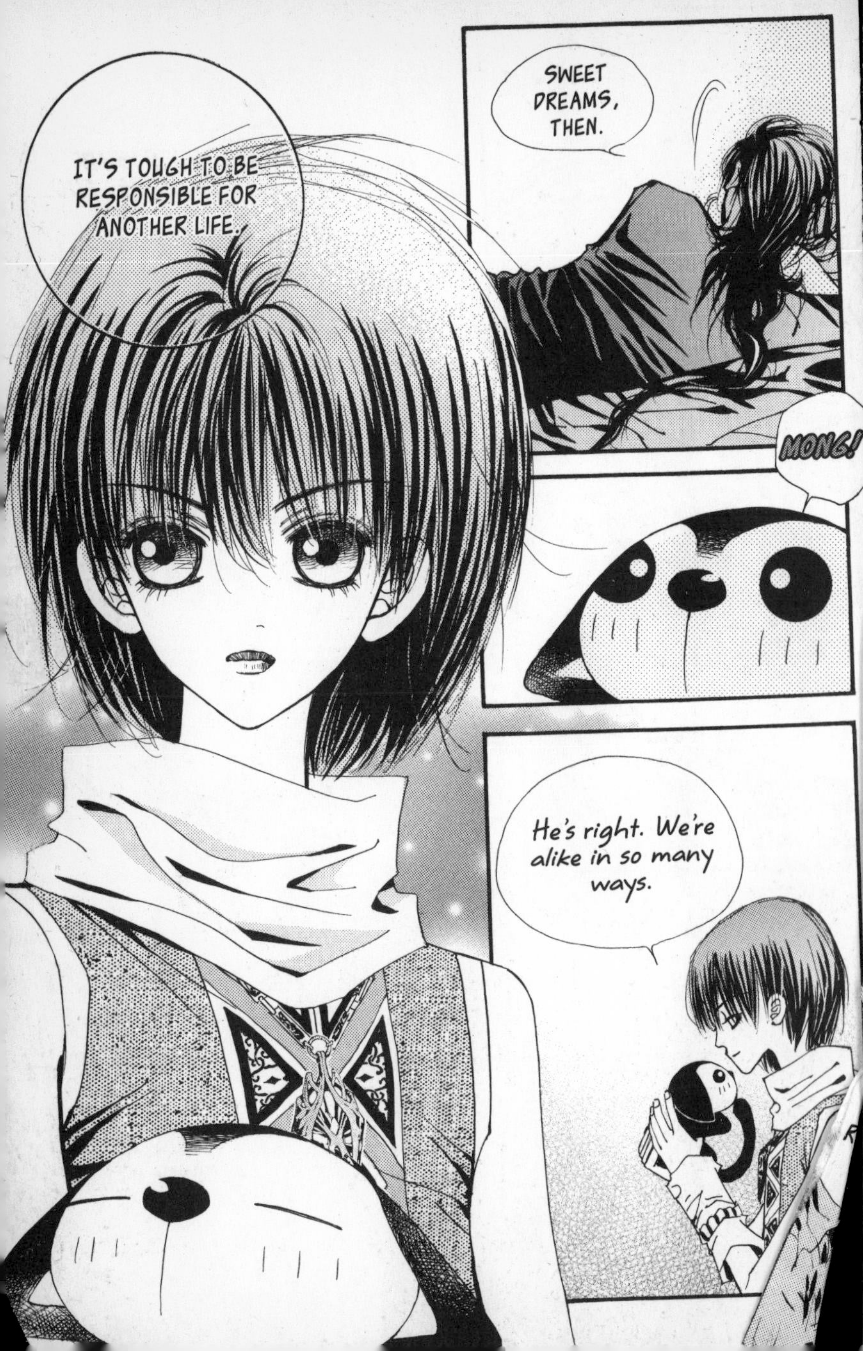
IT'S TOUGH TO BE RESPONSIBLE FOR ANOTHER LIFE.
SWEET DREAMS, THEN.
MONG!
He's right. We're alike in so many ways.
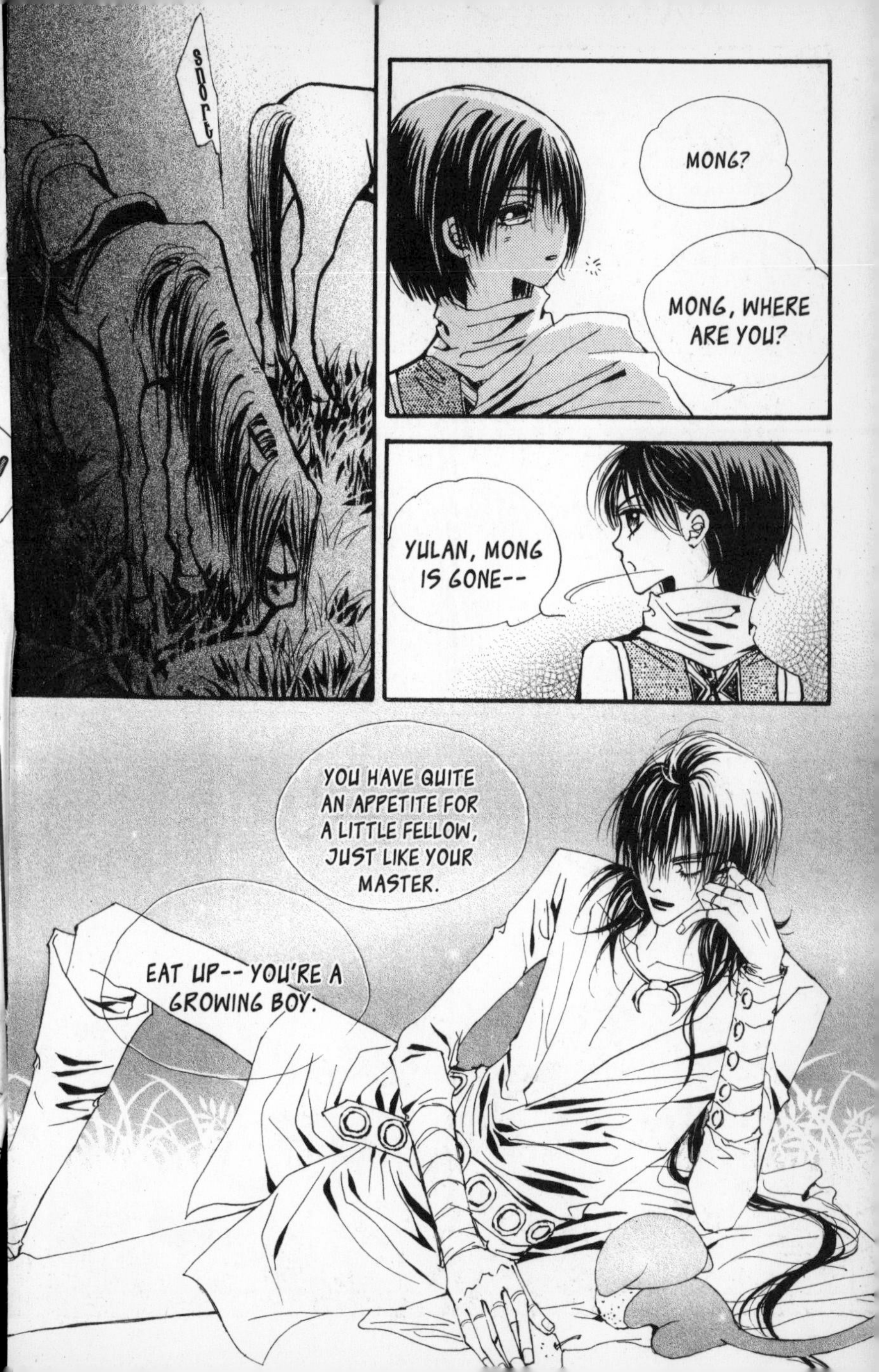
snort
MONG?
MONG, WHERE ARE YOU?
YULAN, MONG IS GONE--
YOU HAVE QUITE AN APPETITE FOR A LITTLE FELLOW, JUST LIKE YOUR MASTER.
EAT UP--YOU'RE A GROWING BOY.

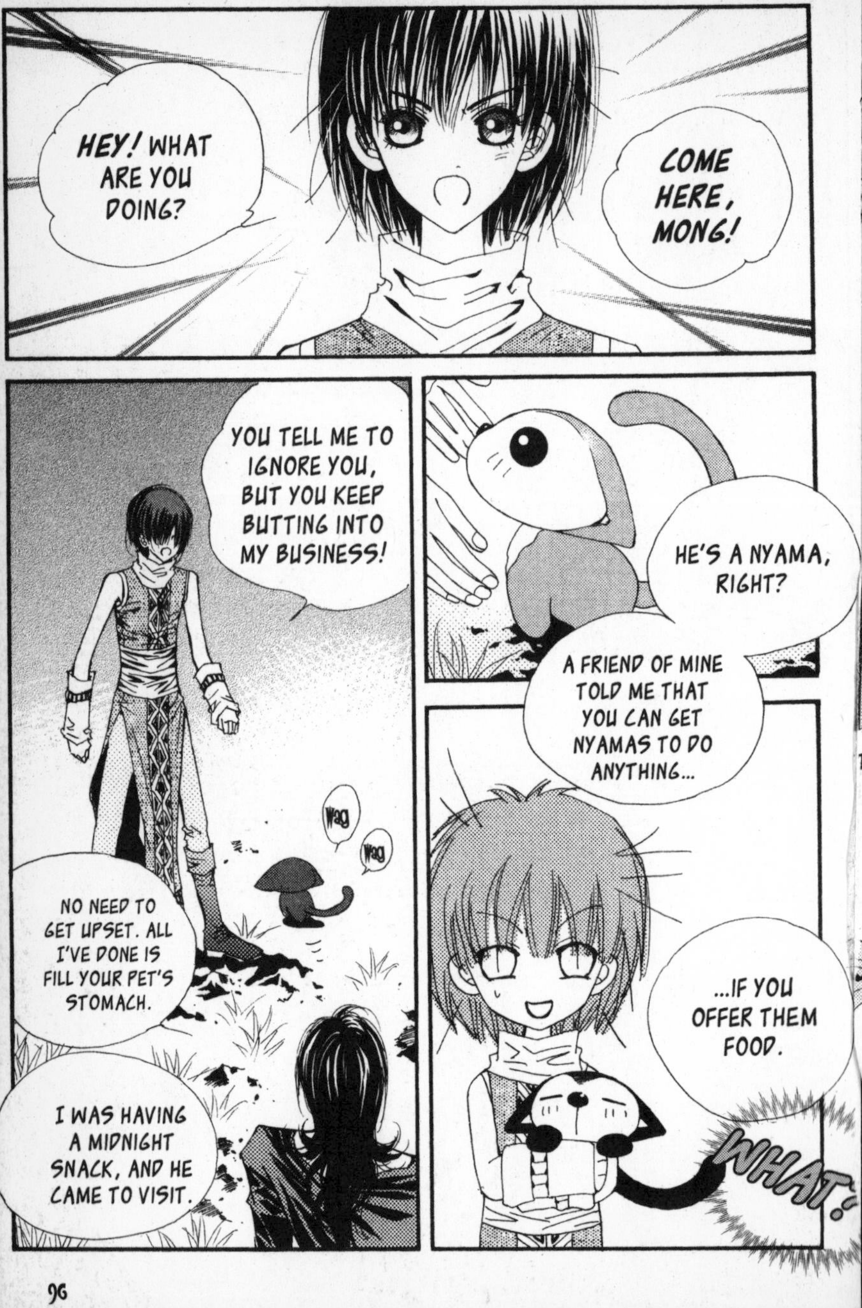
HEY! WHAT ARE YOU DOING?
COME HERE, MONG!
YOU TELL ME TO IGNORE YOU, BUT YOU KEEP BUTTING INTO MY BUSINESS!
Wag
Wag
NO NEED TO GET UPSET. ALL I'VE DONE IS FILL YOUR PET'S STOMACH.
I WAS HAVING A MIDNIGHT SNACK, AND HE CAME TO VISIT.
HE'S A NYAMA, RIGHT?
A FRIEND OF MINE TOLD ME THAT YOU CAN GET NYAMAS TO DO ANYTHING...
...IF YOU OFFER THEM FOOD.
WHAT!

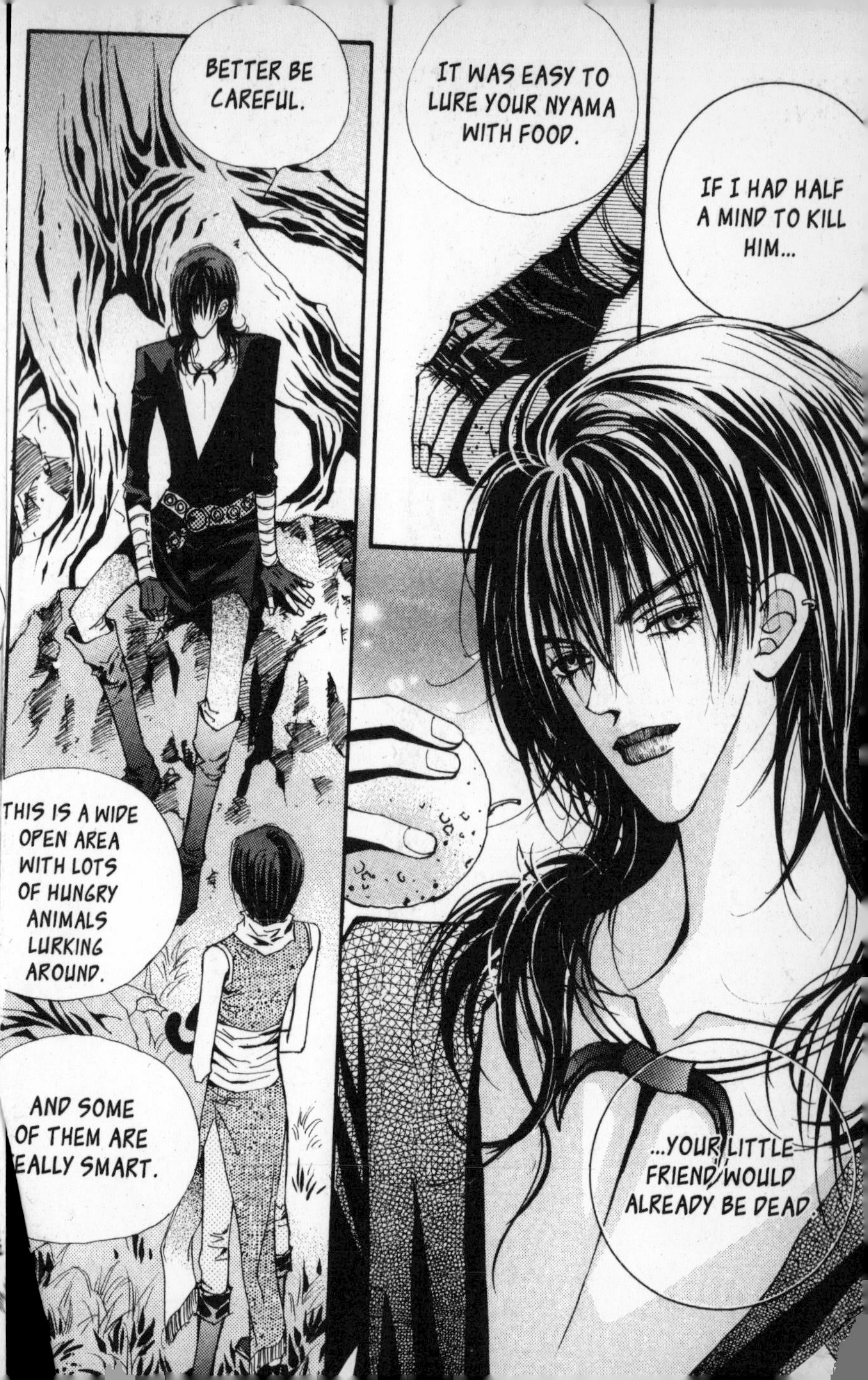
BETTER BE CAREFUL.
THIS IS A WIDE OPEN AREA WITH LOTS OF HUNGRY ANIMALS LURKING AROUND.
AND SOME OF THEM ARE EALLY SMART.
IT WAS EASY TO LURE YOUR NYAMA WITH FOOD.
IF I HAD HALF A MIND TO KILL HIM...
...YOUR LITTLE FRIEND WOULD ALREADY BE DEAD.

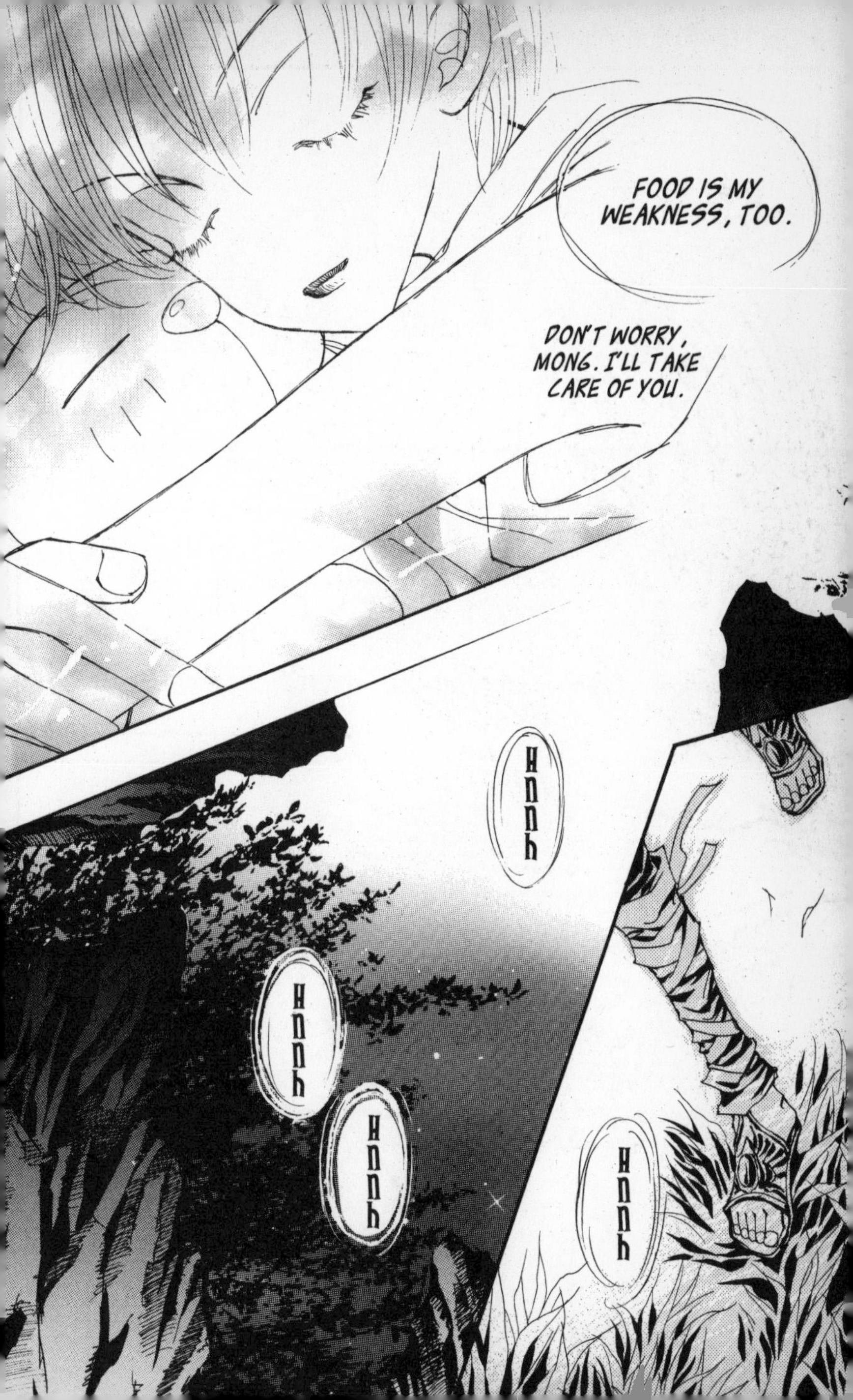
FOOD IS MY WEAKNESS, TOO.
DON'T WORRY, MONG. I'LL TAKE CARE OF YOU.
HNNh
HNNh
HNNh
HNNh

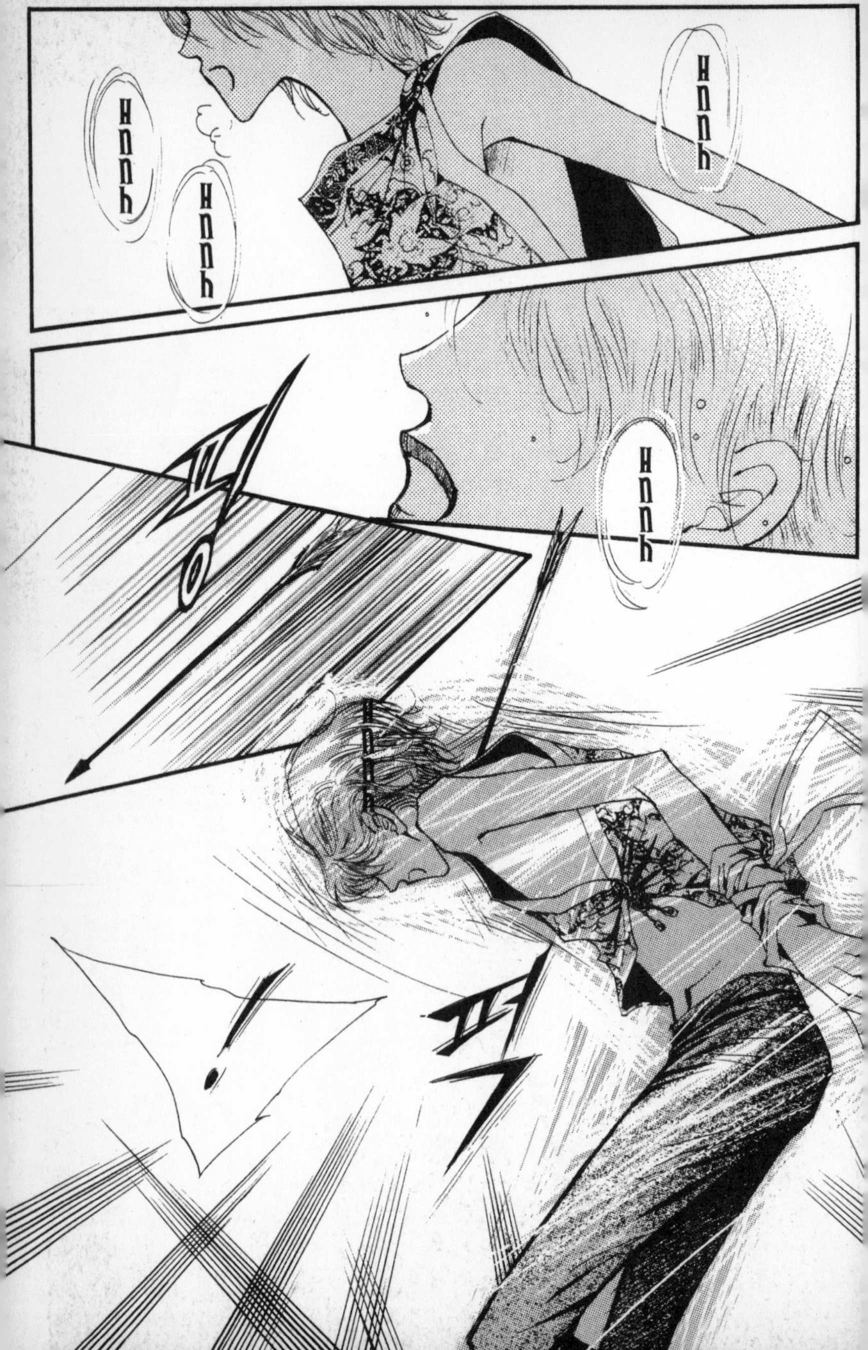
HNNh
HNNh
HNNh
HNNh

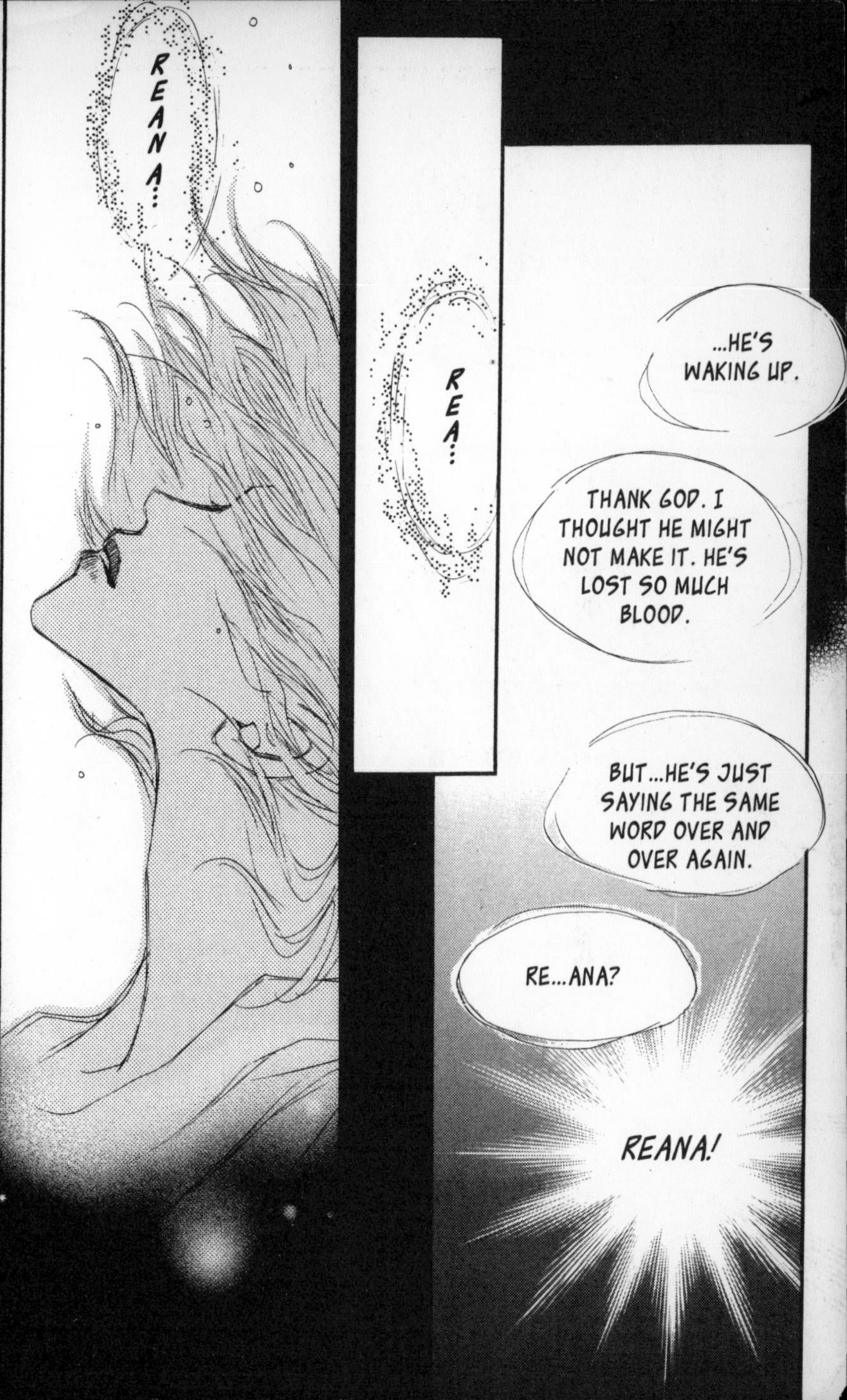
REANA...
REA...
...HE'S WAKING UP.
THANK GOD. I THOUGHT HE MIGHT NOT MAKE IT. HE'S LOST SO MUCH BLOOD.
BUT...HE'S JUST SAYING THE SAME WORD OVER AND OVER AGAIN.
RE...ANA?
REANA!

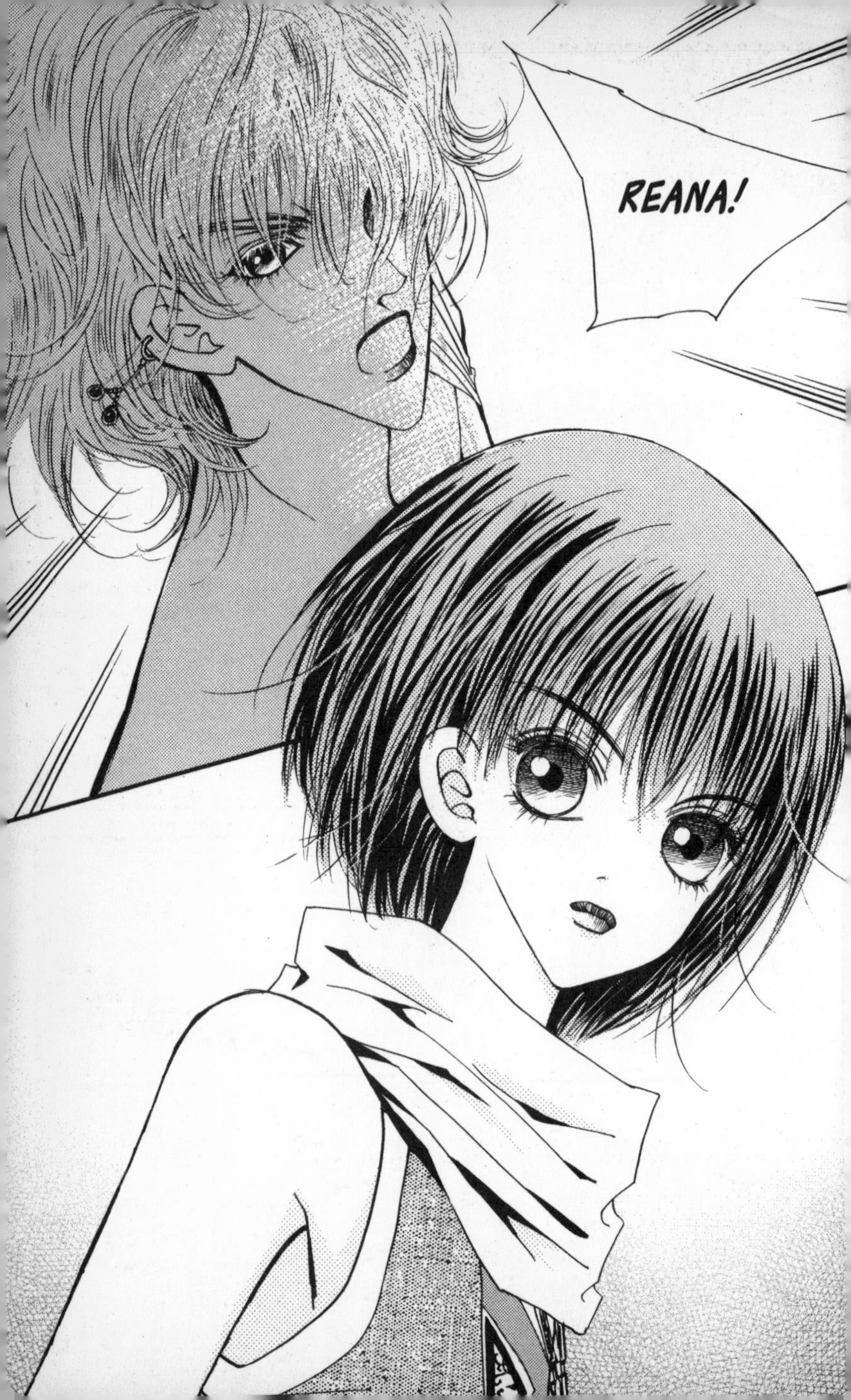
REANA!

OWWW!

DON'T MOVE! THAT WOUND IS DEEP.

WE PUT A SALVE ON IT, BUT THAT WON'T STOP IT FROM HURTING.

HnnH

HnnH

IT'S NOT EASY TO BREATHE, IS IT? THERE'S POISON SPREADING ALL THROUGH YOUR BODY.

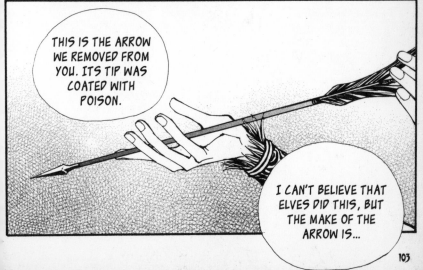

THIS IS THE ARROW WE REMOVED FROM YOU. ITS TIP WAS COATED WITH POISON.

I CAN'T BELIEVE THAT ELVES DID THIS, BUT THE MAKE OF THE ARROW IS...

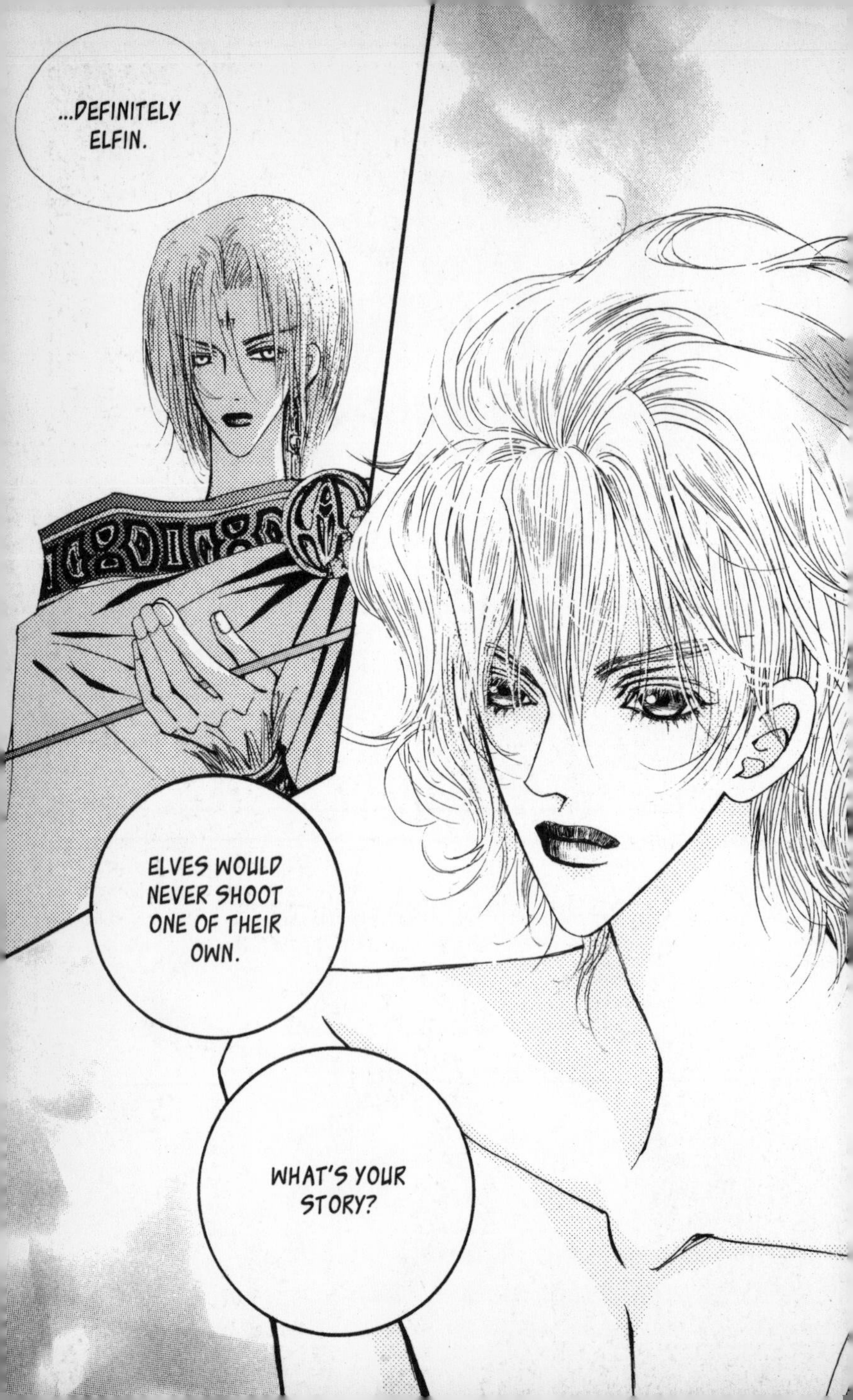
...DEFINITELY ELFIN.
ELVES WOULD NEVER SHOOT ONE OF THEIR OWN.
WHAT'S YOUR STORY?

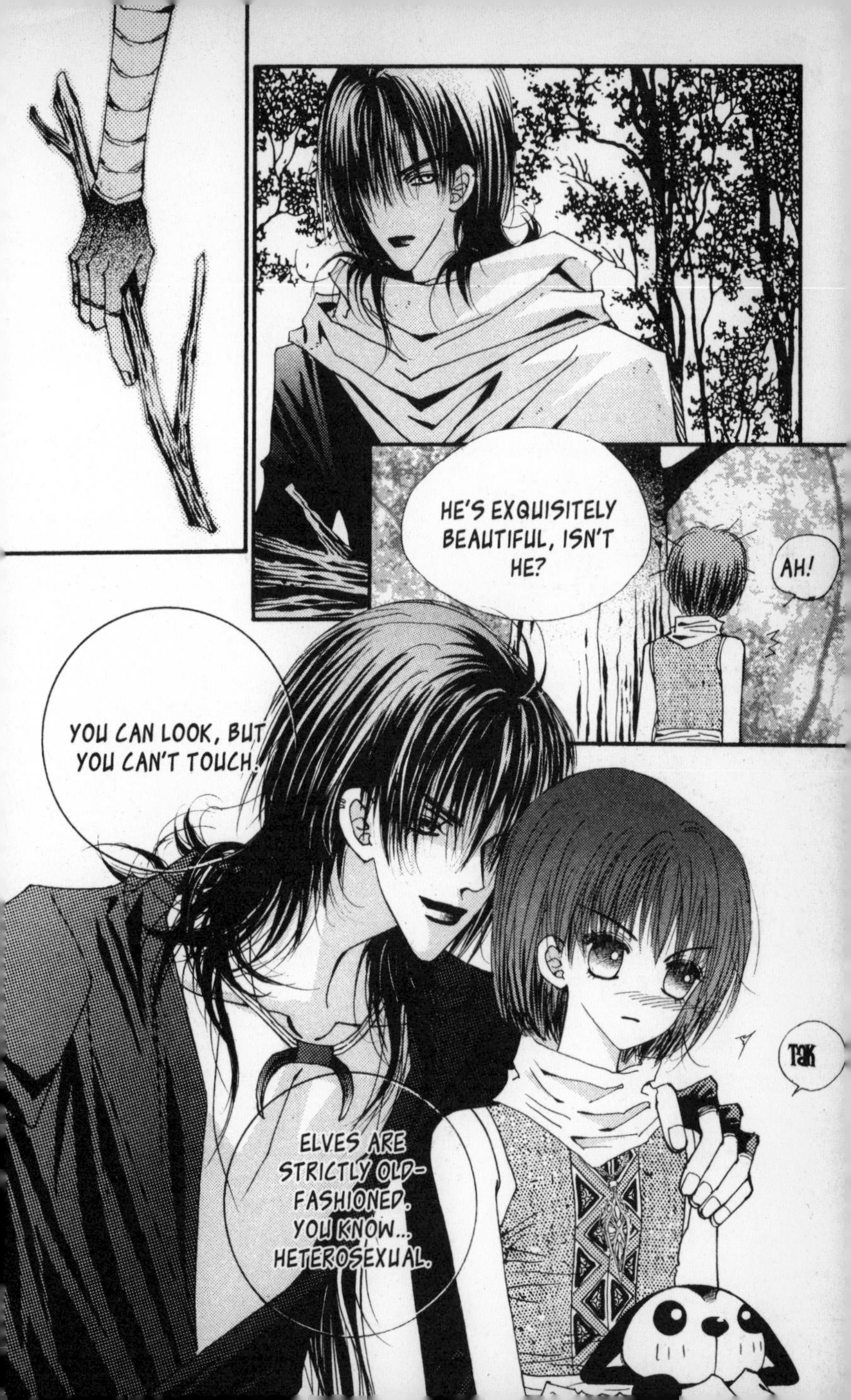
HE'S EXQUISITELY BEAUTIFUL, ISN'T HE?
AH!
YOU CAN LOOK, BUT YOU CAN'T TOUCH.
TAK
ELVES ARE STRICTLY OLD-FASHIONED. YOU KNOW... HETEROSEXUAL.

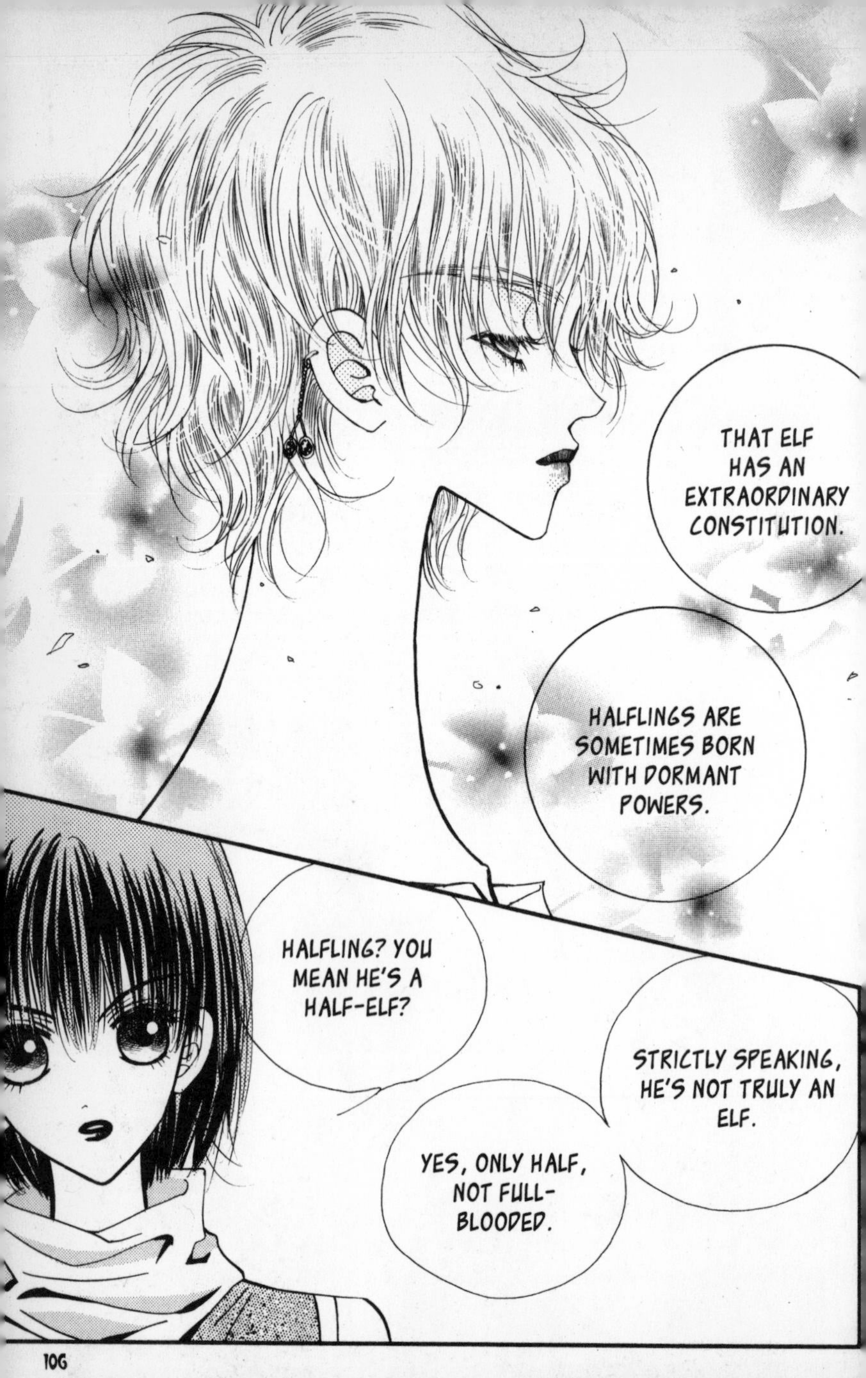
THAT ELF HAS AN EXTRAORDINARY CONSTITUTION.
HALFLINGS ARE SOMETIMES BORN WITH DORMANT POWERS.
HALFLING? YOU MEAN HE'S A HALF-ELF?
STRICTLY SPEAKING, HE'S NOT TRULY AN ELF.
YES, ONLY HALF, NOT FULL-BLOODED.

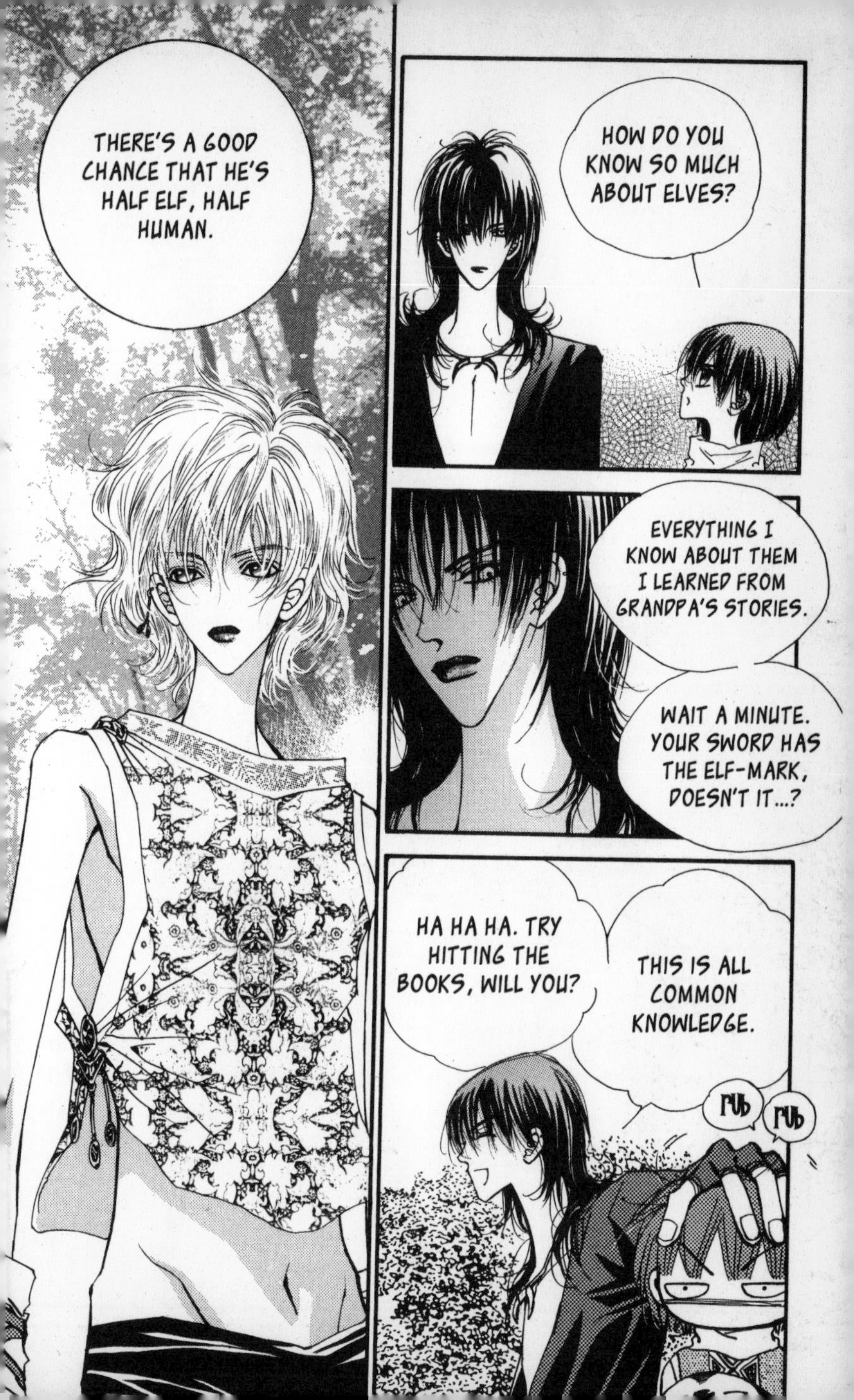
THERE'S A GOOD CHANCE THAT HE'S HALF ELF, HALF HUMAN.
HOW DO YOU KNOW SO MUCH ABOUT ELVES?
EVERYTHING I KNOW ABOUT THEM I LEARNED FROM GRANDPA'S STORIES.
WAIT A MINUTE. YOUR SWORD HAS THE ELF-MARK, DOESN'T IT...?
HA HA HA. TRY HITTING THE BOOKS, WILL YOU?
THIS IS ALL COMMON KNOWLEDGE.
RUB
RUB

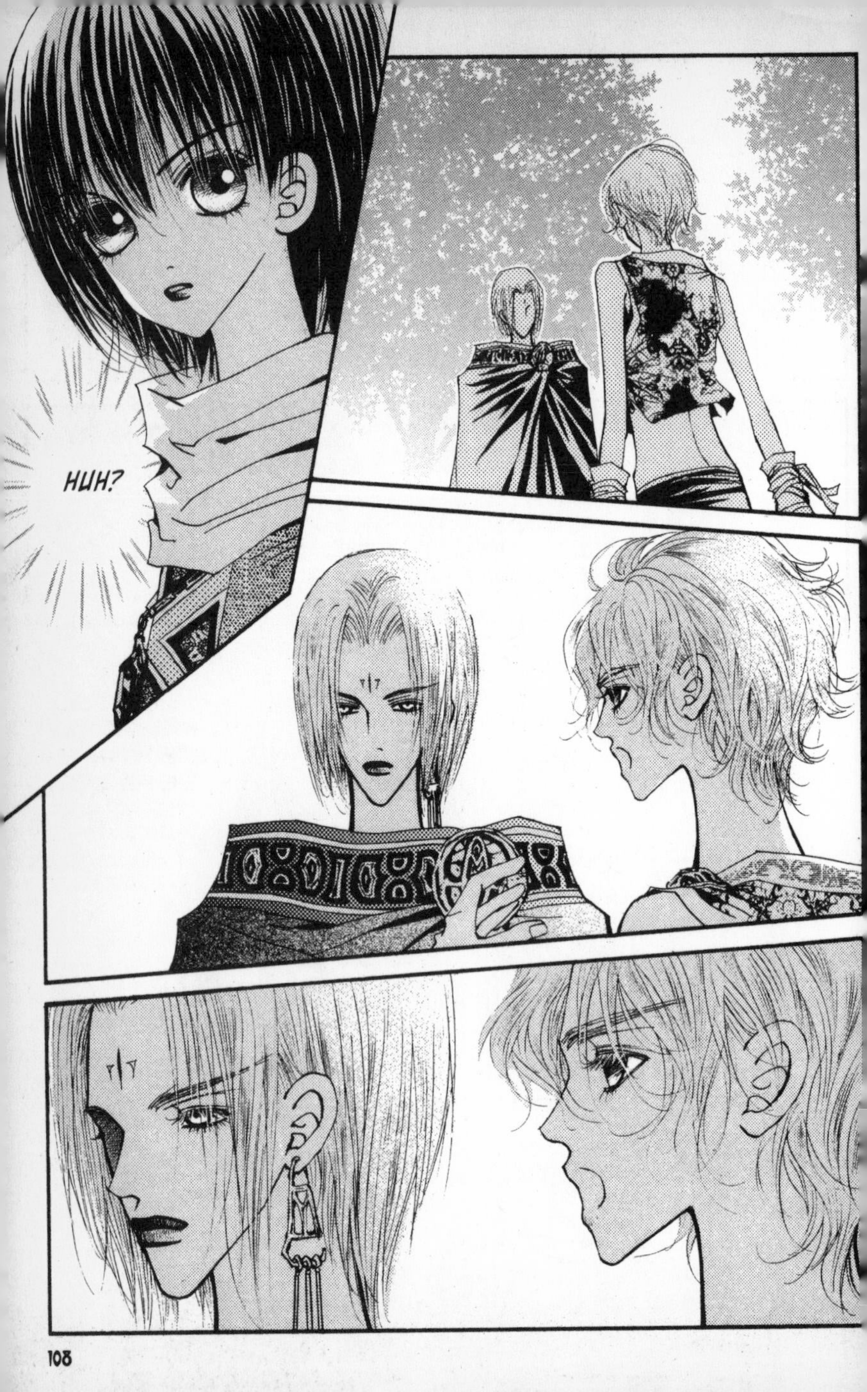
HUH?

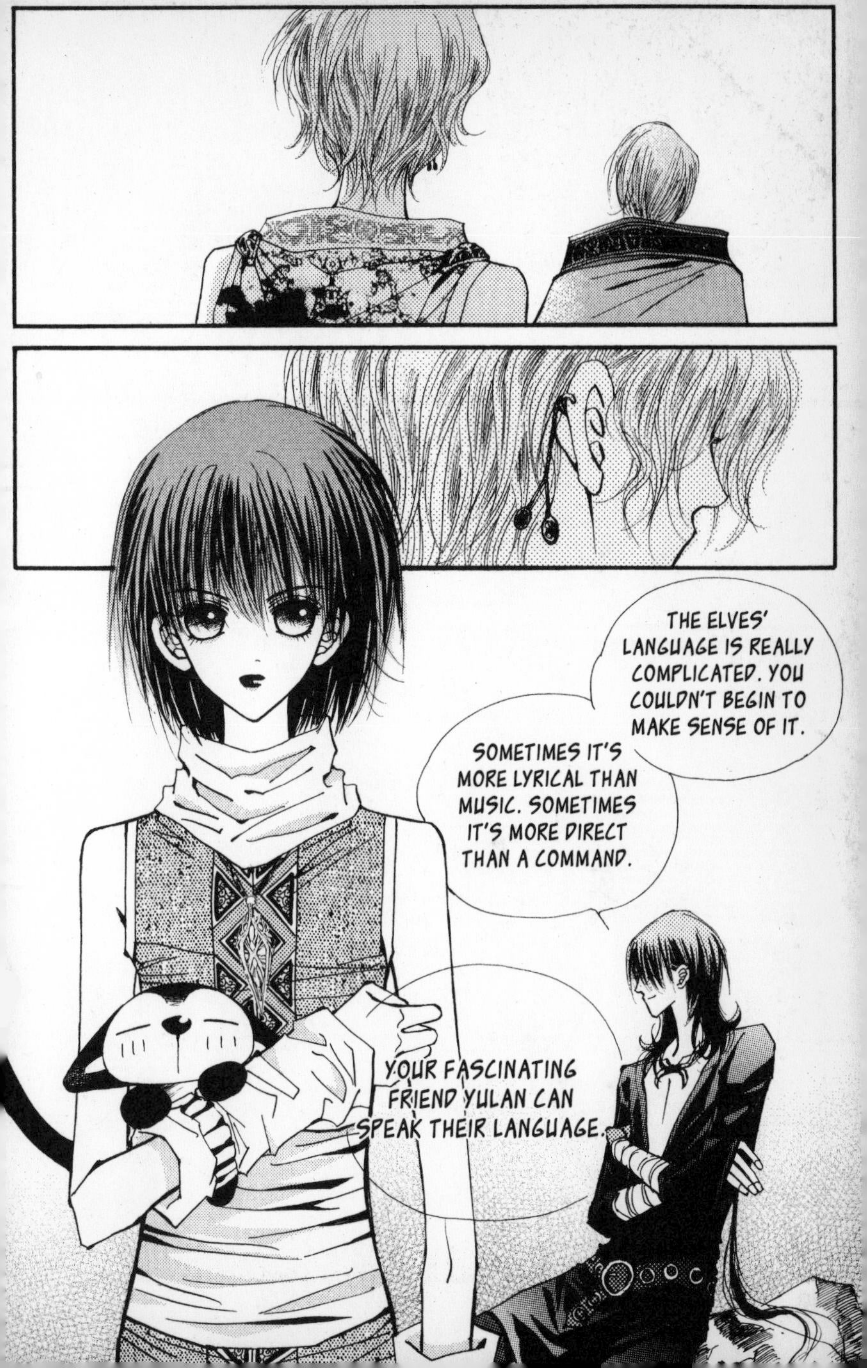
THE ELVES' LANGUAGE IS REALLY COMPLICATED. YOU COULDN'T BEGIN TO MAKE SENSE OF IT.
SOMETIMES IT'S MORE LYRICAL THAN MUSIC. SOMETIMES IT'S MORE DIRECT THAN A COMMAND.
YOUR FASCINATING FRIEND YULAN CAN SPEAK THEIR LANGUAGE.

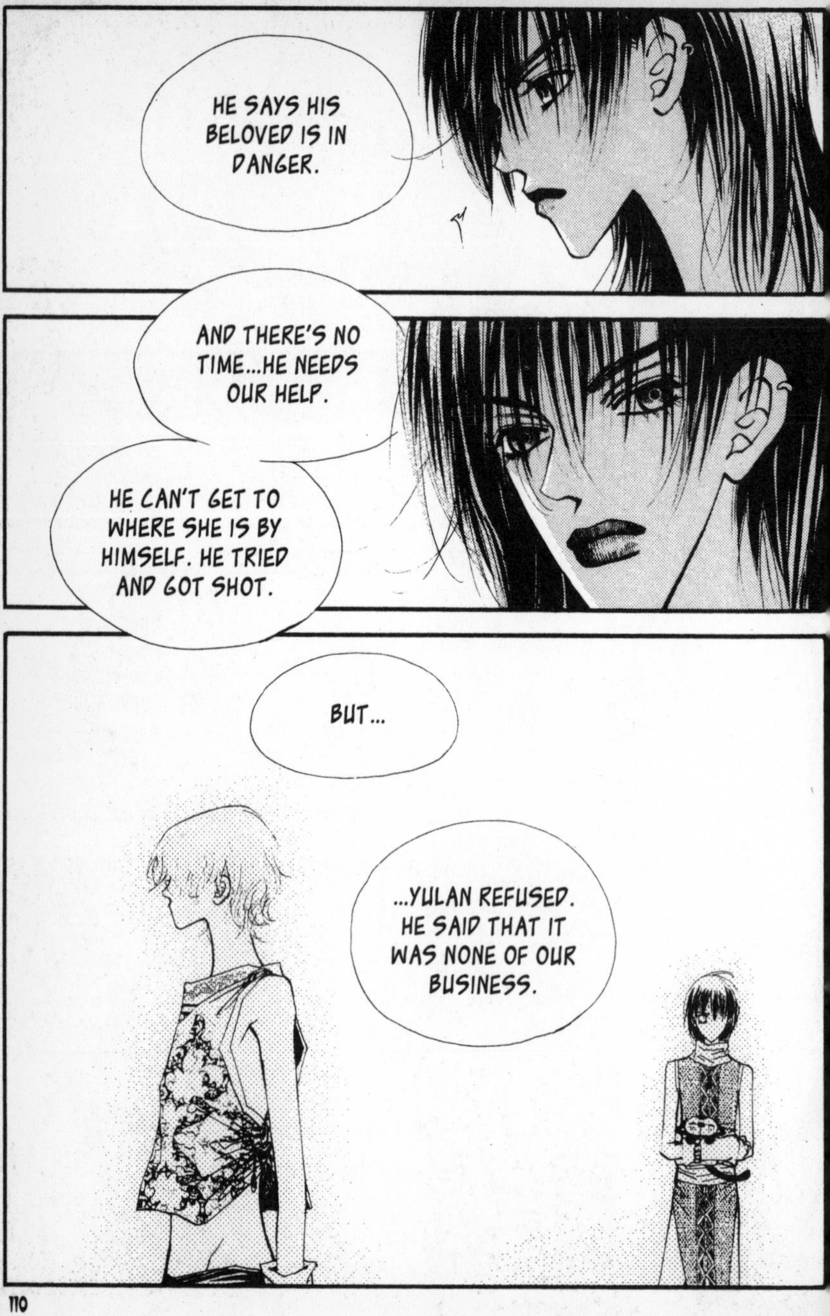
HE SAYS HIS BELOVED IS IN DANGER.
AND THERE'S NO TIME...HE NEEDS OUR HELP.
HE CAN'T GET TO WHERE SHE IS BY HIMSELF. HE TRIED AND GOT SHOT.
BUT...
...YULAN REFUSED. HE SAID THAT IT WAS NONE OF OUR BUSINESS.

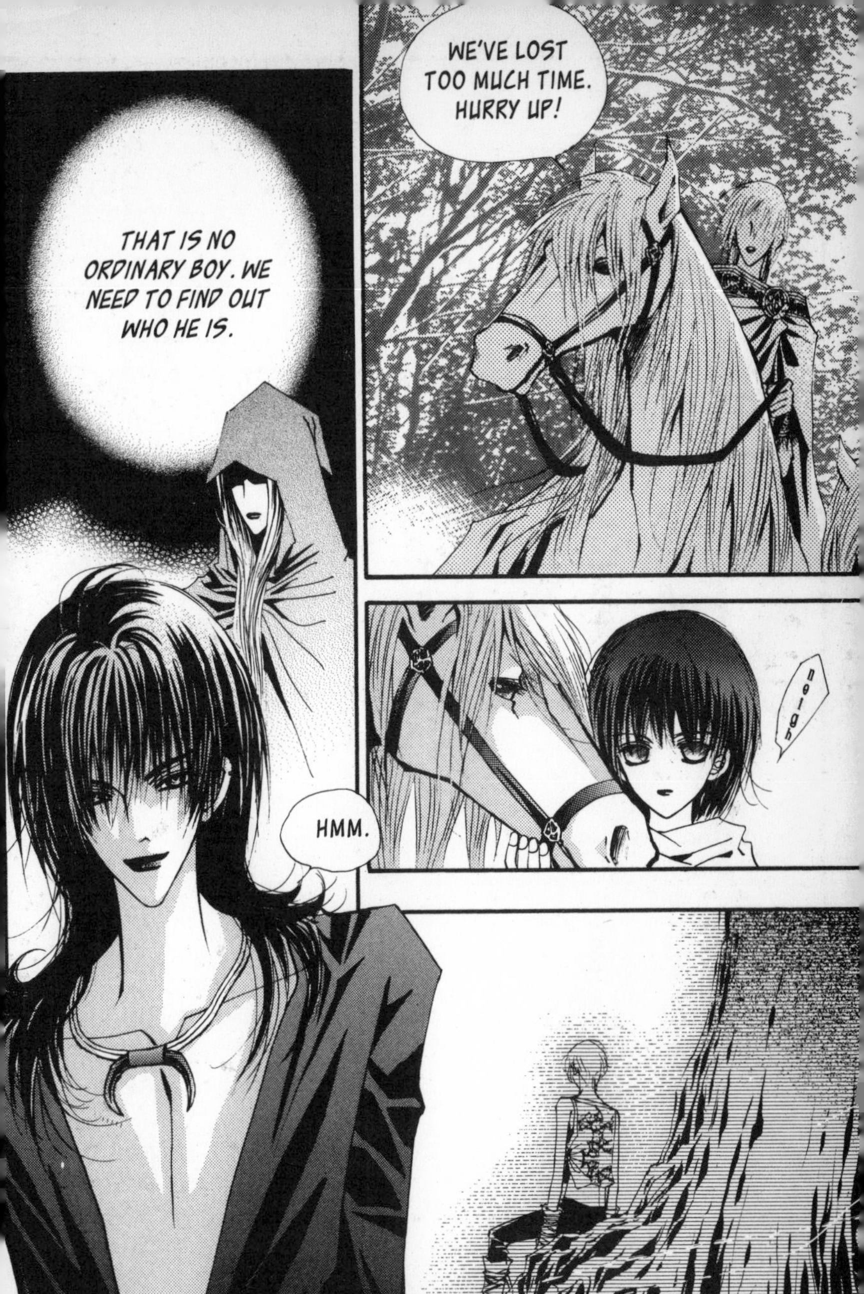
THAT IS NO ORDINARY BOY. WE NEED TO FIND OUT WHO HE IS.
HMM.
WE'VE LOST TOO MUCH TIME. HURRY UP!
neigh

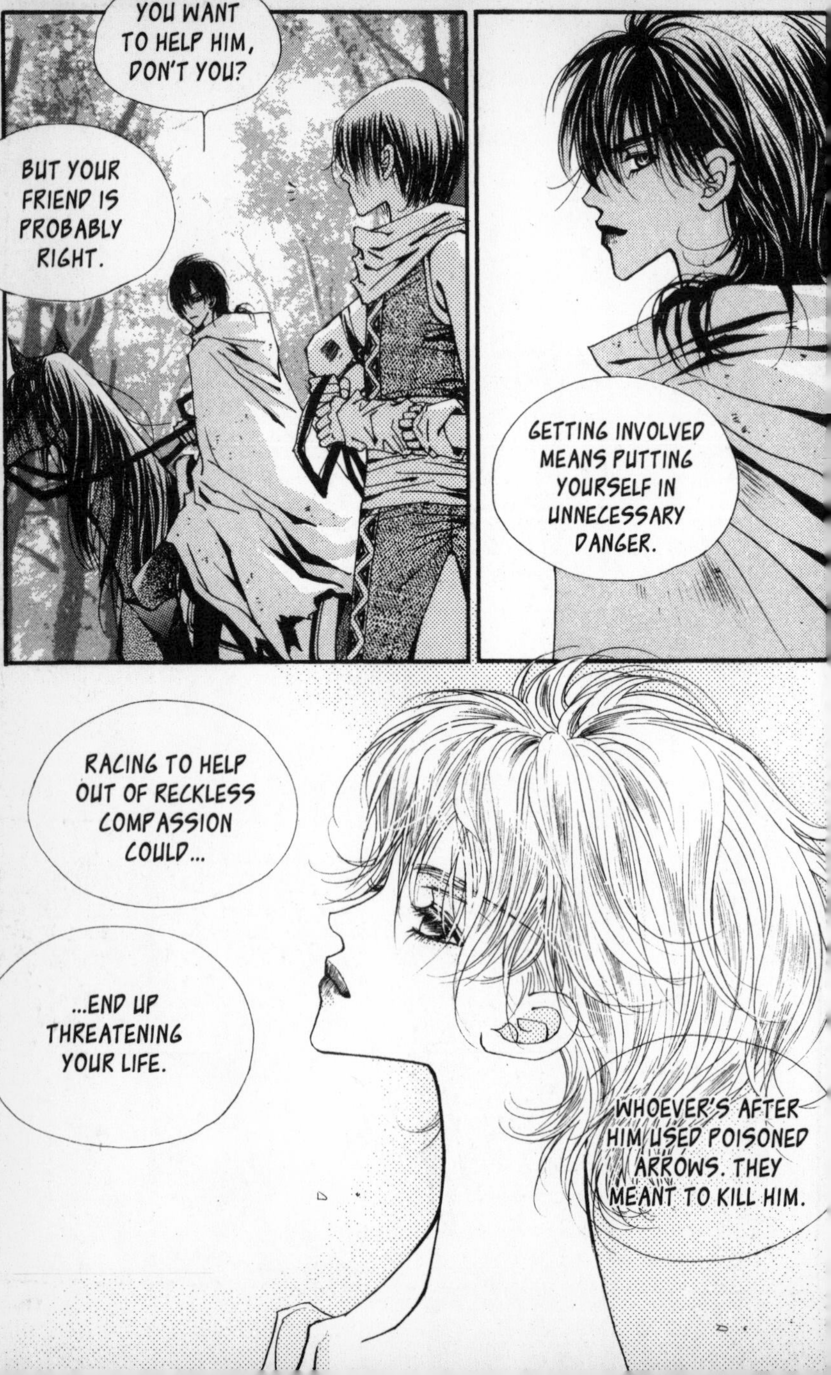
YOU WANT TO HELP HIM, DON'T YOU?
BUT YOUR FRIEND IS PROBABLY RIGHT.
GETTING INVOLVED MEANS PUTTING YOURSELF IN UNNECESSARY DANGER.
RACING TO HELP OUT OF RECKLESS COMPASSION COULD...
...END UP THREATENING YOUR LIFE.
WHOEVER'S AFTER HIM USED POISONED ARROWS. THEY MEANT TO KILL HIM.

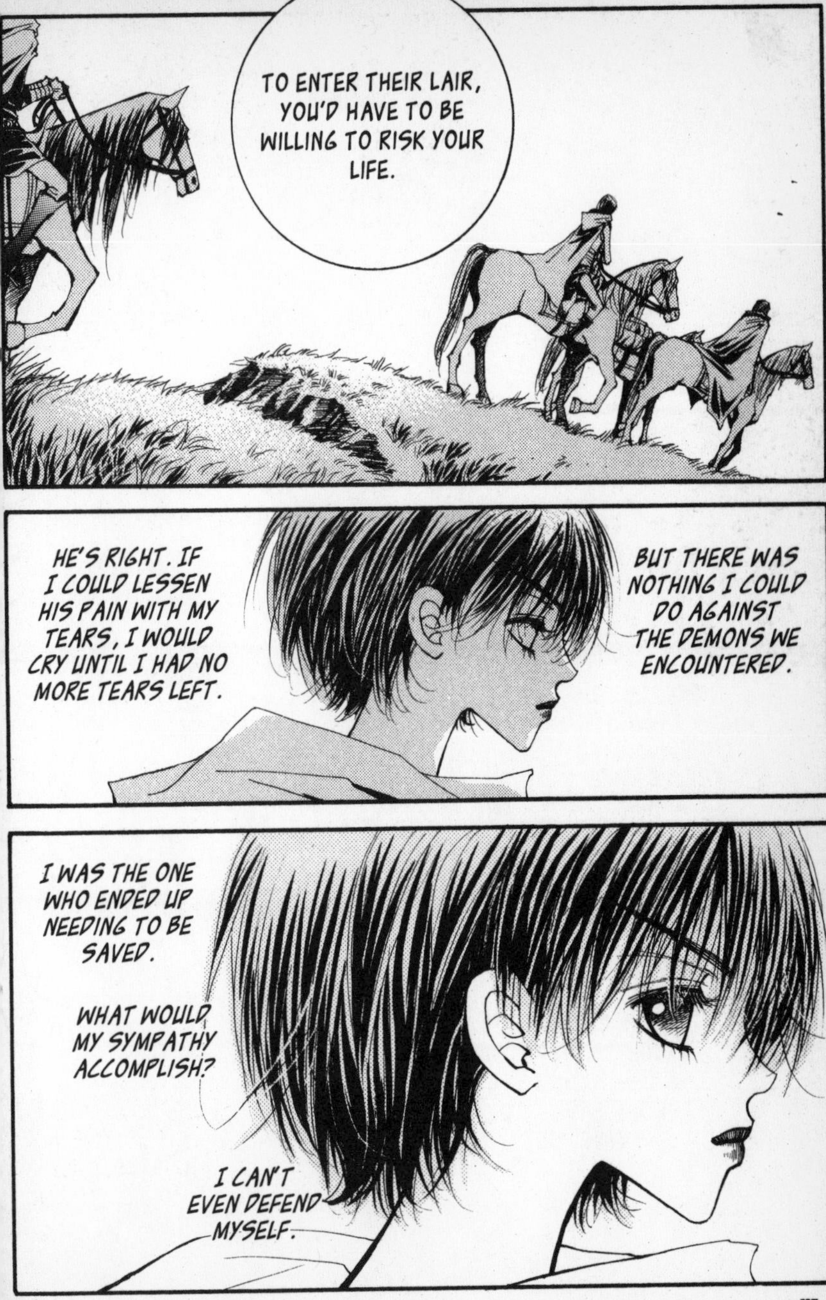
TO ENTER THEIR LAIR, YOU'D HAVE TO BE WILLING TO RISK YOUR LIFE.
HE'S RIGHT. IF I COULD LESSEN HIS PAIN WITH MY TEARS, I WOULD CRY UNTIL I HAD NO MORE TEARS LEFT.
BUT THERE WAS NOTHING I COULD DO AGAINST THE DEMONS WE ENCOUNTERED.
I WAS THE ONE WHO ENDED UP NEEDING TO BE SAVED.
WHAT WOULD MY SYMPATHY ACCOMPLISH?
I CAN'T EVEN DEFEND MYSELF.

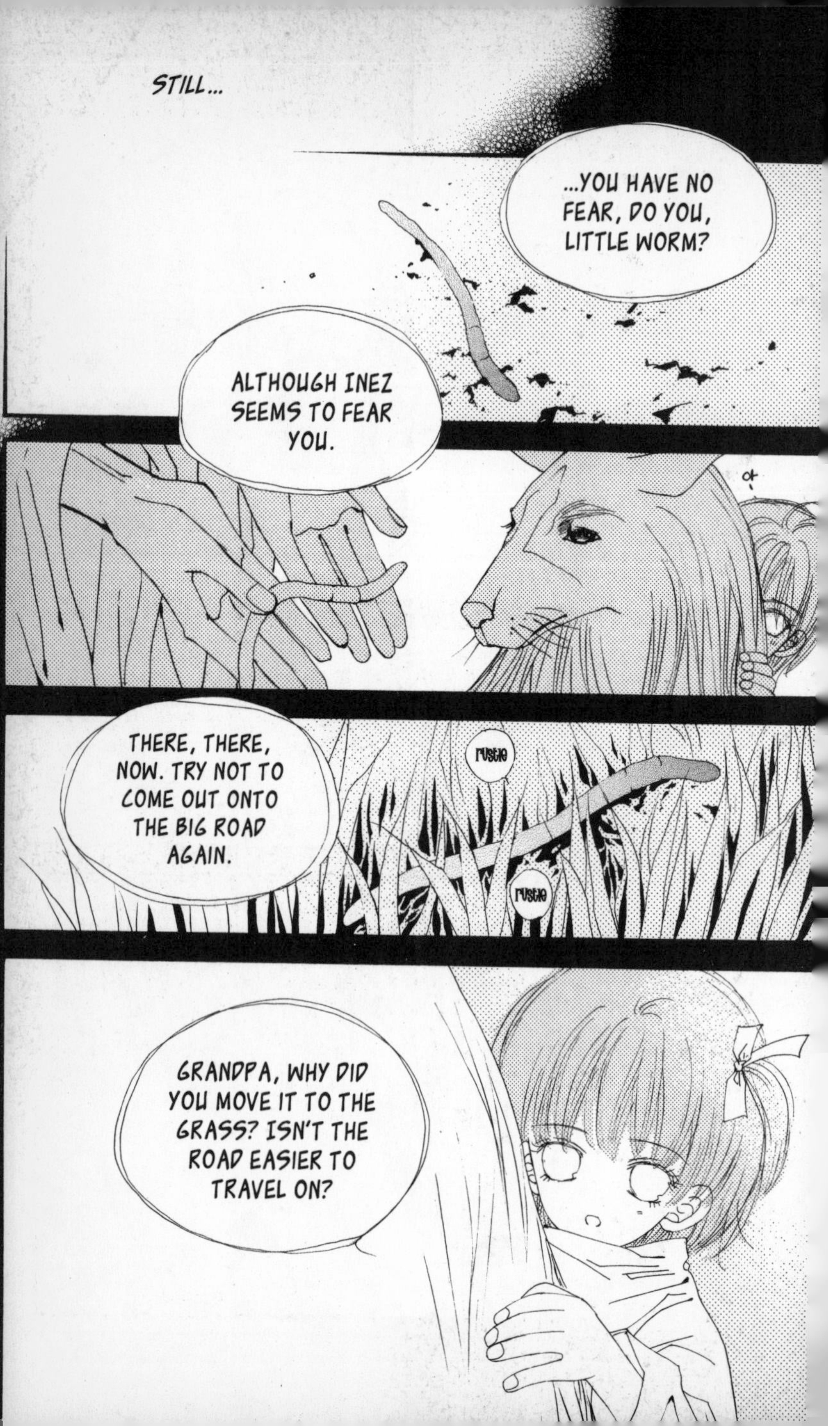
STILL...
...YOU HAVE NO FEAR, DO YOU, LITTLE WORM?
ALTHOUGH INEZ SEEMS TO FEAR YOU.
THERE, THERE, NOW. TRY NOT TO COME OUT ONTO THE BIG ROAD AGAIN.
rustle
rustle
GRANDPA, WHY DID YOU MOVE IT TO THE GRASS? ISN'T THE ROAD EASIER TO TRAVEL ON?

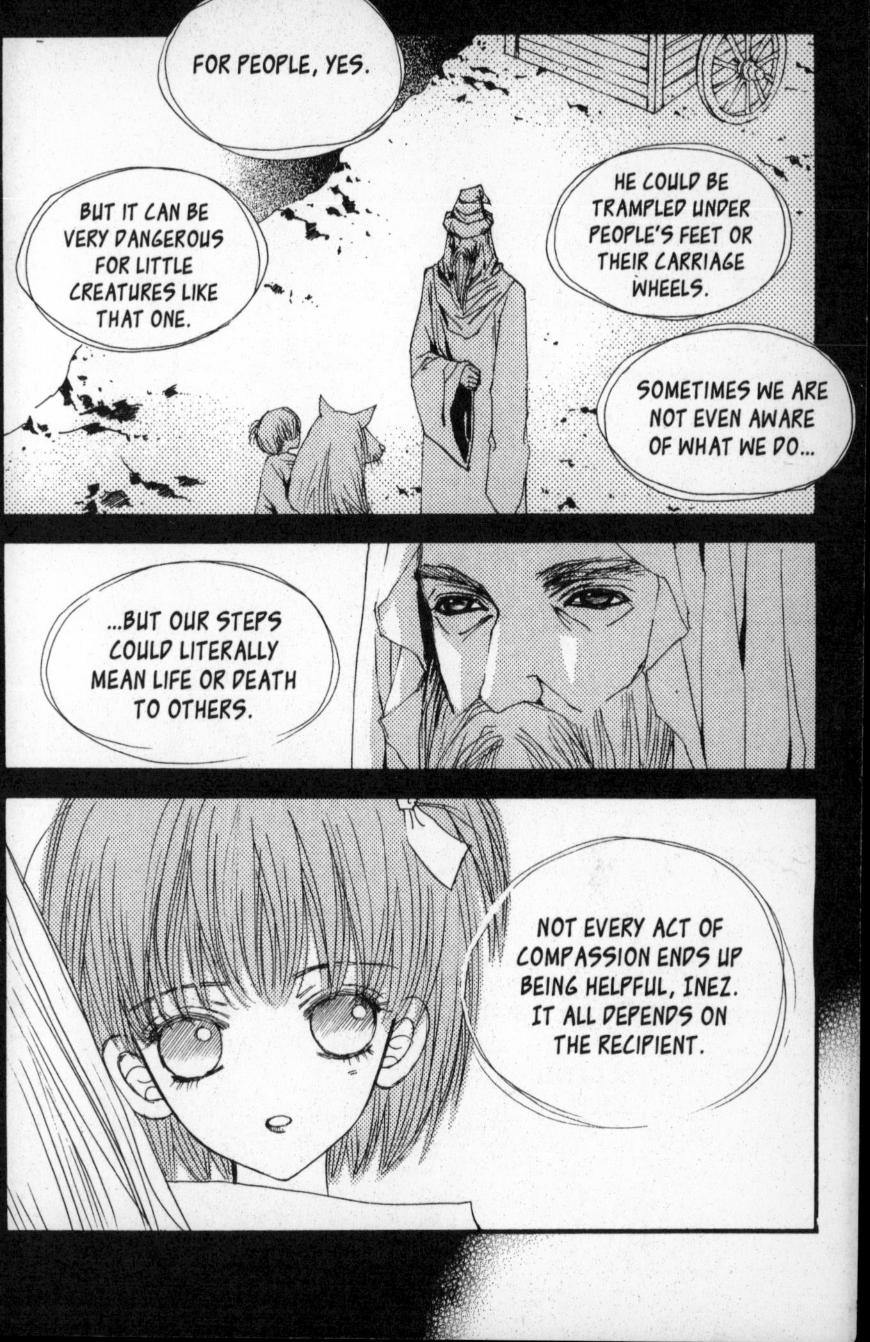
FOR PEOPLE, YES.
BUT IT CAN BE VERY DANGEROUS FOR LITTLE CREATURES LIKE THAT ONE.
HE COULD BE TRAMPLED UNDER PEOPLE'S FEET OR THEIR CARRIAGE WHEELS.
SOMETIMES WE ARE NOT EVEN AWARE OF WHAT WE DO...
...BUT OUR STEPS COULD LITERALLY MEAN LIFE OR DEATH TO OTHERS.
NOT EVERY ACT OF COMPASSION ENDS UP BEING HELPFUL, INEZ. IT ALL DEPENDS ON THE RECIPIENT.

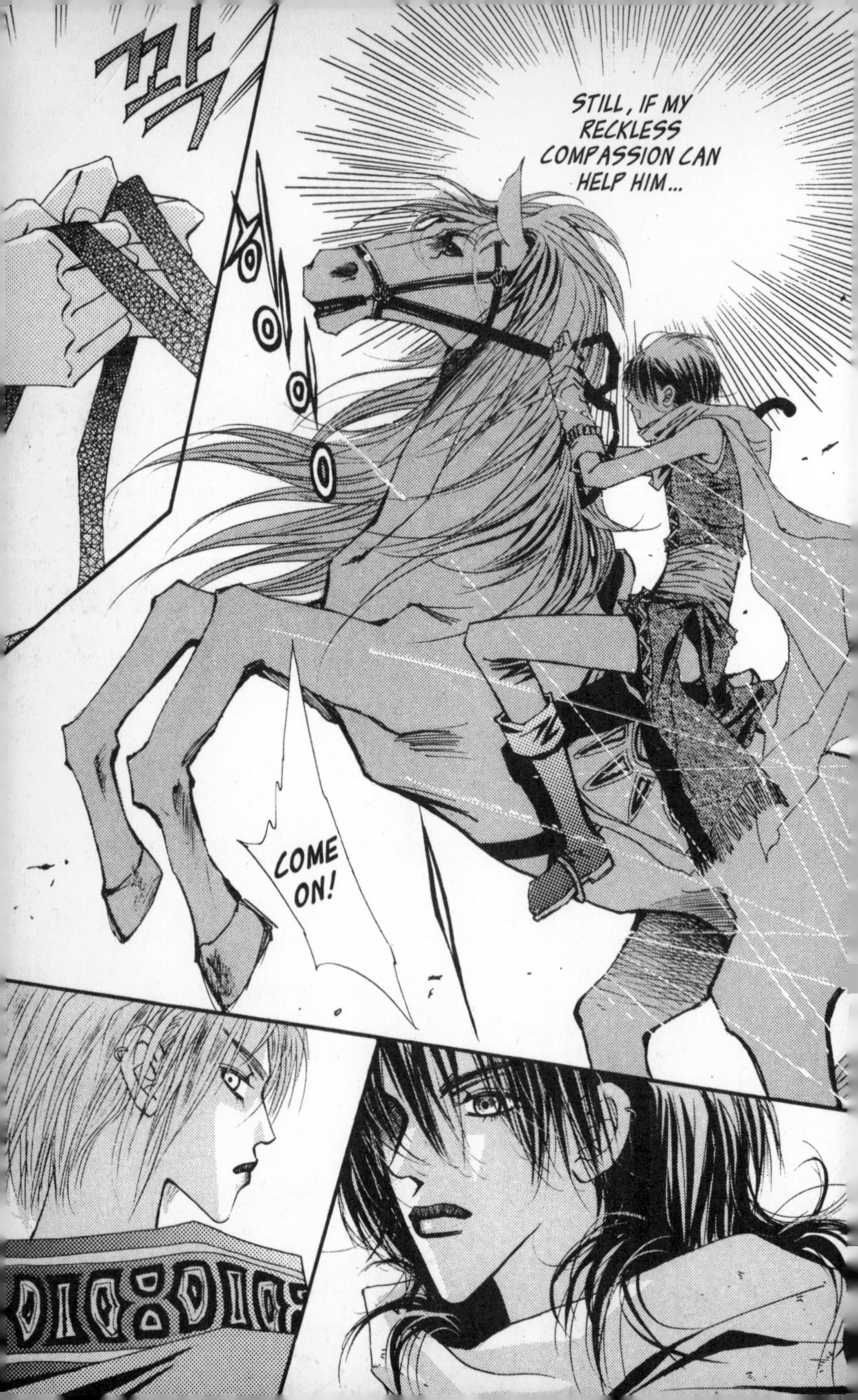
STILL, IF MY RECKLESS COMPASSION CAN HELP HIM...
COME ON!

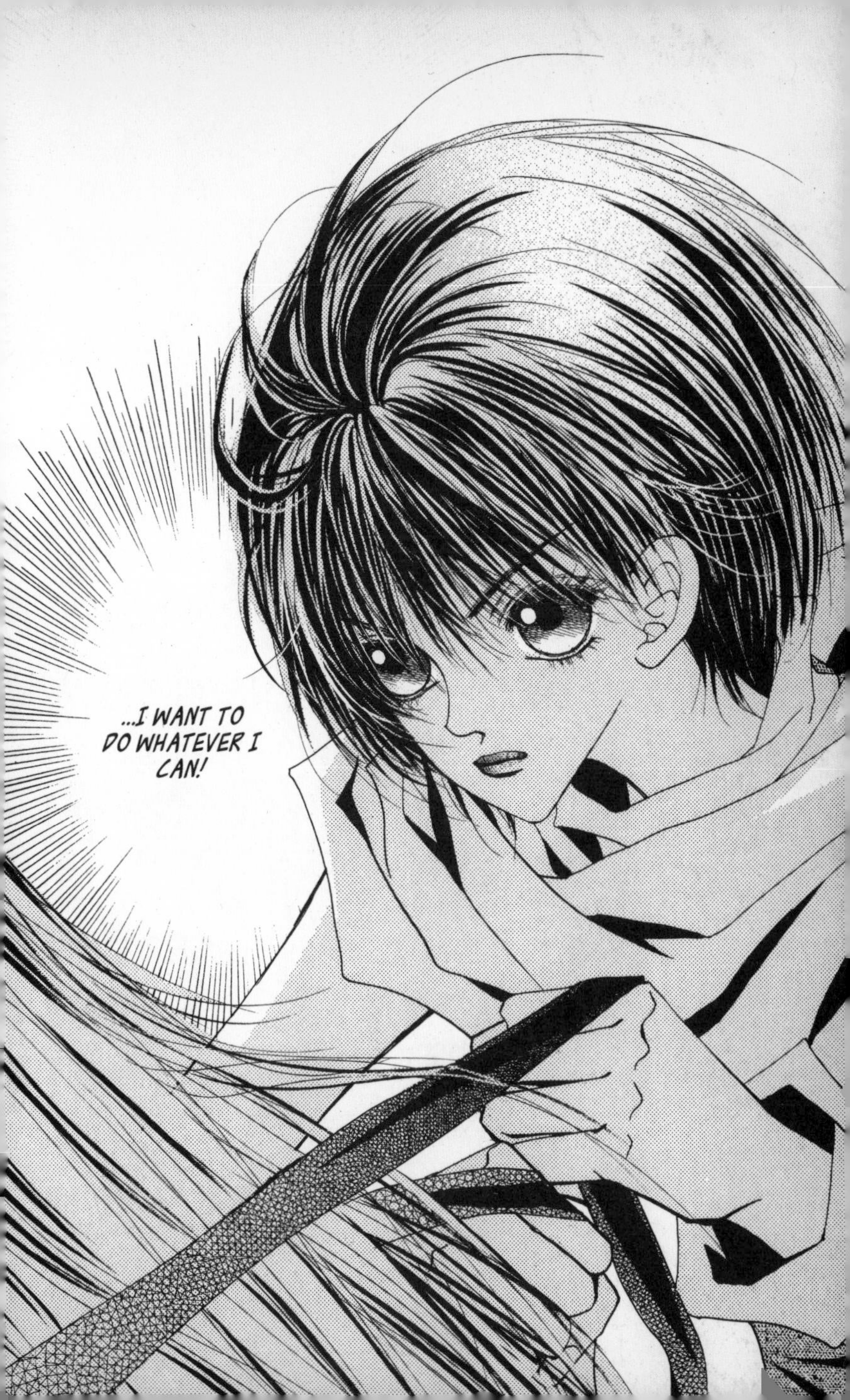
...I WANT TO DO WHATEVER I CAN!

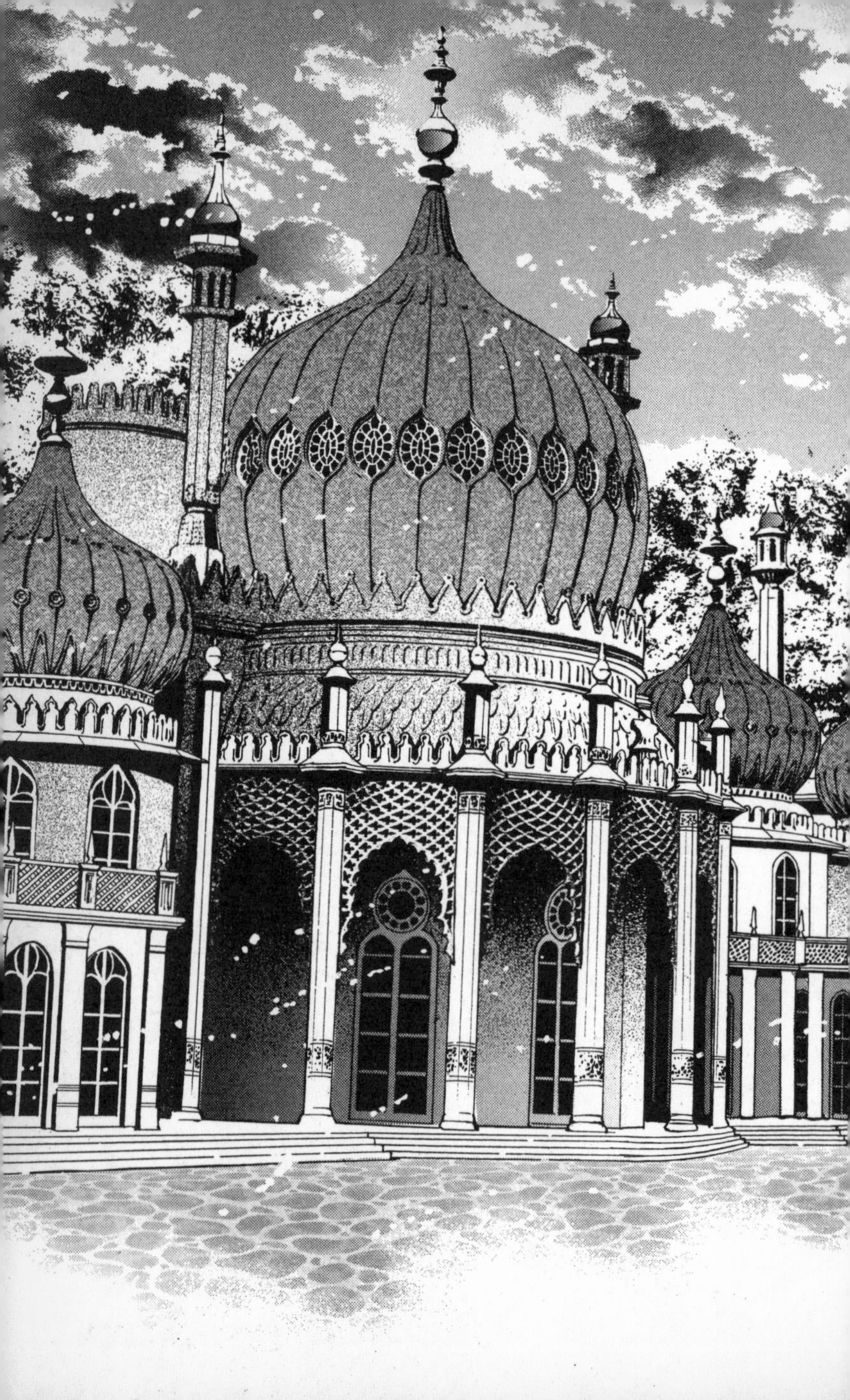

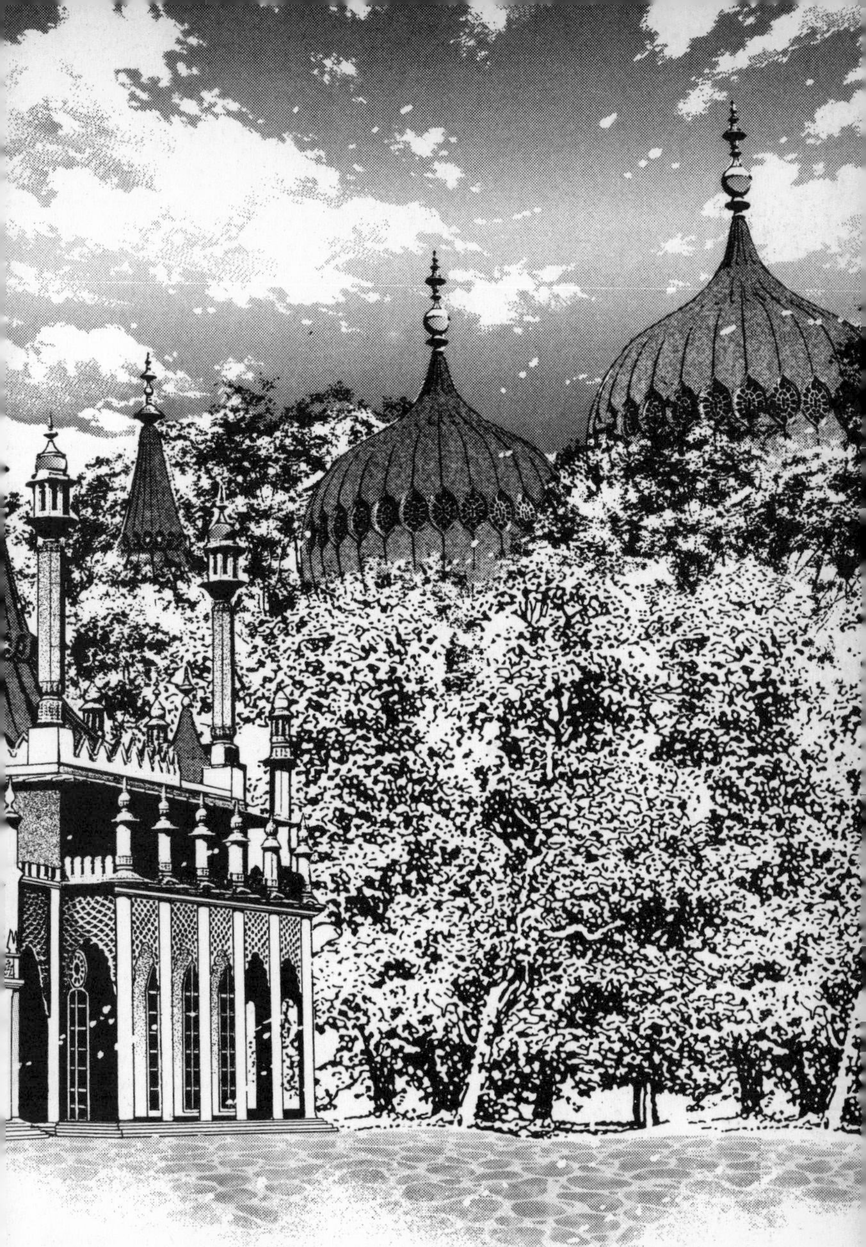

EPISODE 4
EAST GARDEN

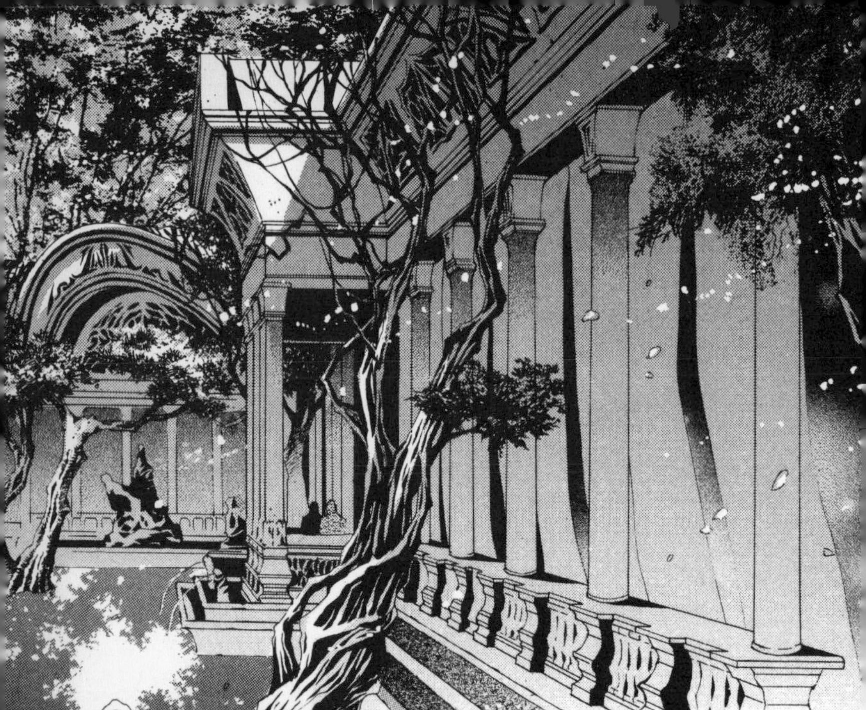

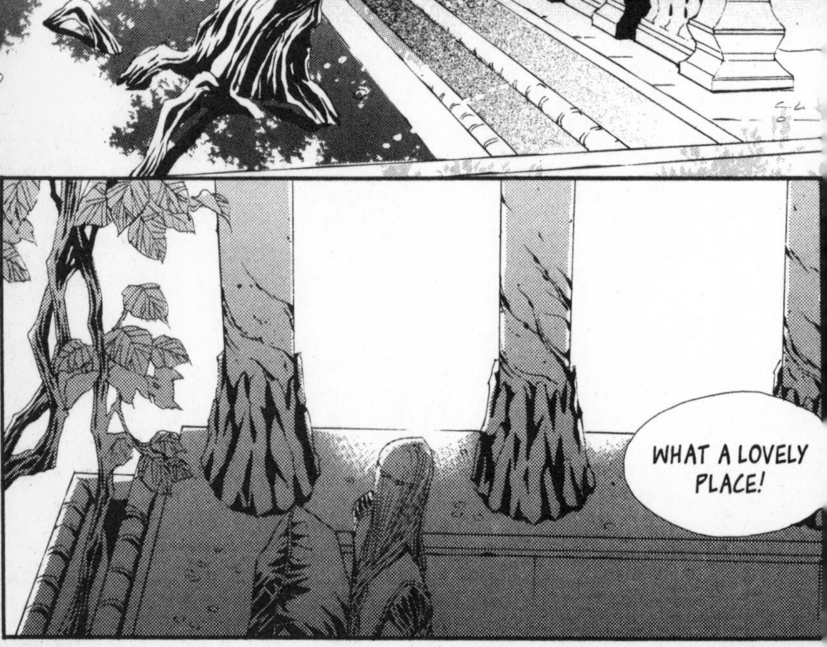
WHAT A LOVELY PLACE!

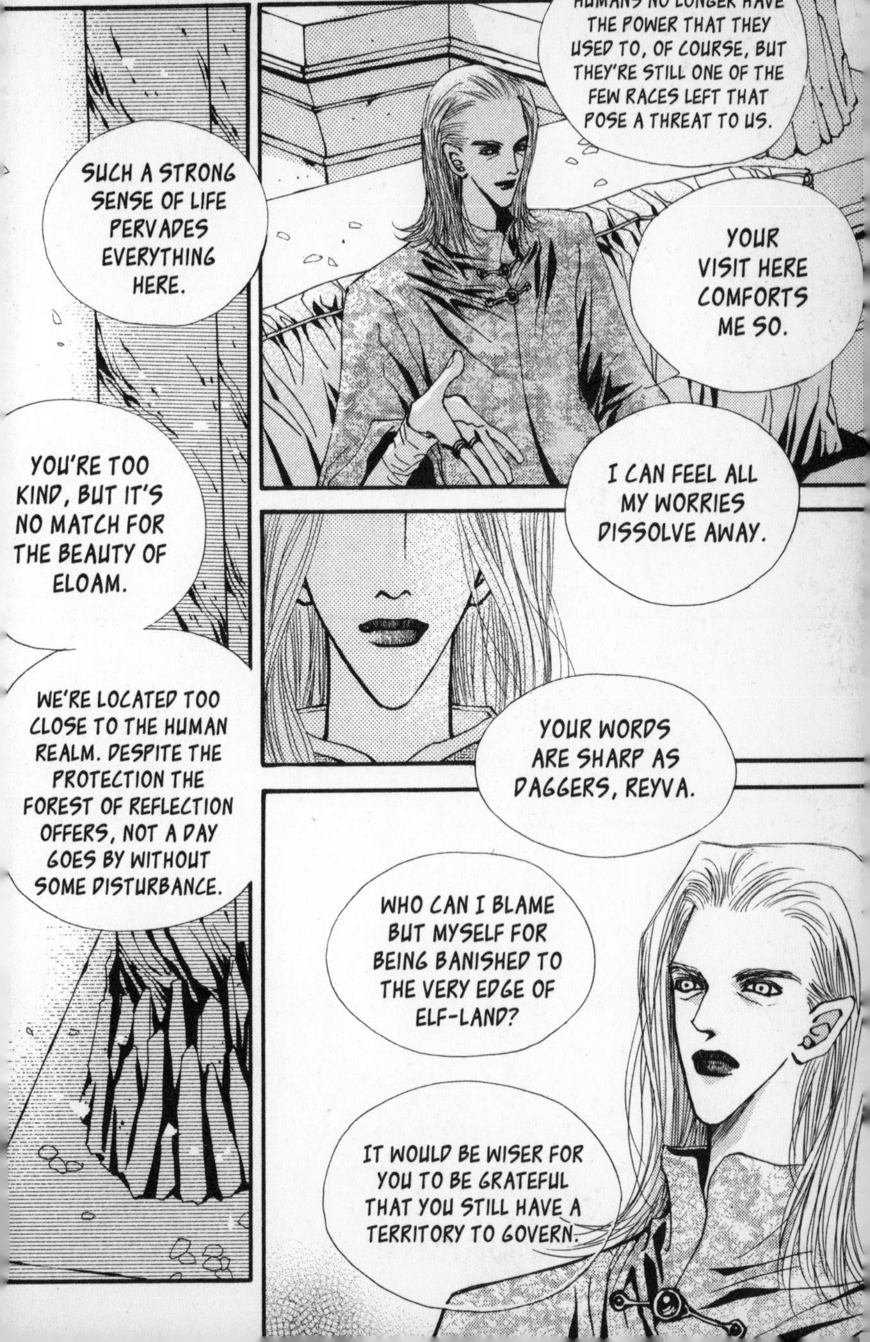
SUCH A STRONG SENSE OF LIFE PERVADES EVERYTHING HERE.
YOU'RE TOO KIND, BUT IT'S NO MATCH FOR THE BEAUTY OF ELOAM.
WE'RE LOCATED TOO CLOSE TO THE HUMAN REALM. DESPITE THE PROTECTION THE FOREST OF REFLECTION OFFERS, NOT A DAY GOES BY WITHOUT SOME DISTURBANCE.
HUMANS NO LONGER HAVE THE POWER THAT THEY USED TO, OF COURSE, BUT THEY'RE STILL ONE OF THE FEW RACES LEFT THAT POSE A THREAT TO US.
YOUR VISIT HERE COMFORTS ME SO.
I CAN FEEL ALL MY WORRIES DISSOLVE AWAY.
YOUR WORDS ARE SHARP AS DAGGERS, REYVA.
WHO CAN I BLAME BUT MYSELF FOR BEING BANISHED TO THE VERY EDGE OF ELF-LAND?
IT WOULD BE WISER FOR YOU TO BE GRATEFUL THAT YOU STILL HAVE A TERRITORY TO GOVERN.

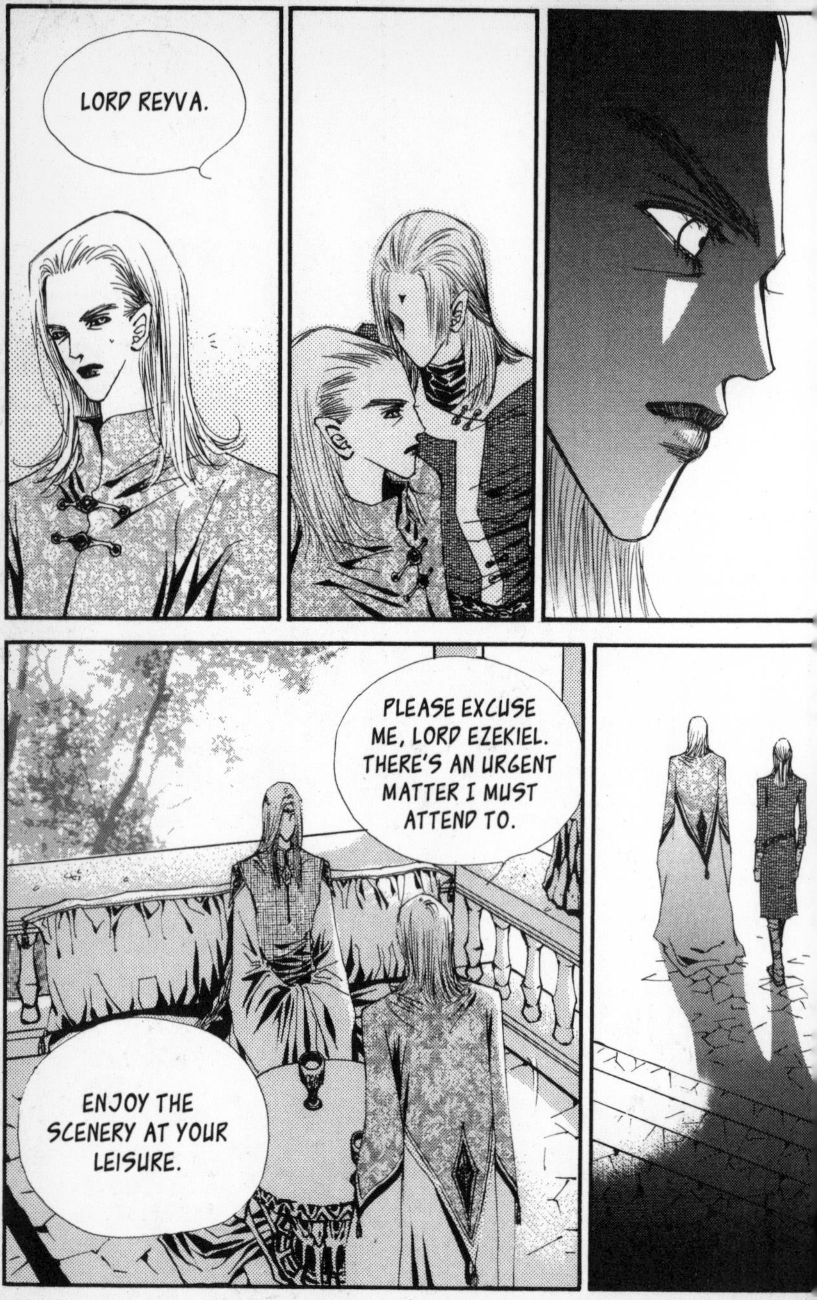
LORD REYVA.
PLEASE EXCUSE ME, LORD EZEKIEL. THERE'S AN URGENT MATTER I MUST ATTEND TO.
ENJOY THE SCENERY AT YOUR LEISURE.

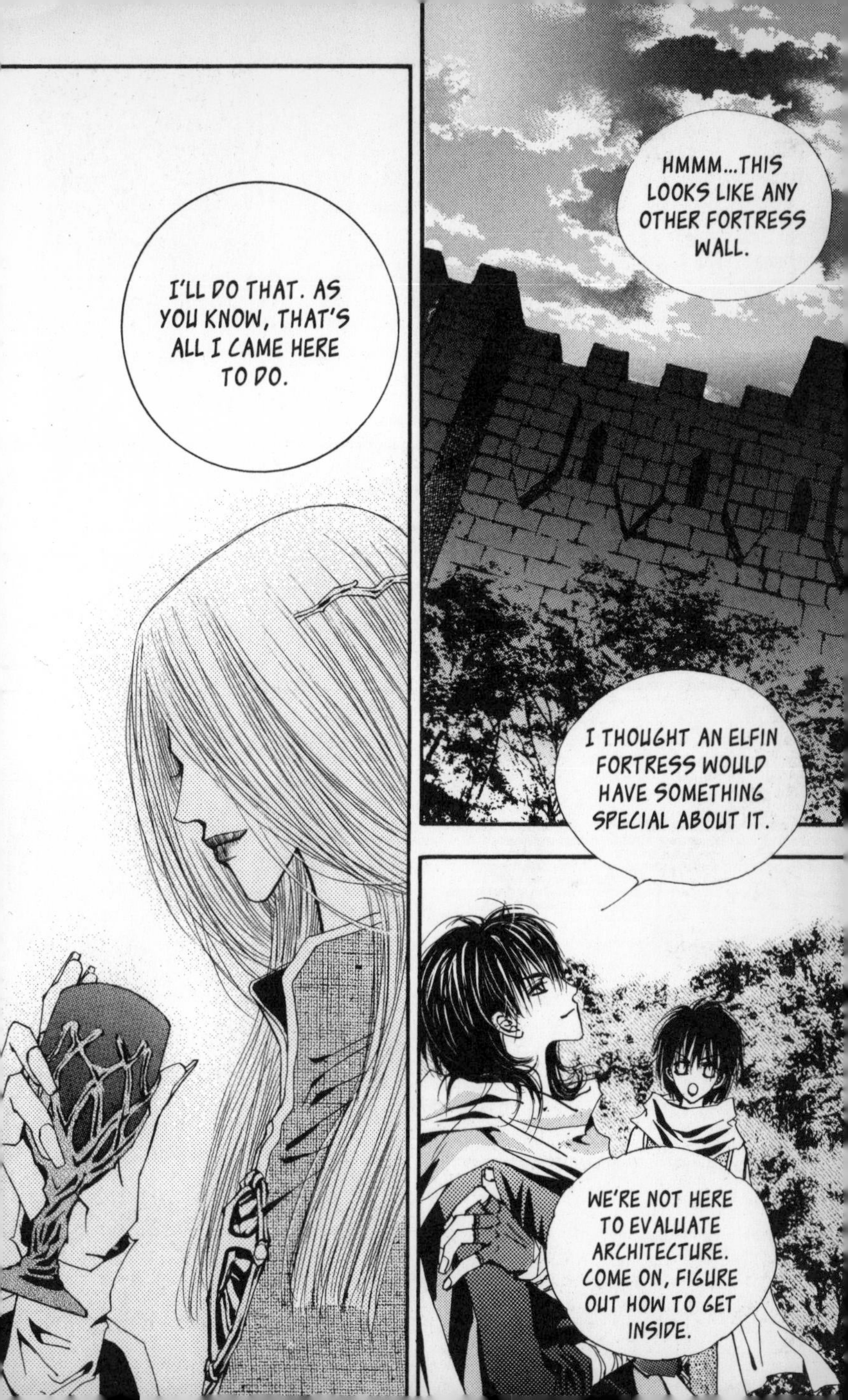
I'LL DO THAT. AS YOU KNOW, THAT'S ALL I CAME HERE TO DO.
HMMM...THIS LOOKS LIKE ANY OTHER FORTRESS WALL.
I THOUGHT AN ELFIN FORTRESS WOULD HAVE SOMETHING SPECIAL ABOUT IT.
WE'RE NOT HERE TO EVALUATE ARCHITECTURE. COME ON, FIGURE OUT HOW TO GET INSIDE.

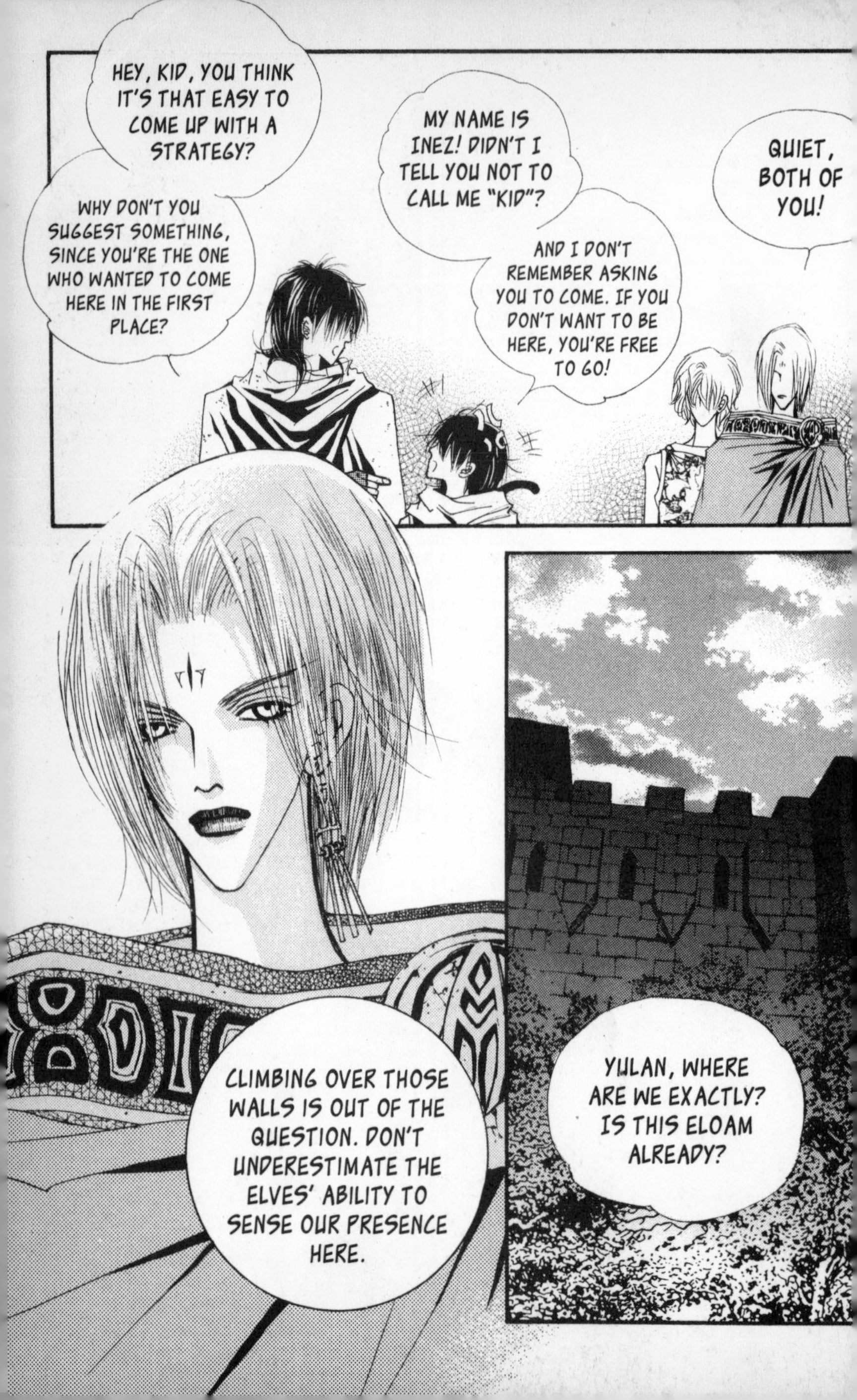
HEY, KID, YOU THINK IT'S THAT EASY TO COME UP WITH A STRATEGY?
WHY DON'T YOU SUGGEST SOMETHING, SINCE YOU'RE THE ONE WHO WANTED TO COME HERE IN THE FIRST PLACE?
MY NAME IS INEZ! DIDN'T I TELL YOU NOT TO CALL ME "KID"?
AND I DON'T REMEMBER ASKING YOU TO COME. IF YOU DON'T WANT TO BE HERE, YOU'RE FREE TO GO!
QUIET, BOTH OF YOU!
CLIMBING OVER THOSE WALLS IS OUT OF THE QUESTION. DON'T UNDERESTIMATE THE ELVES' ABILITY TO SENSE OUR PRESENCE HERE.
YULAN, WHERE ARE WE EXACTLY? IS THIS ELOAM ALREADY?

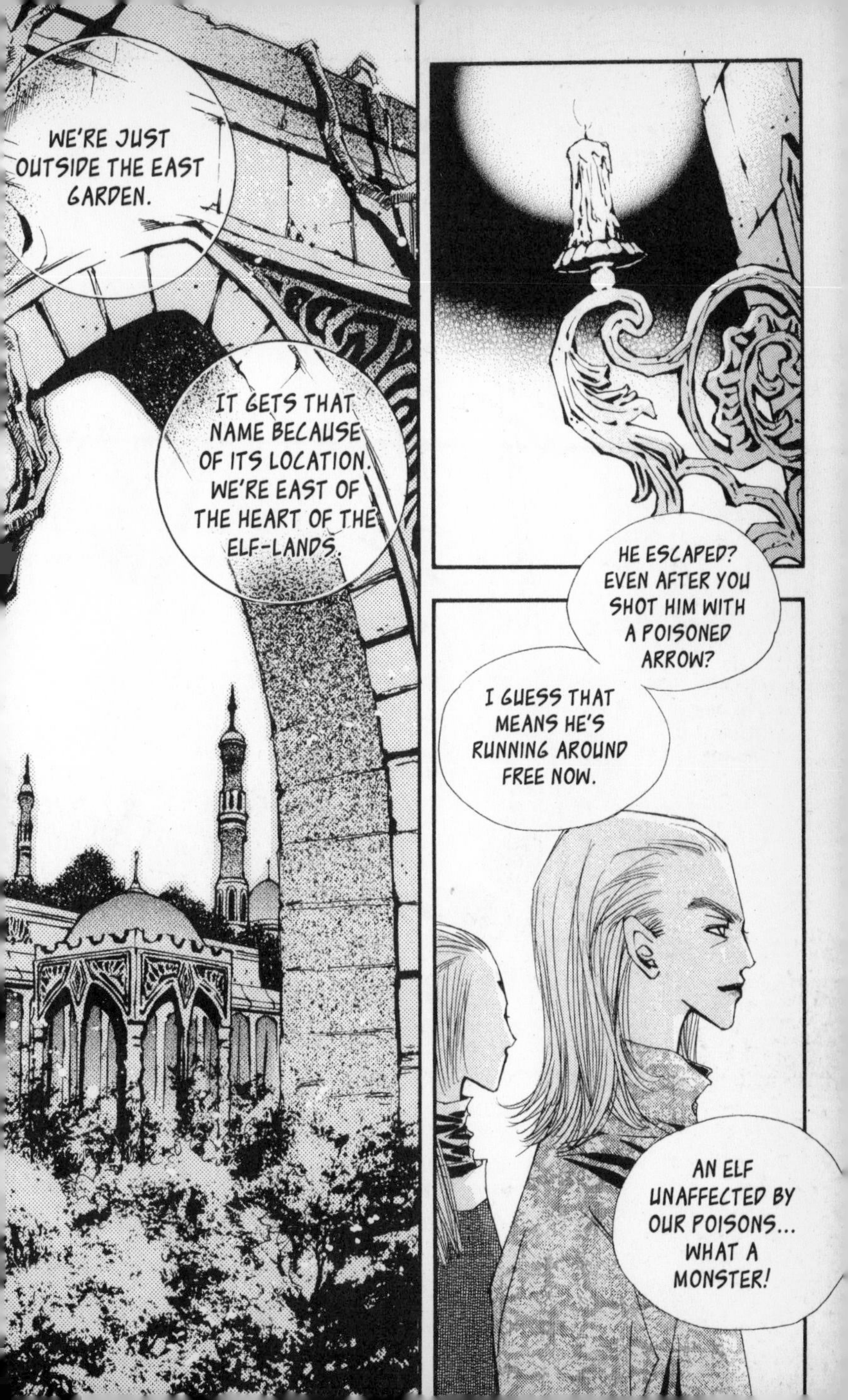
WE'RE JUST OUTSIDE THE EAST GARDEN.
IT GETS THAT NAME BECAUSE OF ITS LOCATION. WE'RE EAST OF THE HEART OF THE ELF-LANDS.
HE ESCAPED? EVEN AFTER YOU SHOT HIM WITH A POISONED ARROW?
I GUESS THAT MEANS HE'S RUNNING AROUND FREE NOW.
AN ELF UNAFFECTED BY OUR POISONS... WHAT A MONSTER!

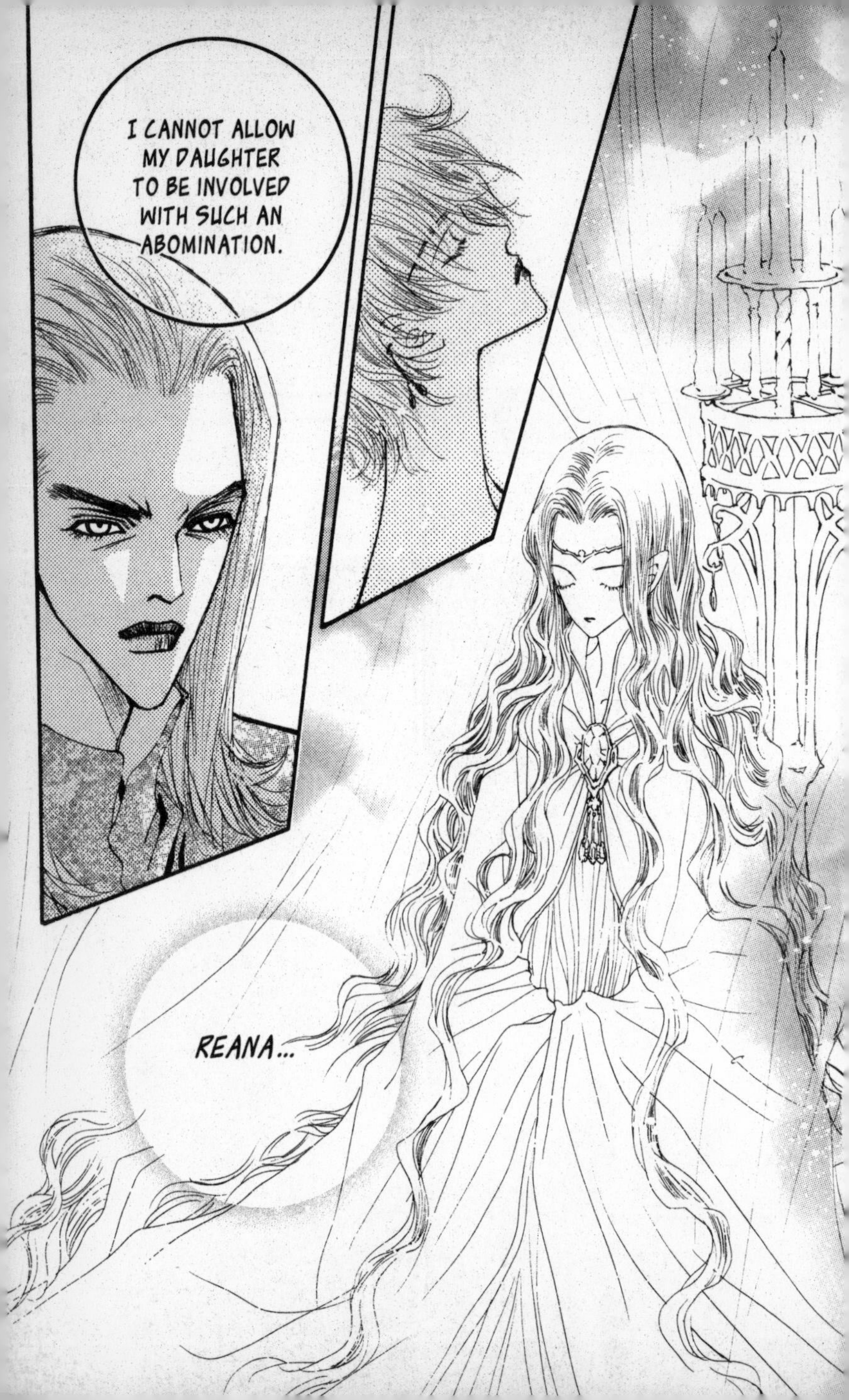
I CANNOT ALLOW MY DAUGHTER TO BE INVOLVED WITH SUCH AN ABOMINATION.
REANA...

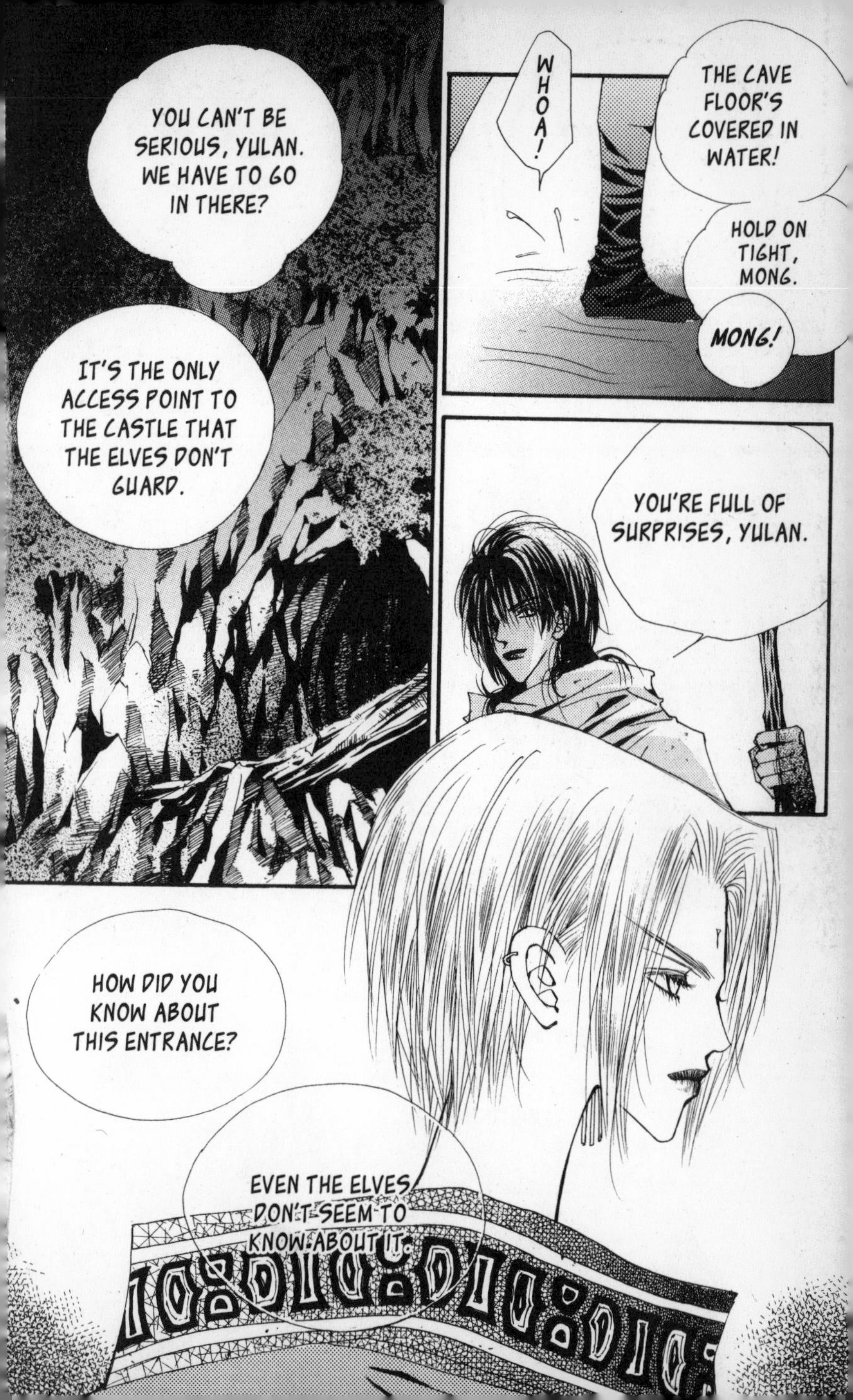
YOU CAN'T BE SERIOUS, YULAN. WE HAVE TO GO IN THERE?
IT'S THE ONLY ACCESS POINT TO THE CASTLE THAT THE ELVES DON'T GUARD.
WHOA!
THE CAVE FLOOR'S COVERED IN WATER!
HOLD ON TIGHT, MONG.
MONG!
YOU'RE FULL OF SURPRISES, YULAN.
HOW DID YOU KNOW ABOUT THIS ENTRANCE?
EVEN THE ELVES DON'T SEEM TO KNOW ABOUT IT.

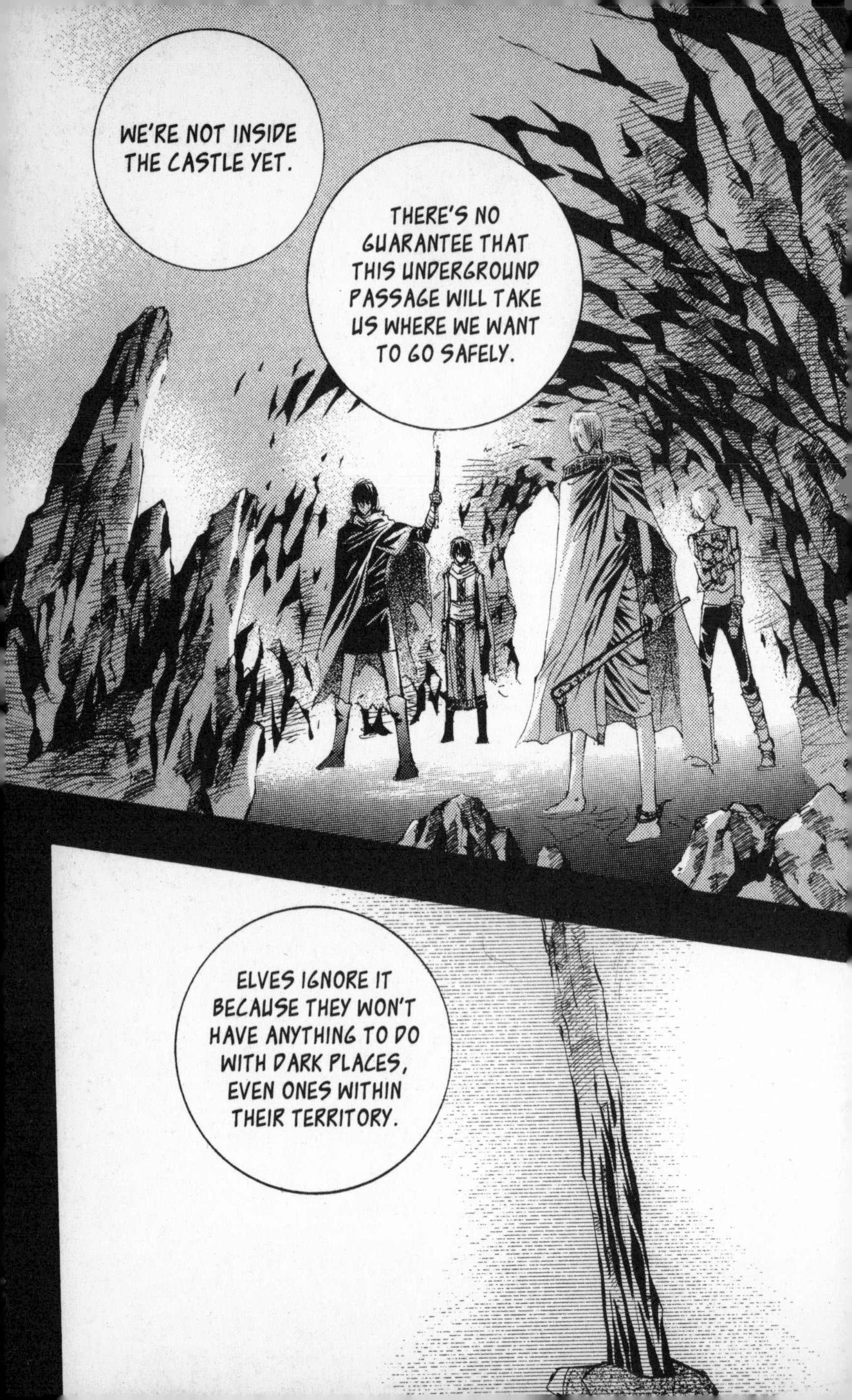
WE'RE NOT INSIDE THE CASTLE YET.
THERE'S NO GUARANTEE THAT THIS UNDERGROUND PASSAGE WILL TAKE US WHERE WE WANT TO GO SAFELY.
ELVES IGNORE IT BECAUSE THEY WON'T HAVE ANYTHING TO DO WITH DARK PLACES, EVEN ONES WITHIN THEIR TERRITORY.

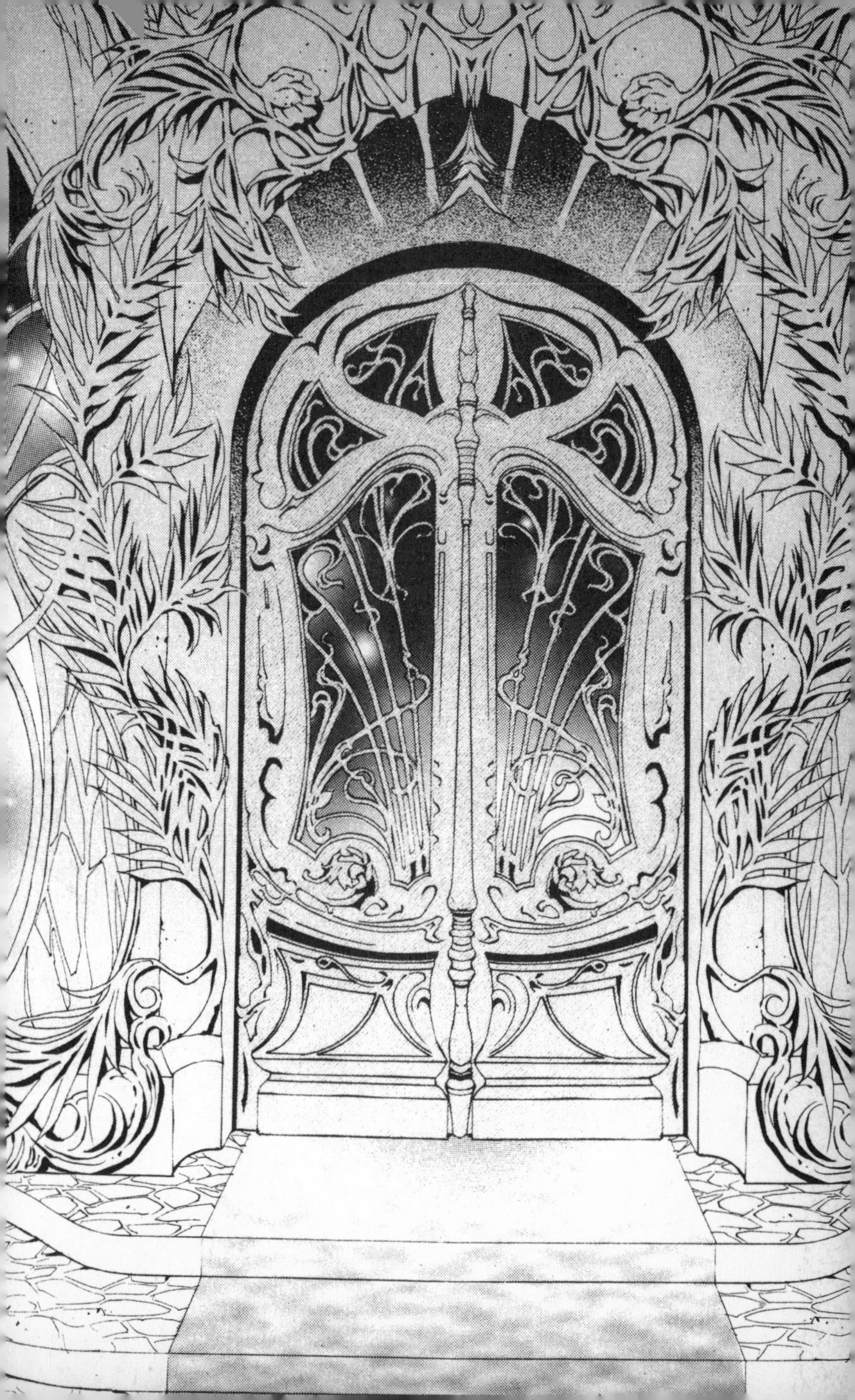

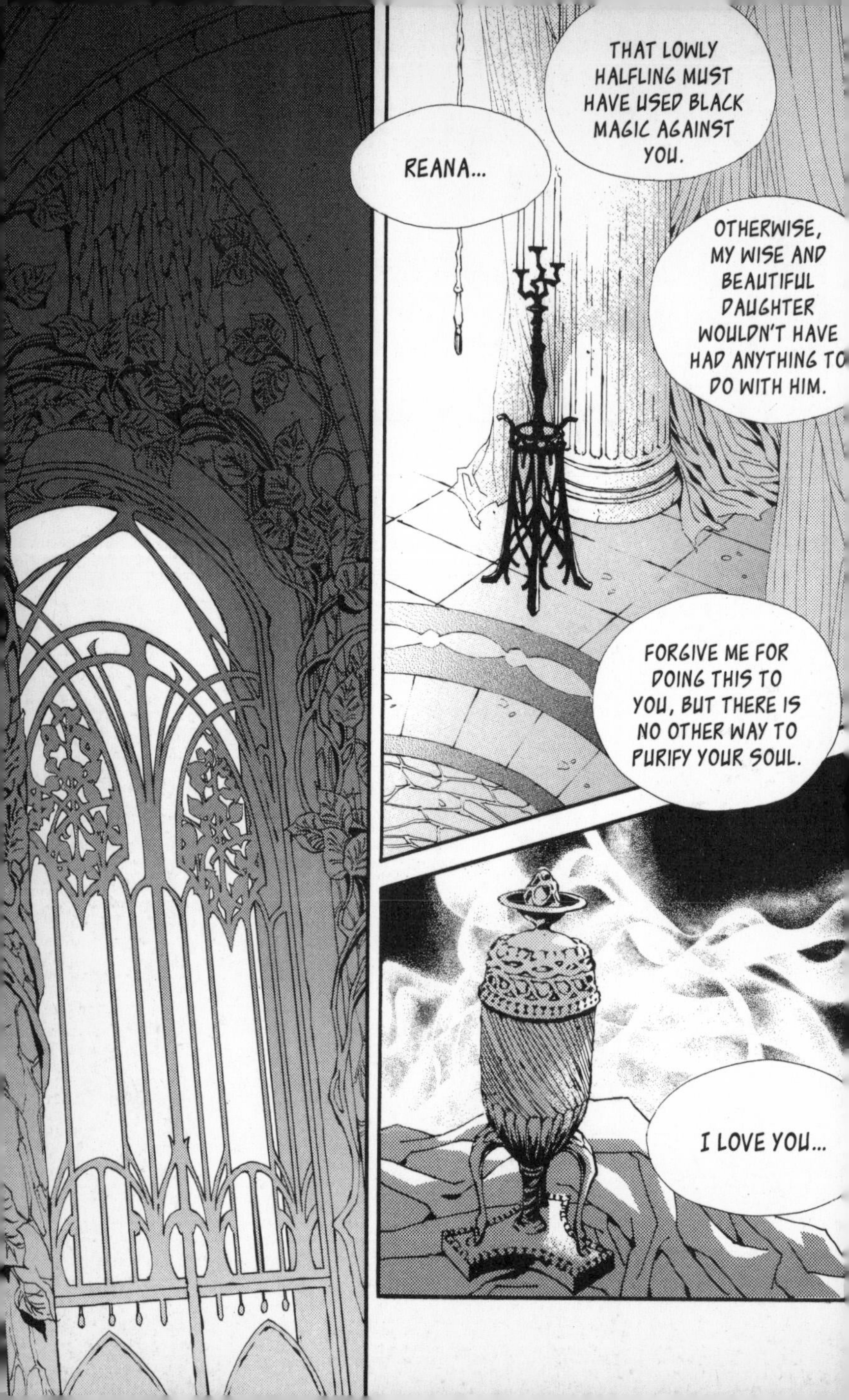
THAT LOWLY HALFLING MUST HAVE USED BLACK MAGIC AGAINST YOU.
REANA...
OTHERWISE, MY WISE AND BEAUTIFUL DAUGHTER WOULDN'T HAVE HAD ANYTHING TO DO WITH HIM.
FORGIVE ME FOR DOING THIS TO YOU, BUT THERE IS NO OTHER WAY TO PURIFY YOUR SOUL.
I LOVE YOU...

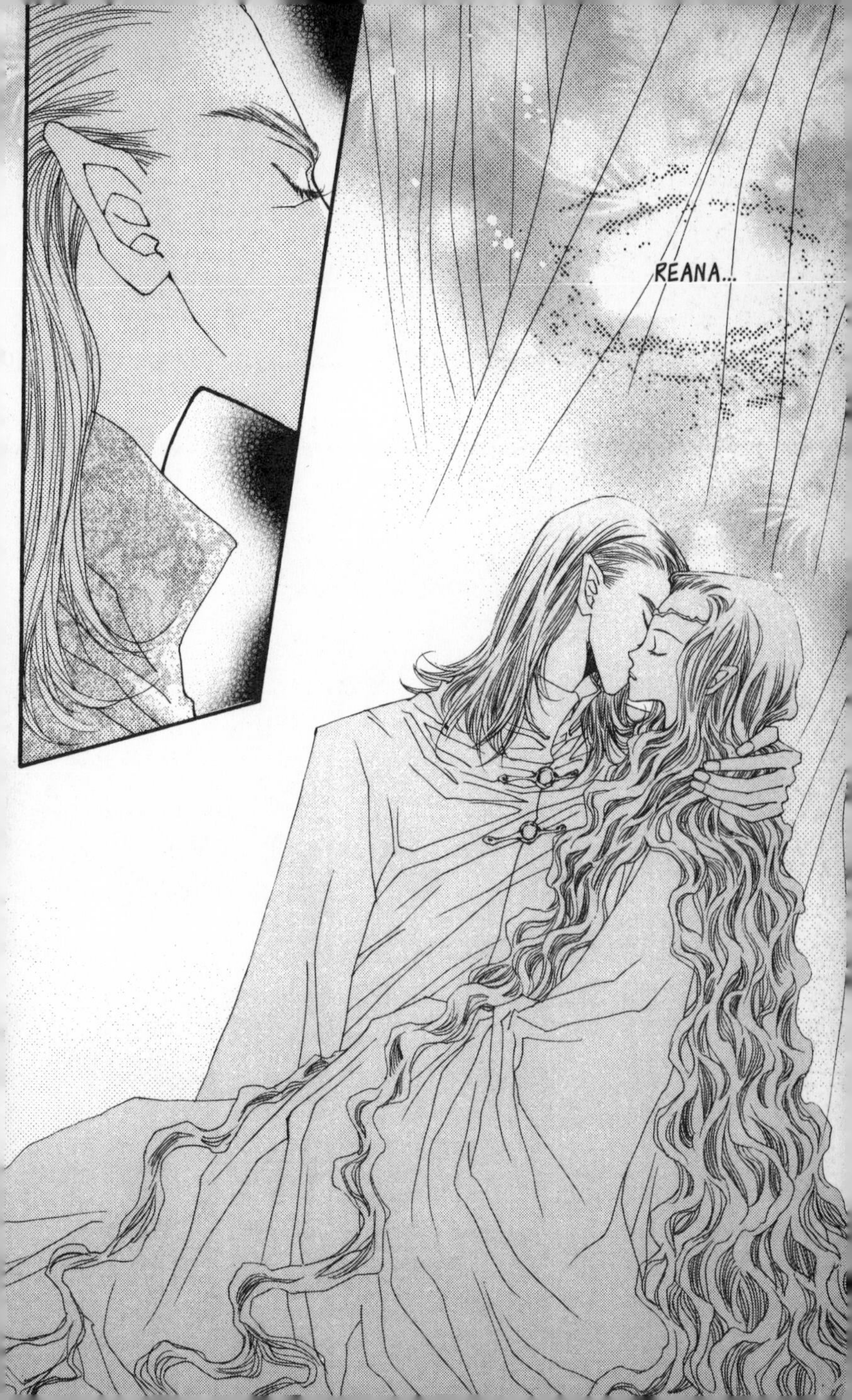
REANA...

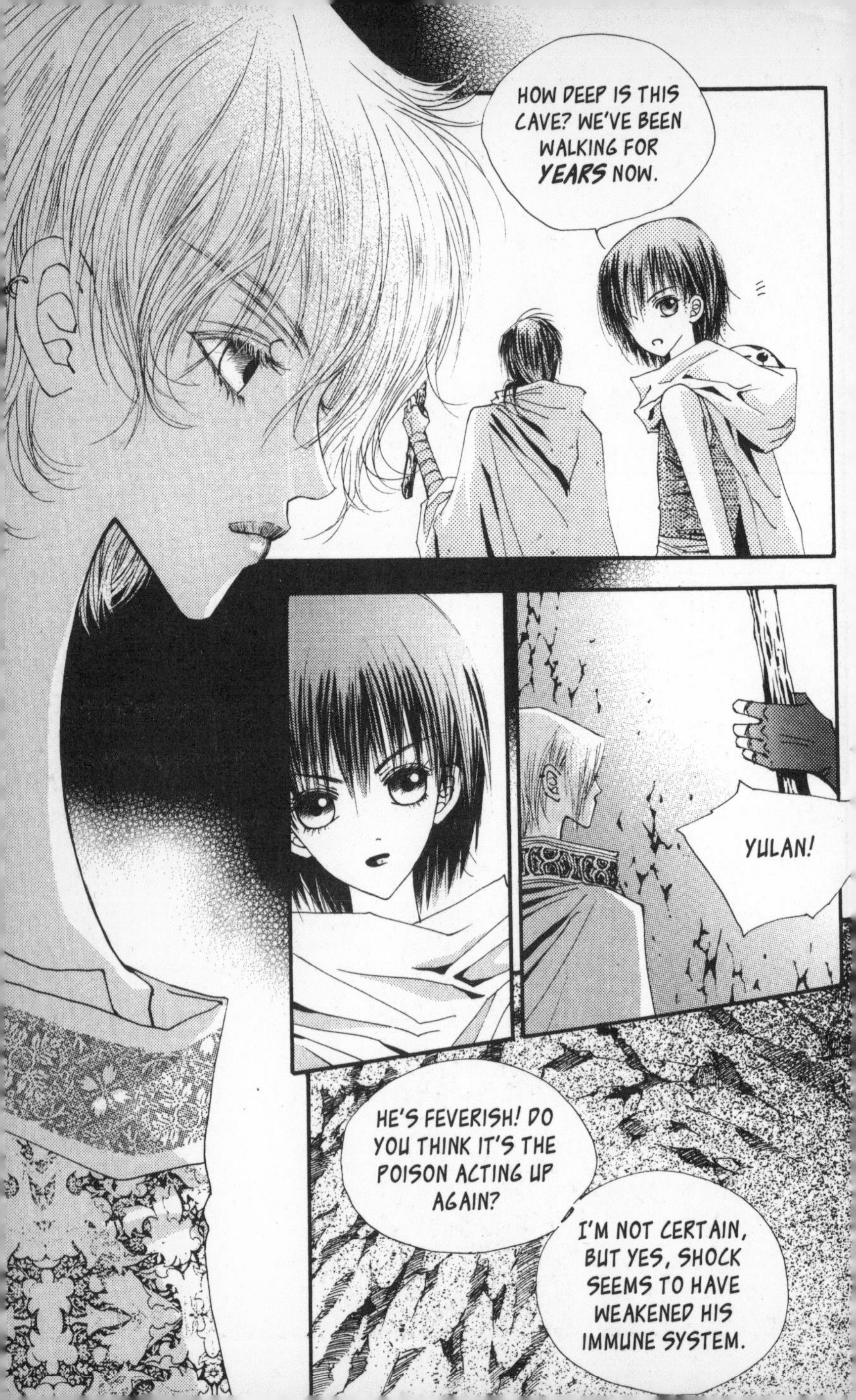
HOW DEEP IS THIS CAVE? WE'VE BEEN WALKING FOR YEARS NOW.
YULAN!
HE'S FEVERISH! DO YOU THINK IT'S THE POISON ACTING UP AGAIN?
I'M NOT CERTAIN, BUT YES, SHOCK SEEMS TO HAVE WEAKENED HIS IMMUNE SYSTEM.

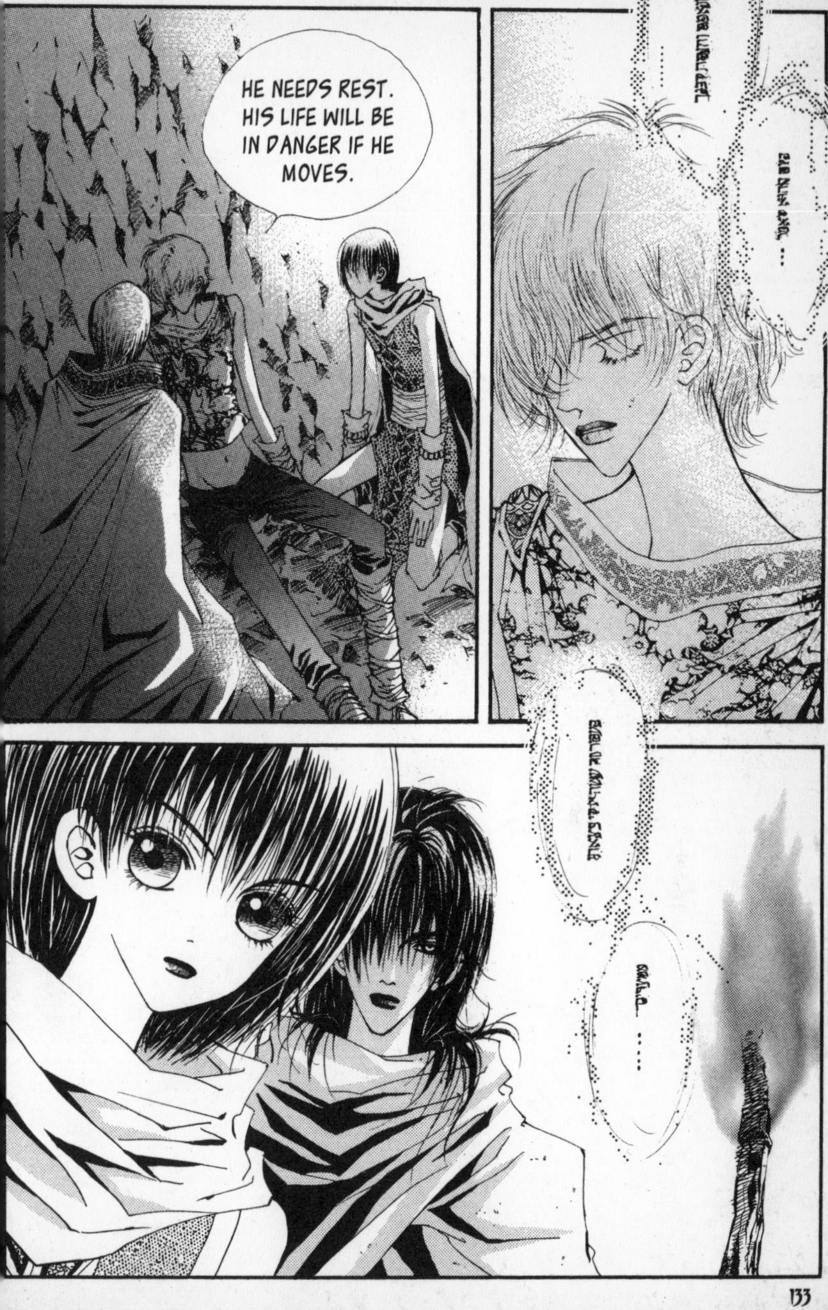
HE NEEDS REST. HIS LIFE WILL BE IN DANGER IF HE MOVES.

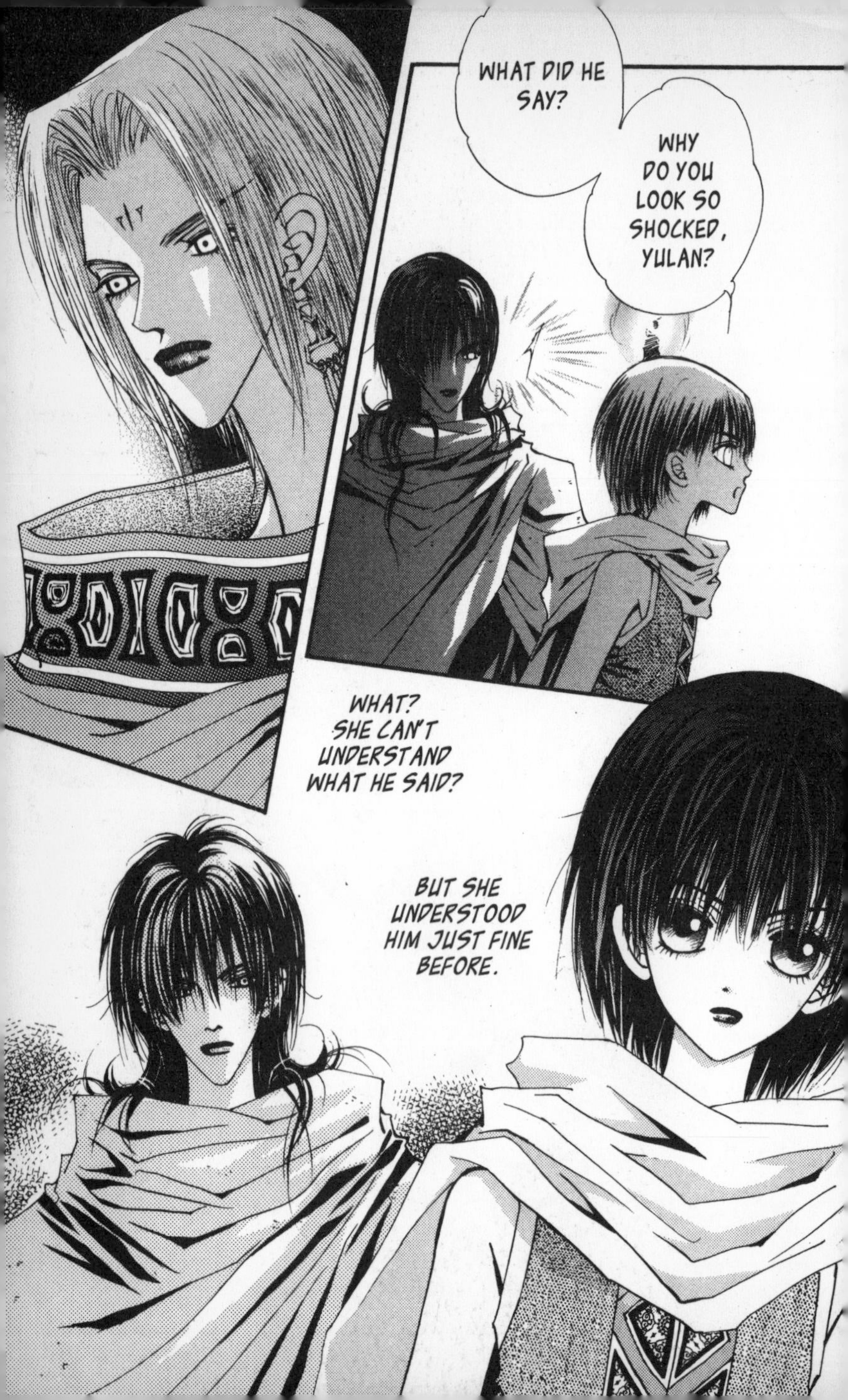
WHAT DID HE SAY?
WHY DO YOU LOOK SO SHOCKED, YULAN?
WHAT? SHE CAN'T UNDERSTAND WHAT HE SAID?
BUT SHE UNDERSTOOD HIM JUST FINE BEFORE.

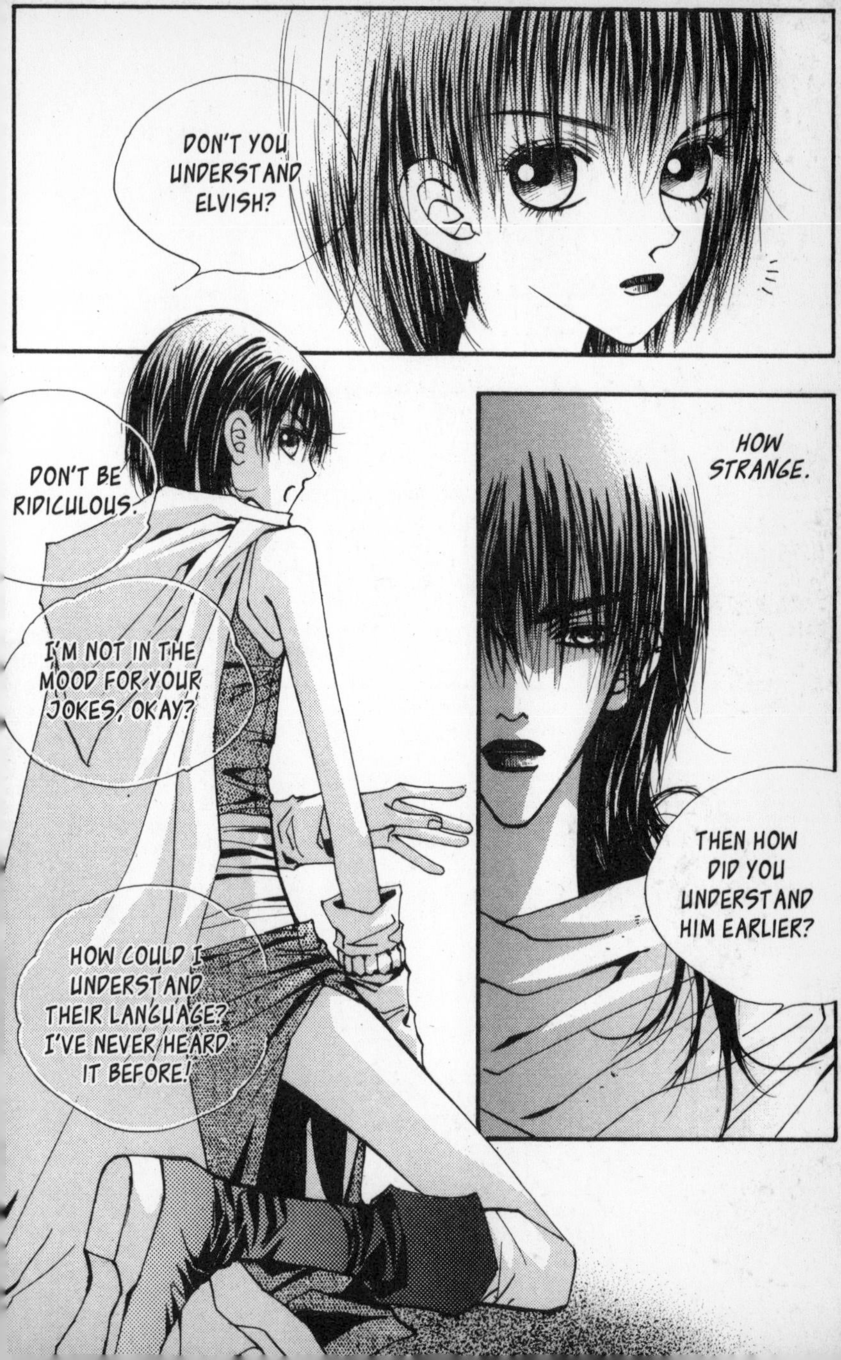
DON'T YOU UNDERSTAND ELVISH?
DON'T BE RIDICULOUS.
I'M NOT IN THE MOOD FOR YOUR JOKES, OKAY?
HOW COULD I UNDERSTAND THEIR LANGUAGE? I'VE NEVER HEARD IT BEFORE!
HOW STRANGE.
THEN HOW DID YOU UNDERSTAND HIM EARLIER?

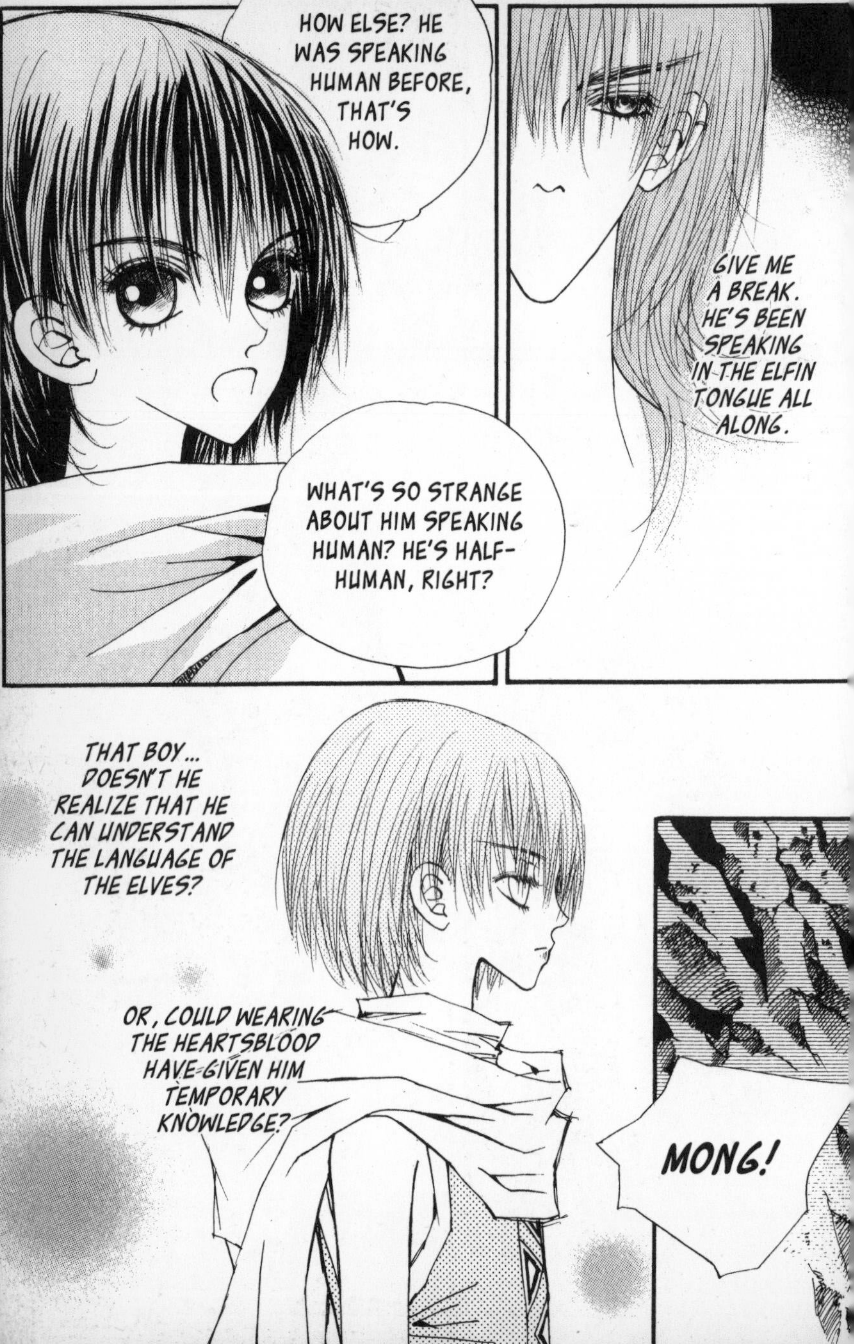
HOW ELSE? HE WAS SPEAKING HUMAN BEFORE, THAT'S HOW.
WHAT'S SO STRANGE ABOUT HIM SPEAKING HUMAN? HE'S HALF-HUMAN, RIGHT?
GIVE ME A BREAK. HE'S BEEN SPEAKING IN THE ELFIN TONGUE ALL ALONG.
THAT BOY... DOESN'T HE REALIZE THAT HE CAN UNDERSTAND THE LANGUAGE OF THE ELVES?
OR, COULD WEARING THE HEARTSBLOOD HAVE GIVEN HIM TEMPORARY KNOWLEDGE?
MONG!

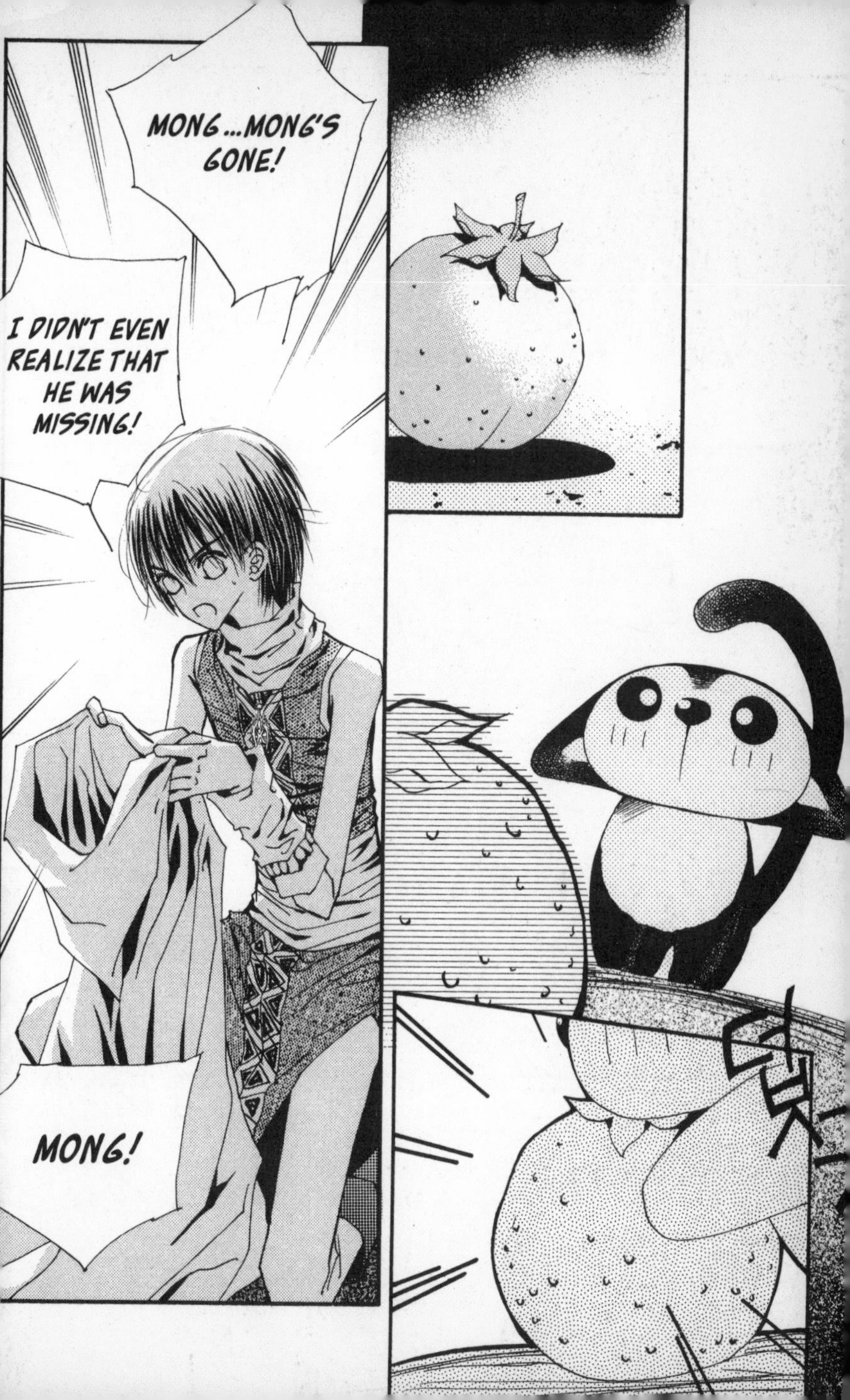
MONG...MONG'S GONE!
I DIDN'T EVEN REALIZE THAT HE WAS MISSING!
MONG!

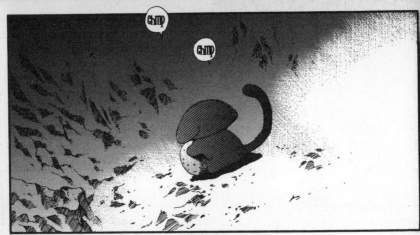

WHAT? WHY ISN'T IT TAKING EFFECT?

COULD IT BE BECAUSE HE'S A BABY?

SHOULD WE JUST ATTACK?

AT ANY RATE, THIS IS A GOLDEN OPPORTUNITY. NYAMAS NEVER MAKE IT OUT TO THESE PARTS.

NO. WE HAVE TO BE PATIENT. THEY'RE FASTER THAN THEY LOOK.

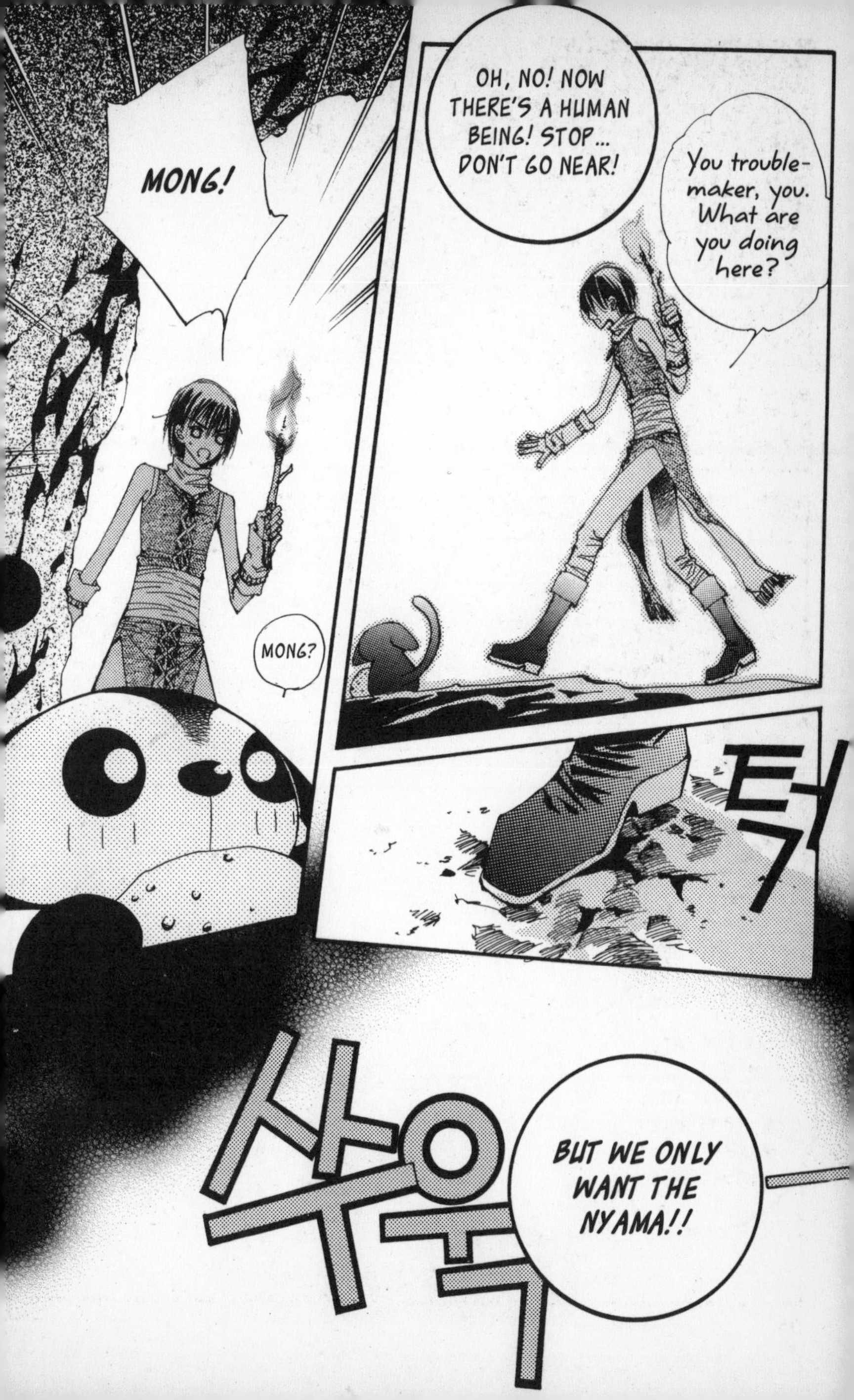
MONG!
MONG?
OH, NO! NOW THERE'S A HUMAN BEING! STOP... DON'T GO NEAR!
You trouble-maker, you. What are you doing here?
BUT WE ONLY WANT THE NYAMA!!

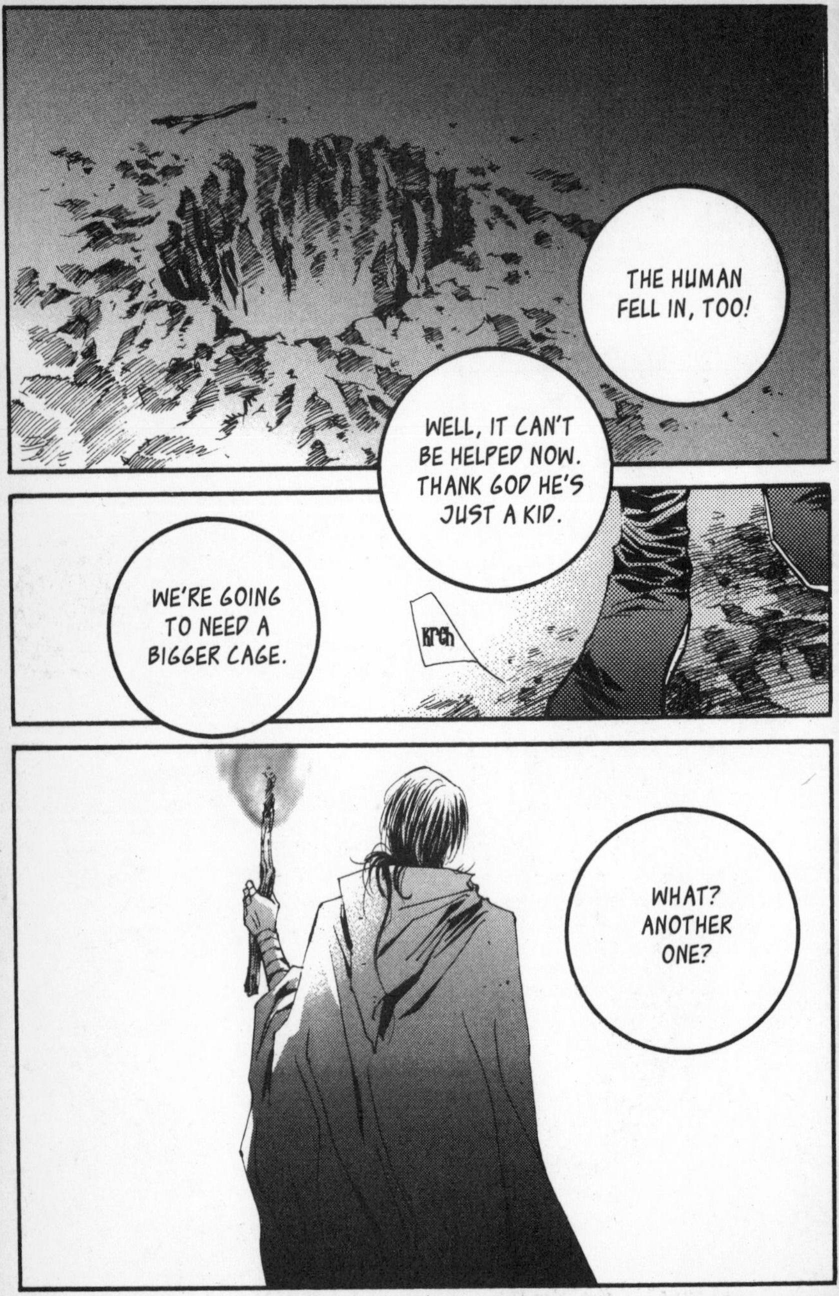
THE HUMAN FELL IN, TOO!
WELL, IT CAN'T BE HELPED NOW. THANK GOD HE'S JUST A KID.
WE'RE GOING TO NEED A BIGGER CAGE.
KRCH
WHAT? ANOTHER ONE?

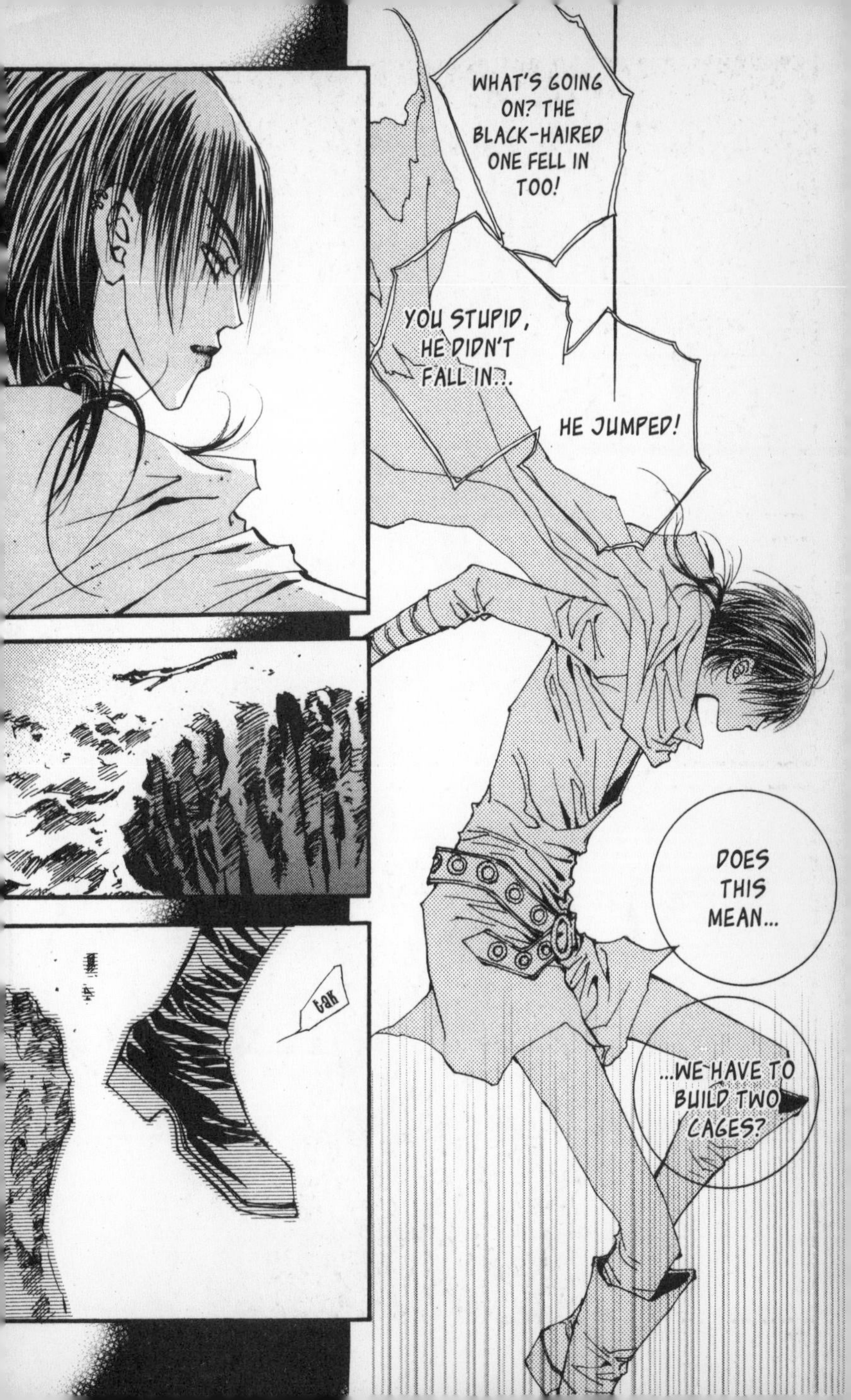
tak
WHAT'S GOING ON? THE BLACK-HAIRED ONE FELL IN TOO!
YOU STUPID, HE DIDN'T FALL IN...
HE JUMPED!
DOES THIS MEAN...
...WE HAVE TO BUILD TWO CAGES?

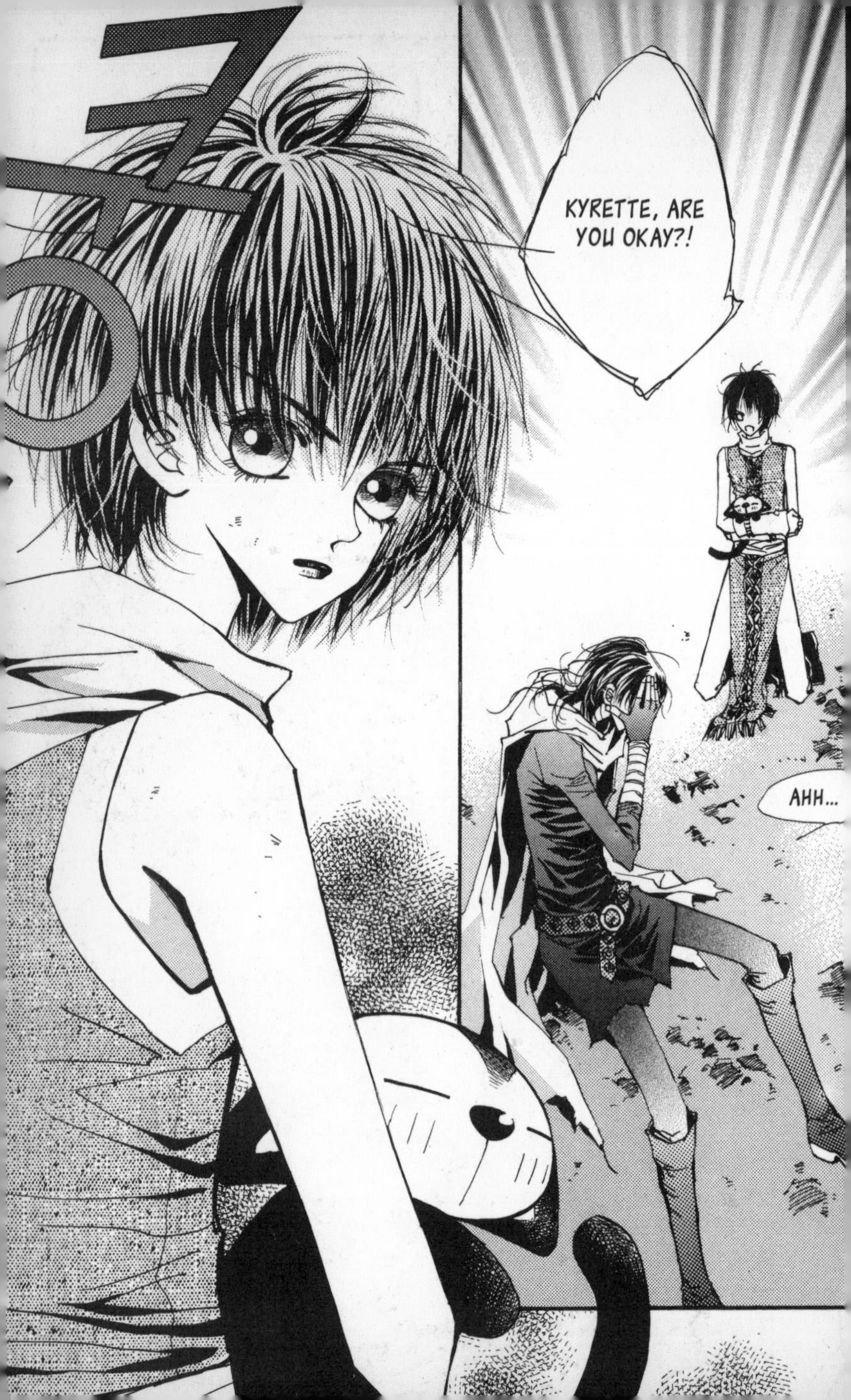
KYRETTE, ARE YOU OKAY?!
AHH...

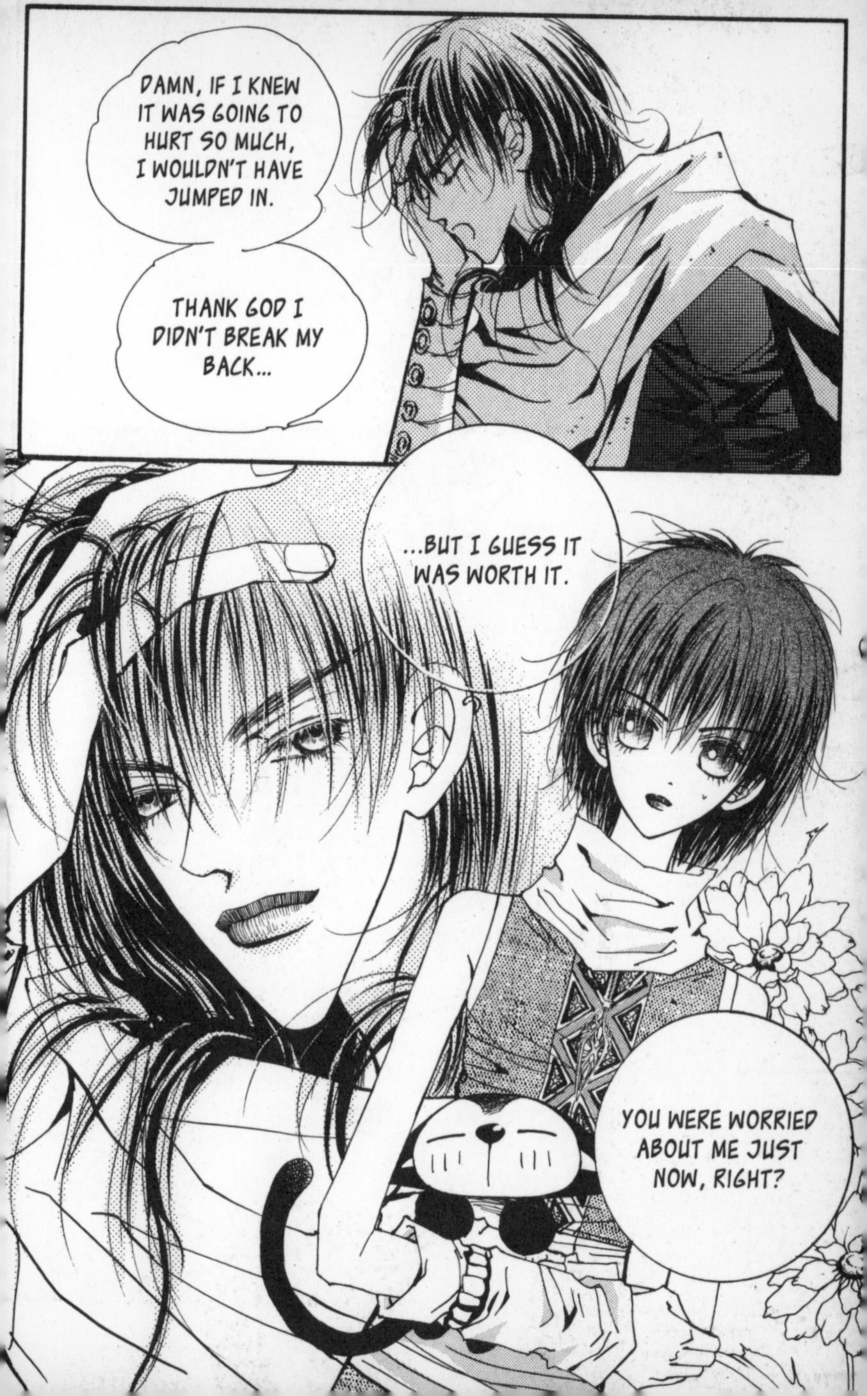
DAMN, IF I KNEW IT WAS GOING TO HURT SO MUCH, I WOULDN'T HAVE JUMPED IN.
THANK GOD I DIDN'T BREAK MY BACK...
...BUT I GUESS IT WAS WORTH IT.
YOU WERE WORRIED ABOUT ME JUST NOW, RIGHT?

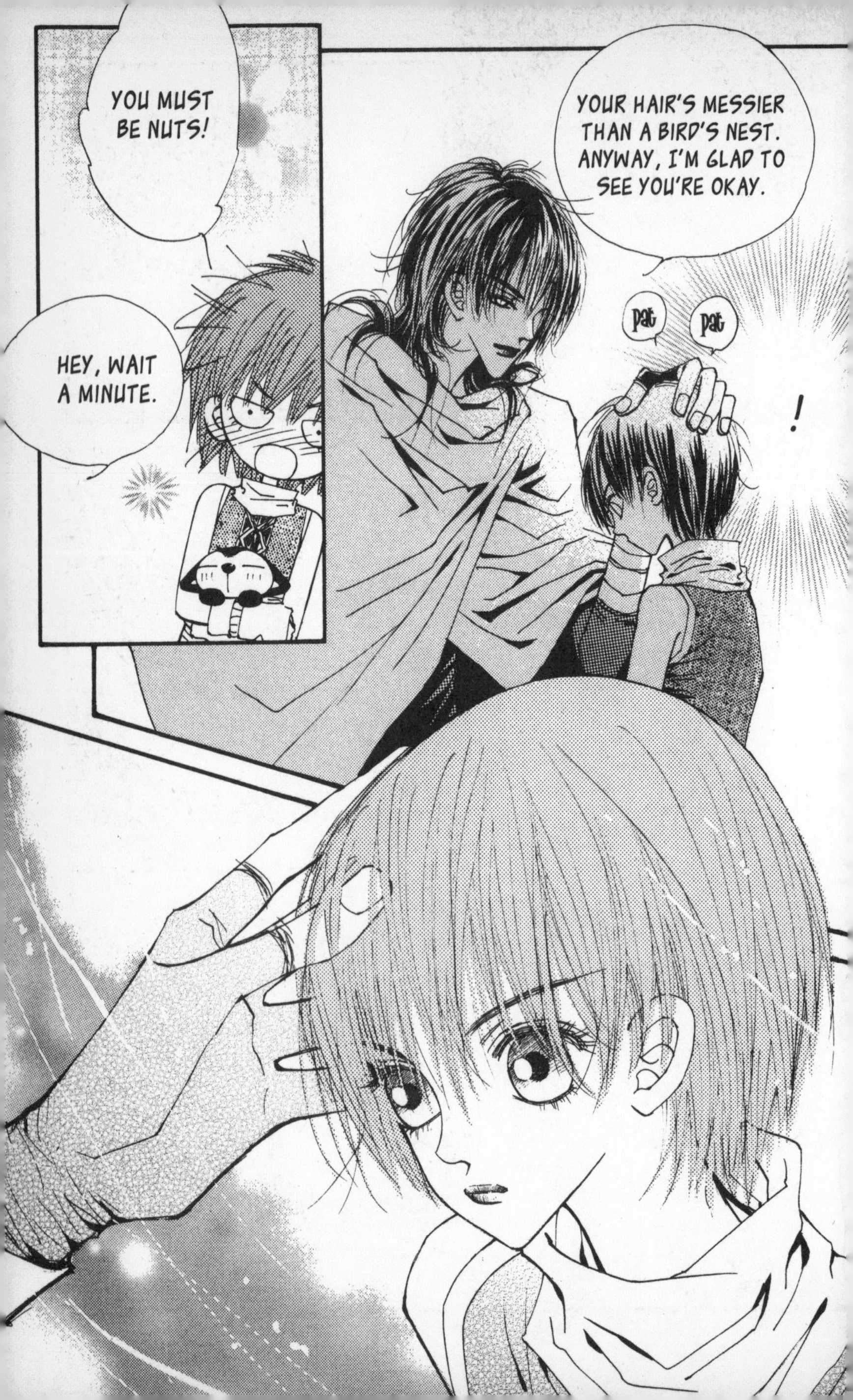
YOU MUST BE NUTS!
HEY, WAIT A MINUTE.
YOUR HAIR'S MESSIER THAN A BIRD'S NEST. ANYWAY, I'M GLAD TO SEE YOU'RE OKAY.
pat
pat
!

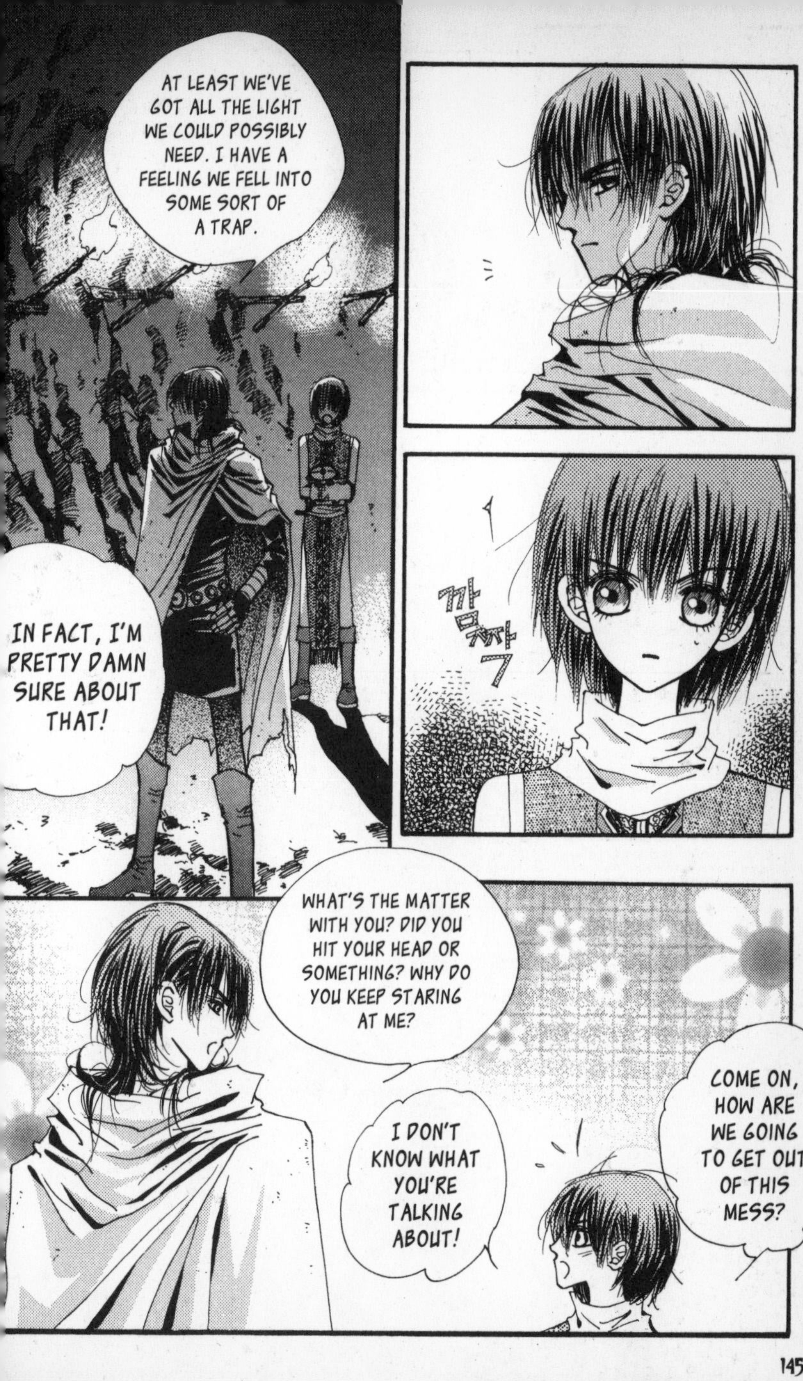
AT LEAST WE'VE GOT ALL THE LIGHT WE COULD POSSIBLY NEED. I HAVE A FEELING WE FELL INTO SOME SORT OF A TRAP.
IN FACT, I'M PRETTY DAMN SURE ABOUT THAT!
WHAT'S THE MATTER WITH YOU? DID YOU HIT YOUR HEAD OR SOMETHING? WHY DO YOU KEEP STARING AT ME?
I DON'T KNOW WHAT YOU'RE TALKING ABOUT!
COME ON, HOW ARE WE GOING TO GET OUT OF THIS MESS?

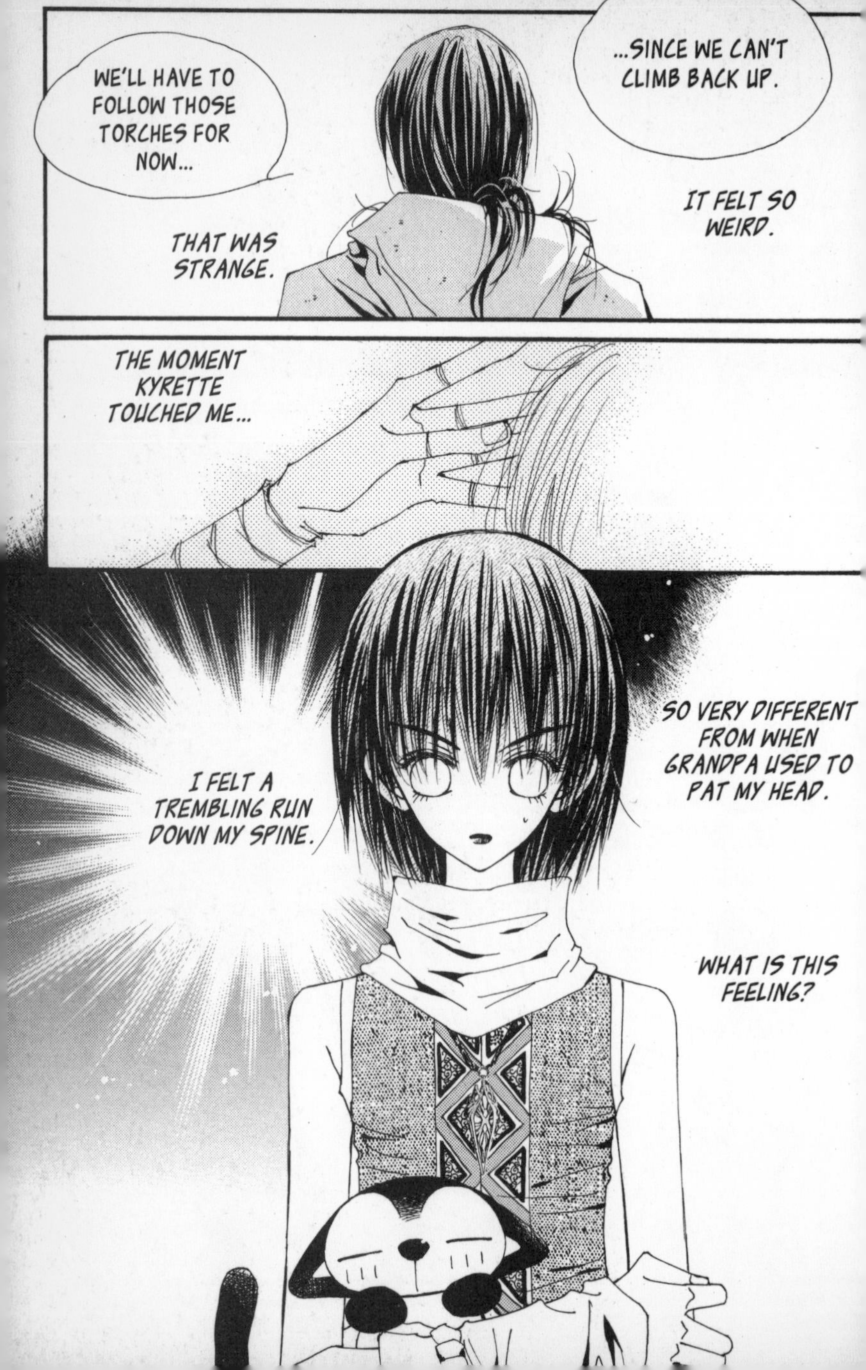
WE'LL HAVE TO FOLLOW THOSE TORCHES FOR NOW...
...SINCE WE CAN'T CLIMB BACK UP.
THAT WAS STRANGE.
IT FELT SO WEIRD.
THE MOMENT KYRETTE TOUCHED ME...
I FELT A TREMBLING RUN DOWN MY SPINE.
SO VERY DIFFERENT FROM WHEN GRANDPA USED TO PAT MY HEAD.
WHAT IS THIS FEELING?

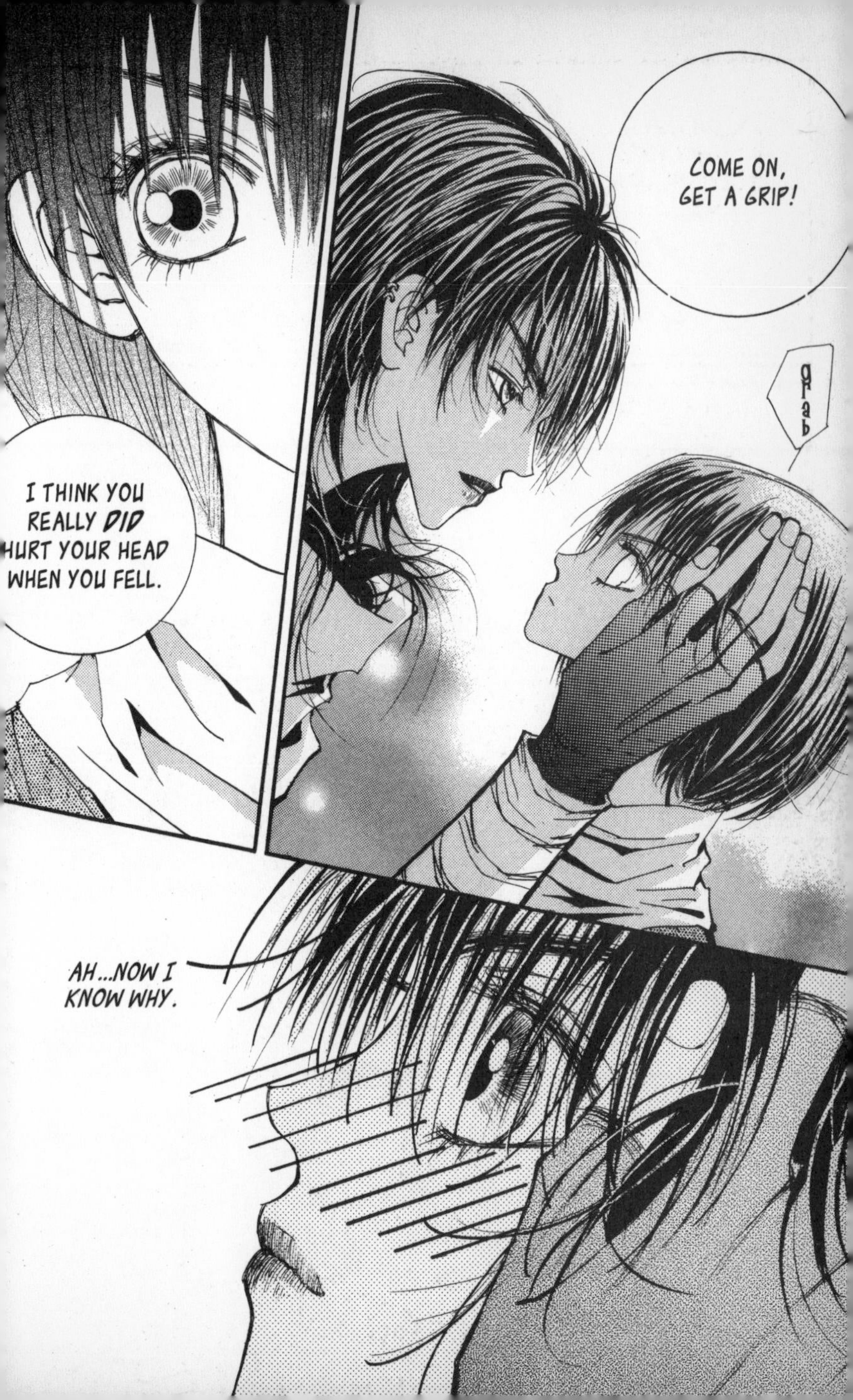
I THINK YOU REALLY DID HURT YOUR HEAD WHEN YOU FELL.
COME ON, GET A GRIP!
grab
AH...NOW I KNOW WHY.

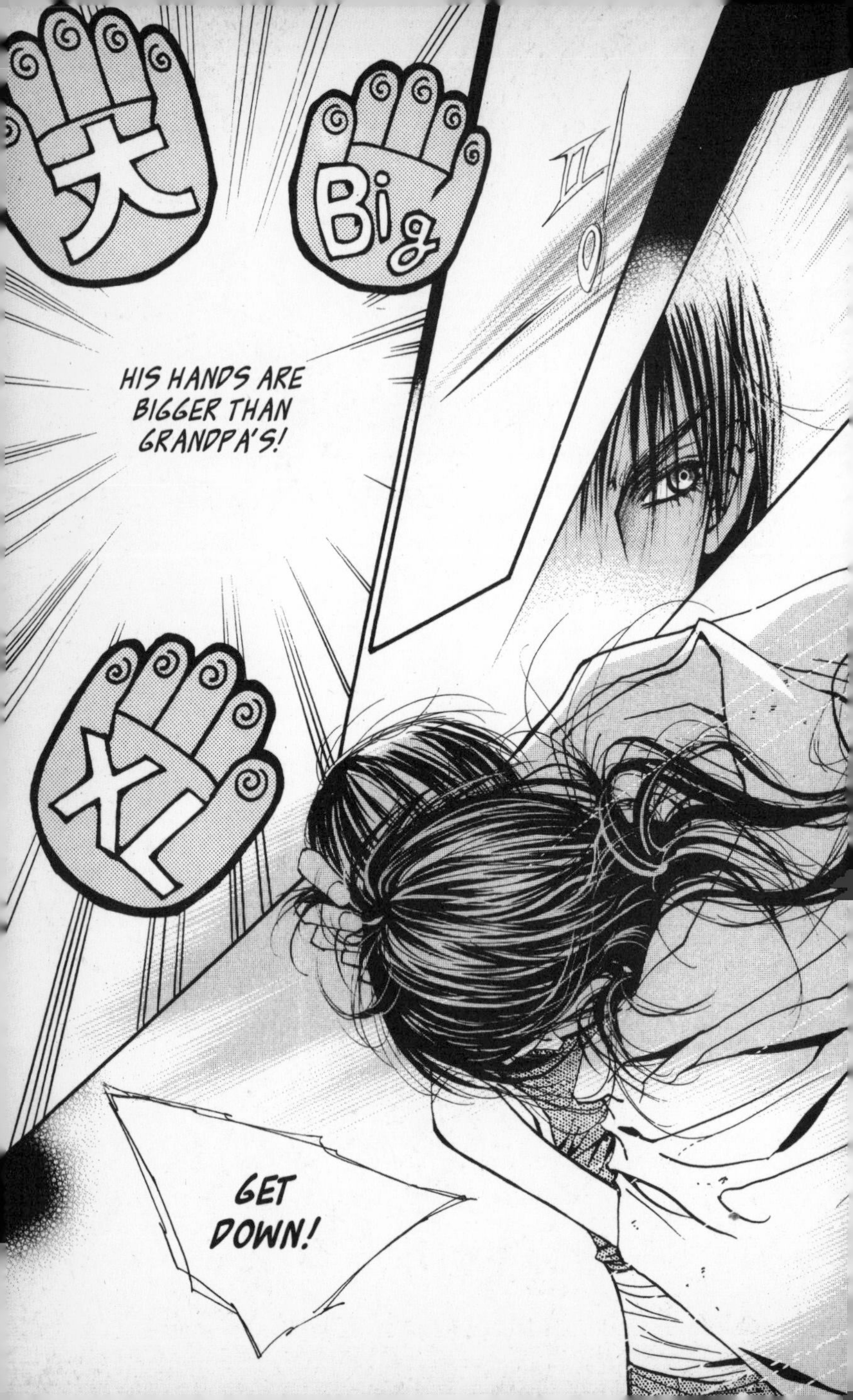
大
Big
大
HIS HANDS ARE BIGGER THAN GRANDPA'S!
GET DOWN!

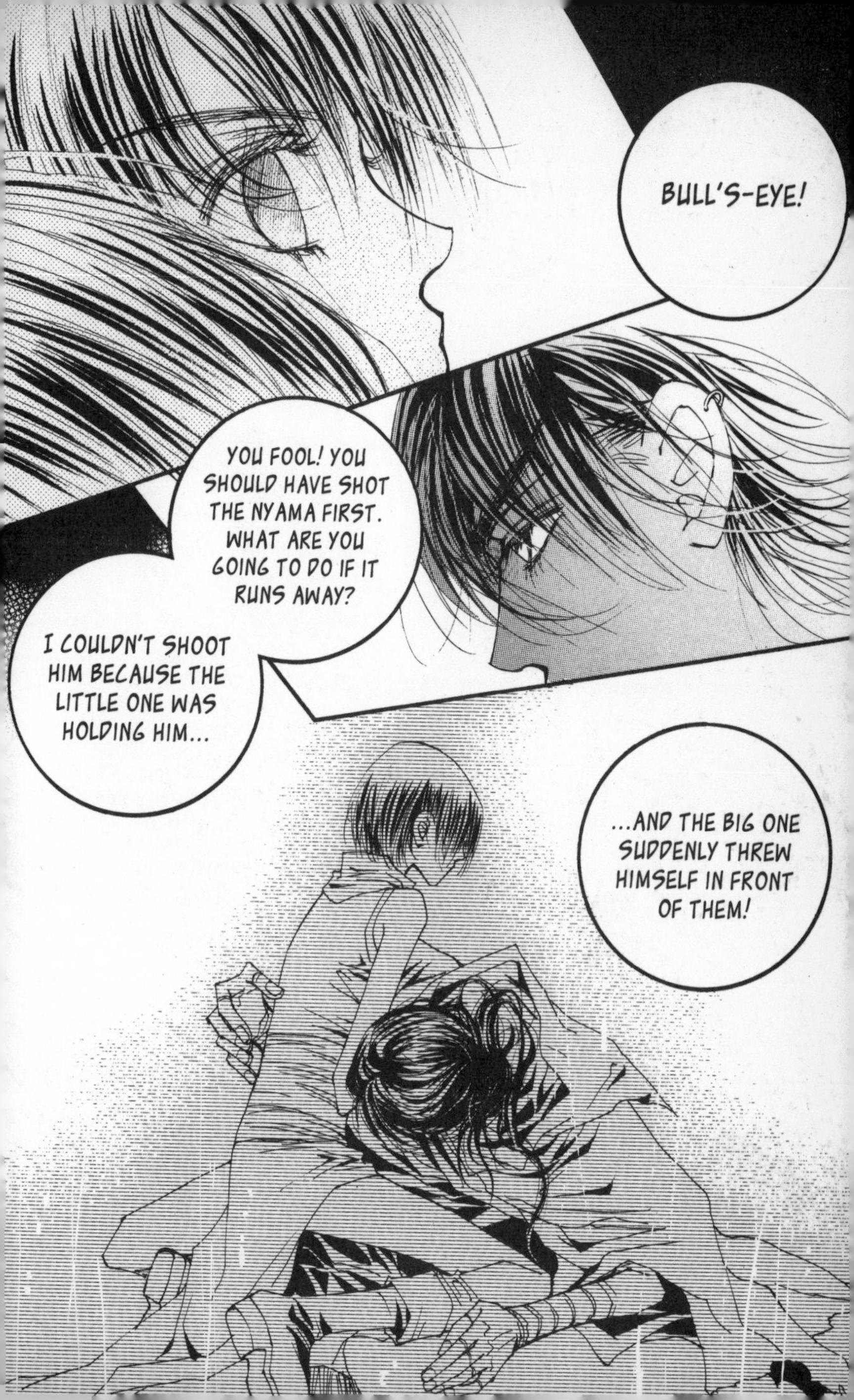
BULL'S-EYE!
YOU FOOL! YOU SHOULD HAVE SHOT THE NYAMA FIRST. WHAT ARE YOU GOING TO DO IF IT RUNS AWAY?
I COULDN'T SHOOT HIM BECAUSE THE LITTLE ONE WAS HOLDING HIM...
...AND THE BIG ONE SUDDENLY THREW HIMSELF IN FRONT OF THEM!

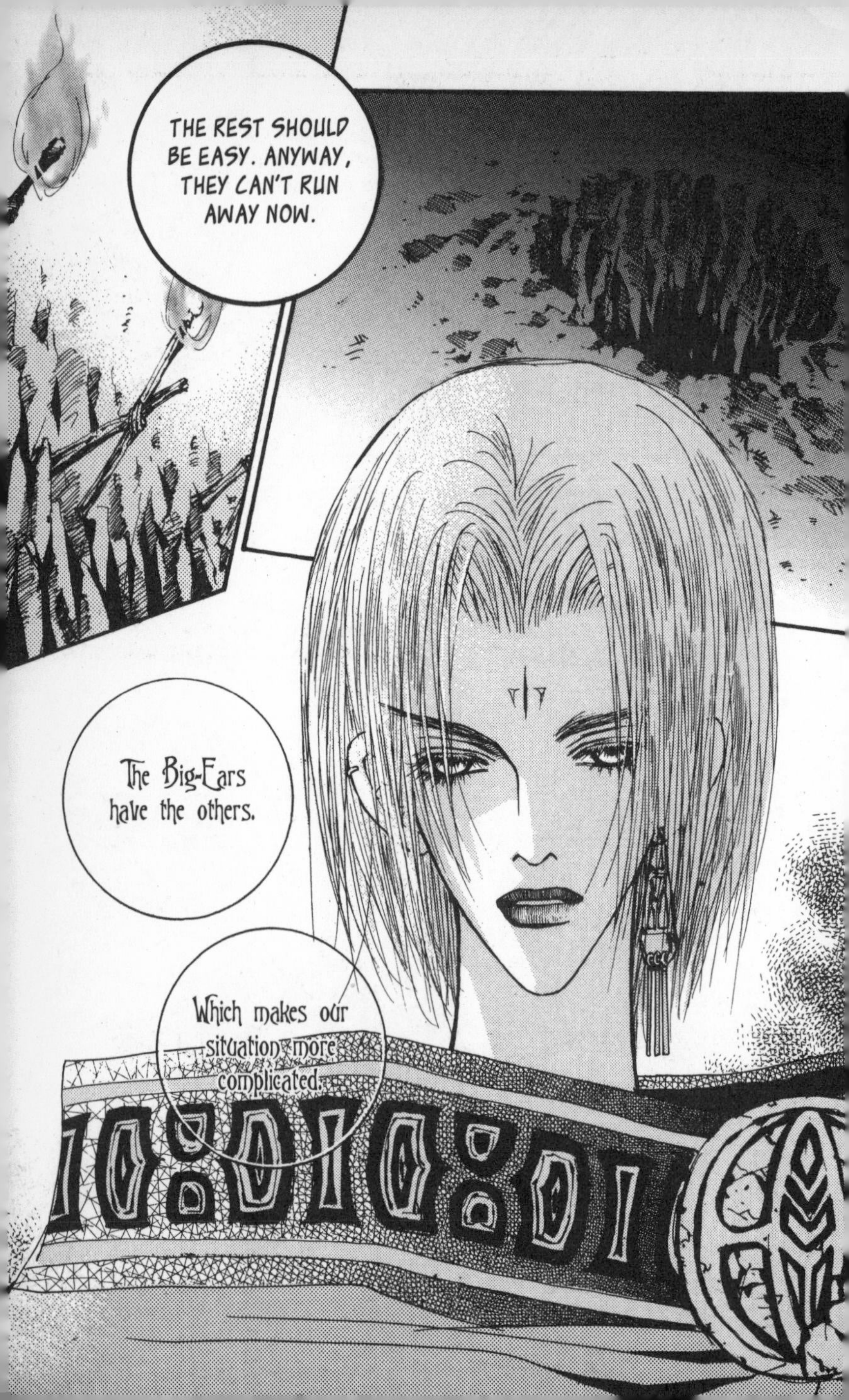
THE REST SHOULD BE EASY. ANYWAY, THEY CAN'T RUN AWAY NOW.
The Big-Ears have the others.
Which makes our situation more complicated.

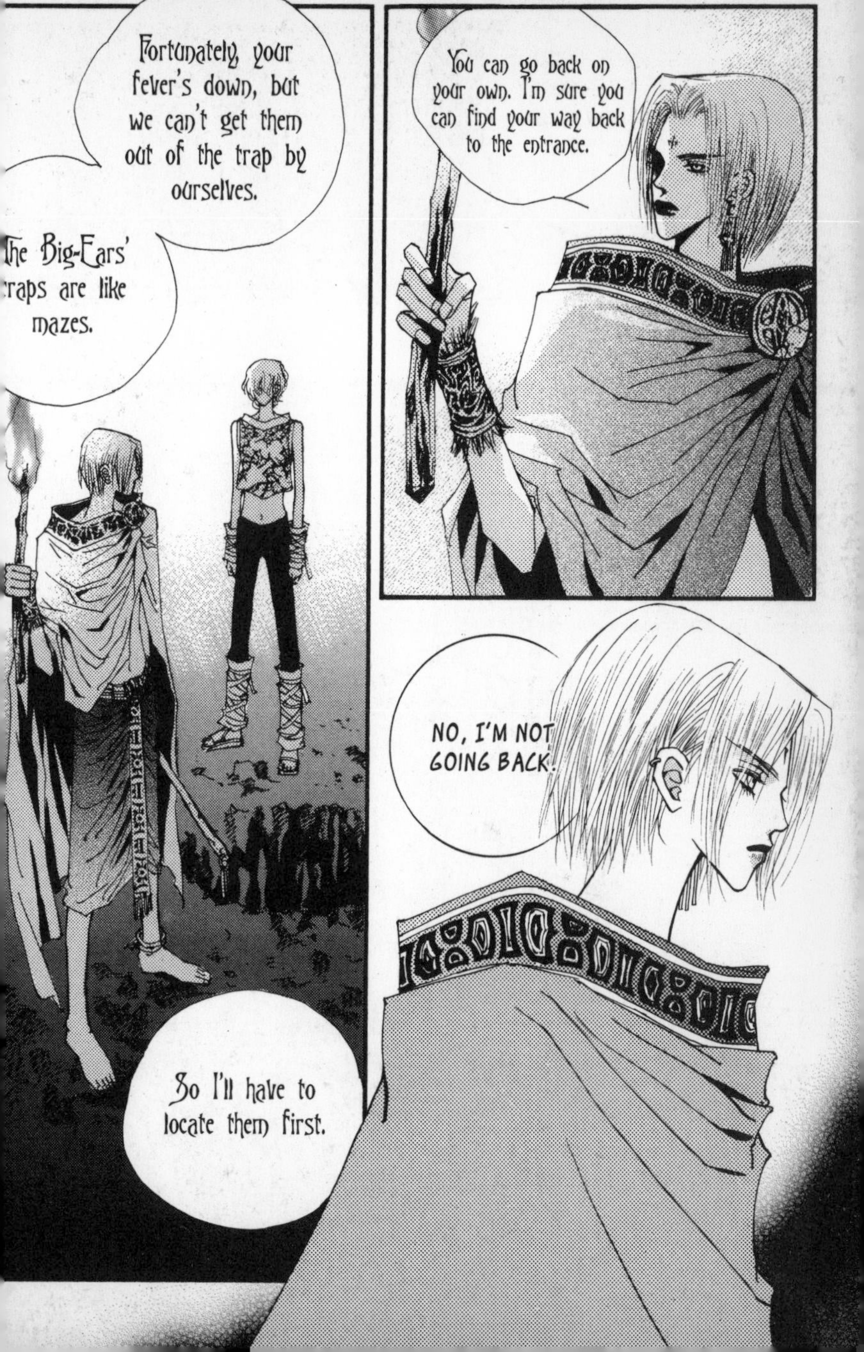
Fortunately, your fever's down, but we can't get them out of the trap by ourselves.
The Big-Ears' traps are like mazes.
So I'll have to locate them first.
You can go back on your own. I'm sure you can find your way back to the entrance.
NO, I'M NOT GOING BACK.

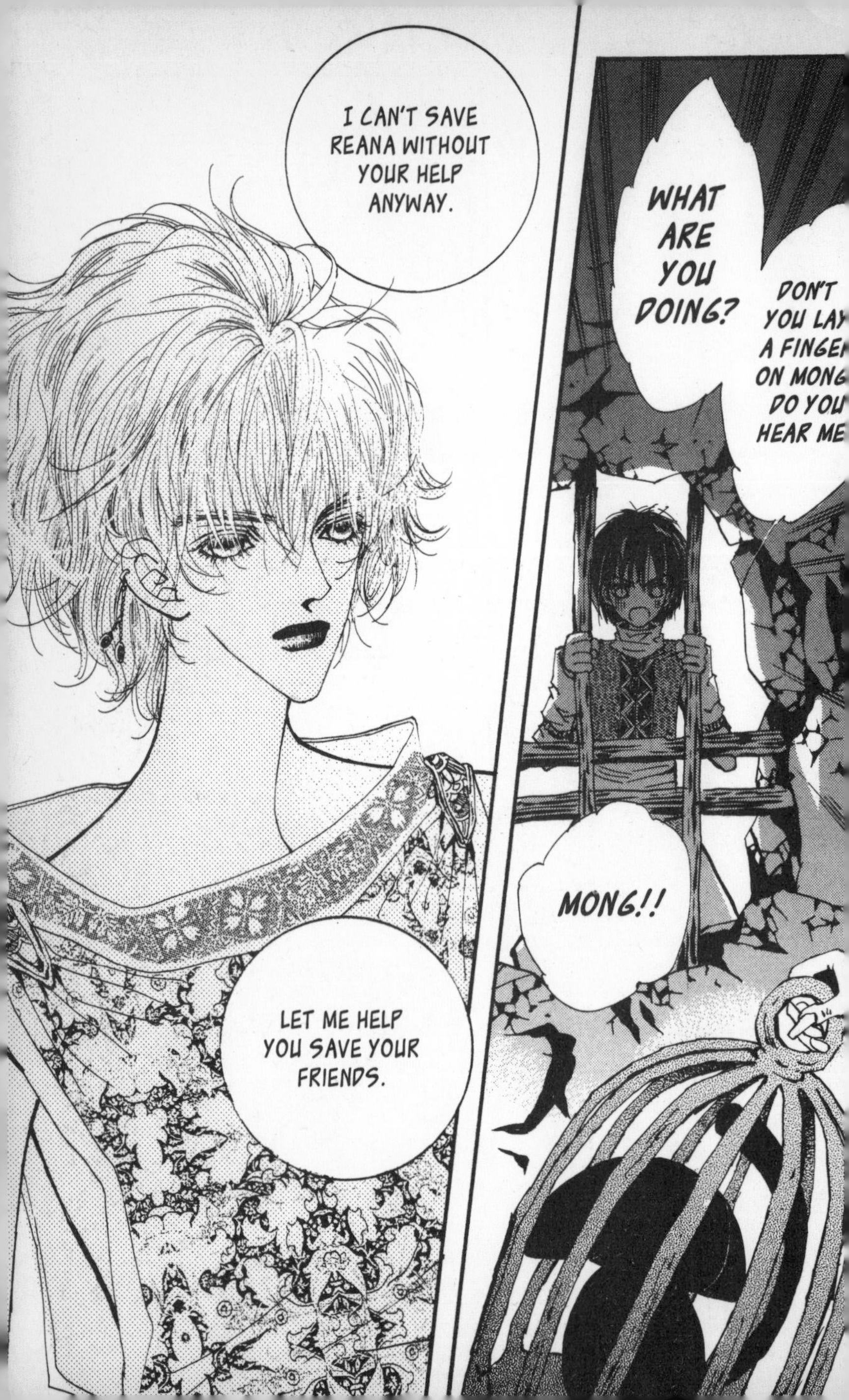
I CAN'T SAVE REANA WITHOUT YOUR HELP ANYWAY.
LET ME HELP YOU SAVE YOUR FRIENDS.
WHAT ARE YOU DOING?
DON'T YOU LAY A FINGER ON MONG DO YOU HEAR ME
MONG!!

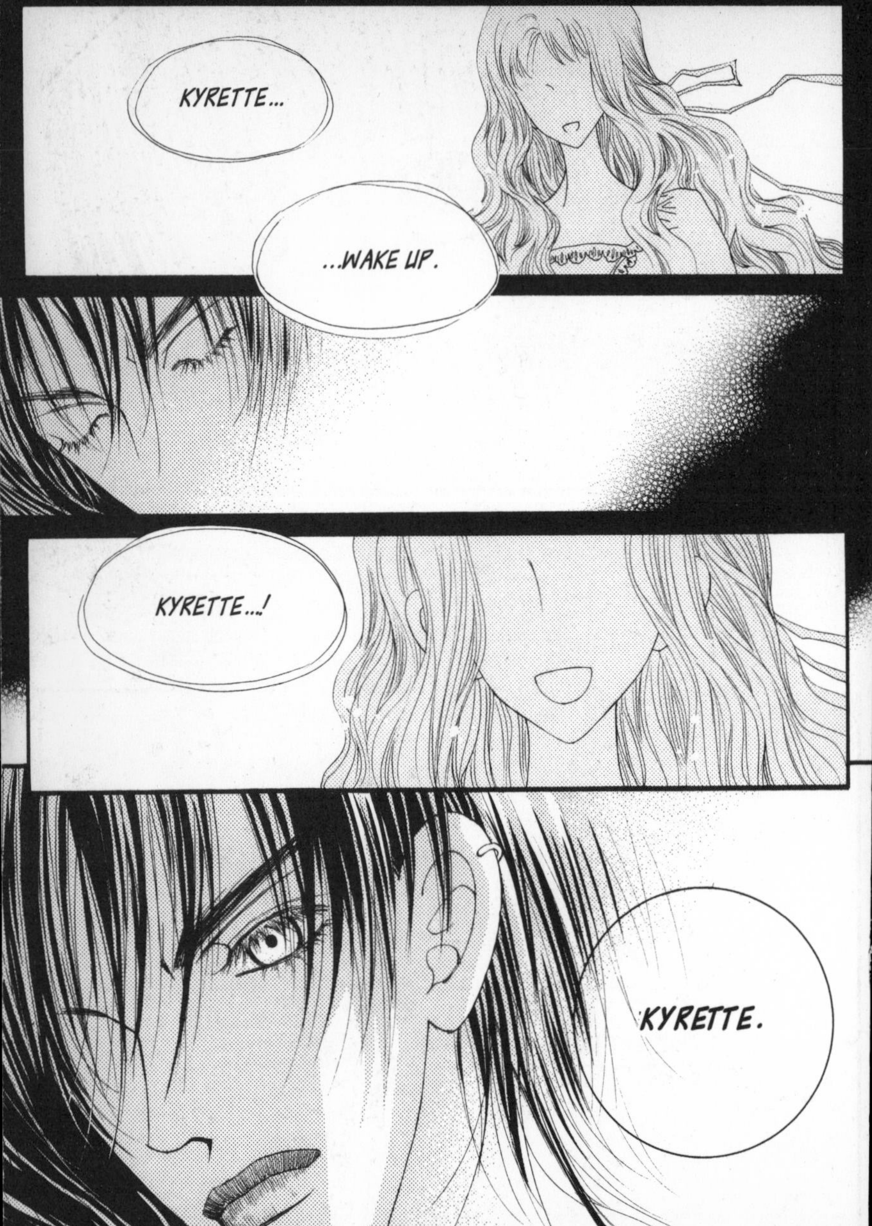

KYRETTE...
...WAKE UP.
KYRETTE...!
KYRETTE.

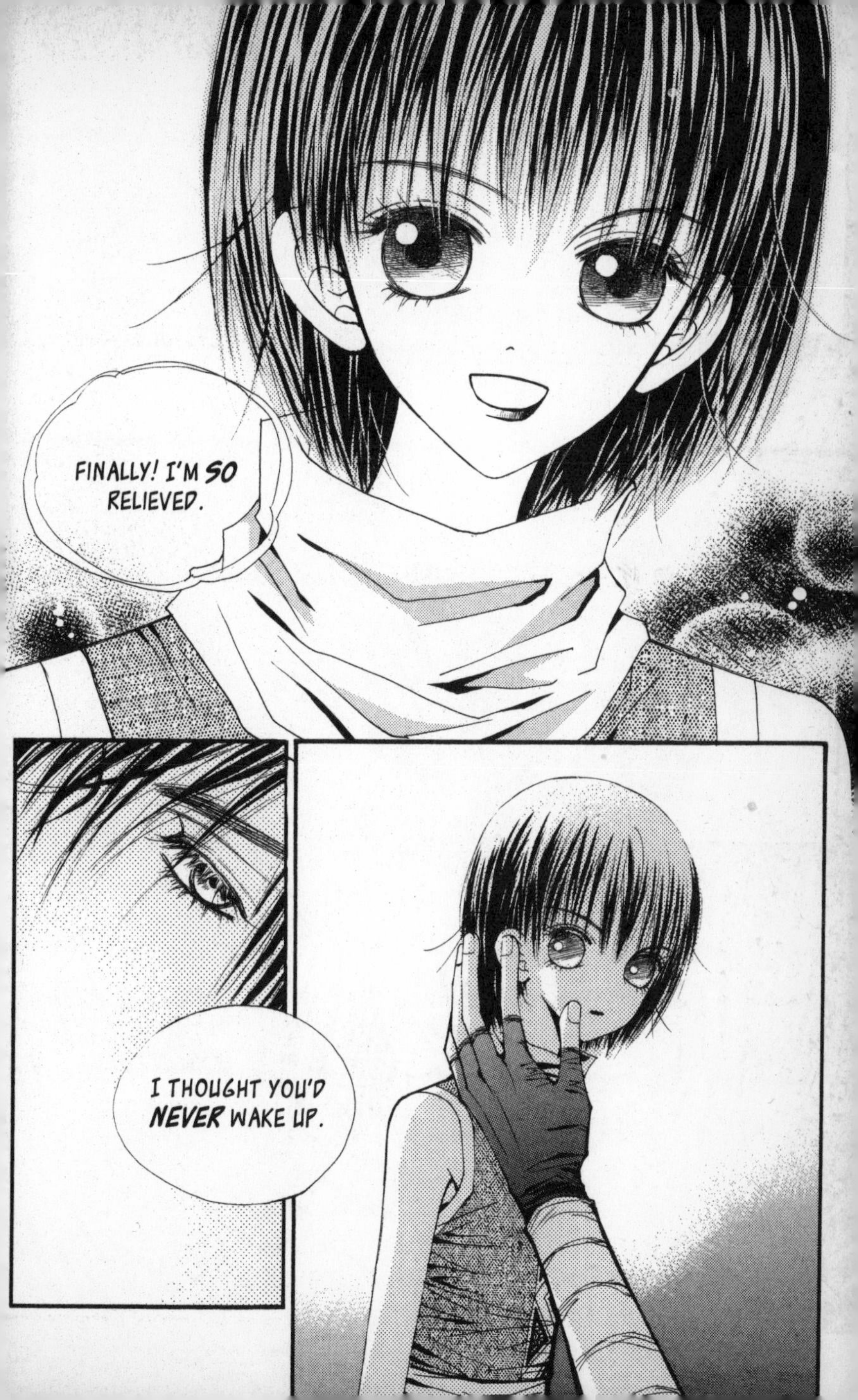
FINALLY! I'M SO RELIEVED.
I THOUGHT YOU'D NEVER WAKE UP.

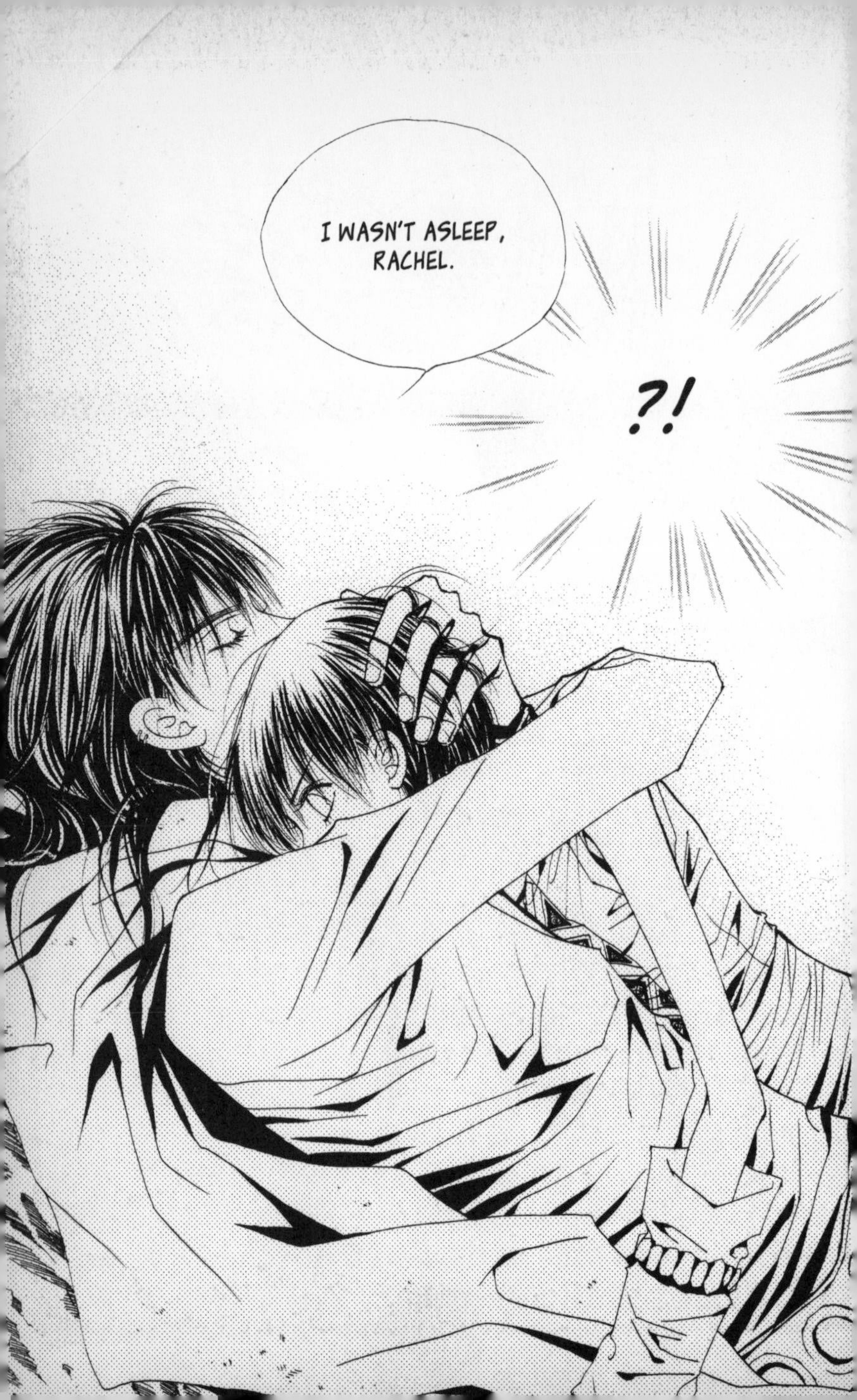
I WASN'T ASLEEP, RACHEL.
?!

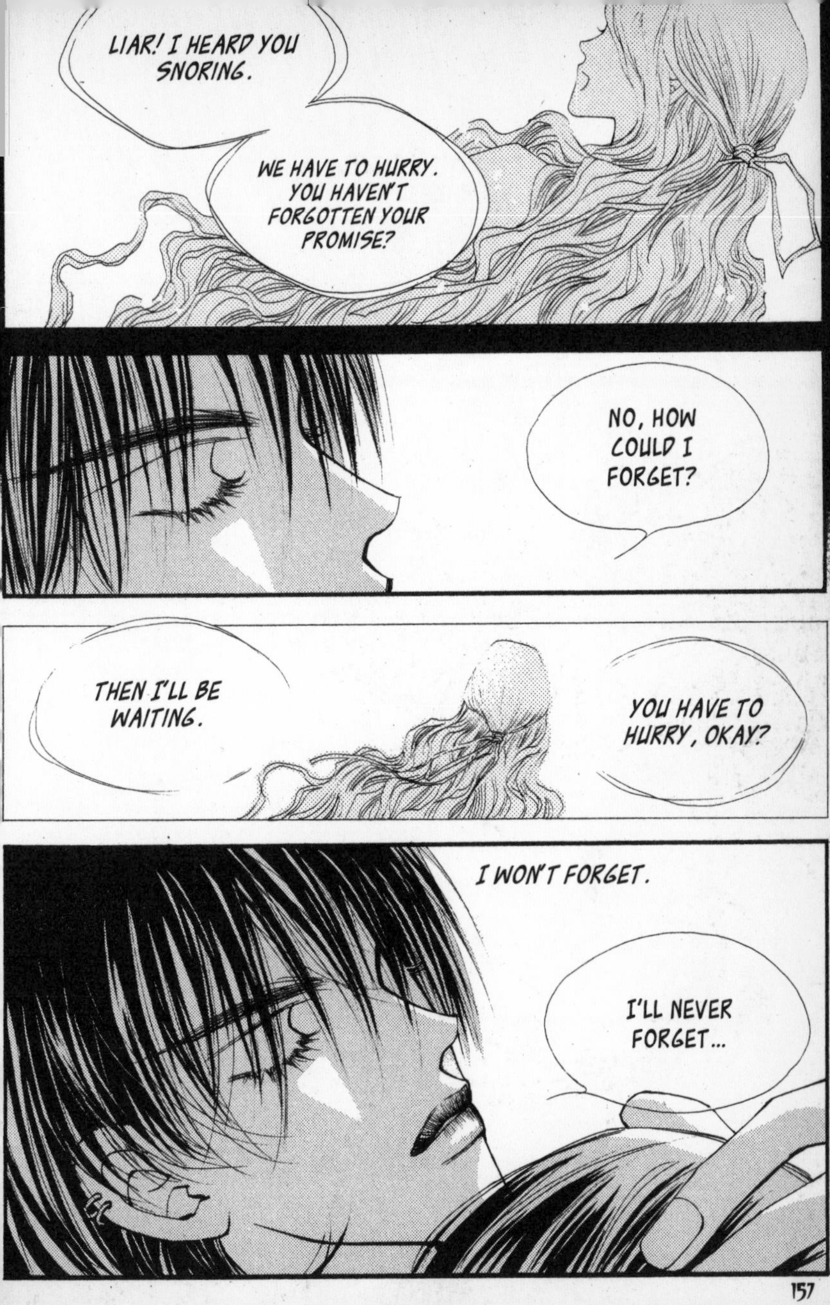

LIAR! I HEARD YOU SNORING.
WE HAVE TO HURRY. YOU HAVEN'T FORGOTTEN YOUR PROMISE?
NO, HOW COULD I FORGET?
THEN I'LL BE WAITING.
YOU HAVE TO HURRY, OKAY?
I WON'T FORGET.
I'LL NEVER FORGET...

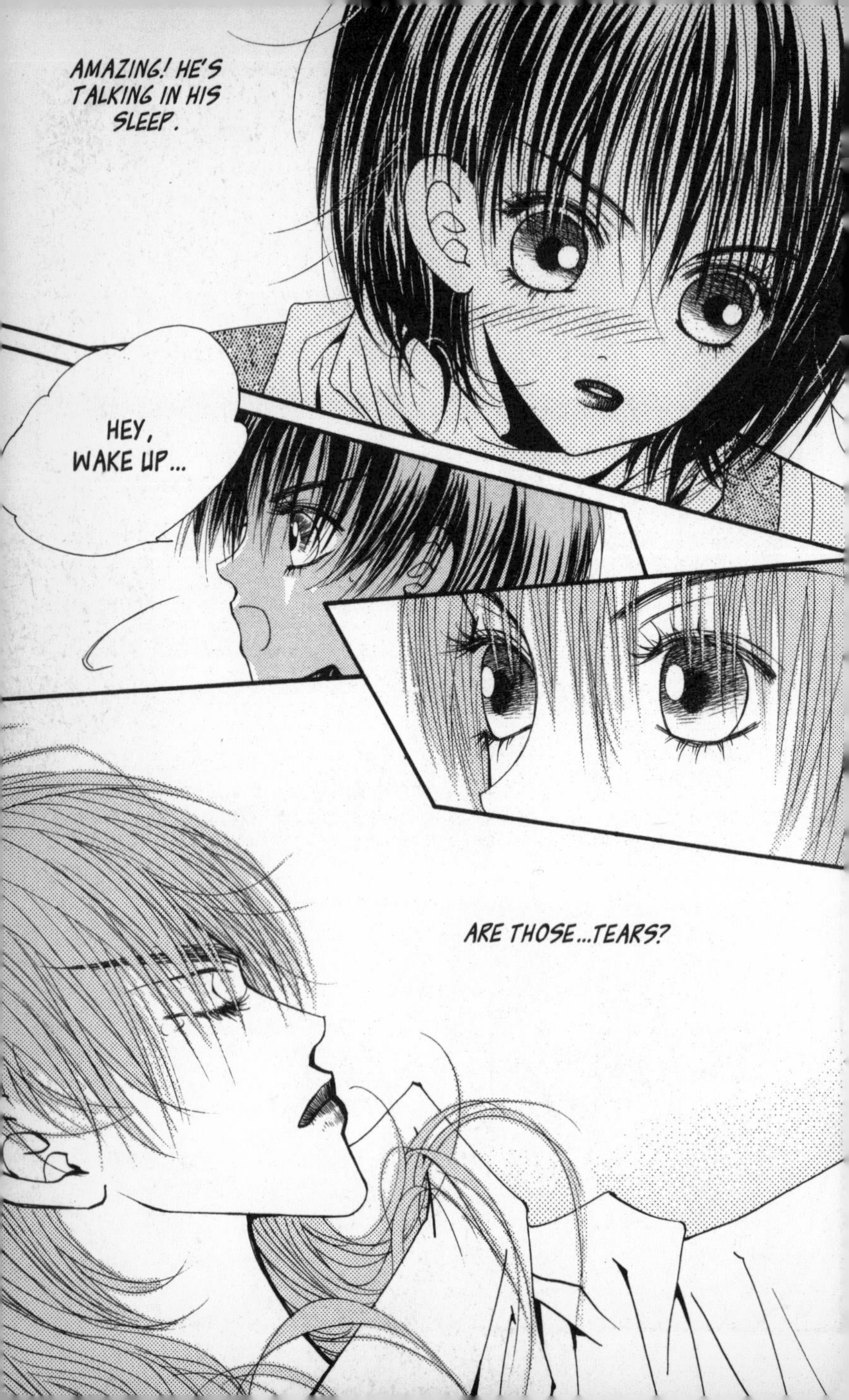
AMAZING! HE'S TALKING IN HIS SLEEP.
HEY, WAKE UP...
ARE THOSE...TEARS?

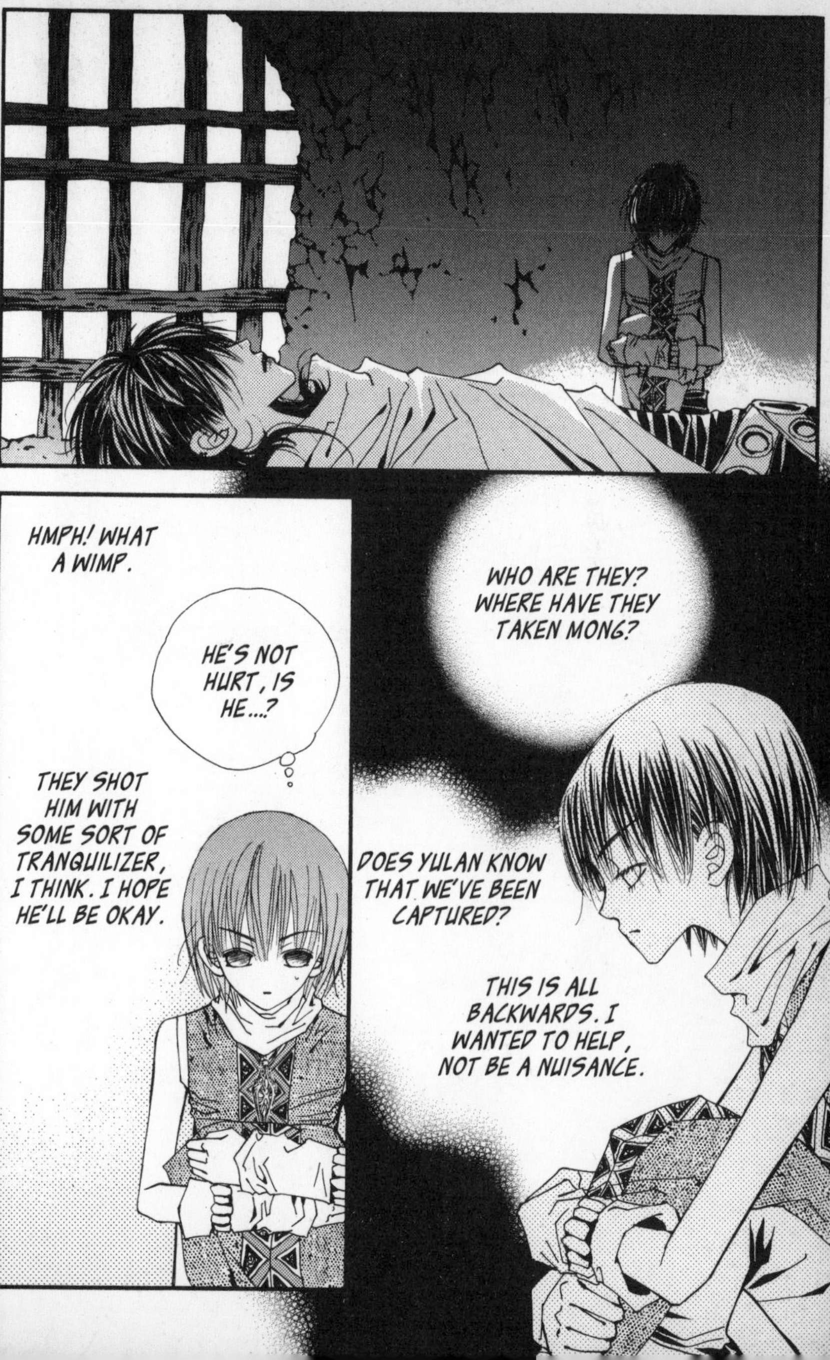
HMPH! WHAT A WIMP.
HE'S NOT HURT, IS HE...?
THEY SHOT HIM WITH SOME SORT OF TRANQUILIZER, I THINK. I HOPE HE'LL BE OKAY.
WHO ARE THEY? WHERE HAVE THEY TAKEN MONG?
DOES YULAN KNOW THAT WE'VE BEEN CAPTURED?
THIS IS ALL BACKWARDS. I WANTED TO HELP, NOT BE A NUISANCE.

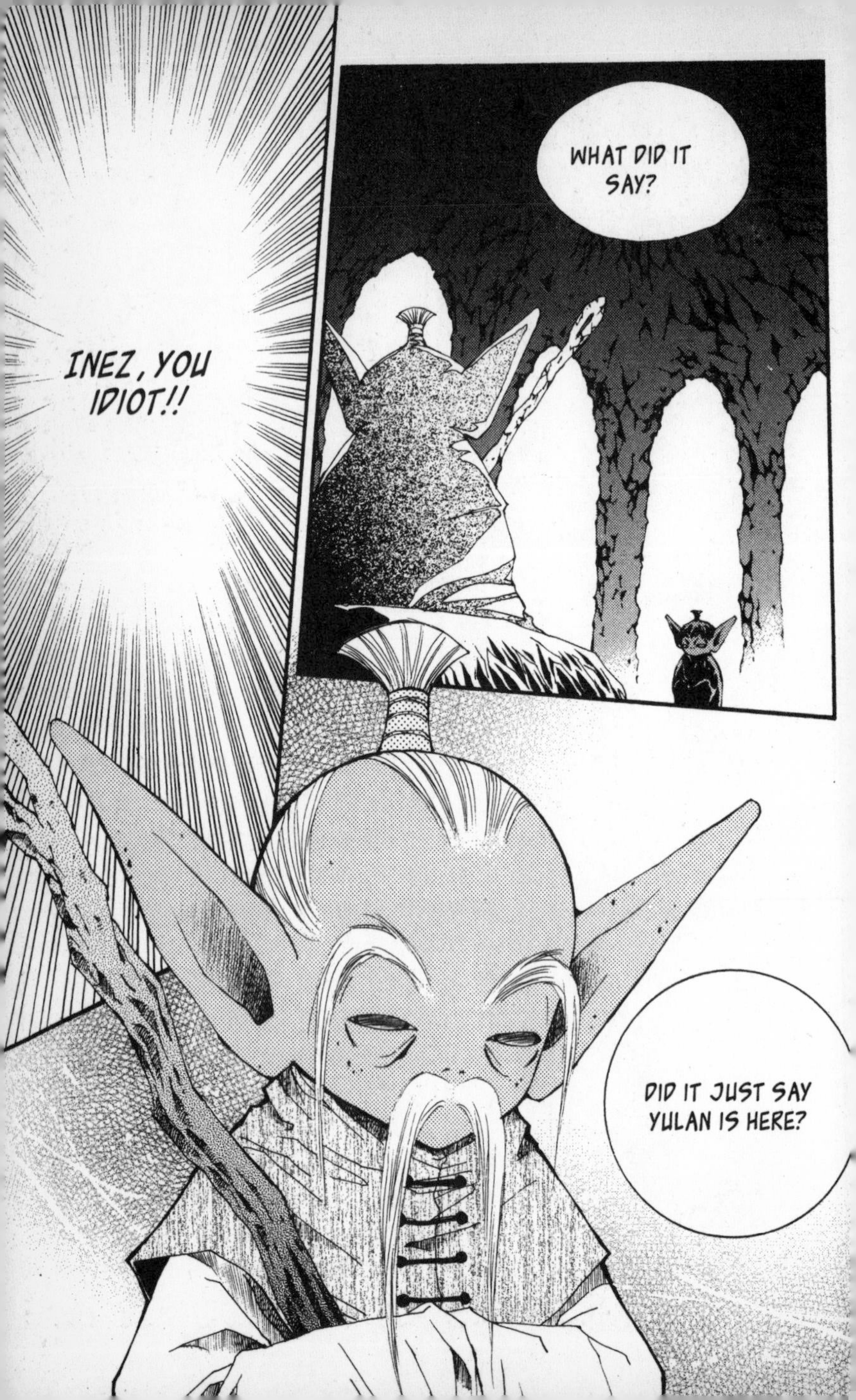
INEZ, YOU IDIOT!!
WHAT DID IT SAY?
DID IT JUST SAY YULAN IS HERE?

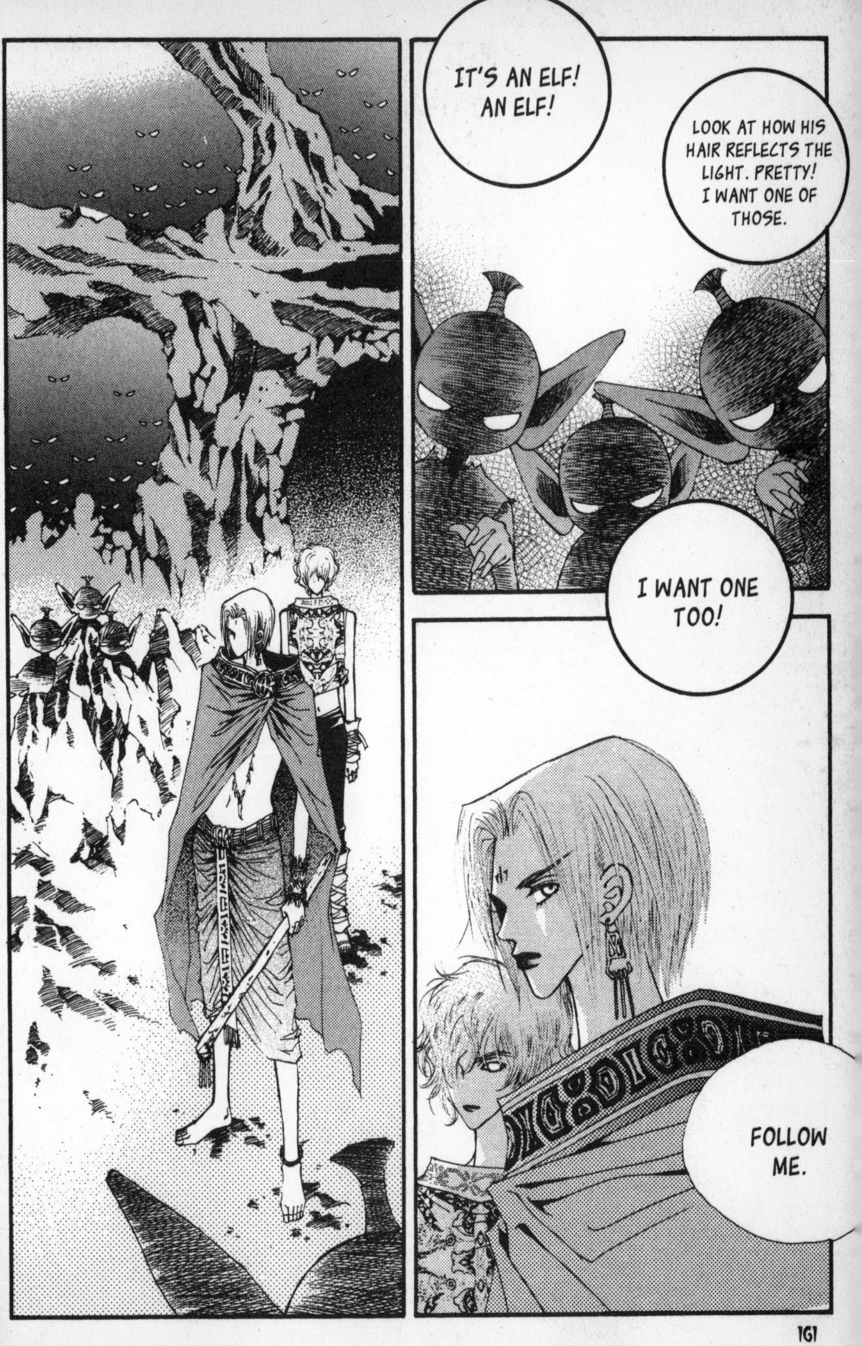
IT'S AN ELF! AN ELF!
LOOK AT HOW HIS HAIR REFLECTS THE LIGHT. PRETTY! I WANT ONE OF THOSE.
I WANT ONE TOO!
FOLLOW ME.

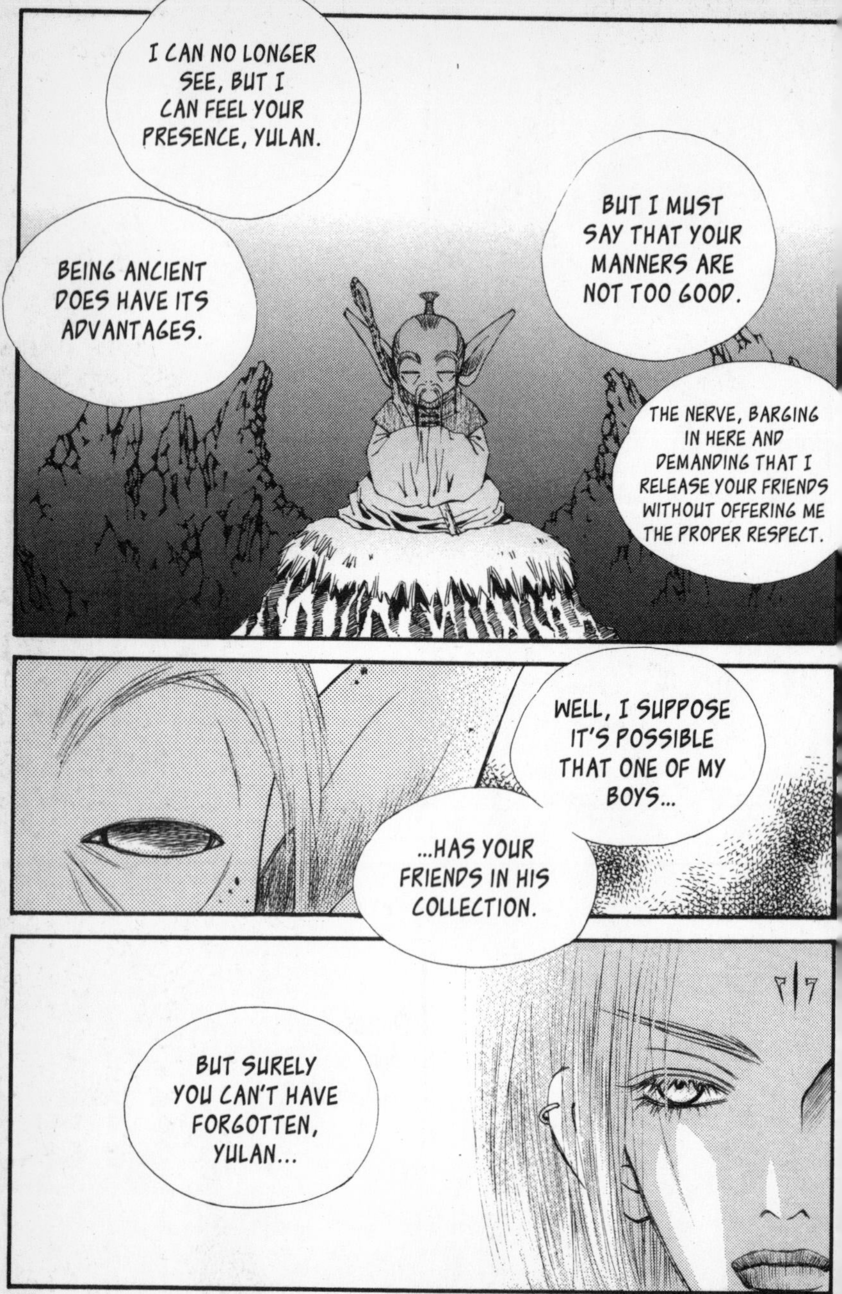
I CAN NO LONGER SEE, BUT I CAN FEEL YOUR PRESENCE, YULAN.
BEING ANCIENT DOES HAVE ITS ADVANTAGES.
BUT I MUST SAY THAT YOUR MANNERS ARE NOT TOO GOOD.
THE NERVE, BARGING IN HERE AND DEMANDING THAT I RELEASE YOUR FRIENDS WITHOUT OFFERING ME THE PROPER RESPECT.
WELL, I SUPPOSE IT'S POSSIBLE THAT ONE OF MY BOYS...
...HAS YOUR FRIENDS IN HIS COLLECTION.
BUT SURELY YOU CAN'T HAVE FORGOTTEN, YULAN...

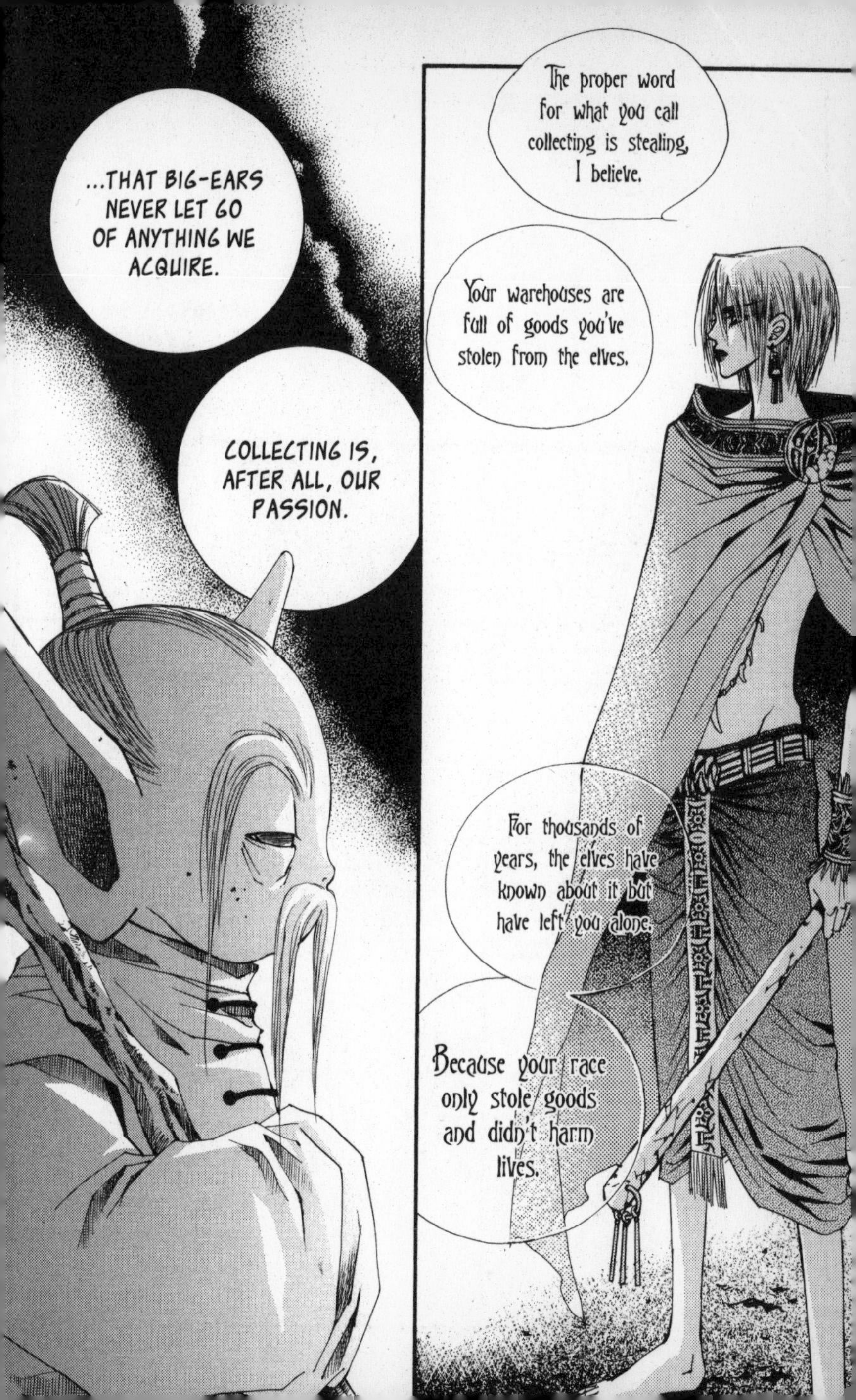
...THAT BIG-EARS NEVER LET GO OF ANYTHING WE ACQUIRE.
COLLECTING IS, AFTER ALL, OUR PASSION.
The proper word for what you call collecting is stealing, I believe.
Your warehouses are full of goods you've stolen from the elves.
For thousands of years, the elves have known about it but have left you alone.
Because your race only stole goods and didn't harm lives.

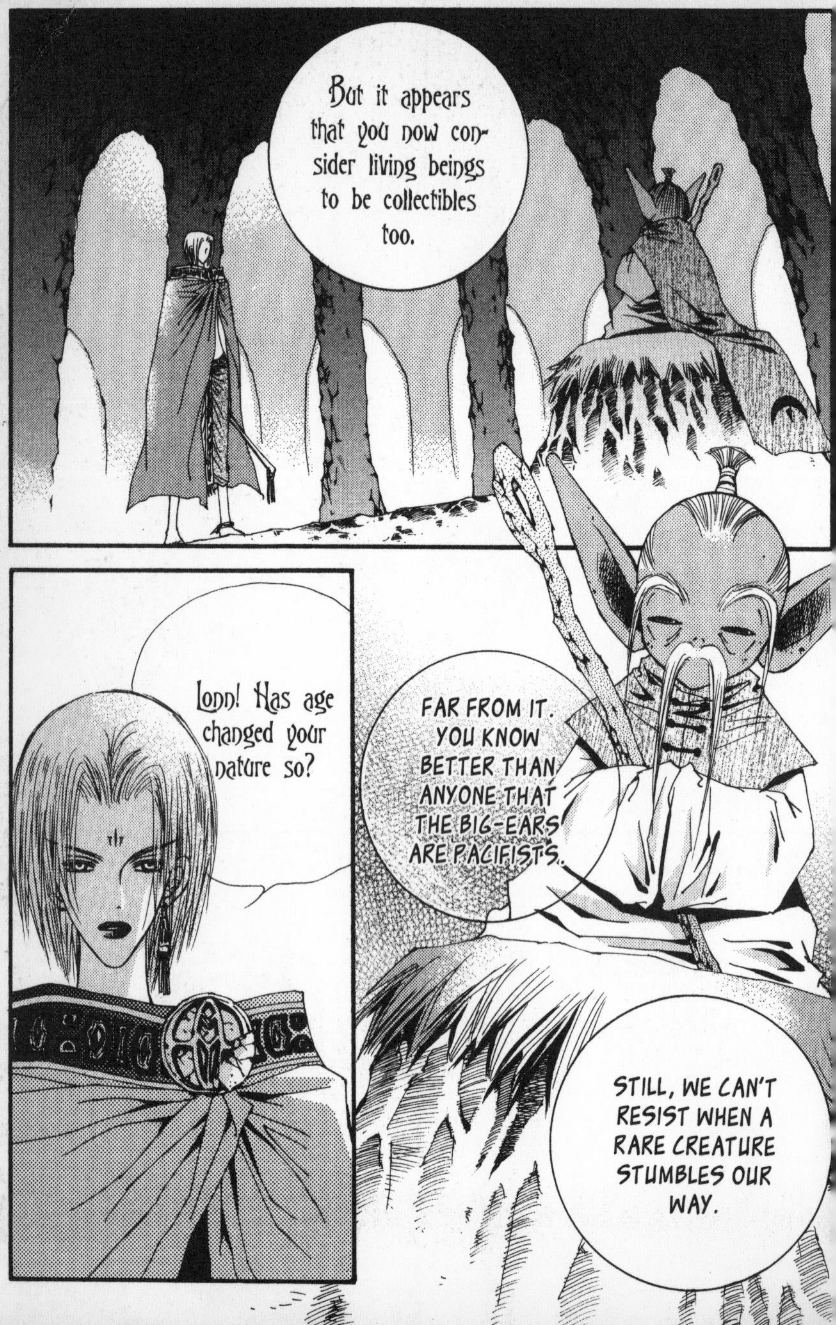
But it appears that you now consider living beings to be collectibles too.
Lonn! Has age changed your nature so?
FAR FROM IT. YOU KNOW BETTER THAN ANYONE THAT THE BIG-EARS ARE PACIFISTS.
STILL, WE CAN'T RESIST WHEN A RARE CREATURE STUMBLES OUR WAY.

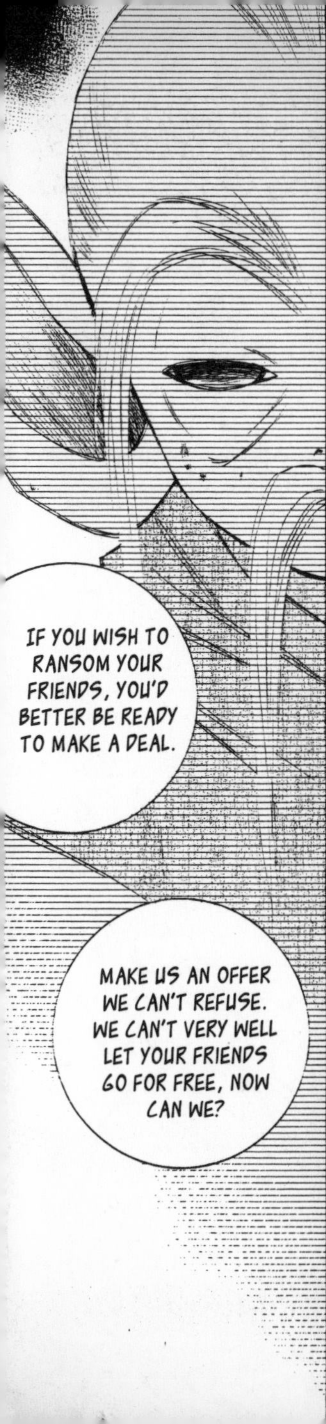
IF YOU WISH TO RANSOM YOUR FRIENDS, YOU'D BETTER BE READY TO MAKE A DEAL.
MAKE US AN OFFER WE CAN'T REFUSE. WE CAN'T VERY WELL LET YOUR FRIENDS GO FOR FREE, NOW CAN WE?
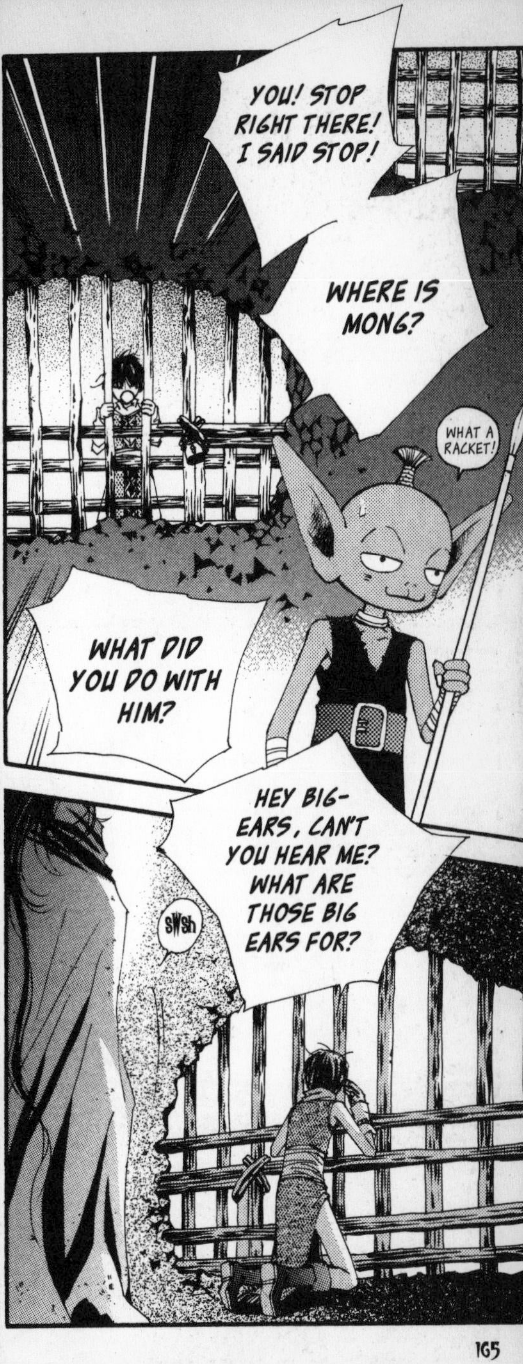
YOU! STOP RIGHT THERE! I SAID STOP!
WHERE IS MONG?
WHAT A RACKET!
WHAT DID YOU DO WITH HIM?
HEY BIG-EARS, CAN'T YOU HEAR ME? WHAT ARE THOSE BIG EARS FOR?
SWSH

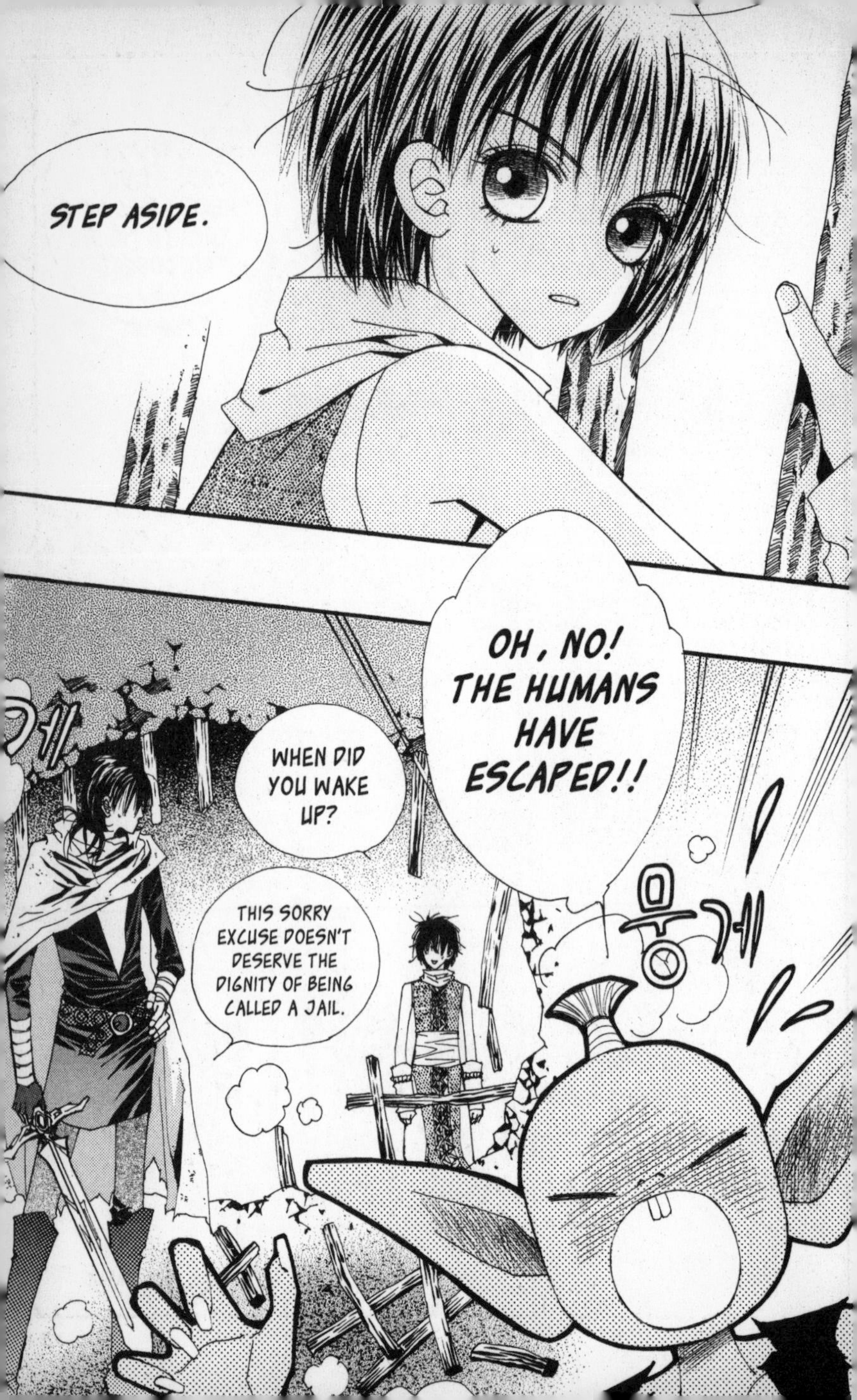

STEP ASIDE.
OH, NO! THE HUMANS HAVE ESCAPED!!
WHEN DID YOU WAKE UP?
THIS SORRY EXCUSE DOESN'T DESERVE THE DIGNITY OF BEING CALLED A JAIL.
웅게

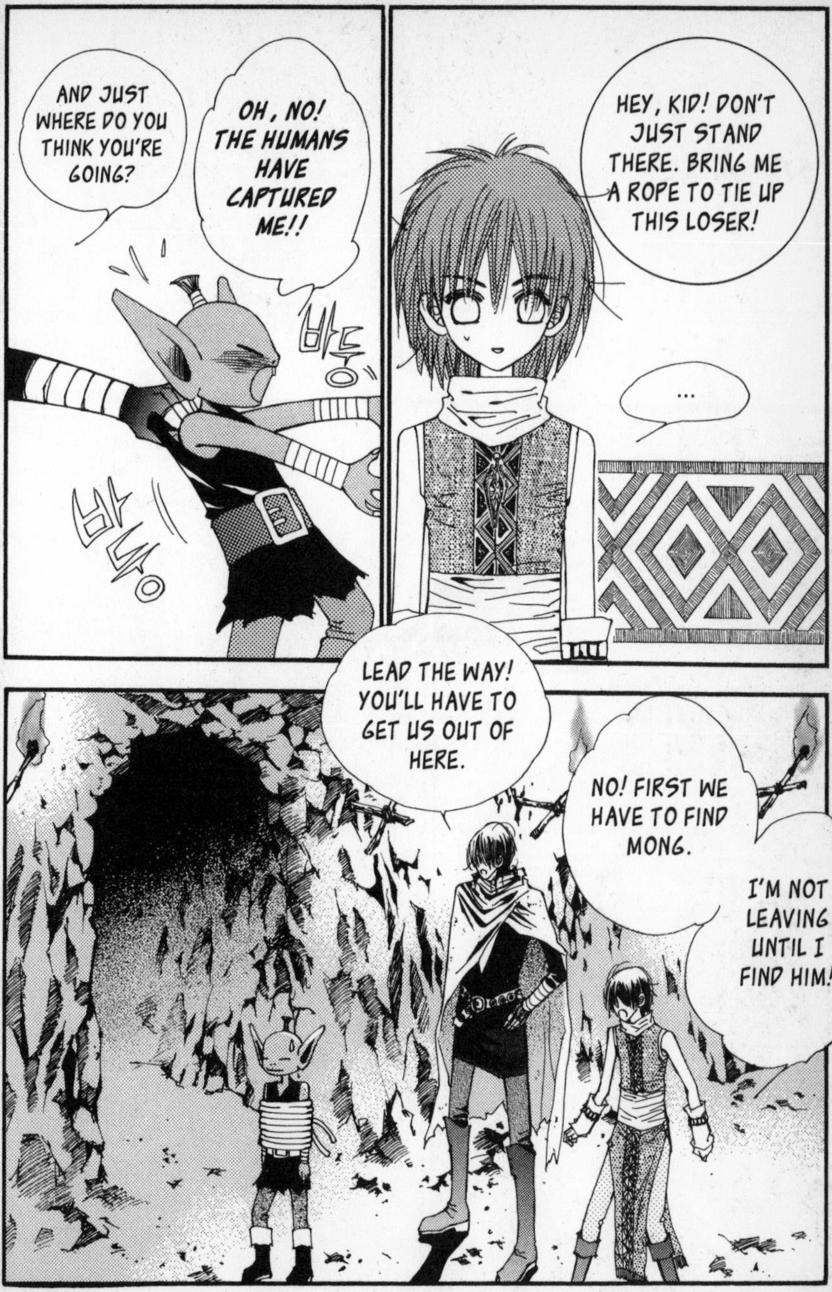

AND JUST WHERE DO YOU THINK YOU'RE GOING?
OH, NO! THE HUMANS HAVE CAPTURED ME!!
바둥
바둥
HEY, KID! DON'T JUST STAND THERE. BRING ME A ROPE TO TIE UP THIS LOSER!
...
LEAD THE WAY! YOU'LL HAVE TO GET US OUT OF HERE.
NO! FIRST WE HAVE TO FIND MONG.
I'M NOT LEAVING UNTIL I FIND HIM!

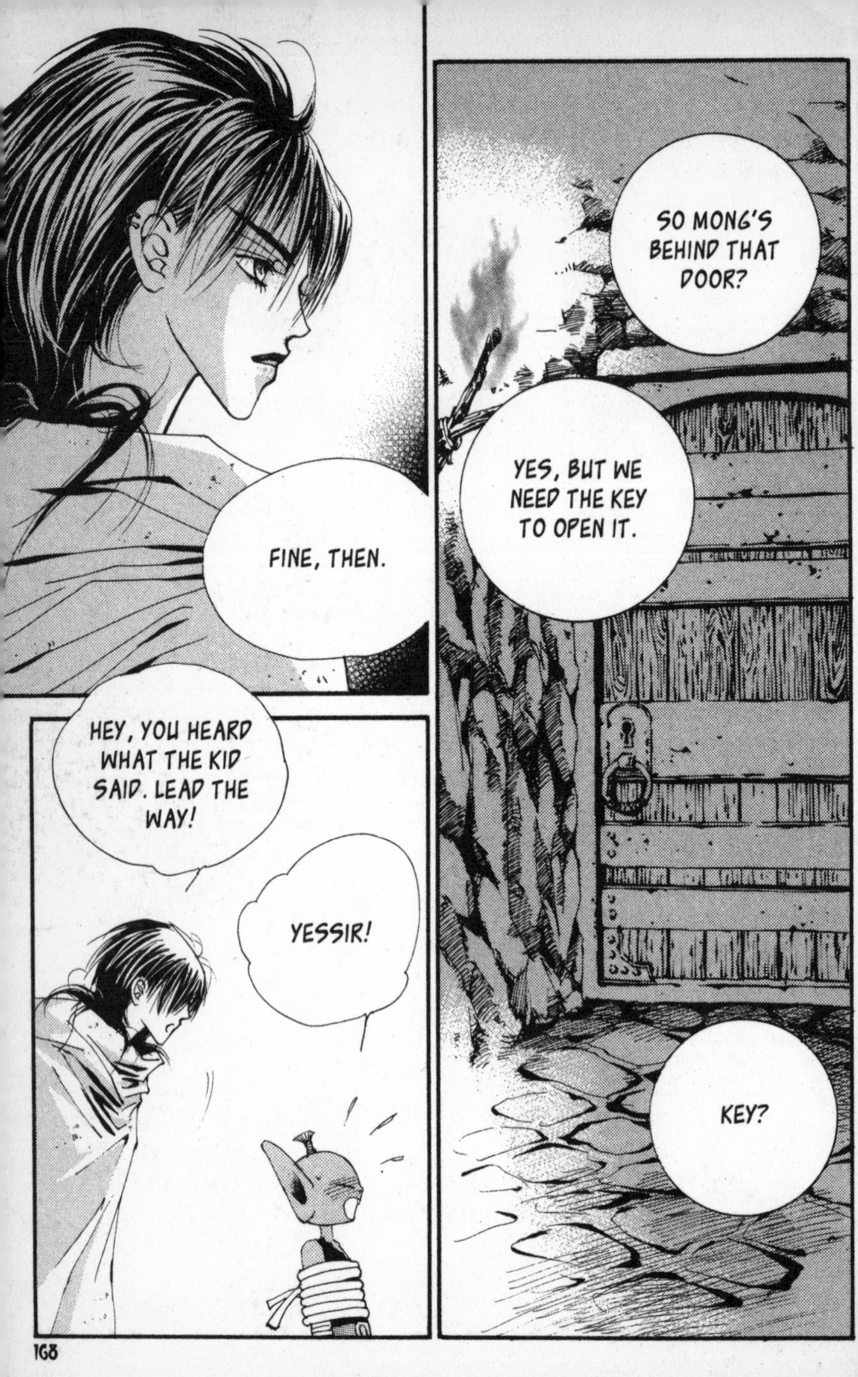
FINE, THEN.
HEY, YOU HEARD WHAT THE KID SAID. LEAD THE WAY!
YESSIR!
SO MONG'S BEHIND THAT DOOR?
YES, BUT WE NEED THE KEY TO OPEN IT.
KEY?

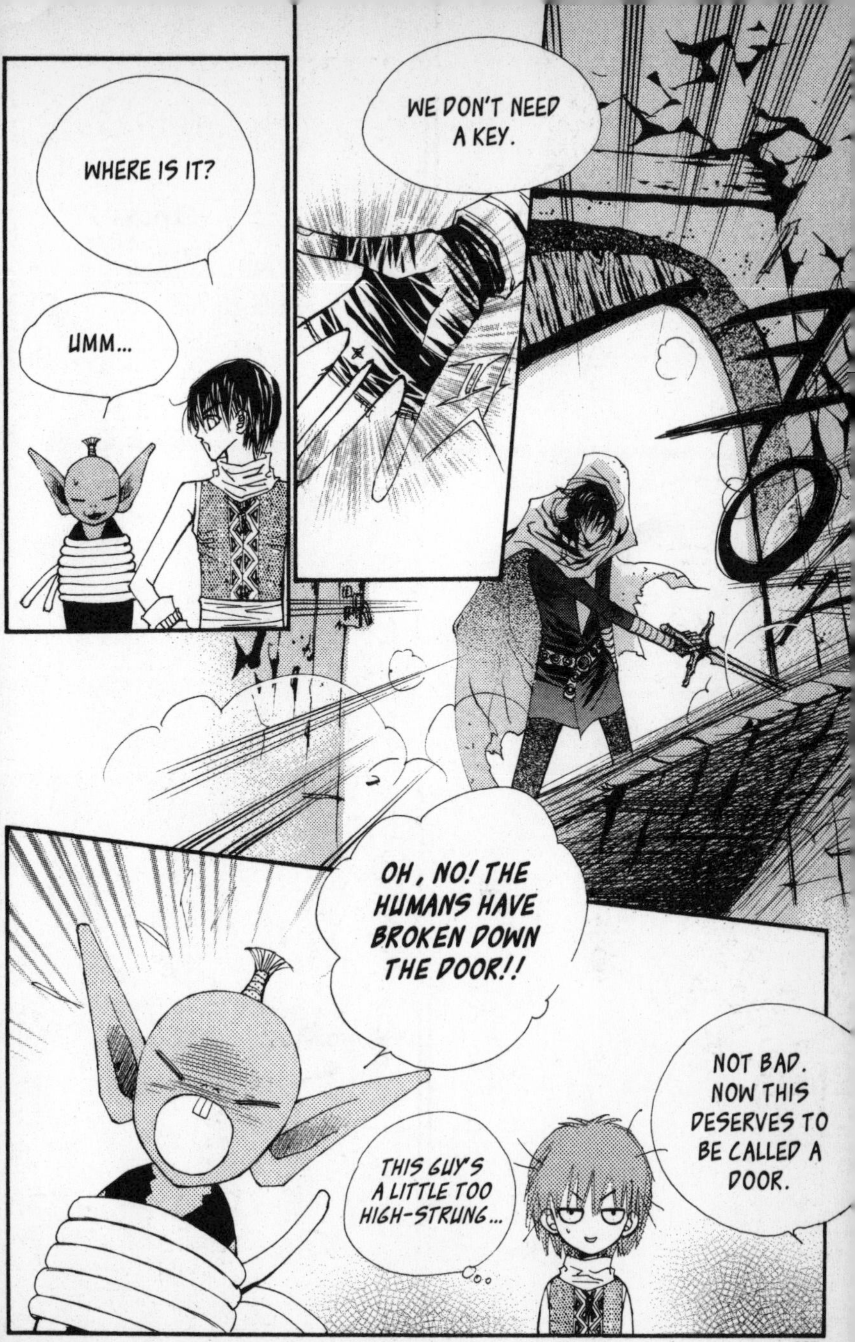
WHERE IS IT?
UMM...
WE DON'T NEED A KEY.
OH, NO! THE HUMANS HAVE BROKEN DOWN THE DOOR!!
THIS GUY'S A LITTLE TOO HIGH-STRUNG...
NOT BAD. NOW THIS DESERVES TO BE CALLED A DOOR.

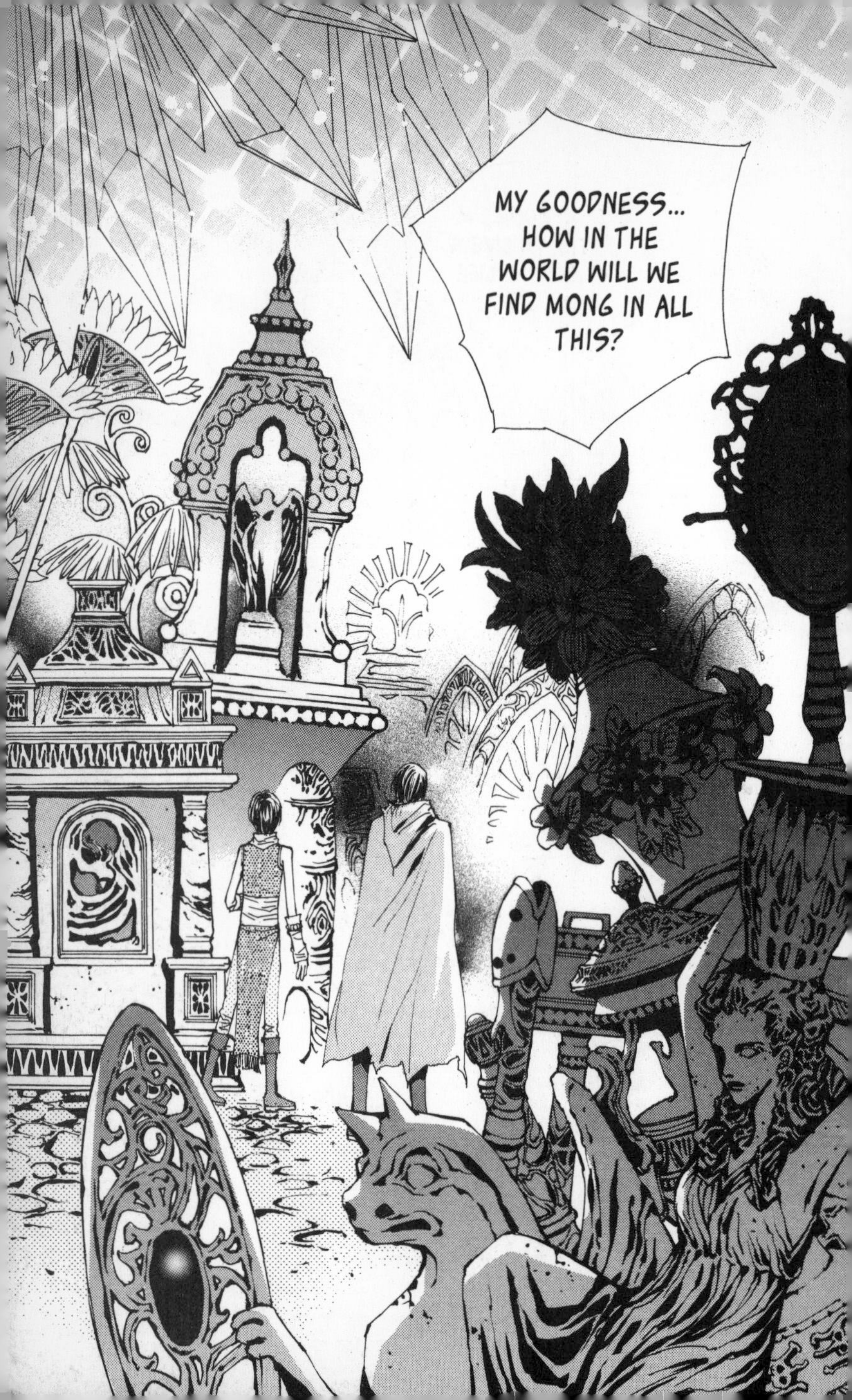
MY GOODNESS... HOW IN THE WORLD WILL WE FIND MONG IN ALL THIS?

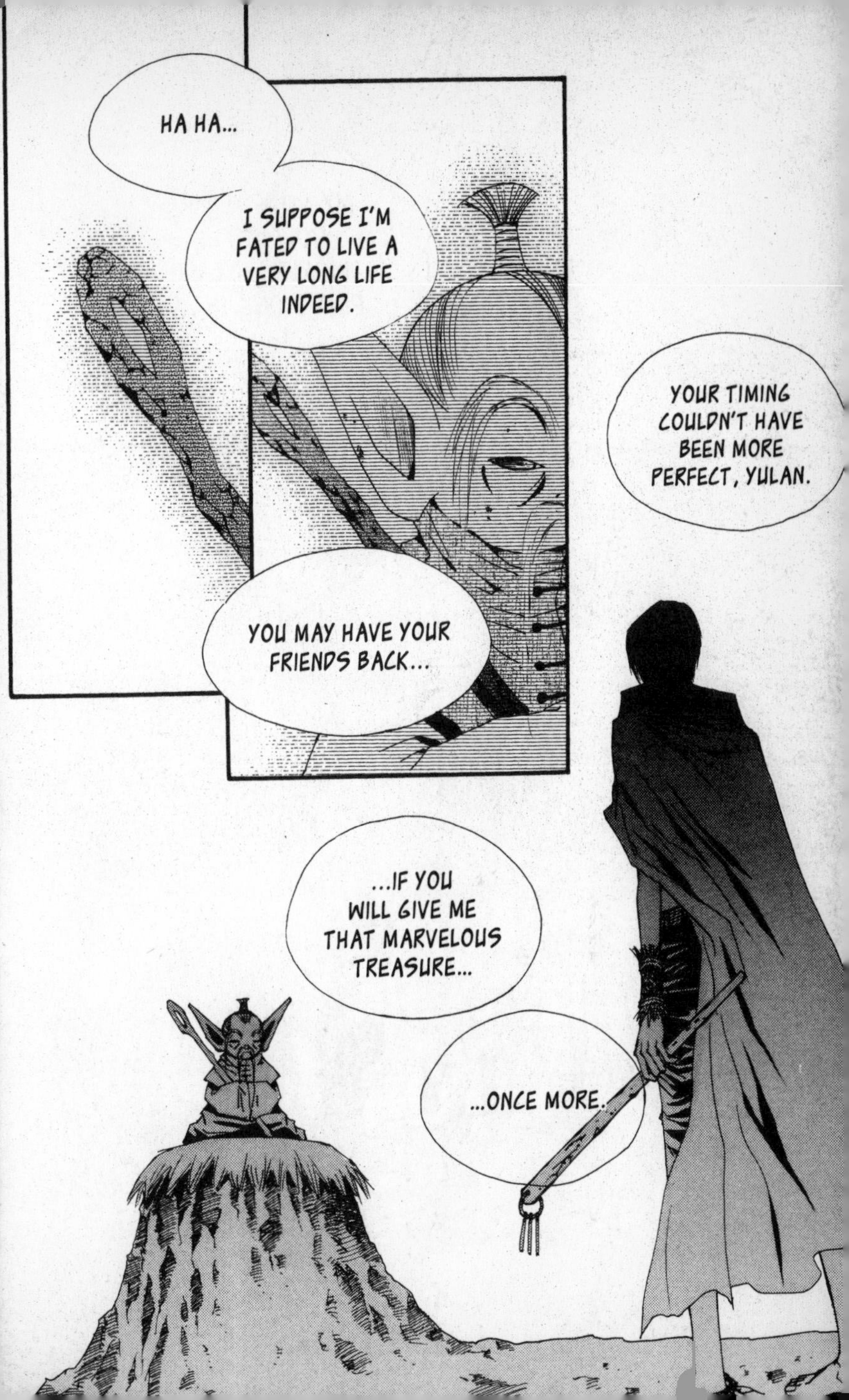
HA HA...
I SUPPOSE I'M FATED TO LIVE A VERY LONG LIFE INDEED.
YOUR TIMING COULDN'T HAVE BEEN MORE PERFECT, YULAN.
YOU MAY HAVE YOUR FRIENDS BACK...
...IF YOU WILL GIVE ME THAT MARVELOUS TREASURE...
...ONCE MORE.

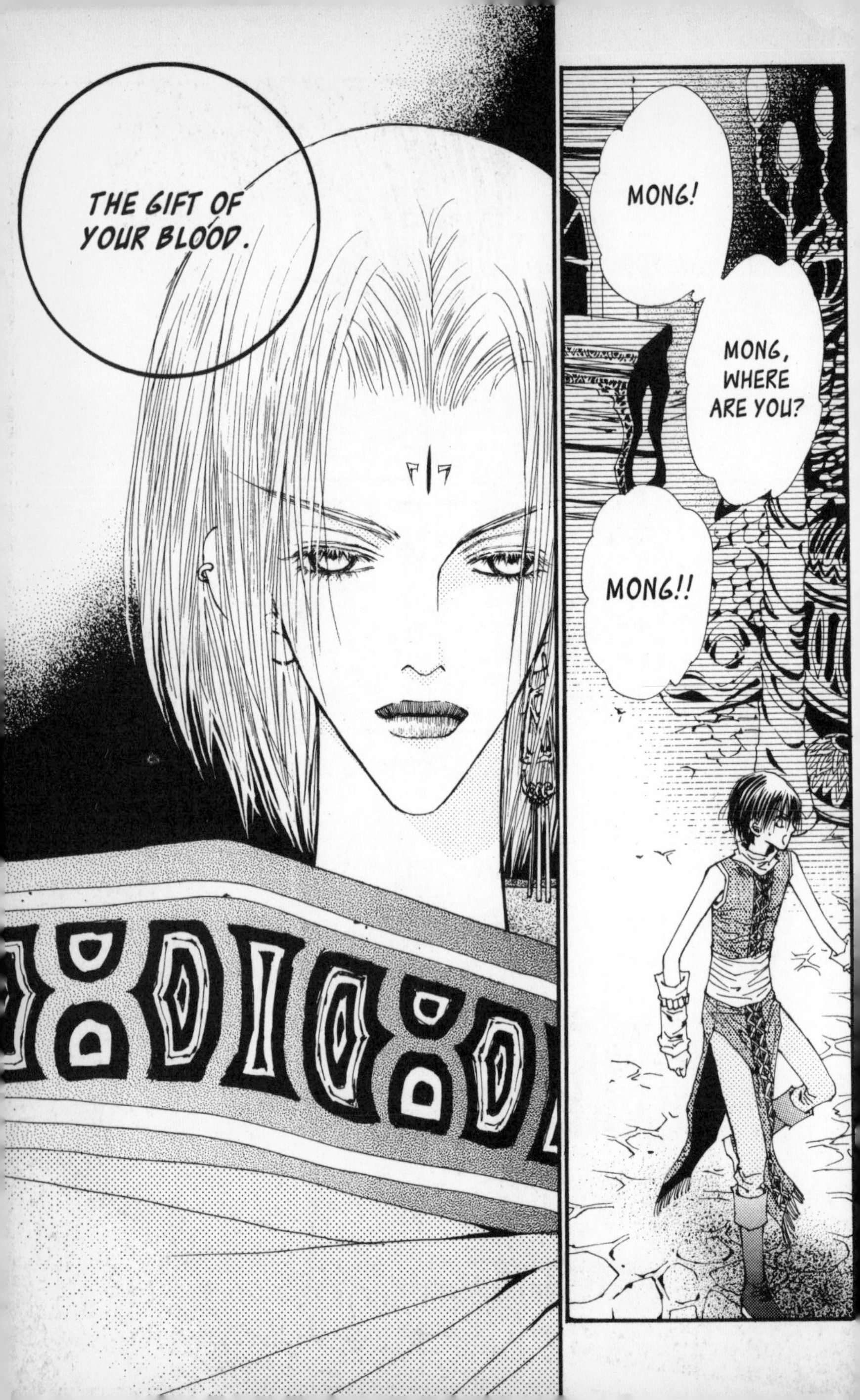
THE GIFT OF YOUR BLOOD.
MONG!
MONG, WHERE ARE YOU?
MONG!!

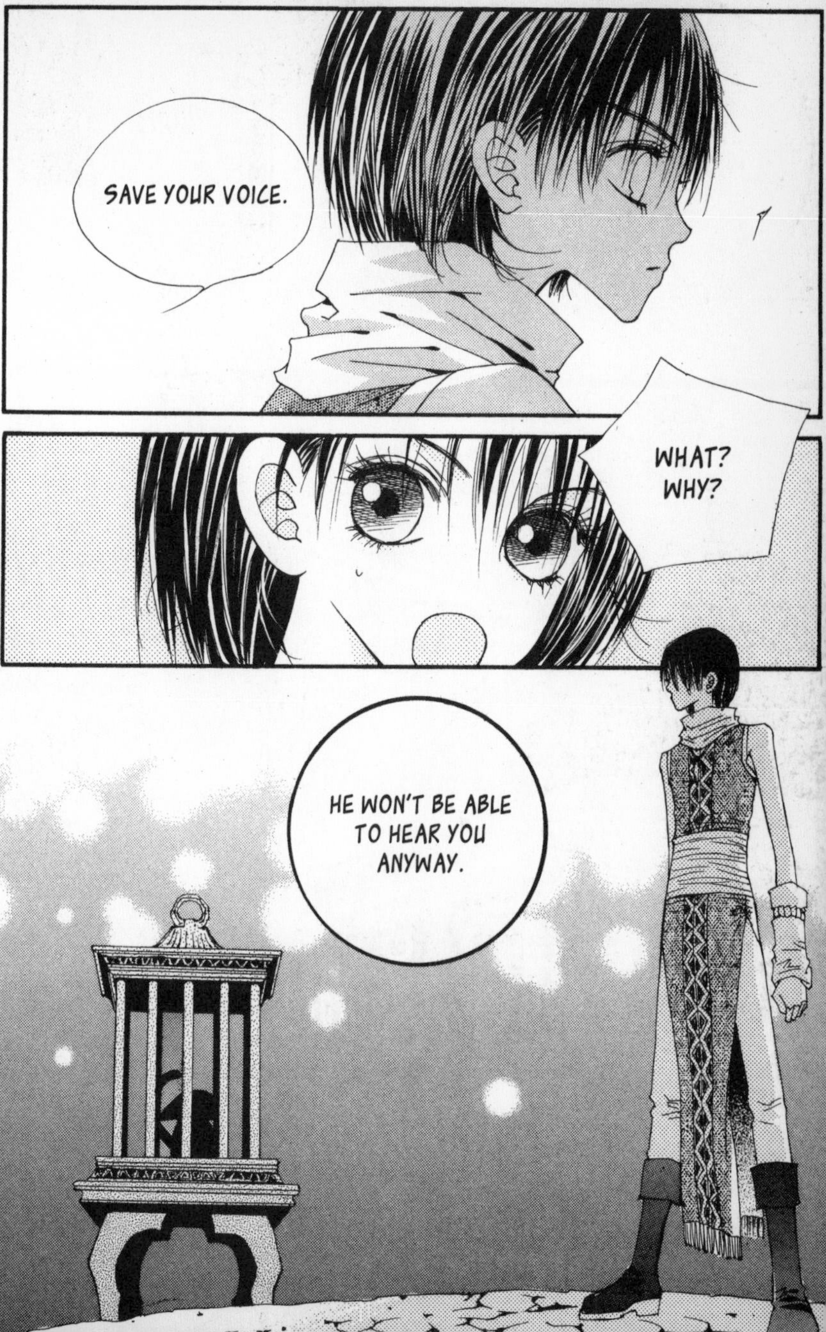
SAVE YOUR VOICE.
WHAT? WHY?
HE WON'T BE ABLE TO HEAR YOU ANYWAY.

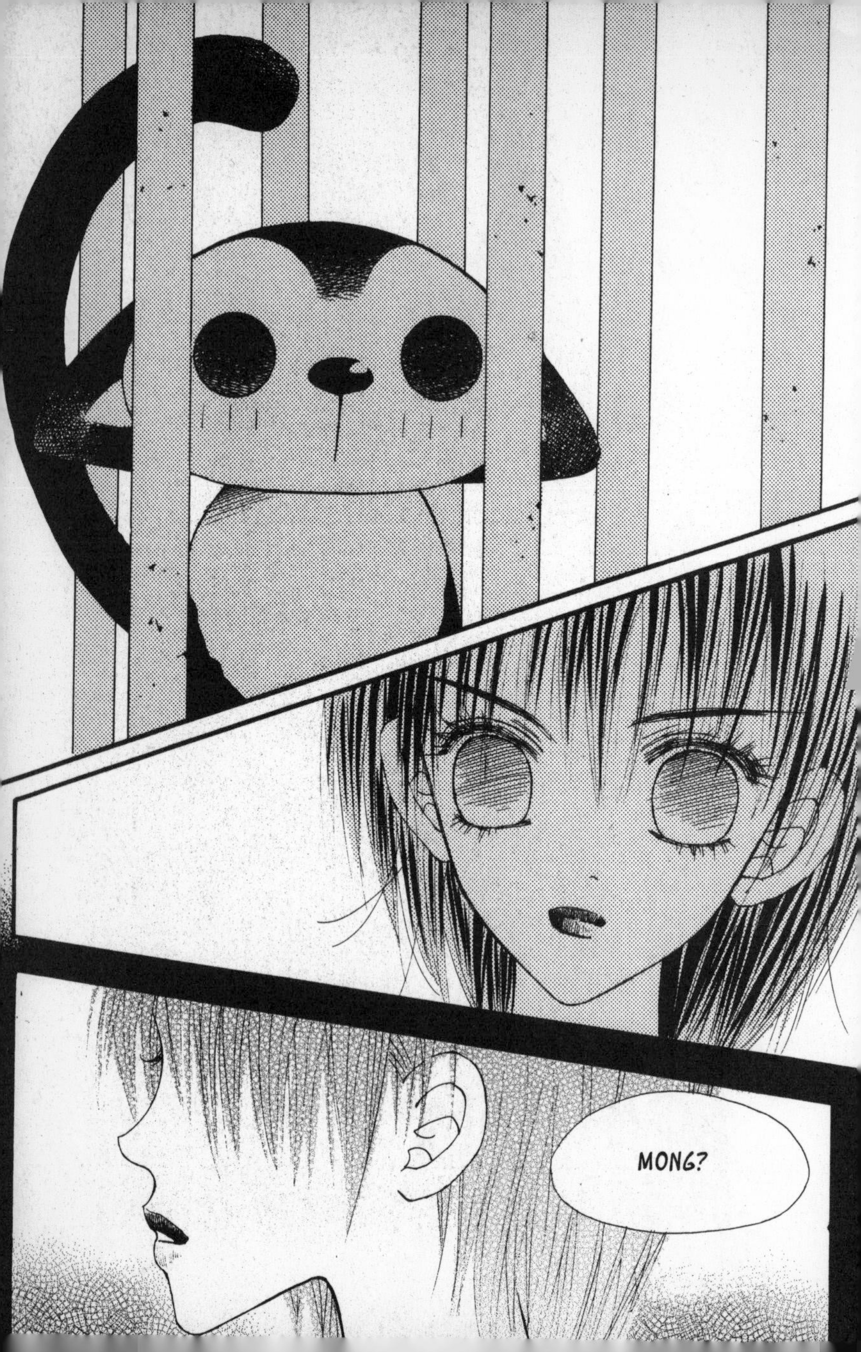
MONG?

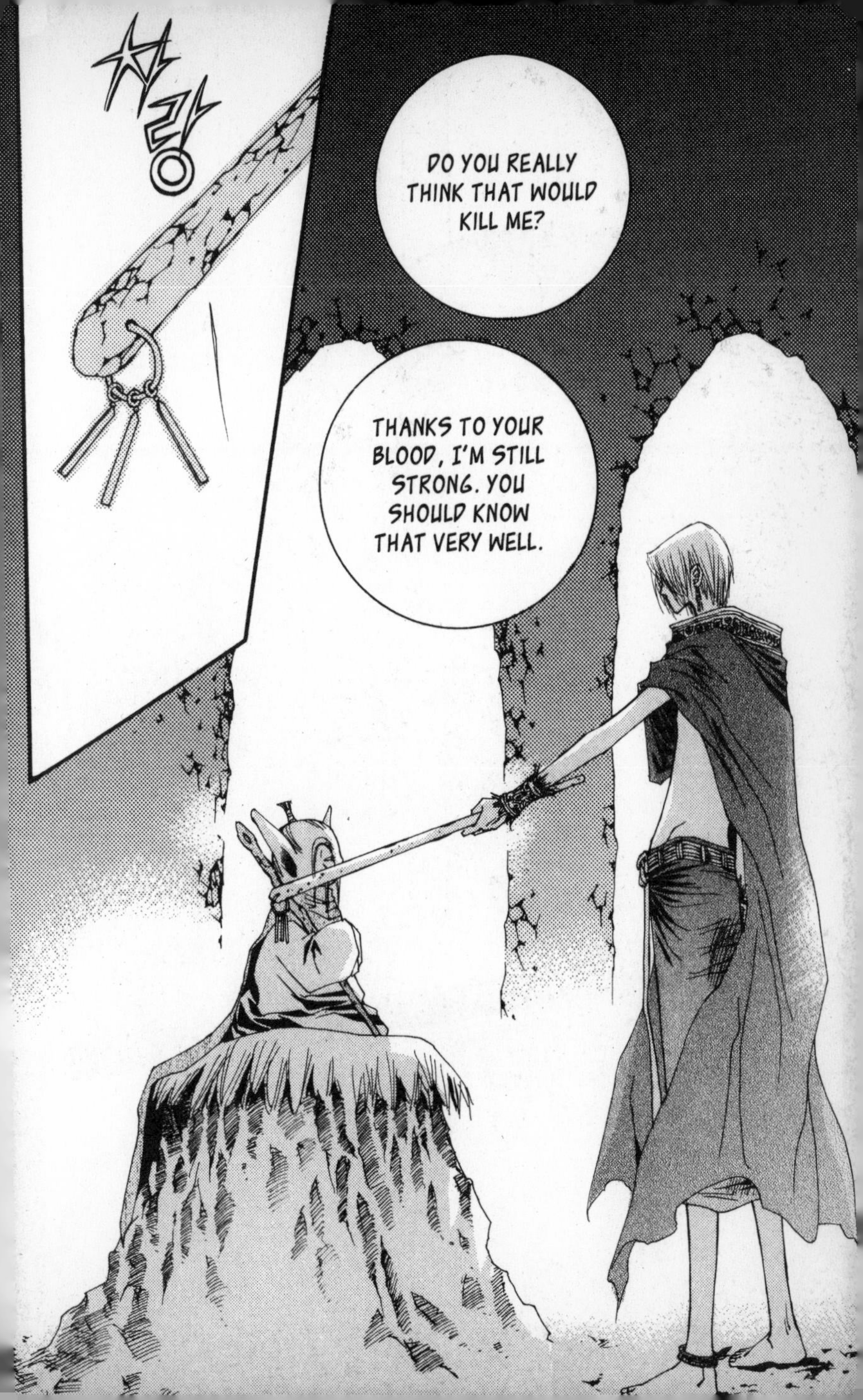
DO YOU REALLY THINK THAT WOULD KILL ME?
THANKS TO YOUR BLOOD, I'M STILL STRONG. YOU SHOULD KNOW THAT VERY WELL.

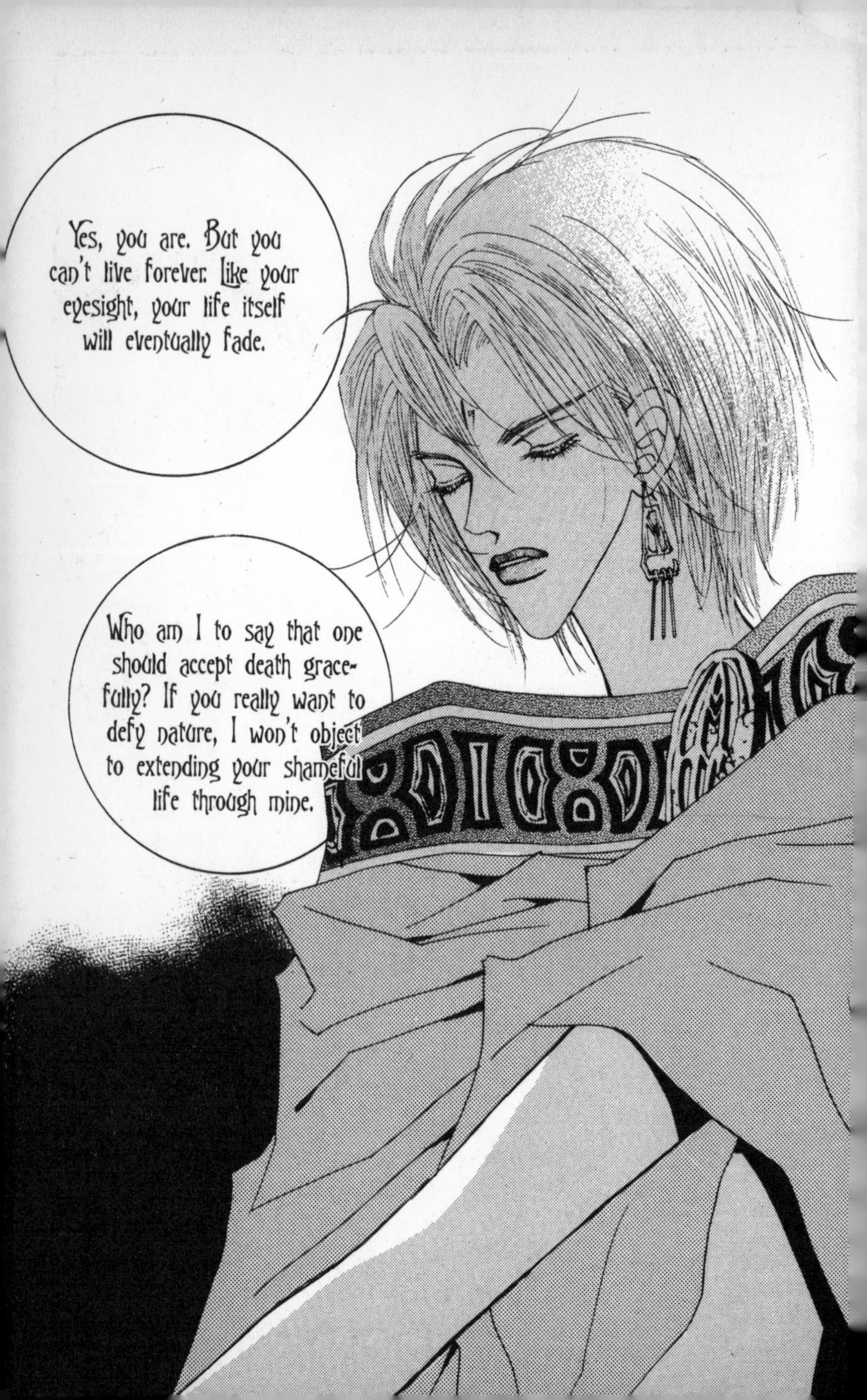
Yes, you are. But you can't live forever. Like your eyesight, your life itself will eventually fade.
Who am I to say that one should accept death gracefully? If you really want to defy nature, I won't object to extending your shameful life through mine.

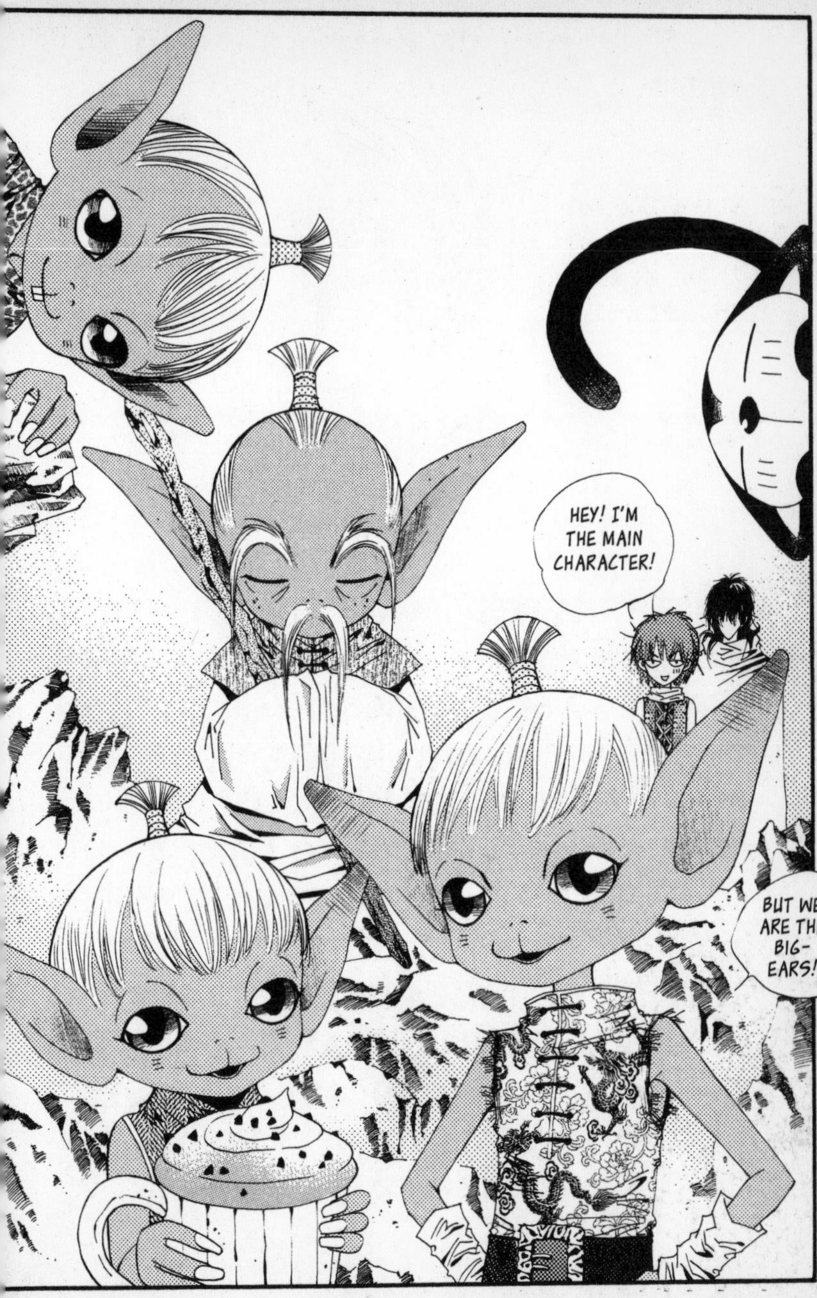
HEY! I'M THE MAIN CHARACTER!
BUT WE ARE THE BIG-EARS!

TO BE CONTINUED IN ARCANA VOLUME 3!

THE QUEST CONTINUES IN

VOLUME 3

AS INEZ TRIES DESPERATELY TO FREE LITTLE MONG FROM HIS CAGE, YULAN MAKES A GREAT SACRIFICE TO LIBERATE HIS COMPANIONS FROM THE CLUTCHES OF THE BIG-EARS. SOON, ALL ROADS LEAD BACK TO THE EAST GARDEN, WHERE REYVA CONTINUES TO MANIPULATE THE DARK ARTS IN AN EFFORT TO KEEP HIS DAUGHTER AND THE HALF-ELF APART. BUT EVEN THE BEST-LAID EVIL SCHEMES DON'T ALWAYS GO ACCORDING TO PLAN. WILL INEZ AND HER FRIENDS BE ABLE TO SAVE THE YOUNG LOVERS? FIND OUT IN THE NEXT VOLUME OF ARCANA!

Written by Keith Giffen, comic book pro and English language adapter of *Battle Royale* and *Battle Vixens*.

Join the misadventures of a group of particularly disturbing trick-or-treaters as they go about their macabre business on Halloween night. Blaming the apples they got from the first house of the evening for the bad candy they've been receiving all night, the kids plot revenge on the old bag who handed out the funky fruit. Riotously funny and always wickedly shocking— who doesn't *love* Halloween?

OT
OLDER TEEN
AGE 16+

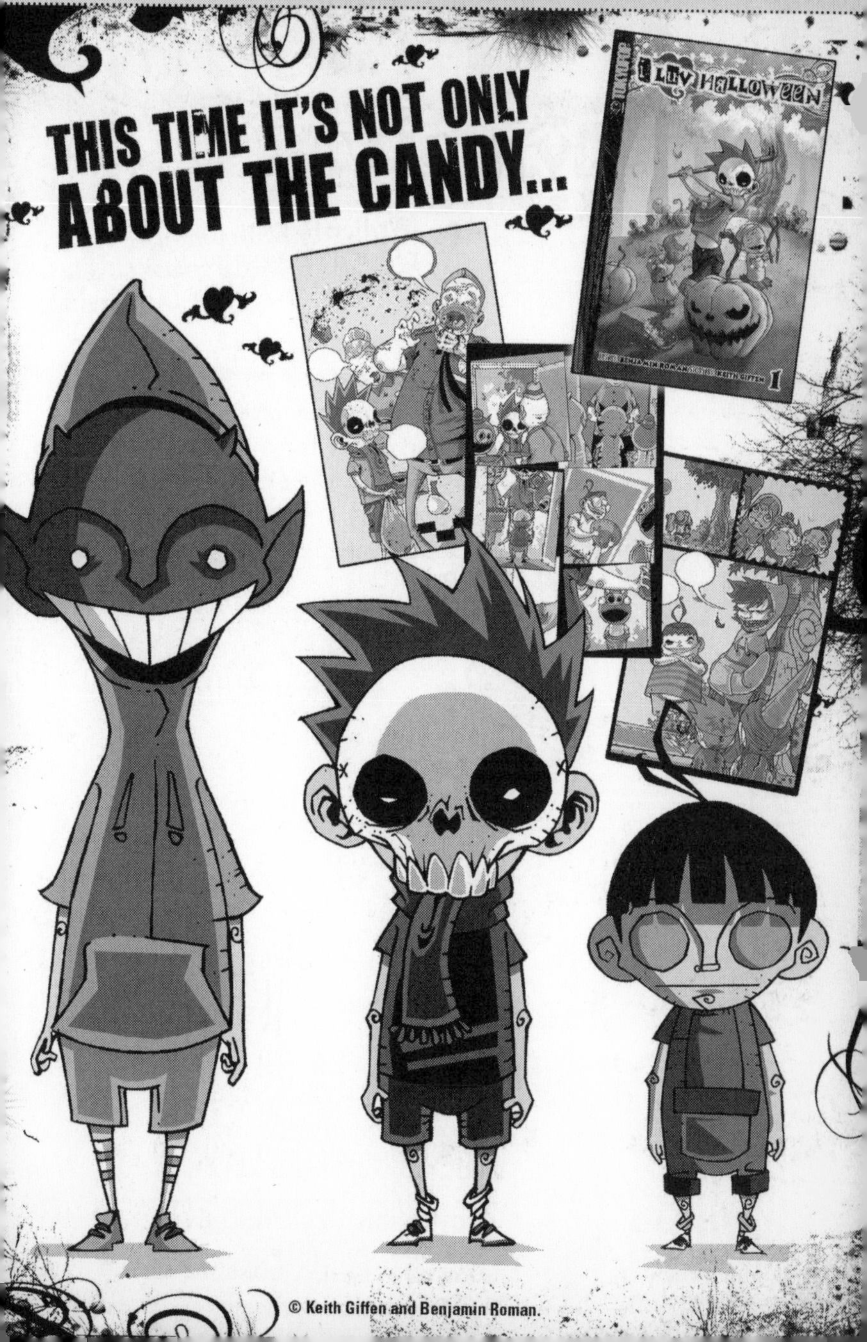
THIS TIME IT'S NOT ONLY
ABOUT THE CANDY...
I LUV HALLOWEEN
1
© Keith Giffen and Benjamin Roman.

TOKYOPOP SHOP

SPOTLIGHT

TOKYOPOP MANGA SUPPLEMENT

SCRAPPED PRINCESS

BY GO YABUKI, ICHIRO SAKAKI, AND YUKINOBU AZUMI

HER BIRTH FORETOLD THE DESTRUCTION OF THE WORLD!

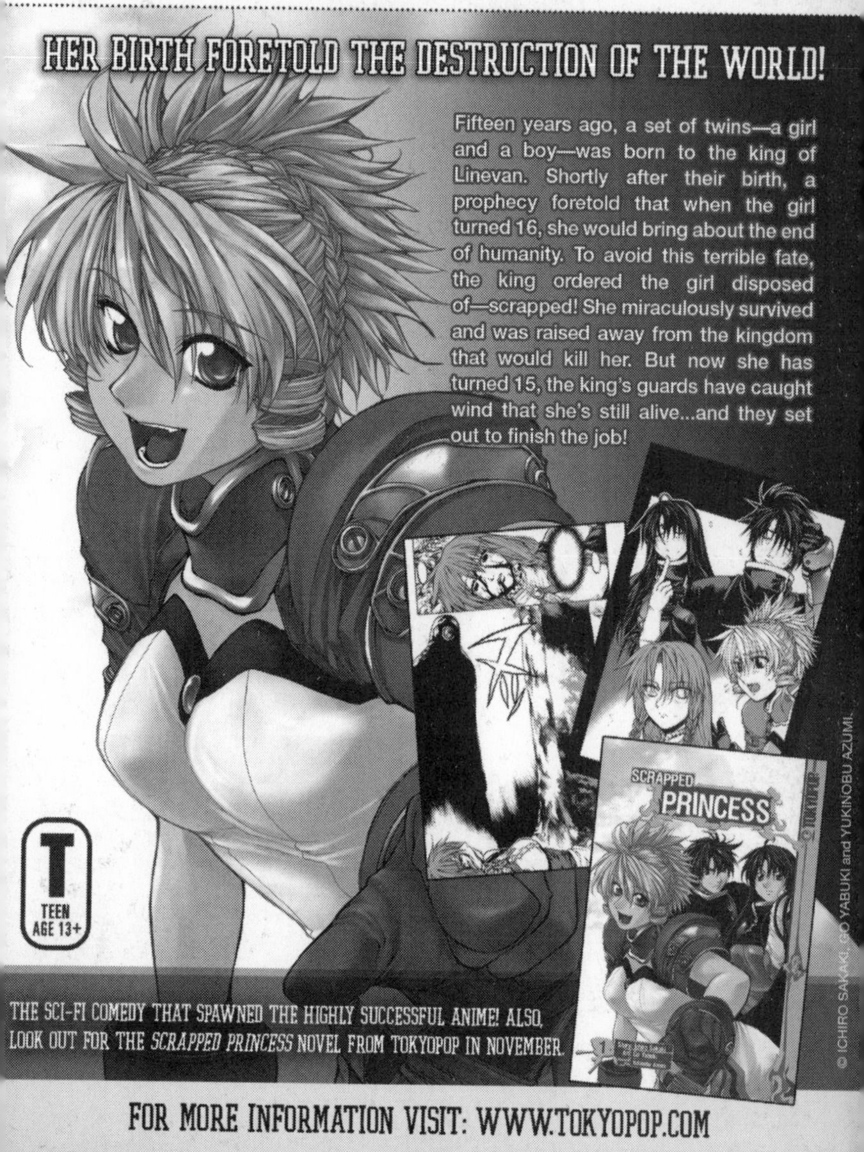
SCRAPPED
PRINCESS

Fifteen years ago, a set of twins—a girl and a boy—was born to the king of Linevan. Shortly after their birth, a prophecy foretold that when the girl turned 16, she would bring about the end of humanity. To avoid this terrible fate, the king ordered the girl disposed of—scrapped! She miraculously survived and was raised away from the kingdom that would kill her. But now she has turned 15, the king's guards have caught wind that she's still alive...and they set out to finish the job!

T
TEEN
AGE 13+

THE SCI-FI COMEDY THAT SPAWNED THE HIGHLY SUCCESSFUL ANIME! ALSO, LOOK OUT FOR THE *SCRAPPED PRINCESS* NOVEL FROM TOKYOPOP IN NOVEMBER.

FOR MORE INFORMATION VISIT: WWW.TOKYOPOP.COM

KAMICHAMA KARIN
BY KOGE-DONBO

Karin is an average girl...at best. She's not good at sports and gets terrible grades. On top of all that, her parents are dead and her beloved cat Shi-chan just died, too. She is miserable. But everything is about to change—little does Karin know that her mother's ring has the power to make her a goddess!

From the creator of *Pita-Ten* and *Digi-Charat!*

Y
YOUTH
AGE 10+

© Koge-Donbo.

KANPAI!
BY MAKI MURAKAMI

Yamada Shintaro is a monster guardian in training—his job is to protect the monsters from harm. But when he meets Nao, a girl from his middle school, he suddenly falls in love...with her neckline! Shintaro will go to any lengths to prevent disruption to her peaceful life—and preserve his choice view of her neck!

A wild and wonderful adventure from the creator of *Gravitation!*

T
TEEN
AGE 13+

© MAKI MURAKAMI.

MOBILE SUIT GUNDAM ÉCOLE DU CIEL
BY HARUHIKO MIKIMOTO

École du Ciel—where aspiring pilots train to become Top Gundam! Asuna, daughter of a brilliant professor, is a below-average student at École du Ciel. But the world is spiraling toward war, and Asuna is headed for a crash course in danger, battle, and most of all, love.

From the artist of the phenomenally successful *Macross* and *Baby Birth!*

T
TEEN
AGE 13+

© Haruhiko Mikimoto and Sostu Agency · Sunrise.